iPod® & iTunes®
FOR
DUMMIES®
2ND EDITION

by Tony Bove and Cheryl Rhodes

WILEY

Wiley Publishing, Inc.

iPod® & iTunes® For Dummies®, 2nd Edition

Published by
Wiley Publishing, Inc.
111 River Street
Hoboken, NJ 07030-5774

Copyright © 2005 by Wiley Publishing, Inc., Indianapolis, Indiana

Published by Wiley Publishing, Inc., Indianapolis, Indiana

Published simultaneously in Canada

WILEY

About the Authors

Tony Bove and **Cheryl Rhodes** have kicked around the computer industry for decades, editing the influential *Inside Report on New Media* newsletter and writing for weekly and monthly magazines, including *Computer Currents, NeXTWORLD, The Chicago Tribune* Sunday Technology Section, and *NewMedia.* They also co-founded and edited *Desktop Publishing/Publish* magazine. Tony and Cheryl have written over a dozen books on computing, desktop publishing, and multimedia, including *iLife All-in-One Desk Reference For Dummies* (Wiley) and *The Art of Desktop Publishing* (Bantam).

Tony and Cheryl produced a CD-ROM interactive documentary in 1996, *Haight-Ashbury in the Sixties.* They also developed the Rockument music site, www.rockument.com, with commentary and radio programs focused on rock music history. As a founding member of the Flying Other Brothers (www.flyingotherbros.com), Tony has performed with Hall-of-Fame rock musicians and uses his iPod to store extensive concert recordings.

Dedication

This book is dedicated to John Paul Bove and James Eric Bove, both of whom contributed tips and spent considerable time testing iPods while turning a vacation into a book project.

Authors' Acknowledgments

John Paul Bove contributed technical expertise and writing for this edition and has certainly earned his new laptop. We want to thank Rich Tennant for his wonderful cartoons; our Wiley project editor Mark Enochs, and Editorial Manager Kevin Kirschner, for ongoing assistance. We also thank Virginia Sanders and Teresa Artman for editing and improving this book immensely. A book this timely places a considerable burden on a publisher's production team, and we thank the production crew at Wiley for diligence beyond the call of reason. We owe thanks and a happy hour to Carole McLendon at Waterside, our agent. And we have acquisitions editor Bob Woerner at Wiley to thank for coming up with the idea for this book. Finally, our heartfelt thanks to members of the Flying Other Brothers (Pete Sears, Barry Sless, Jimmy Sanchez, Bill Bennett, Bert Keely, TBone, and Roger and Ann McNamee) for the music that inspired us while writing this book.

Publisher's Acknowledgments

We're proud of this book; please send us your comments through our online registration form located at www.dummies.com/register.

Some of the people who helped bring this book to market include the following:

Acquisitions, Editorial, and Media Development

Project Editor: Mark Enochs

Acquisitions Editor: Bob Woerner

Copy Editors: Virginia Sanders, Teresa Artman

Technical Editor: Dennis Cohen

Editorial Manager: Kevin Kirschner

Media Development Manager: Laura VanWinkle

Media Development Supervisor: Richard Graves

Editorial Assistant: Amanda M. Foxworth

Cartoons: Rich Tennant, www.the5thwave.com

Composition

Project Coordinator: Maridee Ennis

Layout and Graphics: Andrea Dahl, Denny Hager, Joyce Haughey, Barry Offringa, Lynsey Osborn, Heather Ryan

Proofreaders: Carl William Pierce, Dwight Ramsey, Brian H. Walls, TECHBOOKS Production Services

Indexer: TECHBOOKS Production Services

Publishing and Editorial for Technology Dummies

    Richard Swadley, Vice President and Executive Group Publisher

    Andy Cummings, Vice President and Publisher

    Mary Bednarek, Executive Acquisitions Director

    Mary C. Corder, Editorial Director

Publishing for Consumer Dummies

    Diane Graves Steele, Vice President and Publisher

    Joyce Pepple, Acquisitions Director

Composition Services

    Gerry Fahey, Vice President of Production Services

    Debbie Stailey, Director of Composition Services

Contents at a Glance

Introduction 1

Part 1: Setting Up and Acquiring Music 7
Chapter 1: Getting Started with Your iPod 9
Chapter 2: Setting Up iTunes and Your iPod 31
Chapter 3: Getting Started with iTunes 45
Chapter 4: Buying Music from the iTunes Music Store 53
Chapter 5: Importing Music into iTunes 71
Chapter 6: Sharing Music (Legally) 79
Chapter 7: Using MusicMatch Jukebox 89

Part 11: Managing Your Music 99
Chapter 8: Searching, Browsing, and Sorting in iTunes 101
Chapter 9: Adding and Editing Song Information in iTunes 109
Chapter 10: Organizing Music with Playlists 121
Chapter 11: Updating Your iPod with iTunes 129
Chapter 12: Managing the MusicMatch Jukebox Library 143
Chapter 13: Gimme Shelter for My Music..157
Chapter 14: Burning CDs from iTunes 165

Part 111: Playing Tunes 177
Chapter 15: Playing Your iPod 179
Chapter 16: Getting Wired for Sound 187
Chapter 17: Listening While on the Move 195
Chapter 18: Spinning Tunes Like a DJ 205

Part 1V: Using Advanced Techniques 217
Chapter 19: Choosing Your Encoding Format...219
Chapter 20: Changing Encoders and Encoder Settings 229
Chapter 21: Fine-Tuning the Sound 243
Chapter 22: Recording and Editing Sound 255
Chapter 23: Enhancing Your Music Library 265

Part V: Have iPod, Will Travel 273

Chapter 24: Sleeping with Your iPod 275
Chapter 25: Using the iPod as a Hard Drive 287
Chapter 26: Entering Personal Information 301
Chapter 27: Synchronizing Information with Your iPod 313
Chapter 28: Updating and Troubleshooting 321

Part VI: The Part of Tens 335

Chapter 29: Ten Problems and Solutions for Your iPod 337
Chapter 30: Eleven Tips for the Equalizer 343
Chapter 31: Twelve Web Sources for More iPod Information 347

Index 351

Table of Contents

Introduction *1*

About This Book...2
Conventions Used in This Book 2
And Just Who Are You?...3
A Quick Peek Ahead 3
    Part I: Setting Up and Acquiring Music 3
    Part II: Managing Your Music 4
    Part III: Playing Tunes 4
    Part IV: Using Advanced Techniques 4
    Part V: Have iPod, Will Travel 4
    Part VI: The Part of Tens..5
Icons Used in This Book 5

Part 1: Setting Up and Acquiring Music *7*

Chapter 1: Getting Started with Your iPod **9**

Introducing the iPod 10
Comparing iPod Models 11
    First-generation iPods 12
    Second-generation iPods 12
    Third-generation iPods 13
    iPod mini..14
    Fourth-generation iPods 15
Thinking Inside the Box...16
    Things you have and things you need 16
    Using FireWire or USB cables with a Mac.................17
    Using FireWire or USB cables with a PC 19
Powering Up Your iPod...20
Facing Charges of Battery 21
    Maintaining battery life...22
    Saving power 23
    Replacing your battery 24
Thumbing Through the Menus 24
Pressing the iPod Buttons..26
Setting the Language..27
Resetting Your iPod...28

Chapter 2: Setting Up iTunes and Your iPod 31
  Setting Up iTunes 32
    Setting up iTunes on a Mac 33
    Setting up iTunes for Windows 35
  Setting Up Your iPod with a Mac 38
  Setting Up Your iPod with a Windows PC 40

Chapter 3: Getting Started with iTunes 45
  What You Can Do with iTunes 45
  The iTunes Window 46
  Playing CD Tracks in iTunes 48
    Rearranging and repeating tracks 50
    Skipping tracks..50
    Repeating a song list 50
    Displaying visuals 51

Chapter 4: Buying Music from the iTunes Music Store 53
  Visiting the iTunes Music Store...54
    Setting up an account 56
    Browsing for artists, songs, and albums 57
    Browsing the charts 59
    Power-searching 59
    Playing music videos and movie trailers..............................60
    Browsing celebrity and published playlists...........................61
    Previewing a song 62
  Buying and Downloading Songs 62
    Using 1-Click or the Shopping Cart 62
    Changing your Store preferences 64
    Resuming interrupted downloads..65
    Redeeming gift certificates and prepaid cards 65
  Managing Your Account 66
    Viewing and changing account information...........................66
    Viewing your purchase history..67
    Setting up allowances 67
    Sending gift certificates 68
    Authorizing computers to play purchased music....................69

Chapter 5: Importing Music into iTunes 71
  Setting the Importing Preferences 72
  Ripping Music from CDs..74
  Importing Music Files 76
  Importing Audio Books..77

Chapter 6: Sharing Music (Legally) 79
  Sharing Music from the iTunes Music Store 79
  Sharing Music in a Network 81
  Copying Songs to Other Computers 84
  Copying Songs between PCs and Macs 85

Chapter 7: Using MusicMatch Jukebox 89

What You Can Do with MusicMatch Jukebox 90
Installing MusicMatch Jukebox 91
Importing Music into MusicMatch Jukebox................................93
  Setting the recording format 93
  Ripping songs from a CD 95
  Adding song files from other sources 96
Playing Songs in MusicMatch Jukebox....................................96
  Saving a playlist 97
  Playing albums 98

Part II: Managing Your Music 99

Chapter 8: Searching, Browsing, and Sorting in iTunes 101

Browsing by Artist and Album...101
Understanding the Song Indicators 103
Changing Viewing Options 104
Sorting Songs by Viewing Options 105
Searching for Songs...106

Chapter 9: Adding and Editing Song Information in iTunes 109

Retrieving Information from the Internet..................................110
  Retrieving information automatically 110
  Retrieving information manually 111
Entering Song Information 112
Editing the Information..112
  Editing multiple songs at once.....................................113
  Editing fields for a song 115
  Adding a rating...117
Adding Album Cover Art or Images 118

Chapter 10: Organizing Music with Playlists 121

Creating Playlists...122
  Playlists of songs 122
  Playlists of albums..123
Using Smart Playlists 124
  Creating a smart playlist..124
  Editing a smart playlist 126
Deleting Songs, Albums,
  Artists, and Playlists 126

Chapter 11: Updating Your iPod with iTunes 129

Changing Your Update Preferences 130
Updating Your iPod Automatically.......................................132
  Synchronizing with your library....................................133
  Updating from a library larger than your iPod 133

Updating by playlist 134
Updating selected songs...135
Updating Your iPod Manually 136
Copying music directly 137
Deleting music on your iPod 138
Managing Playlists on Your iPod 139
Creating playlists directly on the iPod 139
Editing playlists 140
Editing Song Information on Your iPod 141

Chapter 12: Managing the MusicMatch Jukebox Library **143**

Managing Song Information 143
Using CD Lookup 144
Editing information tags 144
Adding information about songs 146
Super-tagging songs with information 147
Viewing Your Song Library..148
Browsing the library...148
Changing views of your library.................................148
Searching for songs 149
Updating Your iPod with
MusicMatch Jukebox...150
Updating automatically..150
Updating by MusicMatch playlist 152
Updating manually 153
Deleting Songs 154
Repairing Broken Links to Songs.......................................154

Chapter 13: Gimme Shelter for My Music **157**

Finding the iTunes Library...158
Consolidating the iTunes Library.......................................160
Exporting iTunes Playlists...160
Backing Up the iTunes Library 161
Backing up on the same type of computer..............161
Backing up from Mac to PC or PC to Mac...............162
Backing Up the MusicMatch Jukebox Library.................163
Saving Multiple MusicMatch Jukebox Libraries.............164

Chapter 14: Burning CDs from iTunes **165**

Selecting Recordable CDs..166
What You Can Fit on a CD-R 167
Creating a Burn Playlist 168
Calculating how much music to use 168
Importing music for an audio CD-R 169
Switching import encoders for MP3 CD-R 170

Setting the Burning Preferences 170
    Setting the sound check and gaps................................170
    Setting the format and recording speed 172
Burning a Disc 173
Printing Liner Notes and CD Covers 174
Troubleshooting Burns..174

Part III: Playing Tunes 177

Chapter 15: Playing Your iPod 179

Locating Songs...179
    By artist 180
    By album 180
    By playlist 181
Playing a Song..182
Repeating Songs 182
Shuffling the Song Order 183
Creating On-The-Go Playlists 184
    Selecting songs for the playlist 184
    Clearing songs from the playlist...184
    Saving the playlist in iTunes 185
Adjusting the Volume...186
Bookmarking Audible Audio Books 186

Chapter 16: Getting Wired for Sound 187

Making Connections..188
Connecting to a Home Stereo 190
Connecting Headphones and Portable Speakers 191
Accessories for the iHome 192

Chapter 17: Listening While on the Move 195

Playing Car Tunes...196
    Getting in tune . . . with car adapters...............................196
    Going mobile . . . with car mounts.....................................198
Connecting by Wireless Radio 199
Dressing Up Your iPod for Travel...201
Using Power Accessories 202

Chapter 18: Spinning Tunes Like a DJ 205

Changing the Computer's Output Volume 206
    Adjusting the sound on a Mac 206
    Adjusting the sound in Windows...208

Mixing It Up with iTunes..208
Queuing up tunes with Party Shuffle 209
Cross-fading song playback..211
Playing an iPod through iTunes 212
Connecting your iPod to another computer 213
Using AirTunes for wireless stereo playback..................214
Playing iPod Songs through MusicMatch Jukebox 216

Part IV: Using Advanced Techniques.............................217

Chapter 19: Choosing Your Encoding Format 219

Trading Quality for Space..220
Choosing an Encoder...221
iTunes encoders 221
MusicMatch Jukebox encoders 223
Manic Compression Has Captured Your Song.............................225
Selecting Import Settings 226

Chapter 20: Changing Encoders and Encoder Settings 229

Customizing the Encoder Settings in iTunes 230
Changing AAC encoder settings...230
Changing MP3 encoder settings...232
Changing AIFF and WAV encoder settings........................234
Importing Voice and Sound Effects in iTunes.............................236
Converting Songs to a Different Encoder in iTunes....................236
Changing Recorder Settings in MusicMatch Jukebox................238
Selecting MP3 settings 238
Selecting WAV 239
Using advanced recording options 240

Chapter 21: Fine-Tuning the Sound 243

Adjusting the Sound in iTunes...243
Setting the volume in advance for songs..........................244
Enhancing the sound...245
Sound-checking the iTunes volume 246
Sound-checking the iPod volume 246
Equalize It in iTunes..247
Adjusting the preamp volume...247
Adjusting frequencies 248
Using iTunes' presets 248
Saving your own presets..249
Assigning equalizer presets to songs................................251
Equalize It in Your iPod 252
Choosing an EQ preset on your iPod 253
Applying the iTunes EQ presets 253

Chapter 22: Recording and Editing Sound **255**

Recording Records, Tapes, and Analog Sources 256
  Connecting and setting up audio input 256
  Choosing a sound editing application 259
  Recording in Windows with MusicMatch Jukebox 260
Modifying Songs in iTunes 260
  Setting the start and stop points in a song 261
  Splitting a track into multiple tracks 262

Chapter 23: Enhancing Your Music Library **265**

Downloading Music from Other Sources 265
  Music sources for iTunes and MusicMatch Jukebox 266
  Using the MusicMatch Jukebox Music Guide 267
Playing Streaming Radio in iTunes 269
Changing the MusicMatch Jukebox Look and Feel 271

Part V: Have iPod, Will Travel **273**

Chapter 24: Sleeping with Your iPod **275**

Setting Date, Time, and Sleep Functions 275
Setting the Alarm Clock 277
Choosing Display Settings 278
  Backlight timer 278
  Contrast for better visibility 279
Playing Games 279
  Brick and Parachute 280
  Solitaire 280
  Music Quiz 280
Checking Your Calendar 281
Sorting Your Contacts 281
Speaking into Your iPod 282
  Recording voice memos 282
  Playing back voice memos 283
  Managing voice memos in iTunes 283
Customizing the Menu and Settings 284

Chapter 25: Using the iPod as a Hard Drive **287**

Mounting the iPod as a Hard Drive 288
  Setting up the hard drive iPod on a Mac 288
  Setting up the hard drive iPod on a Windows PC with iTunes 290
  Setting up the hard drive iPod on a Windows PC
    with MusicMatch Jukebox 292
Adding Notes and Text 295
  Using the Notes folder 295
  Adding news feeds, books, and Web pages 296

Storing Photos on Your iPod..296
Taking Your Mac System on the Road 297
Installing Mac OS 9 298
Installing Mac OS X..298
Removing the system..300

Chapter 26: Entering Personal Information 301

Keeping Appointments with iCal on the Mac 302
Setting up an appointment or event....................................303
Adding a To-Do item...305
Creating a custom calendar 305
Keeping Appointments with Microsoft Outlook.......................306
Setting up an appointment or event....................................306
Adding a To-Do task 307
Storing Contacts in the Mac OS X Address Book 308
Adding and editing contact information..............................308
Merging cards...310
Searching in Address Book...310
Managing contacts in groups 310
Storing Contacts in Microsoft Address Book or Outlook.......311

Chapter 27: Synchronizing Information with Your iPod 313

Not 'N Sync? Try iSync (Mac Only)..313
Synchronizing Microsoft Outlook (Windows) 316
Adding Calendars Manually...317
Adding Contacts Manually...318
Using Utilities to Copy Files and Music 319
Mac utilities..319
Windows utilities 320

Chapter 28: Updating and Troubleshooting 321

First Troubleshooting Steps..322
Checking the Hold switch...322
Checking the power...322
Resetting the iPod 323
Draining the iPod battery 323
Hitting the panic button 324
Using iPod Updater 325
Updating the iPod with iPod Updater................................325
Restoring an iPod with iPod Updater..................................327
Troubleshooting iPod for Windows and MusicMatch Jukebox.............329
Updating the iPod with the MusicMatch Jukebox configuration ...329
Restoring an iPod with the MusicMatch Jukebox configuration...330
If your iPod doesn't appear 331

Part VI: The Part of Tens 335

Chapter 29: Ten Problems and Solutions for Your iPod 337
How Do I Get My iPod to Wake Up?...337
How Do I Get My Battery to Last Longer? 338
How Do I Keep My Scroll Wheel from Going Crazy? 338
How Do I Get My Computer to Recognize My iPod? 339
What Do I Do if a Strange Icon Appears on My iPod? 339
How Do I Restore My iPod to its Original Condition from the Factory? ...340
How Do I Update My iPod to Have the Newest Software?.......................340
How Do I Update My iPod with Music When My Library Is Larger
    than My iPod's Capacity?..340
How Do I Cross-Fade Music Playback with My iPod? 341
How Do I Get Less Distortion with Car and Portable Speakers? 342

Chapter 30: Eleven Tips for the Equalizer 343
Setting the Volume to the Right Level 343
Adjusting Another Equalizer..343
Setting Booster Presets 344
Reducing High Frequencies...344
Increasing Low Frequencies...344
Setting Presets for Trucks and SUVs..344
Setting Presets When You're Eight Miles High..344
Reducing Tape Noise and Scratch Sounds 345
Reducing Turntable Rumble and Hum 345
Reducing Off-Frequency Harshness and Nasal Vocals 345
Cranking Up the Volume to Eleven..345

Chapter 31: Twelve Web Sources for More iPod Information 347
The Apple iPod Web Site 347
The Audible Web Site..347
The iTunes Music Store 348
The iPod Support Web Site 348
Apple Software Download 348
The iPod Troubleshooting Guide 348
The MusicMatch Jukebox Site 348
Version Tracker 349
iPodHacks...349
iPoding..349
iPod Lounge 349
Apple Developer Connection 350

Index 351

Introduction

You don't need much imagination to see why we're so happy with our iPods.

Imagine no longer needing CDs. We take road trips that last for weeks, and we never hear the same song twice. We leave our music library safe at home and grab an iPod for a hike or jog and always listen to something different.

Imagine not waiting for hot new music. You can listen to it, purchase it, and load it onto your iPod within minutes of discovering it on the Internet. Be the first in your circle of friends to hear the exclusive new music available from the iTunes Music Store.

Imagine not having to buy music more than once. You can purchase a CD or downloadable music and import the music into a digital library that lasts forever. Imagine never again having to replace an unplayable CD.

Imagine a musician going backstage after a performance and meeting a promoter who says that he can get him ten more gigs if he can confirm the dates *right now*. This musician calmly scrolls through his calendar for the entire year (conveniently stored on his iPod), finding all the details that he needs about gigs and recording sessions, right down to the minute, including travel directions to each gig. "No problem," he says. And of course, he gets the gigs.

Okay, maybe you're not a rock star whose career depends on the information on your iPod. But if rock stars can use them, so can average music lovers.

When we first encountered the iPod, it came very close to fulfilling our dreams as road warriors — in particular, the dream of filling up our cars with music as easily as filling it up with fuel. As we go to press with this edition, another milestone has been reached: BMW has just introduced the first car to sport an iPod-compatible stereo. With the installation of an integrated adapter developed by Apple and BMW, you can now control your iPod or iPod mini through the existing audio system and multifunction steering wheel. Whether you want to be *On the Road* with Jack Kerouac (in audio book form), or "Drivin' South" with Jimi Hendrix, just fill up your iPod and go!

About This Book

We designed *iPod & iTunes For Dummies,* 2nd Edition, as a reference. You can find the information you need when you need it easily. We organized the information so that you can read from beginning to end to find out how to use iTunes and your iPod from scratch. But this book is also designed so that you can dive in anywhere and begin reading because you find all the info you need to know for each task.

We don't cover every detail of every function of the software, and we intentionally leave out some detail so that we don't befuddle you with technospeak when it's not necessary. (Really, engineers can sometimes provide too many obscure choices that no one ever uses.) We write brief but comprehensive descriptions and include lots of cool tips on how to get the best results from using iTunes and your iPod.

Conventions Used in This Book

Like any book that covers computers and information technology, this book uses certain conventions:

- **Choosing from a menu:** In iTunes, when you see "Choose iTunes⇨ Preferences in iTunes," you click iTunes on the toolbar and then click Preferences from the iTunes menu.

  With the iPod, when you see, "Choose Extras⇨Calendars from the iPod main menu," you highlight Extras in the main menu with the scroll wheel, press the Select button to select Extras, and then highlight and select Calendars from the Extras menu.

- **Clicking and dragging:** When you see "Drag the song over the name of the playlist," we mean click the song name, hold the mouse button down, and drag the song with the mouse over to the name of the playlist before lifting your finger off the mouse button.

- **Keyboard shortcuts:** When you see ⌘-I, press the ⌘ key on a Mac keyboard, along with the appropriate shortcut key (in this case, press I, which opens the Song Information window in iTunes). On a Windows PC, the same keyboard shortcut is Ctrl-I (which means press the Ctrl key along with the I key).

- **Step lists:** When you come across steps you need to do in iTunes or on the iPod, the action is in bold, and the explanatory part is underneath. If you know what to do, read the action and skip the explanation. But if you need a little help along the way, check out the explanation.

And Just Who Are You?

You don't need to know anything about audio technology to discover how to make the most of your iPod and the iTunes software that comes with it. Although a course in music appreciation can't hurt, the iPod is designed to be useful even for air-guitar players who barely know the difference between downloadable music and System of a Down. You don't need any specialized knowledge to have a lot of fun with your iPod and the iTunes software while building up your digital music library.

However, we do make some honest assumptions about your computer skills:

- ✔ **You know how to use the Mac Finder or Windows Explorer:** We assume that you already know how to locate files and folders and that you can copy files and folders from one hard drive to another on the computer of your choice: a Mac or a Windows PC.

- ✔ **You know how to select menus and applications on a Mac or a Windows PC:** We assume that you already know how to choose an option from a menu, how to find the Dock on a Mac to launch a Dock application (or use the Start menu in Windows to launch an application), and how to launch an application directly by double-clicking its icon.

For more information on these topics, see that excellent book by Mark L. Chambers, *Mac OS X All-in-One Desk Reference For Dummies,* or the massive tome *Windows XP GigaBook For Dummies,* by Peter Weverka and company (both from Wiley Publishing, Inc.).

A Quick Peek Ahead

This book is organized into six parts, with each part covering a different aspect of using your iPod. Here's a quick preview of what you can find in each part.

Part 1: Setting Up and Acquiring Music

This part gets you started with your iPod, powering it up, recharging its battery, using its menus, and connecting it to your computer. You install and set up the iPod and iTunes software on your Mac or Windows PC. We show you what you can do with iTunes. To acquire music, you can buy music from the iTunes Music Store, or you can rip audio CDs. You also find out how to share your iTunes music. For Windows users, we also provide information about MusicMatch Jukebox. (MusicMatch Jukebox is an alternative to using iTunes and is especially useful for PCs that use older versions of Windows and therefore can't run iTunes.)

Part II: Managing Your Music

This part shows you how to sort the music in your iTunes library by artist, album, duration, date, and other items. You can add and edit iTunes song information. You discover how to arrange songs and albums into iTunes playlists that you can transfer to your iPod. When you have your music organized efficiently, transfer it to the iPod. You can also find out how to do all these things in MusicMatch Jukebox. And, for your peace of mind, we cover backing up your music and burning it to a CD.

Part III: Playing Tunes

We show you how to locate and play songs on your iPod and then we move on to various accessories for connecting your iPod to your home stereo and using your iPod on the road with car stereos and portable speakers. You discover how to play music on your iPod through any computer by using advanced DJ techniques, such as cross-fading song playback and using the iTunes Party Shuffle.

Part IV: Using Advanced Techniques

In this part, you discover digital music encoding and how to change your importing preferences. You can also fine-tune the sound playback with the iTunes equalizer and on your iPod with the iPod equalizer. We describe what you need to record sound and music into your computer from old records and tapes, and how to modify songs in iTunes for playback on your iPod. We cover how to enhance your iTunes or MusicMatch Jukebox library with alternate music sources and Web radio.

Part V: Have iPod, Will Travel

In this part, use your iPod as a road warrior would: setting your alarm clock, sorting your contacts, and recording voice memos, using your iPod as a hard drive and adding notes and text, entering personal information into your computer such as calendar appointments, To-Do lists, and contacts, and synchronizing your iPod with all your personal information. We provide troubleshooting first steps and details about updating and restoring your iPod.

Part VI: The Part of Tens

In this book's Part of Tens chapters, we outline common problems and solutions that happen to most iPods, tips about the iPod equalizer, and Web sources of information to enhance your iPod experience.

Icons Used in This Book

The icons in this book are important visual cues for information you need.

Remember icons highlight important things you need to remember.

Technical Stuff icons highlight technical details you can skip unless you want to bring out the technical geek in you.

Tip icons highlight tips and techniques that save you time and energy, and maybe money.

Warning icons save your butt by preventing disasters. Don't bypass a warning without reading it. This is your only warning!

Part I
Setting Up and Acquiring Music

The 5th Wave   By Rich Tennant

@RICHTENNANT

INTENSE BUT UNINFORMED AUDIOPHILE BILLY WIGGINS ENJOYS HIS CUSTOM BURNED CD COLLECTION OF DIAL UP MODEM WARBLES

In this part . . .

Part I shows you how to do all the essential things with your iPod and iTunes or MusicMatch Jukebox.

- ✔ Chapter 1 gets you started with your iPod. Here you find out how to get the most from your battery, use the menus and buttons, connect your iPod to your Mac or PC, and reset your iPod.

- ✔ Chapter 2 describes how to install the iPod software and iTunes on the Mac or on a Windows PC.

- ✔ Chapter 3 gets you started with iTunes on a Mac or a Windows PC.

- ✔ Chapter 4 covers purchasing music online from the iTunes Music Store.

- ✔ Chapter 5 describes how to import music into iTunes from CDs or other sources (such as the Web).

- ✔ Chapter 6 shows how you can share music (legally) with other iTunes users on your network and copy songs to other computers (even songs purchased online).

- ✔ Chapter 7 describes how to install the iPod software with MusicMatch Jukebox on Windows and how to use MusicMatch Jukebox to import music from audio CDs.

Chapter 1

Getting Started with Your iPod

In This Chapter

▶ Comparing iPod models

▶ Powering up your iPod

▶ Using and recharging your battery

▶ Scrolling through the iPod main menu

▶ Resetting the iPod

*B*ob Dylan and Dave Van Ronk in Greenwich Village, David Bowie and Iggy Pop on the Lower East Side, and the Velvet Underground in the subway. Dire Straits on Wall Street, Steely Dan in Midtown, and Sonny Rollins on the Brooklyn Bridge. The Drifters on Broadway, Miles Davis uptown, John and Yoko on the Upper West Side. Charlie Parker in Harlem, Yo-Yo Ma on the Upper East Side, Primal Fear across Central Park. "The music must change," sang Roger Daltrey of the Who, and the only way you can conveniently carry that much music around while touring the Big Apple in one day is with an Apple iPod.

Music has changed so much during the shift from purchasing music in stores to obtaining music online that the music industry hardly recognizes it, and the Apple iPod music player is one of the major catalysts. The iPod holds so much music that no matter how large your music collection, you will seriously consider putting all your music into digital format on your computer, transferring portions of it to the iPod, and playing music from both your computer and your iPod from now on. You might never stop buying CDs, but you won't have to buy all your music that way. And you'll never again need to replace the music that you already own.

As an iPod owner, you're on the cutting edge of music player technology. This chapter introduces the iPod and tells you what to expect when you open the box. We describe how to power up your iPod and connect it to your computer, both of which are essential tasks that you need to know how to do — your iPod needs power, and your iPod needs music, which it gets from your computer.

Introducing the iPod

The iPod is, essentially, a hard drive and a digital music player in one device, but that device is such a thing of beauty and style and so highly recognizable by now that all Apple needs to do in an advertisement is show it all by itself. Even the 40GB model (the largest capacity as of this writing) weighs less than two CDs in standard jewel cases, and iPod mini is smaller than a cell phone and weighs just 3.6 ounces.

The convenience of carrying music on an iPod is phenomenal. For example, the 40GB iPod model can hold around 10,000 songs. That's more than 21 days of nonstop music. You can put enough music on a 40GB iPod to last three weeks if played continuously, around the clock — or about one new song a day for the next 20 years. And with the iPod's built-in skip protection in every model, you don't miss a beat as you jog through the park or your car hits a pothole.

Although Apple has every right to continue to promote its Macintosh computers, the company saw the wisdom of making the iPod compatible with Windows PCs. Every iPod now comes with the software that you need to make it work with Windows systems as well as Macintosh OS X.

A common misconception is that your iPod becomes your music library. Actually, your iPod is simply another *player* for your music library, which is safely stored on your computer. One considerable benefit of digital music technology is that you can use your computer to serve up your music library and make perfect-quality copies. Copy as much of it as you want onto your iPod, and take it on the road. Two decades from now those digital songs will be the same in quality — the music won't be trapped on a cassette or CD that can degrade over time (CDs can stop working after 15-20 years). The wonderfully remixed, remastered, reconstituted version of your favorite album can be copied over and over forever, just like the rest of your information, and it never loses its sound fidelity. If you save your music in digital format, you will never lose a song and have to buy it again.

The iPod experience includes iTunes (or, in some cases, MusicMatch Jukebox), which lets you organize your music in digital form, make copies, burn CDs, and play disc jockey without discs. Suddenly your music world includes online music stores and free music downloads. Without iTunes (or MusicMatch Jukebox), your iPod is merely an external hard drive. As a result of using iTunes (or MusicMatch Jukebox), your music library is more permanent than it ever was before because you can make backup copies that are absolutely the same in quality. We introduce iTunes in Chapter 2 and describe MusicMatch Jukebox in Chapter 7.

You'll spend only about ten seconds copying an entire CD's worth of music from iTunes on your computer to your iPod. Any iPod can play any song in the most popular digital audio formats, including MP3, AIFF, WAV, and the new AAC format, which features CD-quality audio in smaller file sizes than MP3. The iPod also supports the Audible AA spoken word file format.

The iPod is also a *data player,* perhaps the first of its kind. As an external hard drive, the iPod serves as a portable backup device for important data files. You can transfer your calendar and address book to help manage your affairs on the road, and you can even use calendar event alarms to supplement your iPod's alarm and sleep timer. Although the iPod isn't as fully functional as a personal digital assistance (PDA) — for example, you can't add information directly to the device — you can view the information. You can keep your calendar and address book automatically synchronized to your computer, where you normally add and edit information. We cover using the iPod as a data player in detail in Chapter 24 and as a general-purpose hard drive in Chapter 25.

Comparing iPod Models

Introduced way back in the Stone Age of digital music (2001), the iPod family has grown by three generations and spawned at least one private-label version (the HPod from Hewlett-Packard). Even from the beginning, iPod models were truly innovative for their times. With the MP3 music players of 2001, you could carry about 20 typical songs (or a single live Phish set) with you, but the first iPod could hold more than 1,000 typical songs (or a 50-hour Phish concert).

Today's iPod works with iTunes on either Windows computers or Macs, but that wasn't always the case. The first-generation iPods work only with Macs. In 2002, Apple introduced the second generation — one version for Windows and another for the Mac, using the same design for both. For the third generation (2003), Apple changed the design once again.

Third-generation and fourth-generation models, which are the only models available from Apple as of this writing, work with either Windows or Mac and come in a variety of hard-drive sizes. Some would argue that iPod mini, introduced in early 2004, is part of the fourth generation, but in most ways it is more like a spin-off of the third generation because it has the same capabilities and uses the same software as the third generation. (iPod mini also works with either Mac or Windows.) But they look similar — the fourth-generation iPods, announced just as this book went to press, use the same type of buttons and controls as iPod mini.

By design, you can hold an iPod in your hand while you thumb the *scroll wheel* (our generic term for scroll wheel, scroll pad, touch wheel, or click wheel). The LCD screen on full-size models offers backlighting so that you can see it in the dark. For a nifty chart that shows the differences between iPod models, see the specifications page on the Apple iPod Web site (www.apple.com/ipod/specs.html).

First-generation iPods

Apple doesn't sell first-generation iPods anymore, but you might see a few on eBay. More likely, their proud owners are Mac users who still find them useful. Despite its high price tag ($399) compared with other MP3 players, the first 5GB iPod (offering 5GB of storage space) was an unqualified success when it was introduced in October 2001. Apple sold more than 125,000 units within 60 days. "Listening to music will never be the same again," Apple CEO Steve Jobs told the press at the introduction of the first iPod, and he was right. Months later, Apple introduced the 10GB model.

First-generation iPods work only with Macs, connecting to a Mac with a standard FireWire cable. The first generation offers a distinctive scroll wheel that physically turns with your finger as you use it. These early iPods are hefty at 6.5 ounces and have a stainless-steel back and dual-plastic top casing.

FireWire is called *IEEE 1394* by the engineers who designed it and *DV terminal* by camcorder manufacturers that use it, except Sony, which calls it i.Link.

These models don't offer all the features of newer generations and can't be used with accessories that are designed for newer generations. For example, you can't expect these older models to use extensions such as voice recorders and memory card readers. First-generation models can't be updated to version 2 or newer versions of the iPod software, so they also lack support for features such as adding notes to the iPod and setting up an on-the-go playlist. However, battery life is comparable to newer models, offering up to eight hours before requiring a recharge. (For more about battery life, see "Facing Charges of Battery," later in this chapter.)

Second-generation iPods

Just as enterprising Linux and Windows developers were trying to cobble together ways to make the iPod work with their systems, Apple introduced a second-generation design in the form of two models: the 20GB iPod for the Mac and the 10GB for Windows, which was supplied preformatted for Windows. The Windows model of the second generation shipped with MusicMatch Jukebox (which we describe in Chapter 7).

Second-generation models use an innovative solid-state touch wheel that doesn't physically turn as you use it but instead responds to finger pressure. These models use a standard FireWire connection to connect to the computer with a six-pin FireWire cable.

Second-generation models can't be updated to version 2 of the iPod software, so they don't offer all the features of the third and fourth generation and can't be used with accessories designed for third-generation and fourth-generation models. Although standard FireWire accessories (such as power adapters for automobiles) are available for these models, voice recorders and memory card readers are not (as of this writing).

Third-generation iPods

The third-generation models, many of which are still sold in stores as of this writing, include the 10GB, 15GB, and 30GB models introduced in 2003, and the 20GB and 40GB models introduced later in that same year. All third-generation models and variants, such as iPod mini, share the same basic features and work with the Mac or Windows, and Apple continually provides software updates for these models.

Models of the third generation are thinner than the second generation and use touch-sensitive buttons with audible feedback (replacing the pressure-sensitive buttons of the second generation that offer tactile feedback). Third-generation models also use a *dock connector* to connect to a computer or power supply (see Figure 1-1). The dock keeps your iPod in an upright position while connected and lets you connect a home stereo or headphones through the dock, which makes it convenient as a base station when you're not traveling with your iPod — you can slip the iPod into the dock without connecting cables.

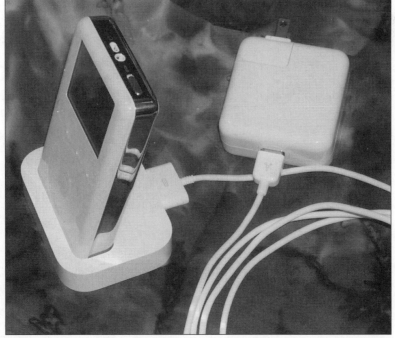

Figure 1-1:
The third-generation iPod in its dock connected to the power adapter.

The dock doesn't come standard with the 15GB model, but you can order it as an extra from the Apple Store.

The supplied cables connect to the dock on one end (or to the iPod itself, if you don't use a dock) and connect to a computer or power supply on the other end, using standard FireWire or USB 2.0 (some models may not include the USB cable, but you can order it from the Apple Store for about $20). (PC users crave choice — you can read about USB in the sidebar "FireWire or USB: That is the question" in this chapter.)

iPod mini

The third generation also includes iPod mini, as shown in Figure 1-2, which is small enough to fit in a shirt pocket. Its smooth, ultra-thin, anodized aluminum case comes in five different colors and houses a 4GB drive that can hold about 1,000 songs — as much as the original 5GB model. (An iPod mini can fit more songs in the same amount of space because Apple introduced a better compression format called AAC in second-generation models, as described in Chapter 19. The AAC format can also be used in older models, so in effect when Apple introduced AAC the capacity of all models increased.)

Figure 1-2:
iPod mini fits
in a shirt
pocket.

Besides its smaller size (and therefore, smaller dock), another of iPod mini's distinguishing characteristic is the click wheel, which offers the same functions as the touch wheel but is more suitable for such a small device. The click wheel combines the scroll wheel and buttons, with pressure-sensitive buttons underneath the top, bottom, left, and right areas of the circular pad of the wheel.

iPod mini has the same software features as the full-size, third-generation iPods except that it uses a different set of accessories because of its size. We describe both types of iPods and their accessories throughout this book.

Fourth-generation iPods

In 2004, Apple just introduced a fourth-generation iPod, shown in Figure 1-3, that uses the same click wheel and buttons as iPod mini, and offers several new features with the new software update (version 3.0) of the iPod software. This includes the ability to randomly shuffle the playback of songs with the press of a button and to charge up the iPod through the USB connection to your computer (previously only FireWire connections to the computer provided power). The fourth-generation iPods are available in 40GB and 20GB models.

Figure 1-3: The fourth-generation iPod uses the same click wheel as iPod mini.

The fourth generation units also offer up to 12 hours of battery time between charges. The battery is the same type as used in other models — the improvement is in how the software manages power in the iPod. Like third-generation iPods, the fourth generation also uses a dock connector to connect the iPod to a computer or power supply, and the dock itself is available separately from the Apple Store. The fourth-generation iPods connect to computers using either FireWire or USB connections.

The fourth generation iPod models differ from earlier models by offering a top-level Music choice in the main menu and the ability to create multiple on-the-go playlists. You can also play audio books at slower or faster speeds while maintaining natural-sounding pitch.

iPod shuffle

If the regular iPod models are not small enough to fit into your lifestyle, try the newest model — called the iPod shuffle — which is as much a fashion statement as a state-of-the-art music player because this one you can wear! The iPod shuffle is 3.3 inches long, less than 1 inch wide, and about a ⅛ inch thick. It's so tiny that it weighs only 0.78 of an ounce, which is little more than a car key or pack of gum (see Figure 1-4). You can hang it from your ears using the supplied earbuds and wear it around your neck like a necklace.

The 512MB iPod shuffle can hold 120 songs, and the 1GB model can hold 240 — assuming an average of four minutes per song, using the AAC format at the High Quality setting (as described in Chapter 19). Remember, the iPod shuffle is not for storing music permanently — you use it just to play selections from the iTunes library on your computer. It has no display, but that's actually a good thing, because it keeps the size and weight down to a minimum. And needs to display to play a couple of hundred songs in random or sequential order.

Figure 1-4:
The iPod shuffle weighs less than an ounce and offers skip-free playback.

With skip-free playback, lightweight design, and no need for a display, you can easily use the iPod shuffle while skiing, snowboarding, or even skydiving (and if you're at a high altitude, try "Expecting to Fly" by Buffalo Springfield, or "Astral Traveling" by Pharoah Sanders). That's because it uses flash memory rather than a hard drive — you can shake it as hard as you want without a glitch. The iPod shuffle's battery, similar to the ones used in other fourth-generation iPods, offers up to 12 hours of power between charges.

Unlike other iPods, the iPod shuffle can't play tunes in the AIFF or Apple Lossless formats, which consume a lot of storage space but are higher in sonic quality. You can play songs in the AAC format (including songs from the online iTunes Music Store) or the MP3 format; both formats compress the music to use much less space.

To turn on the iPod shuffle, use the three-position toggle switch on the back; a green stripe below the switch helps you see what position the switch is in. Operation and controls are simple, as follows:

- ✔ The top position turns the iPod shuffle off; the middle position starts playing the list of songs from beginning to end in sequential order; and the bottom position shuffles through songs randomly — you don't know what song will come next, and that's its appeal. You may want a little randomness in your life.

- ✔ By using the buttons that look like standard CD-player buttons on the front, you can skip forward to the next song or skip back to the previous one. The center button either starts or pauses playback. The plus (+) button turns the volume up, and the minus (-) button turns it down.

The iPod shuffle shines a yellow LED on the front side to show when the player is charging, and a green LED when the shuffle is completely charged. A blinking green LED indicates that the player is on pause. On the back, just below the toggle switch, is a Battery Status button that, when pressed, flashes an LED to indicate how much battery juice remains: green is a good charge; yellow is a low charge; red is a *very* low charge. No glow at all means no power remains.

Underneath the cap on the tip of the iPod shuffle is a convenient USB 2.0 connector that links the iPod shuffle to a computer or to an optional power supply and supplies power for recharging its battery. You don't need a separate cable. And the iPod shuffle charges its battery from your computer, so you don't need the optional power supply. You can also get optional the $29 iPod shuffle External Battery Pack, which provides 20 additional hours of playtime with two AAA batteries.

FireWire or USB: That is the question

If you use a Mac, FireWire is the choice to make unless your Mac offers USB 2.0 and you're using an iPod mini. If you use a PC, you can choose between FireWire and USB 2.0 depending on which one you already have and whether you need to use the ports for something else.

Why so complicated? It's a question of speed and convenience. FireWire can hustle data at rates up to 400 Mbps over its cable. That's typically fast enough — with FireWire, you can transfer an entire CD's worth of music in less than ten seconds.

But engineers are never happy; they keep making things better. USB (Universal Serial Bus) has been around for a while, connecting hundreds of nifty devices to PCs. Such nifty devices include keyboards, pointing devices, external hard drives, keychain-sized flash drives, printers, scanners, and much more. USB proponents envied FireWire, which is more than 30 times faster than USB version 1.1, which offers a speed of only 12 Mbps. So they developed a more advanced generation of USB. Version 2.0 has a transfer rate of 480 Mbps — that's 40 times faster than the first version — but since USB in practice does not sustain that rate for the entire data transfer, as FireWire does, FireWire is still faster.

Both FireWire and USB 2.0 connections are plug-and-play: You can plug them in at any time whether your computer is on or off. Depending on the device that you use with these connections, FireWire or USB 2.0 can provide power to the device.

The horse race between FireWire and USB 2.0 has left some computers in the dust, such as older Macs and PCs. Many Mac models now sport USB 2.0 connectors, but when it comes to iPods, only iPod mini supports USB 2.0 for the Mac. So, for most Mac users, FireWire is the only choice. Many desktop PCs and laptops offer PCI and/or CardBus slots for adding FireWire or USB 2.0 cards, and some PCs offer built-in FireWire or USB 2.0.

You can add FireWire to your PC with an expansion card such as the FireCard 400 CardBus card from Unibrain (www.unibrain.com), which plugs into a PC desktop or laptop CardBus slot. Laptop PCs made as far back as 1999 offer CardBus slots. Desktop PCs typically let you add expansion cards inside the PC, and there are many IEEE 1394 expansion cards available on the market. Before you buy a FireWire/IEEE 1394 card, make sure that it's compatible with your hardware and operating system. Apple offers approved FireWire expansion cards at the online Apple Store (http://store.apple.com/1-800-MY-APPLE/WebObjects/AppleStore).

If you have trouble installing your FireWire or USB 2.0 card or using your iPod with it, see Chapter 28 for troubleshooting tips.

Thinking Inside the Box

Don't destroy the elegantly designed box while opening it; you might want to place it prominently in your collection of Equipment That Ushered in the 21st Century. Before going any further, check the box and make sure that all the correct parts came with your iPod.

Things you have and things you need

The iPod box includes a CD-ROM with the iTunes software for the Mac and PC and the FireWire and USB cables you can use to connect your iPod to a computer. All models come with a FireWire-compatible power adapter for connecting either the older iPod or the newer iPod-in-dock to an AC power source.

With most models, you also get a set of earbud headphones and a remote controller that connects to the iPod by wire. The accessories don't stop there — you might also have a carrying case and some other goodies. Optional accessories, many of which we describe in this book, are available at the online Apple Store (www.apple.com/store).

You also need a few things that don't come with the iPod:

- **A PC or Mac:** With a Mac, iTunes requires Mac OS X 10.1.5 or newer for connecting with FireWire (OS X 10.3.4 for connecting via USB), a 400 MHz G3 processor or better and at least 256MB of RAM. You also need QuickTime, which you can download from the Apple Web site for free (but most Macs already have it). On a PC, iTunes requires Windows 2000 or XP, a 500 MHz Pentium-class processor or faster, and 256MB of RAM. You can alternatively use the iPod with MusicMatch Jukebox and a 300 MHz or faster PC with at least 96MB of RAM running Windows Me, 2000, or XP (with at least 128MB of RAM).

- **FireWire or USB connection on a PC:** All Macs provide FireWire, so you're all set. PCs running Windows must have FireWire also called IEEE 1394) or USB 2.0. See the sidebar "FireWire or USB: That is the question" in this chapter for more information about FireWire and USB 2.0 connections on PCs.

- **iTunes 4.6 or newer:** You can download Mac or Windows versions for free from the Apple Web site (www.apple.com/itunes). The CD-ROM that's supplied with newer iPods should have both versions of iTunes as well, but some may have iTunes 4.5 — which is fine, because version 4.5 works (it just doesn't have all the features of 4.6), and you can download the 4.6 version at any time to replace it. CD-ROMs supplied with some older iPod models provided MusicMatch Jukebox instead. You can use MusicMatch Jukebox if you don't meet the requirements to run iTunes (see Chapter 7).

- *Optional:* Mac users can install iSync, which is a free utility program from Apple for synchronizing your iPod (and PDAs and cell phones) with your address book and calendar, and iCal for creating and editing your calendar. Both are available for free from www.apple.com.

Using FireWire or USB cables with a Mac

If you have a Mac, the choice is easy: FireWire has been a part of every Mac since at least 2000, and it's much faster than the USB connections typical on Macs. (To find out about FireWire, see the sidebar "FireWire or USB: That is the question" in this chapter.) However, differences exist between iPod generations.

Current (third-generation and fourth-generation) models offer a special cable with a flat dock connector to connect the dock — or the iPod itself — to the Mac's FireWire port. The dock includes a cable with a flat dock connector on one end and a FireWire (or optional USB) connector on the other. (An optional cable is available from the Apple Store that offers USB). You can connect the FireWire or USB end of the cable to the computer (to synchronize with iTunes and play iPod music in iTunes) or to the power adapter.

The connection on the bottom of the iPod is the same as the connection on back of the dock. Plug the flat connector of the cable into the iPod or dock, and then plug the six-pin FireWire connector on the other end to the FireWire port on your Mac (marked the Y symbol that resembles a radiation symbol), or plug the USB connector to the USB port on your Mac.

The full-size third-generation iPods don't support USB 2.0 on the Mac, but iPod mini and fourth-generation models support it if your Mac offers USB 2.0, and a USB cable is provided. You need OS X 10.3.4 for connecting via USB 2.0 to a Mac.

First-generation and second-generation models offer only a standard FireWire connection, so you can use a standard Mac-style FireWire cable to connect the iPod to the Mac's FireWire connection. Plug the six-pin connector of a standard FireWire cable into the iPod, and plug the six-pin connector on the other end to the FireWire port on your Mac. (The six-pin connector is marked by the Y symbol that resembles a radiation symbol.)

Using FireWire or USB cables with a PC

If you have a Windows PC you can use FireWire (called IEEE 1394 in PC circles), or USB 2.0, which is available on most current desktop PCs and laptops.

FireWire/IEEE 1394 expansion cards are available in various formats: Some offer the standard six-pin port found on Macs, and some offer a four-pin port that is also used in camcorders. If your card has a six-pin port, you can plug your iPod cable directly into it.

For cards with four-pin ports, Apple provides the FireWire cable adapter, as shown in Figure 1-5, and you can hook it up to the Mac-standard six-pin connector at the end of your FireWire cable. The small four-pin connector on the adapter plugs into the four-pin port on the FireWire card. Then plug the other end of your cable to your iPod or your dock. You can purchase a special FireWire/IEEE 1394 cable that has a six-pin plug on one end and a four-pin plug on the other — look for it in well-stocked electronics stores that sell digital camcorders, as many camcorders use such a cable.

The FireWire cable adapter is supplied with full-size iPods but not with iPod mini. You can purchase one from the Apple Store.

If you use USB 2.0 with your PC, you can use the USB 2.0 cable supplied with your iPod or iPod mini. The USB 2.0 cable that has a flat dock connector on one end and a USB 2.0 connector on the other. Apple also offers a combination FireWire/USB 2.0 cable with a dock connector on one end and a cable that forks into two connectors — one for FireWire and one for USB 2.0.

Figure 1-5:
The FireWire cable adapter for connecting to a FireWire card that has a four-pin port.

Powering Up Your iPod

All iPods come with essentially the same requirement: power. Fortunately, it also comes with a cable and an AC power adapter that works with voltages in North America and many parts of Europe and Asia. (See Chapter 17 for information about plugging into power in other countries.)

First-generation and second-generation iPod models offer a Mac-style FireWire connection on the top of the iPod. The power adapter also sports a FireWire connection, so all you need is a standard six-pin FireWire cable to plug in.

Third-generation and fourth-generation models and iPod mini can use a dock that offers FireWire and USB connections. The dock can also connect to your home stereo through a line-out connection.

A FireWire connection to a Mac provides power to the iPod and recharges the battery as long as the Mac isn't in sleep mode. A FireWire connection to a FireWire/IEEE 1394 card in a PC might not be able to provide power — check with the card manufacturer. The smaller 4-pin connections for FireWire/IEEE 1394 cards typically don't supply power to the iPod.

If your iPod shows a display but doesn't respond to your touch, don't panic — check the Hold switch on top of the unit and make sure that it's set to one side so that the orange bar disappears (the normal position). You use the Hold switch for locking the buttons, which prevents accidental activation.

You might notice that the iPod's display turns iridescent when it gets too hot or too cold, but this effect disappears when its temperature returns to normal. iPods can function in temperatures as cold as 50 degrees and as warm as 95 degrees (Fahrenheit) but work best at room temperature (closer to 68 degrees).

If you leave your iPod out in the cold all night, it might have trouble waking from sleep mode, and it might even display a low battery message. Plug the iPod into a power source, wait until it warms up, and try it again. If it still doesn't wake up or respond properly, try resetting the iPod as we describe in "Resetting Your iPod," later in this chapter.

Facing Charges of Battery

You can take a six-hour flight from Pennsylvania to California and listen to your iPod the entire time. All iPod models use the same type of built-in rechargeable lithium ion battery; the first-, second-, and third-generation iPods offer up to eight hours of battery power, and the fourth generation offers up to 12 hours.

However, keep in mind that playback battery time varies with the type of encoder that you use for the music files in iTunes — Chapter 19 has more information about encoders. It also varies depending on how you use your iPod controls and settings.

The iPod battery recharges automatically when you connect the iPod to a power source — for example, it starts charging immediately when you insert it into a dock that's connected to a power source (or to a computer with a powered FireWire connection). It takes only four hours to recharge the battery fully. Need power when you're on the run? Look for a power outlet in the airport terminal or hotel lobby — you can fast-charge the battery to 80-percent capacity in one hour. If you can wait four hours, your iPod is fully charged.

WARNING!

Don't fry your iPod with some generic power adapter — use *only* the power adapter supplied with the iPod from Apple.

A battery icon in the top-right corner of the iPod display indicates with a progress bar how much power is left. When you charge the battery, the icon turns into a lightning bolt inside a battery. If the icon doesn't animate, the battery is fully charged. You can also use your iPod while the battery is charging, or disconnect it and use it before the battery is fully charged.

Maintaining battery life

The iPod's built-in rechargeable lithium ion battery is, essentially, a life-or-death proposition. After it's dead, it can be replaced, but the replacement may cost more than $50 (some services may charge less for older models). If your warranty is still active, you can have Apple replace it — but you don't want to do that yourself because opening the iPod invalidates the warranty.

Fortunately the battery is easy to maintain. We recommend *calibrating* the battery once soon after you get your iPod — that is, run it all the way down (a full discharge) and then charge it all the way up (which takes four hours). Although this doesn't actually change battery performance, it does improve the battery gauge so that the iPod displays a more accurate indicator.

Unlike batteries that require you to fully discharge and then recharge in order to get a fuller capacity, the iPod lithium ion battery prefers a partial rather than a full discharge, so avoid frequent full discharges after the initial calibration (frequent full discharges can lower battery life). Lithium ion batteries typically last three years or more and are vulnerable to high temperatures, which decrease their life spans considerably. Don't leave your iPod in a hot place, such as on a sunny car dashboard, for very long.

For an excellent technical description of how to maintain rechargeable lithium ion batteries, see the BatteryUniversity.com Web site (www.battery university.com/parttwo-34.htm).

The bottom of the iPod warms up when it's powered on. The bottom functions as a cooling surface that transfers heat from inside the unit to the cooler air outside. The iPod's carrying case acts as an insulator, so be sure to remove the iPod from its carrying case before you recharge it.

Keeping the iPod encased in its carrying case when charging is tempting but also potentially disastrous. The iPod needs to dissipate its heat, and you could damage the unit by overheating it and frying its circuits, rendering it as useful as a paperweight. To get around this problem, you can purchase one of the heat-dissipating carrying cases available in the Apple Store. For example, Marware (`www.marware.com/`) offers the SportSuit Convertible case ($39.95).

Even when not in use, your iPod drinks the juice. If your iPod is inactive for 14 days, you must recharge its battery — perhaps the iPod gets depressed from being left alone too long.

Saving power

Your iPod is a hard drive, and whatever causes the hard drive to spin causes a drain on power. Your iPod also has a *cache* — a memory chip holding the section of music to play next. The iPod uses the cache not only to eliminate skipping when something jostles the hard drive but also to conserve power because the drive doesn't have to spin as much.

If you use the AIFF or WAV formats for importing music into iTunes (or MusicMatch Jukebox), don't use these formats with your iPod — convert the music first, as we describe in Chapter 20. These formats take up way too much space on the iPod hard drive and fill up the iPod cache too quickly, causing skips when you play them and using too much battery power because the drive spins more often. (See Chapter 5 for importing with iTunes, or flip to Chapter 7 for importing with MusicMatch Jukebox. Chapter 19 provides detailed information about these formats.)

The following are tips on power saving while using your iPod:

- **Pause:** Pause playback when you're not listening. Pausing (stopping) playback is the easiest way to conserve power.

- **Back away from the light:** Use the iPod backlight sparingly. Press and hold the Menu button to turn off the backlight, or select Backlight from the iPod main menu to turn it on or off. For a solution that lasts longer, turn the Backlight Timer setting to Off on the Settings menu. Don't use the backlight in daylight.

✔ **Hold it:** Flip the Hold switch to the lock position (with the orange bar showing) to make sure that controls aren't accidentally activated. You don't want your iPod playing music in your pocket and draining the battery when you're not listening.

✔ **You may continue:** Play songs continuously without using the iPod controls. Selecting songs and using Previous/Rewind and Next/Fast-Forward requires precious energy. Not only that, but the hard drive has to spin more often when searching for songs, using more power than during continuous playback.

Always use the latest iPod software and update your software when updates come out. Apple is always trying to improve the way your iPod works, and many of these advancements relate to power usage.

Replacing your battery

Apple customers aren't always happy campers. Early iPods came with batteries that couldn't be replaced, but all it took were a few premature battery failures and quite a few customer complaints for Apple to institute a battery replacement service. Apple also offers a special AppleCare warranty for iPods.

You can't remove or replace the iPod internal battery yourself — you need Apple to replace it if it dies.

If your iPod isn't responding after a reset (see "Resetting Your iPod" in this chapter for how to reset your iPod), follow the troubleshooting steps in Chapter 28. If these steps don't restore your iPod to working condition, you might have a battery problem. Go to the Apple support page for the iPod (www.apple.com/support/ipod/index.html) and click the iPod service FAQ link to read frequently asked questions and answers about iPod support. Then click the iPod service request form link on the support page and follow the instructions to request service and return your iPod for a replacement.

The only time we had to do this (with a 30GB iPod), Apple required us to send just the iPod unit itself, without the power adapter or any other accessories, to Apple's service facility. Within a week, Apple sent back a brand new iPod (same model).

Thumbing through the Menus

After you import music into the iPod, you're ready to play music. The design of the iPod lets you hold it in one hand and perform simple operations by thumb. Even if you're all thumbs when pressing small buttons on tiny devices, you can still thumb your way to iPod heaven.

The iPod's unique circular scroll wheel makes scrolling through an entire music collection quick and easy. With your finger or thumb, scroll clockwise on the wheel to scroll down a list, or counter-clockwise to scroll up. As you scroll, options on the menu are highlighted. Use the Select button at the center of the scroll wheel to select whatever is highlighted in the menu display.

In full-size third-generation models, the touch-sensitive buttons above the scroll wheel perform simple functions when you touch them. (First-generation and second-generation models aren't touch-sensitive, so you need to press them.)

iPod mini and fourth-generation iPods provide a click wheel that offers the same functions as the scroll wheel *and* the clickable buttons. It has pressure-sensitive buttons underneath the top, bottom, left, and right areas of the circular pad of the wheel. These areas tilt as you press them, activating the buttons.

The iPod main menu for the newer fourth-generation models, shown in Figure 1-6, offers the following selections:

- **Music:** Select music by playlist, artist, album, song, genre, or composer, or select an audio book.
- **Extras:** View and set the clock and alarm clock, view contacts, view your calendar, view notes, and play games.
- **Settings:** Set display settings, menu settings, the backlight timer, the clicker, and the date and time.
- **Shuffle Songs:** Play songs from your music library in random order.
- **Backlight:** Turn on or off the backlighting for the iPod display.
- **Now Playing:** This appears only when a song is playing — it takes you to the Now Playing display.

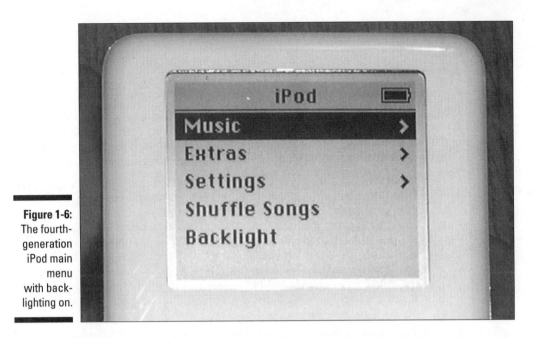

Figure 1-6:
The fourth-
generation
iPod main
menu
with back-
lighting on.

The main menu for first, second, and third generation iPods, and iPod mini, replace the Music selection above with the following:

- ✔ **Playlists:** Select a playlist to play.
- ✔ **Browse:** Select by artist, album, song, genre, or composer.

Pressing the iPod Buttons

The buttons do various tasks for song playback:

- ✔ **Previous/Rewind:** Press once to start a song over. Press twice to skip to the previous song. Press and hold to rewind through a song.
- ✔ **Menu:** Press once to go back to the previous menu. Each time you press, you go back to a previous menu until you reach the main menu. Press and hold the button to turn on the backlight.
- ✔ **Play/Pause:** Press to play the selected song, album, or playlist. Press Play/Pause when a song is playing to pause the playback.
- ✔ **Next/Fast-Forward:** Press once to skip to the next song. Press and hold Next/Fast-Forward to fast-forward through the song.

The buttons and scroll wheel can do more complex functions when used in combination:

- ✓ **Turn on the iPod.** Press any button.

- ✓ **Turn off the iPod.** Press and hold the Play/Pause button.

- ✓ **Disable the iPod buttons.** To keep from accidentally pressing the buttons, push the Hold switch to the other side so that an orange bar appears (the Hold position). To reactivate the iPod buttons, push the Hold switch back to the other side so that the orange bar disappears (the normal position).

- ✓ **Reset the iPod.** Set the Hold switch to the Hold position, and then move it back to normal. Then, on first-, second-, or third-generation iPods or iPod mini, press the Menu and Play/Pause buttons simultaneously for about five seconds until the Apple logo appears in the iPod display; for the newer fourth-generation iPods, press the Menu and Select buttons simultaneously for six seconds. You can reset the iPod if it gets hung up for some reason. (For example, it might get confused if you press the buttons too quickly.) This operation resets the iPod, essentially restarting the iPod's hard drive. It doesn't change the music or data on the iPod. See "Resetting Your iPod," later in this chapter.

- ✓ **Turn the backlight on and off.** Press and hold the Menu button (or select the Backlight option from the main menu).

- ✓ **Change the volume.** While playing a song (the display reads Now Playing), adjust the volume with the scroll wheel — clockwise turns the volume up, counterclockwise turns the volume down. A volume slider appears on the iPod display, indicating the volume level as you scroll.

- ✓ **Skip to any point in a song.** While playing a song (the display says Now Playing), press and hold the Select button until the progress bar appears to indicate where you are in the song, and then use the scroll wheel to scroll to any point in the song. Scroll clockwise to move forward, and counterclockwise to move backward.

Setting the Language

Wiedergabelisten? Übersicht? (Playlists? Browse?) If your iPod is speaking in a foreign tongue, don't panic — you're not in the wrong country. You might have purchased an iPod that's set to a foreign language. More likely, someone set it to a different language accidentally or on purpose (as a practical joke). Fortunately, you can change the setting without having to know the language that it's set to.To set the language, no matter what language the menu is using, follow these steps:

1. **Press the Menu button repeatedly until pressing it doesn't change the words on the display.**

If pressing the Menu button no longer changes the display, you're at the main menu.

2. **Choose the third option from the top on the newer fourth-generation iPods, or the fourth option on iPod mini and older models (in English, this is the Settings option).**

   Scroll clockwise until the item is highlighted, and then press the Select button. The Settings menu appears.

3. **Choose the thirteenth option from the top on the newer fourth-generation iPods, or the twelfth option on older models (which, in English, is the Language option).**

   The Language menu appears.

4. **Choose the language that you want to use. (English is at the top of the list.)**

If these steps don't do the trick, the menu may have been customized (something you can discover how to do in Chapter 24). Someone could have customized it previously, or perhaps you accidentally pressed buttons that customized the menu. To get around this problem, you can reset all the iPod settings back to the defaults. (Unfortunately, resetting your iPod settings back to the defaults wipes out any customizations that you've made; you have to redo any repeat/shuffle settings, alarms, backlight timer settings, and so on.)

Follow these steps to reset all your settings, no matter what language displays:

1. **Press the Menu button repeatedly until pressing it doesn't change the words on the display.**

   If pressing the Menu button no longer changes the display, you're at the main menu.

2. **Choose the third option from the top on the newer fourth-generation iPods, or the fourth option on iPod mini and older models (in English, this is the Settings option).**

   The Settings menu appears.

3. **Choose the option at the bottom of the menu (in English, the Reset All Settings option).**

   The Reset All Settings menu appears.

4. **Choose the second menu option (in English, the Reset option; the first menu option is Cancel).**

   The Language menu appears.

5. **Choose the language you want to use. (English is at the top of the list.)**

The language you choose now applies to all the iPod menus. But don't go pulling that joke on someone else!

Resetting Your iPod

If your iPod doesn't turn on, don't panic — at least not yet. First check the Hold switch's position on top of the iPod. If it's in the locked position (with orange showing), slide it to the normal position. If it still doesn't work, check whether the iPod has enough juice. Is the battery charged up? Connect the iPod to a power source and see whether it works.

There are times when your iPod freezes up or seems confused, and it just won't start up. Pressing more than one iPod button at the same time might have caused this problem, or perhaps you disconnected the iPod from your computer before it had a chance to display the iPod's main menu (or in older models, the message saying it's okay to disconnect). In situations like this, you can *reset* the iPod.

Resetting the iPod isn't the same as resetting the *settings* of your iPod. If all you need to do is reset the settings on the Settings menu, you can choose Settings⇨Reset All Settings⇨Reset from the main menu. (We cover the settings on the Settings menu in Chapter 24.) All your menu and display settings return to their original values.

This section is about a different kind of reset — similar to pressing a reset button on a computer. This operation resets the operating system of the iPod and restarts the system. Sometimes when your iPod gets confused or refuses to turn on, you can fix it by resetting it. Follow these steps:

1. **Toggle the Hold switch to the locked position and then back to the unlocked position.**

   This step is like the beginning of a secret handshake.

2. **On the new fourth-generation models, press the Menu and Select buttons simultaneously; on older models, press the Menu and Play/Pause buttons simultaneously. Hold these buttons for at least six seconds until the Apple logo appears; then release the buttons when you see the Apple logo.**

   The appearance of the Apple logo signals that your iPod is resetting itself, so you no longer have to hold down the buttons.

   Releasing the Menu and Select buttons (or Play/Pause on older models) as soon as you see the Apple logo is important. If you continue to hold down the buttons after the logo appears, the iPod displays the low battery icon (which looks like a slashed battery), and you must connect it to a power source before using your iPod again.

After resetting, everything should be back to normal, including your music and data files.

Chapter 2

Setting Up iTunes and Your iPod

- -

In This Chapter

▶ Downloading the iTunes and iPod installers

▶ Setting up iTunes on a Mac

▶ Setting up iTunes on a PC running Windows

▶ Installing iPod software for a Mac

▶ Installing iPod software for Windows

- -

An iPod without iTunes is like a CD player without CDs. Sure, you can use applications and utilities from sources other than Apple to put music on an iPod. (See Chapter 23 if you don't believe us.) But iTunes gives you access to the vast online iTunes Music Store, and it's excellent for managing music on your computer and synchronizing your music library with your iPod.

On the Mac, iTunes is practically the only jukebox in town — it's not profitable to compete with something that's free. And yet, Apple hasn't abused its position by putting out a less-than-functional program. On Windows, iTunes has plenty of competition but is still one of the top five audio players.

This chapter explains how to set up your iPod with iTunes on the Mac or for Windows. You have to choose one or the other, at least for the moment — to see how to switch from one type of computer to another, flip to Chapter 28.

If you don't use Windows 2000 or Windows XP on your PC, you can't use iTunes for Windows — you have to install MusicMatch Jukebox from the iPod CD-ROM. (We describe MusicMatch Jukebox in Chapter 7.) You might want to use MusicMatch Jukebox for other reasons, such as its compatibility with other audio formats and its own MusicMatch MX radio — but you must choose because your iPod can synchronize with only iTunes *or* MusicMatch Jukebox.

Setting Up iTunes

If your Mac is rather new, you probably already have iTunes installed because all Macs sold since 2003 (and many before that time) are preinstalled with iTunes and Mac OS X (version 10.1.5 or newer). The most up-to-date version of iTunes as of this writing is version 4.6. If you've never used iTunes before, when you first launch it, you automatically get the iTunes Setup Assistant.

The version of iTunes that's provided with your iPod on a CD-ROM might be the newest version; then again, it might not be. Software updates occur very rapidly. If you really want the latest version, go directly to the Apple Web site to get it. You can download iTunes for free. Install iTunes first, and then install the iPod software.

You can set your Mac to automatically download the latest version of iTunes when it becomes available. Simply use Software Update from the Mac OS X System Preferences window. Click the Check Now button to check for a new version. If one exists, it appears in a window for you to select. Click the check mark to select it, and then click Install to download and install it.

If you use a PC with Windows, you most likely don't have iTunes yet. Go directly to the Apple Web site and download the latest version.

iPods that were sold before iTunes became available for Windows (in the fall of 2003) don't include iTunes on the CD-ROM. The older iPod CD-ROMs install MusicMatch Jukebox. If you plan on using iTunes for Windows, which requires Windows XP or Windows 2000, download the newer iTunes and iPod installers from the Apple Web site.

When you get your iPod, you might be tempted to go ahead and install from the CD-ROM. Our experience, especially with Windows PCs, is that you're better off going to the Apple Web site first and downloading the latest versions of the iTunes and iPod installers for Windows. Install iTunes first, and then install the iPod software.

To download iTunes for Mac or Windows, go to the Apple iTunes page on the Web (www.apple.com/itunes), select the appropriate version (Mac or Windows), and then click the Download iTunes button, as shown in Figure 2-1. Follow the instructions to download the installer to your hard drive. Pick a location on your hard drive to save the installer.

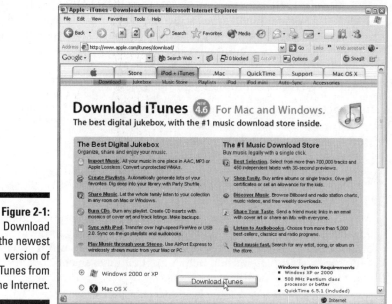

Figure 2-1:
Download
the newest
version of
iTunes from
the Internet.

Setting up iTunes on a Mac

If you downloaded the iTunes installer, launch the installer to unpack and install iTunes. To install iTunes from the CD-ROM, open the iTunes folder on the CD-ROM, and then double-click the iTunes package file (it has an `.mpkg` extension) to unpack and install it.

The Mac version installs iTunes in the Applications folder on the Mac OS X startup drive. Mac users can proceed by directly launching iTunes and setting it up with the iTunes Setup Assistant. Follow these steps:

1. **Launch iTunes.**

   Double-click the iTunes application or click the iTunes icon in the Dock.

2. **If this is the first time you've used iTunes, click the Agree button for Apple's License Agreement.**

   Apple's License Agreement appears only when you start iTunes for the first time.

Optional: Before you click the Agree button, you have a few other options. You can click the Save button to save the license agreement as a document, the Print button to print it, the Decline button to quit iTunes immediately, or simply go with the Agree button. No lawyers are present when you do this; it's all up to you.

3. **Click Next in the iTunes Setup Assistant opening screen.**

   The iTunes Setup Assistant takes you through the process of setting up iTunes for the Internet. After clicking Next, the iTunes Setup Assistant displays a window with questions.

4. **Select Yes or No to answer the following questions:**

   • Would you like to use iTunes to handle audio content from the Internet?

   We suggest selecting Yes, allowing iTunes to handle audio content, because iTunes offers more features than you typically find with browser plug-ins from other companies. On the other hand, if you're happy with your plug-ins and helper applications, select No and leave your Internet settings untouched.

   • Do you want iTunes to automatically connect when it's necessary?

   If you use an always-on broadband Internet service, you probably want iTunes to connect automatically, and you can select Yes. If you use a dial-up modem, if your Internet service is intermittently off, or if your Internet service charges when you use it, you probably don't want this connection to be automatic. Selecting No forces iTunes to ask first.

   After you click Done, the iTunes Setup Assistant also asks whether you want iTunes to search your home folder for music files. You might want to click the No button for now because iTunes might find files that you don't want to add to your library (such as music for games).

5. **The assistant asks whether you want to keep your iTunes music folder organized. Select Yes or No, and then click Next.**

   This seems like a no-brainer — the default is Yes, which tells iTunes to keep your music files organized — iTunes renames and moves files into appropriate folders when you edit the artist name, song title, album name, or track number. If you don't want this type of organization, select No.

6. **The assistant asks whether you want to go straight to the iTunes Music Store. Select Yes or No, and then click Next.**

   We suggest selecting No. However, if you can't wait to go shopping, Chapter 4 gives you the scoop on the iTunes Music Store.

7. **Click Done.**

   That's it — the iTunes window appears. (We unravel the wonders of this window in Chapter 3.) You can drag the bottom-right corner of your iTunes window to make it larger or smaller on your screen.

Whether or not you set iTunes to automatically connect to the Internet, be sure to connect to the Internet with iTunes at some point. Doing so allows you to buy music online and listen to Web radio. You can even retrieve track information when you insert a CD so that you don't have to type the information yourself.

Setting up iTunes for Windows

Before installing iTunes for Windows, make sure that you're logged on as a Windows Administrator user if you're using Windows 2000 or Windows XP. Quit all other applications before installing and disable any virus protection software.

To install iTunes for Windows, download the iTunesSetup.exe file from the Apple Web site, as we describe earlier in this chapter (refer to Figure 2-1).

If for some reason you can't download this software from the Internet, and you know for certain that the CD-ROM includes iTunes for Windows, you can use the CD-ROM to install iTunes. The CD-ROM installation process installs both iTunes for Windows and the iPod Updater for Windows. See the section "Setting Up Your iPod with a Windows PC" for information about installing iTunes for Windows from the CD-ROM.

To install iTunes for Windows, follow these steps:

1. **Double-click the** iTunesSetup.exe **file, which you can download from the Apple Web site.**

   The installer comes to life, displaying its opening screen.

2. **Click Next to begin installing iTunes for Windows.**

   After clicking Next, the installer displays a pane in the window with questions about the type of setup, as shown in Figure 2-2.

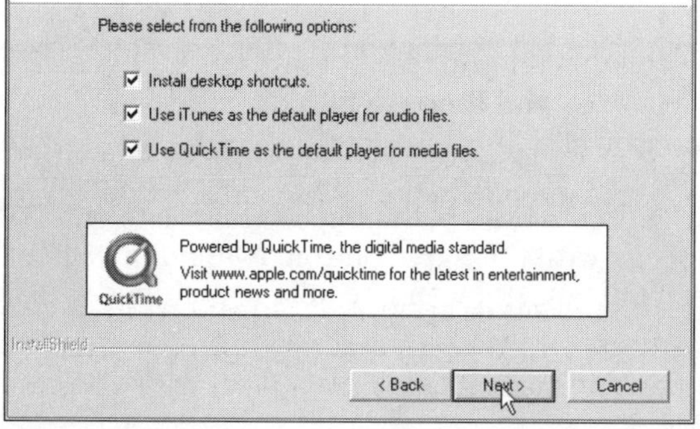

Figure 2-2: Setup options for the iTunes installation in Windows.

3. **Select the appropriate options for your iTunes setup, and then click Next.**

   The options are

   - **Install Desktop Shortcuts:** You can install shortcuts for your Windows desktop for iTunes.

   - **Use iTunes as the Default Player for Audio Files:** We suggest turning this on — allowing iTunes to be the default audio content player — because iTunes offers more features than you typically find with players and browser plug-ins from other companies. On the other hand, if you're happy with your audio player, you can deselect this option, leaving your default player setting unaffected.

   - **Use QuickTime as the Default Player for Media Files:** We suggest turning this on — allowing QuickTime to be the default audio multimedia (including video and audio) player — because QuickTime for Windows can play just about any media format and is comparable to players and browser plug-ins from other companies. On the other hand, if you're happy with your media player, you can deselect this option, leaving your default media player setting unaffected.

4. **In the Choose Destination Location pane, select a destination folder for iTunes, and then click Next.**

   By default, the installer assumes that you want to store the program in the Program Files folder of your C: drive (which is an excellent place to store it, unless you have other ideas). If you want to use a different folder, click Browse to use Windows Explorer to locate the desired folder.

   After you click Next, the installer proceeds with its task.

5. **When the installer finishes, click Done.**

   iTunes for Windows is now installed on your PC.

To set iTunes up for your Internet connection and start using it, double-click the iTunes program or use your Start menu to locate iTunes and launch it. After that, follow these steps:

1. **If this is the first time you've used iTunes, click the Agree button for Apple's License Agreement.**

   Apple's License Agreement appears only when you start iTunes for the first time.

   Optional: Before you click the Agree button, you have a few other options. You can click the Save button to save the license agreement as a document, the Print button to print it, the Decline button to quit iTunes immediately, or simply go with the Agree button. If you don't agree, you can consult a lawyer, but you still won't be able to continue with the setup.

2. **Click Next in the iTunes Setup Assistant opening screen.**

   The iTunes Setup Assistant takes you through the process of setting up the Windows version of iTunes for the Internet. After clicking Next, the Setup Assistant displays a pane that helps you find music files on your PC, as shown in Figure 2-3.

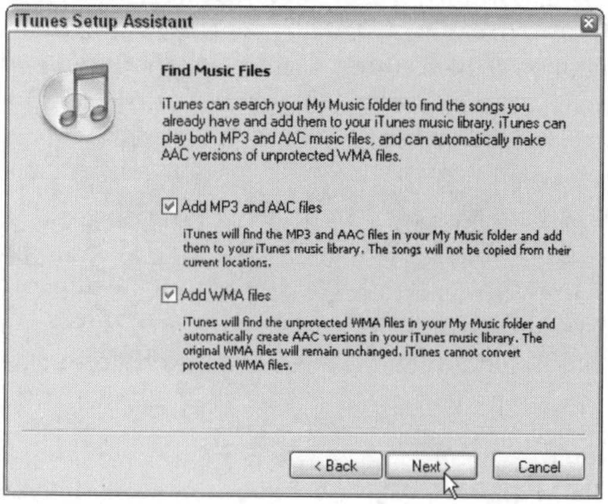

Figure 2-3:
Finding
music files
using iTunes
Setup
Assistant.

3. **Select or deselect the following options for finding music (by default they are selected):**

   • **Add MP3 and AAC Files:** Select this option if you already have music files in the AAC format that's used by iTunes and the iPod — this option copies those files automatically into iTunes. You might want to turn this off, however, because iTunes might find MP3 files that you don't want to add to your library (such as music for games).

   • **Add WMA Files:** Select this option if you want to add unprotected Windows Media audio files to your iTunes library. This option automatically converts the WMA files to the AAC format. (For more information about formats, see Chapter 19.) The original WMA files are left untouched.

4. **The assistant asks whether you want to keep your iTunes music folder organized. Select Yes or No, and then click Next.**

   The default is Yes, which tells iTunes to keep your music files organized — iTunes renames and moves files into appropriate folders when you edit the artist name, song title, album name, or track number. If you don't want this type of organization, click No.

5. **The assistant asks whether you want to go straight to the iTunes Music Store. Select Yes or No, and then click Next.**

   We suggest selecting No until you are ready to go to the store. (Chapter 4 covers the iTunes Music Store in depth.)

6. **Click Finish.**

   That's it — the iTunes window appears. (Chapter 3 gives you the full scoop on this window.) You can drag the bottom-right corner or the edges of your iTunes window to make it larger or smaller on your screen.

Setting Up Your iPod with a Mac

To set up your iPod with a Mac, connect it to the Mac by using your FireWire cable — unless you use an iPod mini and have a Mac that offers USB 2.0, in which case you can use the USB cable. We describe connecting to a Mac in Chapter 1.

As with the iTunes software, the version of the iPod software that's provided with your iPod on CD-ROM might not be the newest version. Even minor changes to the software might mean new iPod features or better performance with your battery. Updates to the iPod software occur frequently. If you want the latest version, go directly to the Apple Web site to get it. You can download the iPod software for free.

You can set your Mac to automatically download the latest version of the iPod software when it becomes available — just use Software Update from the Mac OS X System Preferences window. Click the Check Now button to check for a new version. If one exists, it appears in a window for you to select. Select it and click Install to download and install it.

To download the iPod software, go to Apple's iPod download page on the Web (www.apple.com/ipod/download) and select the appropriate version (Mac or Windows). Follow the instructions to download the installer to your hard drive. Pick a location on your hard drive to save the installer. Then launch the installer to unpack and install the iPod software.

Apple pre-installs the iPod software on Apple-branded models so that you can use it right away with iTunes on a Mac. The extra step of downloading and installing iPod software ensures that you have the newest version and that you can restore the iPod if necessary (as we describe in Chapter 28).

When you first connect your iPod to a Mac, the iTunes Setup Assistant appears like a butler, ready to help you set it up, as shown in Figure 2-4. In this dialog you can give your iPod a name, which is a good idea if you plan on sharing several iPods among several computers.

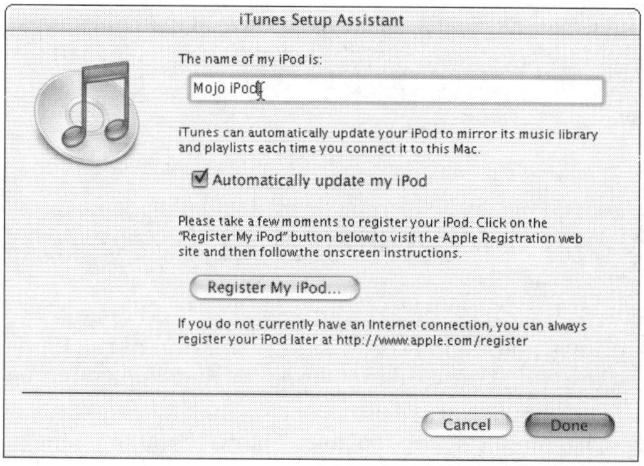

Figure 2-4: Set up your iPod with the iTunes Setup Assistant.

In the iTunes Setup Assistant, you can decide whether to update your iPod automatically or manually. If this is your first time using an iPod, you probably want to fill it up right away, so leave the Automatically Update My iPod option selected. (Don't worry. You can always change it later; see Chapter 11.) If you want to copy only a portion of your library to the iPod, deselect (clear) this option.

The iTunes Setup Assistant allows you to register your iPod with Apple to take advantage of Apple support. When you reach the last dialog, click Done. iTunes automatically launches, and your iPod's name appears in the iTunes Source pane under the Music Store. If you selected the automatic update feature in the iTunes Setup Assistant, the iPod name appears grayed out in the Source pane, and you can't open it. However, your iPod quickly fills up with the music from your iTunes music library — that is, if you *have* music in your library.

If you deselected the automatic update feature, the iPod name appears just like any other source in the Source pane, and you can open it and play songs on the iPod through iTunes and your Mac speakers, as we describe in Chapter 18. Of course, if you're just starting out, you probably have no tunes in your library. Your next step is to import music from CDs, buy music online, or import music from other sources.

After finishing setup, the iPod icon also appears on the Finder Desktop. If you leave your iPod connected to the Mac, the iPod appears on the Desktop and in iTunes whenever you start iTunes.

To see how much free space is left on the iPod, click the iPod icon on the desktop and choose File➪Get Info. The Finder displays the Get Info window with information about capacity, amount used, and available space. You can also use the About command on the iPod, which is available in the Settings menu: Choose Settings➪About. The iPod information screen appears with capacity and available space.

Setting Up Your iPod with a Windows PC

To use an iPod with Windows, you have to run the iPod installer to reformat the iPod for Windows and install the Windows version of the iPod software. Before installing the iPod software for Windows, make sure that you're logged on as a Windows Administrator user if you're using Windows 2000 or Windows XP. Quit all other applications before installing, and disable any virus protection software.

The version of the iPod software for Windows provided on the CD-ROM with your iPod might not be the newest version. Therefore, we recommend going directly to the Apple Web site and downloading the latest version.

If you bought your iPod before the fall of 2003, the CD-ROM that came with it installs MusicMatch Jukebox. Don't use the CD-ROM from older iPods if you plan on using iTunes for Windows — download the newer iTunes and iPod installers from the Apple Web site.

If you use Windows 2000 or Windows XP, you can use iTunes for Windows. If you use any other Windows version, you need to install MusicMatch Jukebox from the iPod CD-ROM. (We cover MusicMatch Jukebox in Chapter 7.)

To download the iPod software for Windows, go to Apple's iPod download page on the Web (www.apple.com/ipod/download) and click the <u>iPod software</u> link. Follow the instructions to download the installer to your hard drive. Pick a location on your hard drive to save the installer.

To install the iPod software for Windows, follow these steps:

1. **Double-click the** Setup.exe **file, which you can download from the Apple Web site.**

2. **In the first dialog that appears, choose the language that you want to use, and then click OK.**

   The language shortcut menu lets you choose from quite a number of different languages. After clicking OK, the InstallShield Wizard so familiar to Windows users takes over and launches the installer.

3. **Click Next (or Cancel to quit).**

4. **In the Choose Destination Location pane, select a destination folder for the iPod Update folder, and then click Next.**

   The iPod folder contains the iPod Update folder that in turn contains the iPod Updater program. By default, the installer assumes that you want to store the iPod folder in the Program Files folder of your C: drive (which is just peachy, unless you like to defy the system designers at Microsoft by putting programs in other places). Click Browse to use Windows Explorer to locate a different folder if you dare. After selecting a folder (or keeping the default), click Next.

5. **Select the Yes option or the No option to determine whether your system restarts after finishing your installation, and then click Finish.**

   By all means, select the Yes option to restart your computer — after all, you don't know where it's been or what it was doing before you arrived with this new software. Restarting cleans out memory and starts Windows over again. Select the No option only if you prefer to live dangerously or need to install more software.

As of this writing, the CD-ROMs that are supplied with iPods offer iTunes for Windows and the iPod Updater program in one installation. However, the CD-ROM might not contain the newest versions of these programs. The Apple Web site offers free downloads.

If you have no other choice, you can install from the CD-ROM and then update your software later from the Apple Web site. The CD-ROM's AutoPlay feature starts the installation process; if the installer doesn't open automatically, right-click the CD-ROM icon in the My Computer window and choose AutoPlay from the shortcut menu that appears (see Figure 2-5). Follow the instructions to type in your iPod serial number, and click Next for each window. The CD-ROM installation performs the same process as installing iTunes and the iPod software separately.

After your system starts up, you can launch the iPod Updater program by double-clicking the program icon or choosing it from the Start menu (Start⇨ iPod⇨iPod Updater). If you install from the CD-ROM, the iPod Updater program launches automatically.

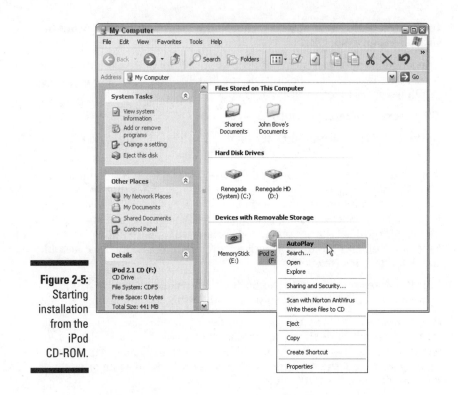

Figure 2-5: Starting installation from the iPod CD-ROM.

Connect your iPod by using a FireWire or a USB 2.0 hookup, which are available on most desktop PCs and laptops. To read more about this choice, see Chapter 1.

After connecting your iPod to the PC, the iPod Updater displays a dialog asking whether you want to configure the iPod. Click OK, and the iPod Updater displays a dialog for updating or restoring your iPod, as shown in Figure 2-6. The only option with a new iPod is to click Restore.

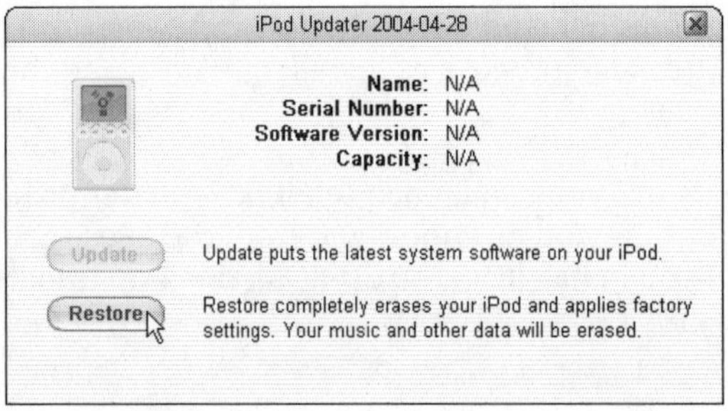

Figure 2-6: Use the iPod Updater to restore the iPod to factory conditions for Windows.

iPod Updater 2004-04-28

Name: N/A
Serial Number: N/A
Software Version: N/A
Capacity: N/A

Update — Update puts the latest system software on your iPod.

Restore — Restore completely erases your iPod and applies factory settings. Your music and other data will be erased.

The Restore function clears all settings and reformats the iPod to the Windows hard drive format, preparing it for use. After you click Restore, the iPod Updater displays a warning dialog.

Click Restore to continue with the restoration. If you're restoring an iPod that you bought prior to 2004, the iPod Updater displays the message in Figure 2-7, asking you to disconnect your iPod and connect it to a power supply so that it can do a firmware refresh. (*Firmware* is software encoded in hardware.) Disconnect your iPod carefully, and then connect it to your power adapter. The iPod performs a firmware refresh operation that takes a few minutes.

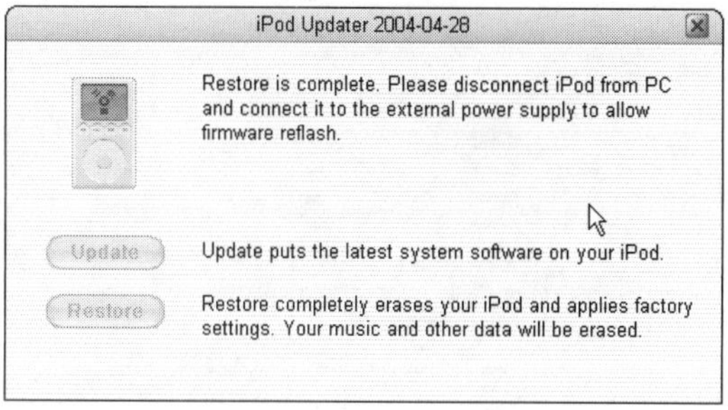

Figure 2-7:
Disconnect
an older
iPod for a
firmware
refresh.

iPod Updater 2004-04-28

Restore is complete. Please disconnect iPod from PC and connect it to the external power supply to allow firmware reflash.

Update   Update puts the latest system software on your iPod.

Restore   Restore completely erases your iPod and applies factory settings. Your music and other data will be erased.

After the operation is complete, the iPod Updater displays its opening dialog. Close the iPod Updater by clicking the X-marked close box in the upper-right corner.

Chapter 3

Getting Started with iTunes

In This Chapter

▶ Finding out what you can do with iTunes

▶ Playing music tracks on a CD

▶ Skipping and repeating music tracks

▶ Displaying visuals while playing music

More than half a century ago, jukeboxes were the primary and most convenient way for people to select the music they wanted to hear and share with others, especially newly released music. Juke joints were hopping with the newest hits every night; however, you still had to insert coins to play songs. Possibly, you could afford records and a turntable, but you had to throw a party to share the music with others.

Today, using iTunes, you can create a digital jukebox and conveniently click a button to play a song. Connect your computer to a stereo amplifier in your home or connect speakers to your computer, and suddenly your computer is the best jukebox in the neighborhood.

This chapter explains how iTunes changes your music-playing and -buying habits for the better, and it covers how to set up and configure iTunes for your Internet connection. It also describes playing music tracks on a CD. (If you plan on using MusicMatch Jukebox on your Windows PC instead of iTunes, see Chapter 7.)

What You Can Do with iTunes

You can listen to a new song on the Internet and download it to iTunes immediately. You can also buy music online at the iTunes Music Store. iTunes downloads music from the store and puts it in your library, making it immediately available for playing, burning onto a CD, or transferring to an iPod. You can even use iTunes to listen to Web radio stations and add your favorite stations to your music library.

Transferring songs from a CD to your computer is called *ripping* a CD (to the chagrin of the music industry old-timers who think that users intend to destroy the discs or steal the songs). Ripping an entire CD's worth of songs is quick and easy, and track information, such as artist name and title, arrives automatically over the Internet.

iTunes gives you the power to organize songs into playlists and burn any set of songs in your library to CD, in any order. You can even set up dynamic smart playlists that reflect your preferences and listening habits. iTunes offers an equalizer with preset settings for all kinds of music and listening environments, and it gives you the ability to customize and save your own personalized settings with each song.

The Mac and Windows versions of iTunes are virtually identical, with the exception that dialogs look a bit different between the two operating systems. There are also a few other differences, mostly related to the different operating environments — the Windows version lets you import Windows Media (WMA) songs, while the Mac version, like most Mac applications, can be controlled by Applescripts. Nevertheless, as Apple continues to improve iTunes, the company releases upgrades to both versions at the same time, and the versions are free to download.

The iTunes Window

You can run iTunes anytime to add music and manage your music library. You don't have to connect your iPod until you're ready to transfer music to it (as we describe in Chapter 11), or play the music on the iPod rather than the music in the library (as we describe in Chapter 18).

When you launch iTunes, your music library and other sources of music appear. Figure 3-1 shows the iTunes window on the Mac, and Figure 3-2 shows it in Windows.

The iTunes window offers a view of your music library and your sources for music, as well as controls for organizing, importing, and playing music, as follows:

✔ **Source pane:** Displays the source of your music — Library (your music library), Party Shuffle (a dynamic playlist), Radio (access to Web radio), Music Store (the iTunes Music Store), your iPod (if it's connected), and your playlists.

✔ **Song List pane and Browse pane:** Depending on the source that's selected in the Source pane, these panes display the songs in your music library, your playlist, your iPod, or Web radio stations. The Browse button in the upper-right corner toggles between Browse view (with the Song List pane below and the Browse pane above with genre, artist, and album) and the Song List pane by itself.

✔ **Status pane:** When a song is playing, this displays the name of the artist and song (if known) and the elapsed time.

✔ **Search field:** Type characters in this field to search your music library.

✔ **Player buttons — Forward/Next, Play/Pause, and Previous/Rewind:** Control the playback of songs in iTunes.

✔ **Playlist buttons — Add, Shuffle, Repeat:** Add playlists, and shuffle or repeat playback of playlists.

✔ **Miscellaneous buttons — Show/Hide Artwork, Equalizer, Turn on visual effects, Eject:** Display or hide song artwork (supplied with purchased songs), the equalizer, and visual effects. The Eject button ejects a CD or iPod — while a CD will actually pop out of some computers, iPods are hard drives, and ejecting them simply removes (or *un-mounts*) the drives from the system.

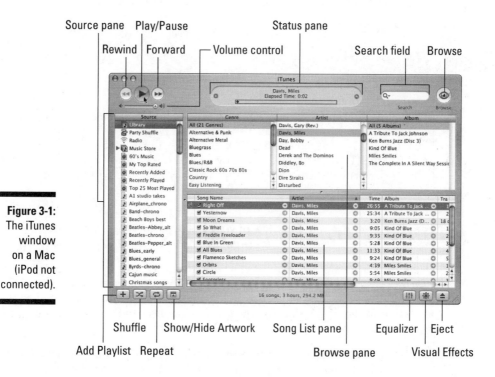

Figure 3-1:
The iTunes window on a Mac (iPod not connected).

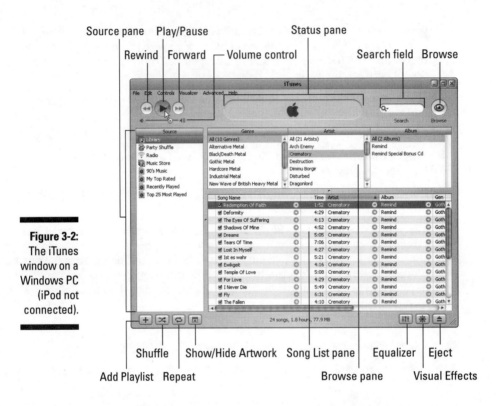

Source pane   Play/Pause   Status pane

Rewind Forward Volume control   Search field Browse

Figure 3-2:
The iTunes
window on a
Windows PC
(iPod not
connected).

Shuffle   Show/Hide Artwork   Song List pane   Equalizer   Eject

Add Playlist Repeat   Browse pane   Visual Effects

If you don't like the width of the Source pane, you can adjust it by dragging the shallow dot on the vertical bar between the Source pane and the Song List pane and Browse pane. You can also adjust the height of the Song List and Browse panes by dragging the shallow dot on the horizontal bar between them. To resize the iTunes window in Windows, drag the edges of the window horizontally or vertically. On a Mac, drag diagonally from the bottom-right corner.

Playing CD Tracks in iTunes

iTunes needs music. You can get started right away with ripping music from CDs into your library, but for more instant gratification, you can *play* music right off the CD without importing it. Maybe you don't want to put the music into your library yet. Maybe you just want to hear it first, as part of your Play First, Rip Later plan.

Insert any music CD or even a CD-R that someone burned for you. The music tracks appear in the iTunes song list. The Browse button changes to an Import button when a CD is inserted, in anticipation of importing (or *ripping*) the CD.

The songs first appear in your song list as generic unnamed tracks. If your computer is connected to the Internet, and you selected Yes for the Automatically Connect to the Internet question in the iTunes Setup Assistant (see Chapter 2), you can usually get real song information immediately without having to type anything. After you insert the CD, iTunes displays a message about accessing the Gracenote CDDB database on the Internet, and then presents the track information for each song automatically, as shown in Figure 3-3. (Gracenote CDDB is a song database on the Internet that knows the track names of commercial CDs. You can read about it and editing song information, in Chapter 9.)

Figure 3-3:
CD track info appears after iTunes consults the Internet.

When you play a CD in iTunes, it's just like using a CD player. To play a CD from the first track, click the Play button. (If you clicked somewhere else after inserting the disc, you may have to click the first track to select it before clicking the Play button.) The Play button then turns into a Pause button, and the song plays.

When the song finishes, iTunes continues playing the songs in the list in sequence until you click the Pause button (which then toggles back into the Play button). You can skip to the next or previous song by using the arrow keys on your keyboard, or by clicking the Forward button or the Back button next to the Play button. You can also double-click another song in the list to start playing it.

You can press the space bar to perform the same function as clicking the Play button; pressing it again is just like clicking the Pause button.

The Status pane above the list of songs tells you the name of the artist or the song title (if known), as well as the elapsed time of the track. When you click the artist name, the artist name disappears, and the song title appears; if you click the song title, the artist name comes back up. If you click the Elapsed Time status, the status changes to the remaining time and then, with another click, to the total time. (One more click brings you back to the elapsed time.)

Eject a CD by clicking the Eject button or by choosing Controls⇨Eject Disc. Another way to eject the CD is to click the eject icon next to the CD's name in the Source pane. You can also right-click the CD's name and choose Eject from the contextual menu.

Rearranging and repeating tracks

You can rearrange the order of the tracks to automatically play them in any sequence you want — similar to programming a CD player. Click the upward-pointing arrow at the top of the first column in the song list, and it changes to a downward-pointing arrow, and the tracks appear in reverse order.

To change the order of tracks that you're playing in sequence, just click and hold on the track number in the leftmost column for the song, and then drag it up or down in the list. You can set up the tracks to play in a completely different sequence.

Skipping tracks

To skip tracks so that they don't play in sequence, deselect the check box next to the song names. iTunes skips deselected songs when you play the entire sequence.

To remove all check marks from a list, simultaneously hold down the ⌘ key on a Mac (or the Ctrl key in Windows) while clicking a check mark. Select an empty check box while pressing ⌘/Ctrl to add check marks to the entire list.

Repeating a song list

You can repeat an entire song list by clicking the Repeat button below the Source pane on the left side of the iTunes window (or by choosing Controls⇨Repeat All). When it's selected, the Repeat button icon changes to show blue highlighting. Click the Repeat button again to repeat the current song (or choose Controls➪Repeat One). The icon changes to include a blue-highlighted numeral 1. Click it once more to return to normal playback (or choose Controls➪Repeat Off).

The Shuffle button, located to the left of the Repeat button, plays the songs in the list in a random order, which can be fun. You can then press the arrow keys on your keyboard or click the Back and Forward buttons to jump around in random order.

Displaying visuals

The visual effects in iTunes can turn your display into a light show that's synchronized to the music in your library. You can watch a cool visual display of eye candy while the music plays — or leave it on like a lava lamp. You can also add more visual effects as plug-ins to iTunes, as we describe in Chapter 23.

Click the Visual Effects button on the bottom-right side of the iTunes window to display visual effects. The visual animation appears in the iTunes window and synchronizes with the music.

In addition to the animation replacing the iTunes song list, an Options button replaces the Import button in the upper-right corner of the iTunes window. You can click the Options button to open the Visualizer Options dialog, as shown in Figure 3-4.

Figure 3-4: Set options for visual effects.

The Visualizer Options dialog offers the following options that affect the animation (but not the performance of iTunes when it's playing music):

- ✔ **Display Frame Rate:** Displays the frame rate of the animation along with the animation.

- ✔ **Cap Frame Rate at 30 fps:** Keeps the frame rate at 30 fps (frames per second) or lower, which is the speed of normal video.

- ✔ **Always Display Song Info:** Displays the song name, artist, and album for the song currently playing, along with the animation.

- ✔ **Use OpenGL:** You can choose to use OpenGL, the most widely used standard for three-dimensional graphics programming, to display very cool animation with faster performance.

- ✔ **Faster but Rougher Display:** The animation plays faster, with rougher graphics. Select this option if your animation plays too slowly.

The Visualizer menu in iTunes gives you even more control over visual effects. You can choose Visualizer➪Small or Visualizer➪Medium to display the visual effects in a rectangle inside the iTunes window, or choose Visualizer➪Large to fill the iTunes window. Choosing Visualizer➪Full Screen sets the visual effects to fill up the entire screen. When displaying the full-screen visual effects, you can click the mouse or press Escape (Esc) to stop the display and return to iTunes. Choosing Visualizer➪Turn Visualizer On is the same as clicking the Visual Effects button: It displays the visual effects.

While the animated visual effects play, press Shift-/ (like when you type a question mark) to see a list of keyboard functions. Depending on the visual effect, you might see more choices of keyboard functions by pressing Shift-/ again.

To turn off the visual effects display, click the Visual Effects button again. You can leave the effects on (except when in full-screen mode) even while opening the equalizer because you still have access to the playback controls.

Chapter 4

Buying Music from the iTunes Music Store

In This Chapter

▶ Setting up an account with the iTunes Music Store

▶ Previewing and buying songs

▶ Sending and receiving gift certificates

▶ Setting up allowance accounts

▶ Authorizing computers to play purchased music

*W*hen Apple announced its new music service, Apple chairman Steve Jobs remarked that other services put forward by the music industry tend to treat consumers like criminals. Steve had a point. Many of these services cost more and add a level of copy protection that prevents consumers from burning CDs or using the music they bought on other computers or portable MP3 players.

Record labels had been dragging their feet for years, experimenting with online sales and taking legal action against online sites, such as Napster, that allowed free downloads and music copying. Although the free music attracted millions of listeners, the free services were under legal attack in several countries, and the digital music that was distributed wasn't of the highest quality (not to mention the widespread and sometimes intentional misspellings in the song information and artist names). Consumers grew even warier when the Record Industry Association of America (RIAA), a legal organization looking out for the interests of record companies, began legal proceedings against people for illegal copyright infringement — people who possibly thought they were downloading free music.

No one should go to jail for being a music junkie. Consumers and the industry both needed a solution, so Apple did the research on how to make a service that worked better and was easier to use, and the company forged ahead with the iTunes Music Store. By all accounts, Apple has succeeded in offering the easiest, fastest, and most cost-effective service for buying music online for your computer and your iPod. The iTunes Music Store even offers gift certificates that you can e-mail to others and allowance accounts that you can set up for others (such as children) with credit limits but without the need to use a credit card. Apple adds new features to the store almost every week.

In this chapter, we show you how to sign in and take advantage of what the iTunes Music Store has to offer.

Visiting the iTunes Music Store

You can visit the iTunes Music Store by connecting to the Internet and using either iTunes or America Online (AOL).

As of this writing, the iTunes Music Store offers at least a half-million songs, with most songs available for download at the price of 99 cents each and entire albums available for download at less price than the CD. You can play the songs on up to five different computers, burn your own CDs, and use them on players, such as the iPod. The store also offers audio books from Audible.com.

The iTunes Music Store is part of iTunes version 4 and newer. If you're running an older version of iTunes, download the newest version, as we describe in Chapter 2.

You can preview any song for up to 30 seconds, and if you have an account set up, you can buy and download the song immediately. We don't know of a faster way to get a song.

To open the iTunes Music Store, you have three options:

- ✔ **Click the Music Store option in the Source pane.** This opens the Music Store's home page, as shown in Figure 4-1.

- ✔ **Follow a music link in iTunes.** Click the *music link* (the gray-circled arrow next to a song title, artist name, or album title) to go to a Music Store page related to the song, artist, or album. iTunes performs a search in the Music Store by using the song information. If nothing closely related turns up, at least you end up in the Music Store, and you might even find music you like that you didn't know about.

✔ **Go to iTunes on AOL and click the iTunes link.** If you use AOL, you can browse or search the AOL music area for songs and click the <u>iTunes</u> link to automatically launch iTunes and go to the Music Store.

If you need to fire up your modem and log on to your Internet service to go online, do so before clicking the Music Store option or following a music link.

The Music Store replaces the iTunes Song List and Browse panes. You can check out artists and songs to your heart's content although you can't buy songs unless you have a Music Store account set up. You can use the Choose Genre pop-up menu to specify music genres, or click links for new releases, exclusive tracks, and so on — just like any other music service on the Web.

Genre pop-up   Forward   Music Store pages

Music Store links Back   Music Store home page   Search field Account sign-in Browse

Figure 4-1:
The iTunes
Music Store
home page.

We use the term *pop-up menu* for menus on the Mac that literally pop up from dialogs and windows; the same type of menu in Windows actually drops down and is also called a *drop-down menu*. We use pop-up menu for both.

The iTunes Music Store also provides buttons on a gray bar just above the Song List pane and Browse pane. The left and right triangle buttons work just like the Back and Forward buttons of a Web browser, moving back a page or forward a page. The button with the Home icon takes you to the iTunes Music Store home page. The Browse button in the upper-right corner switches the view between Browse view (with the Song List and Browse panes both open) and Song List view (with only the Song List pane open).

Setting up an account

To create an iTunes Music Store account, follow these steps:

1. **In iTunes, click the Music Store option in the Source pane or follow a music link.**

   The Music Store's home page appears (refer to Figure 4-1), replacing the iTunes Song List pane and Browse pane.

2. **Click the Sign In button in the upper-right area of the window to create an account or sign in to an existing account.**

   If you don't have an account, the button next to Account on the gray bar reads "Sign In." If you already have an account, the account name appears in place of the Sign In button. You need an account to buy music. After clicking the Sign In button, iTunes displays the account sign-in dialog, as shown in Figure 4-2.

Figure 4-2:
Sign in to
the iTunes
Music Store.

Sign In to buy music on the iTunes Music Store
To create an Apple Account, click Create New Account.

(Create New Account)

If you have an Apple Account (from the Apple Store or .Mac, for example), enter your Apple ID and password. Otherwise, if you are an AOL member, enter your AOL screen name and password.

Apple ID:
bove

Example: steve@mac.com

Password:

(Forgot Password?)

(Cancel) (Sign In)

If you already set up an account with the Apple Store, with the .Mac service, or with AOL, you're halfway there. Type in your ID and password, and then click the Sign In button. Apple remembers the personal information that you put in previously, so you don't have to re-enter it every time you visit the Music Store. If you forgot your password, click the Forgot Password? button, and iTunes provides a dialog to answer your test question. If you answer correctly, iTunes then e-mails your password to you.

3. If you aren't signed up yet, click the Create New Account button.

iTunes displays a new page, replacing the iTunes Music Store home page with the terms of use and an explanation of steps to create a new account.

4. Click the Agree button, and then fill in your personal account information.

iTunes displays the next page of the setup procedure, which requires you to type your e-mail address, password, test question and answer (in case you forget your password), birth date, and privacy options.

5. Click the Continue button to go to the next page of the account setup procedure, and then enter your credit card information.

The entire procedure is secure, so you don't have to worry. The Music Store keeps your personal information (including your credit card information) on file, and you don't have to type it again.

6. Click Done to finish the procedure.

You can now use the iTunes Music Store to purchase and download music to play in iTunes and use on an iPod.

If you use AOL and the AOL Wallet feature, you can assign payment for your Music Store account to your AOL Wallet. AOL Wallet contains your billing and credit card information for purchases. Use AOL Wallet to fill out your personal information. AOL Wallet automatically fills information into the text boxes of the account setup pages so that you don't have to.

Browsing for artists, songs, and albums

The iTunes Music Store home page is loaded with specials and advertisements to peruse. You can also use the Genre pop-up menu to see only those specials and ads for a particular genre. You can click just about anything on the home page to get more information: today's top ten songs, exclusive offerings, albums, artists' names, and more.

What if you're just looking for a song or album by a particular artist? You can browse the store by genre and artist name in a method similar to browsing your iTunes library. To browse the store, click the Browse button in the top-right corner of the iTunes window. iTunes displays the store's offerings categorized by genre, and within each genre, by artist and album. Click a genre in the left column, then an artist in the middle column, and then an album in the right column, which takes you to the list of songs from that album that are available to preview or purchase, as shown in Figure 4-3.

Figure 4-3:
Browsing
the Music
Store for
artists and
albums.

To see more information about a song or the album that it came from, click the music link (one of the gray-circled arrow buttons in the song list):

- ✔ Clicking the arrow in the Artist column takes you to the artist's page of albums.

- ✔ Clicking the arrow in the Album column takes you to the album page.

- ✔ Clicking the arrow in the Genre column takes you back to the genre's specials page (or the home page).

Our only complaint about browsing by artist is that artists are listed alphabetically by first name — you have to look up Bob Dylan under *Bob*.

If you know specifically what you're looking for, you can search rather than browse. The Search field in the top-right corner of the iTunes window lets you search the iTunes Music Store for just about anything. First make a selection in the Genre column, type the name of an artist, and then press Return. Type more letters of the song title or artist name to narrow your search or use the Power Search feature. (See the "Power-searching" section, later in this chapter.)

Browsing the charts

What do Louis Armstrong, Roy Orbison, the Beach Boys, Dean Martin, and Mary Wells have in common? Each one had a top-ten hit in the charts for 1964. So says *Billboard,* the weekly magazine for the entertainment industry that has kept tabs on song popularity for more than half a century. The iTunes Music Store offers pop charts for each year going back to 1946, so you can probably find some of the songs that you grew up with.

You can't find *every* song that made the charts — only the songs that the iTunes Music Store offers. Although the store has over half a million songs, the store has still many more millions of songs not yet licensed for sale.

To find the charts, click the Billboard Charts link in the list of Music Store links on the home page, or browse the store and select Charts at the very top of the Genre column. From the Charts column, you can select Billboard Hot 100, Billboard Top Country, or Billboard Top R&B.

Don't like the songs that *Billboard* chose? Try selecting Radio Charts from the Genre column, and then pick a city in the United States in the middle column. Now you can find out what songs are hits in your hometown, no matter where you are at the moment.

Power-searching

You're serious about music, and you want the power to search for exactly what you want. Click the Power Search link on the iTunes Music Store home page to go to the Power Search page, as shown in Figure 4-4.

You can fill in the song title, the artist name, and the album title, or just fill in one of those text boxes (for example, if all you know is the song title). You can narrow your search by picking a genre from the Genre pop-up menu and by adding a composer name. After you fill in as much as you know, click the Search button.

Figure 4-4:
Use Power
Search
to find a
song in the
Music Store.

Playing music videos and movie trailers

Music videos and movie trailers are just a click away, and they're free to watch. The Music Video link on the iTunes Music Store home page takes you to a Music Store page. Click a thumbnail or title to select a video, and then select a small video window size (240 x 180 pixels) for quicker downloading or a large video window size (480 x 360 pixels).

It might take some time to download the video before it starts to play. After the QuickTime player controls appear in the iTunes window, as shown in Figure 4-5, you can click the movie's Play button (the right triangle next to the Sound button) to play the video.

You can play music in your iTunes library while waiting for a Music Store page or video to download over the Internet. Double-click the Music Store option in the Source pane to open the Music Store in a separate window. With two windows, you can use the first window to play music in your library while using the second to browse the Music Store and download a video. The first windows stops playing music when you use the second window to play a video or select a song to preview or buy.

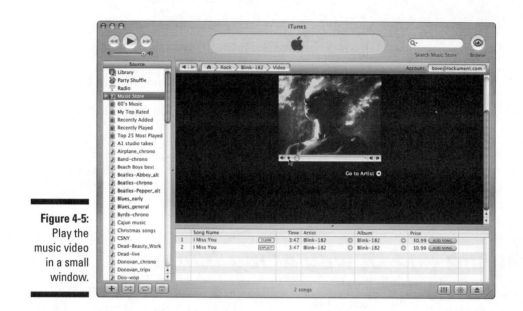

Figure 4-5:
Play the
music video
in a small
window.

Browsing celebrity and published playlists

Do you want to be influenced? Do you want to know what influenced some of today's music celebrities and buy what they have in their record collections? Scroll down the iTunes Music Store home page and click a celebrity name in the Celebrity Playlists panel, or click the Celebrity Playlists link to go to the page of celebrity playlists.

A typical celebrity playlist offers about an album's worth of songs from different artists. You can preview or buy any song in the list or follow the music links to the artist or album page.

The Music Store home page lists some of the celebrity playlists, but a lot more aren't listed there (78 the last time we checked). To see all the celebrity playlists, click the See All button at the bottom of the panel of Celebrity Playlist links on the home page.

You can also be influenced by other Music Store buyers and do a little influencing yourself. Click the iMix link on the Music Store home page to check out playlists that have been contributed by other consumers and published in the Music Store. iMixes offer 30-second previews of any songs in the playlist.

Previewing a song

The cool thing about record stores, besides being able to hang out and meet people, is the ability to preview CDs before you buy them. You can't meet flesh-and-blood people in the online iTunes Music Store, but you can preview songs before you buy them. To preview a song, click the song title in the song list, and then click the Play button or press the space bar.

By default, the previews play on your computer off the Internet in a stream, so you might hear a few hiccups in the playback. Each preview lasts about 30 seconds. Just when you start really getting into the song, it ends — but if the song is irresistible, you can buy it on the spot.

Buying and Downloading Songs

After setting up an account, you can purchase songs and download each one to your computer immediately, or gather them in a virtual shopping cart first, to see your choices and decide whether or not to purchase them before downloading them all at once.

Depending on how you set up your account, you can download the song immediately with the 1-Click option or place the song in your Music Store Shopping Cart temporarily, to purchase and download later. You can change your Music Store shopping method at any time.

After the song downloads, it appears in your iTunes song list. Purchased songs also appear in a special Purchased Music playlist under the Music Store option in the Source pane. You can see the list of all the songs that you purchased by clicking the triangle to expand the Music Store option in the Source pane, and then clicking the Purchased Music option. The Song List pane and Browse pane change to show the list of songs that you purchased.

Using 1-Click or the Shopping Cart

Apple offers 1-Click technology in the iTunes Music Store so that with one click, the song immediately starts downloading to your computer — and the purchase is done.

With 1-Click, you select a song and click the Buy Song button at the far right of the song. (You might have to scroll down your iTunes Music Store window.) The store displays a warning dialog to make sure that you want to buy the song, and you can then go through with it or cancel. If you click the Buy button to purchase the song, the song downloads automatically and shows up in your iTunes library. The Music Store keeps track of your purchases over a 24-hour period and charges a total sum rather than for each single purchase.

1-Click seems more like two clicks. If you really want to use only one click to buy a song, select the Don't Warn Me About Buying Songs option in the warning dialog so that you never see it again.

You don't have to use the 1-Click technology. Instead, you can add songs to the Shopping Cart to delay purchasing and downloading until you're ready. With the Shopping Cart, the store remembers your selections, allowing you to browse the store at different times and add to your Shopping Cart without making any purchases final. You can also remove items from the cart at any time. When you're ready to buy, you can purchase and download the songs in your cart at once.

Your decision to download each song immediately or add to a Shopping Cart and download later is likely based on how your computer connects to the Internet. If you have a slow connection such as a phone line, you probably want to use the Shopping Cart, so that you don't tie up the phone with each download.

If you switch to the Shopping Cart method (see the following section, "Changing your Store preferences"), the Buy Song button toggles to an Add Song button. After adding songs, you can view your Shopping Cart by clicking the triangle next to the Music Store option in the Source pane to show the Music Store selections (see Figure 4-6), and click the Shopping Cart option. The Shopping Cart appears with your purchases listed in the Song List pane, and recommendations from the store appear along the top of the window.

When you're ready to purchase everything in your Shopping Cart, click the Buy Now button in the lower-right corner of the Shopping Cart window to close the sale and download all the songs at once. You can alternatively click the Buy (for an album) or Buy Song buttons for each item that you want to purchase.

To delete items from your Shopping Cart, select them and press Delete/ Backspace. A warning appears asking whether you're sure that you want to remove the selected items. Click Yes to go ahead and remove the selections from your Shopping Cart.

Figure 4-6:
Viewing
your
Shopping
Cart before
checking
out of the
Music Store.

Changing your Store preferences

You can change your shopping method by choosing iTunes⇨Preferences on
the Mac or by choosing Edit⇨Preferences on a Windows PC. In the Preferences
window, click the Store button. The Store Preferences window appears. You
can set the following features:

✔ Change from 1-Click to Shopping Cart or vice versa. 1-Click is the default.

✔ If you select the Play Songs After Downloading option, the songs that
you buy start playing as soon as they complete download to your iTunes
library.

✔ For better playing performance (fewer hiccups) with previews over slow
Internet connections, select the Load a Complete Preview before Playing
option. (It's deselected by default.)

If you use more than one computer with your Music Store account, you can set
the preferences for each computer differently and still use the same account.
For example, your home computer might have a faster connection than your
laptop on the road, and you can set your iTunes preferences accordingly —
the home computer could be set to 1-Click, and the laptop could be set to
Shopping Cart.

Resuming interrupted downloads

All sales are final — you can't return the digital merchandise. However, you have to receive all of it before the Music Store charges you for the purchase. If for any reason the download is interrupted or fails to complete, your order remains active until you connect to the store again.

iTunes remembers to continue the download when you return to iTunes and connect to the Internet. If for some reason the download doesn't continue, choose Advanced⇨Check for Purchased Music to continue the interrupted download. You can also use this command to check for any purchased music that hasn't downloaded yet.

If your computer's hard drive crashes and you lose your information, you also lose your songs — you have to purchase and download them again. However, you can mitigate this kind of disaster by backing up your music library, which we describe in detail in Chapter 13. You can also burn your purchased songs onto an audio CD, as we describe in Chapter 14.

Redeeming gift certificates and prepaid cards

If you're the fortunate recipient of an iTunes Music Store gift certificate, all you need to do is go to the Music Store in iTunes and set up a new account if you don't already have one. Recipients of gift certificates can set up new accounts without having to provide a credit card number. As a recipient of a gift, you can simply click None for the credit card option and use the gift certificate as the sole payment method.

You can receive gift certificates on paper, delivered by the postal service, or by e-mail; you can also receive a prepaid card with a fixed balance. To redeem a certificate, click the Gift Certificate link on the iTunes Music Store home page, and then click the Redeem Now button. Then type the number printed on the lower-right edge of the certificate or supplied in the e-mail, click the Redeem button to credit your account, and then sign in to your account or set up an account. To redeem the amount of a prepaid card, click the Prepaid Cards link on the iTunes Music Store home page, click the Redeem button now, and then sign in or set up your account.

If you use Apple's Mail program, you can redeem a gift certificate that was sent by e-mail by clicking the Redeem Now button at the bottom of the e-mail message. This button launches iTunes with the Music Store option selected in the Source pane, and the certificate's number shows up automatically. Click the Redeem button to credit your account, and then sign in to your account (if you already have an account), or set up an account (see "Setting up an account," earlier in this chapter).

The balance of your gift certificate (how much you have left to spend) appears right next to your account name in the iTunes Music Store window and is updated as you make purchases.

Managing Your Account

Online stores record necessary information about you, such as your credit card number, your billing address, and so forth. You can change this information at any time, and you can also take advantage of Music Store account features, such as sending gift certificates and setting up allowance accounts.

Viewing and changing account information

Life is unpredictable. As John Lennon sang in "Beautiful Boy (Darling Boy)," "Life is what happens to you while you're busy making other plans." So if your billing address changes, or you need to switch to another credit card, or you need to change your password for any reason, you can edit your account information at any time.

To see your account information in the Music Store, click the Account button that shows your account name. iTunes displays a dialog for you to enter your account password. You then click the View Account button to see your account in the store.

Your account page displays your Apple ID, the last four digits of the credit card that you use for the account, your billing address, your most recent purchase, and your computer authorizations. (See "Authorizing computers to play purchased music," later in this chapter.) You can click buttons to edit your account information and credit card and to buy or redeem gift certificates and set up allowances.

Viewing your purchase history

In the rock 'n' roll lifestyle, you might recall songs from the 60s but not remember what you bought last week. To view your purchase history, go to your account page by clicking the Account button and typing your password in the dialog that appears. Click the View Account button, and on your account page, click the Purchase History button.

The Music Store displays the songs that you purchased, starting with the most recent.

If you bought a lot of songs, not all of them appear on the first page. To see the details of previous purchases, click the arrow to the left of the order date. After viewing your history, click Done at the bottom of the history page to return to your account page.

Setting up allowances

Do you trust your kids with your credit card? You don't have to answer that — you can sidestep the entire issue by providing an *allowance account* for that special someone who wants to buy music on your credit card. With an allowance account, you can set the amount of credit to allow for the account each month — from $10–$200 in increments of $10. You can change the amount of an allowance or stop it at any time.

To use an allowance account, the recipient must be using iTunes version 4 or newer and live in a country where the iTunes Music Store is available on the Internet (such as the United States).

You can set up the allowance account yourself or define an allowance on an existing account. The recipient signs in to the account and types his or her password — no credit card required. When the recipient reaches the limit of the allowance, that account can't buy anything else until the following month. iTunes Music Store saves any unused balance until the next Music Store purchase.

To set up an allowance account, click the <u>Allowance</u> link on the Music Store home page. iTunes takes you to the Allowance page in the Music Store, where you can enter your name, your recipient's name, the monthly allowance amount (using the Monthly Allowance pop-up menu), and your recipient's Apple ID and password.

Click Continue to proceed with the account setup process, and then follow the instructions to finish setting up the account.

To stop an allowance or change the amount of an allowance account, go to your account page by clicking the Account button that shows your account name, and then type your password in the dialog that appears. Click the View Account button and scroll the account page until you see the Setup Allowance button; click this button to go to the Allowance page.

Sending gift certificates

A song is a gift that keeps on giving every time the recipient plays the song. You can't go wrong giving a Music Store gift certificate to that special person who has everything. New songs are introduced every day, and another half-million songs are available spanning every type of musical genre.

Before sending a gift certificate, first make sure that the recipient can run iTunes 4. (You might want to subtly suggest to the future recipient, in an e-mail, that it's time to download iTunes, just to find out whether he or she has the requisite system configuration.) On a Mac, iTunes requires Mac OS X 10.1.5 or newer, a 400 MHz G3 processor or better, and at least 256MB of RAM. The recipient also needs iTunes version 4 or newer (4.6 is the newest as of this writing) and QuickTime, which anyone can download from the Apple Web site for free (but most Macs already have it). On a PC, iTunes requires Windows 2000 or XP, a 500 MHz Pentium-class processor or faster, and 256MB of RAM.

To buy a gift certificate to send to someone, click the Gift Certificate link on the Music Store home page. iTunes takes you to the Gift Certificate page in the Music Store.

Click the Buy Now button to purchase a gift certificate. You can send a printed certificate by snail mail or as an e-mail message. Supply the address, set the amount of the gift certificate, and even add a personal message if you want; then click Continue and follow the instructions to finish the process.

To set up or change the amount of a gift certificate, go to your account page by clicking the Account button that shows your account name and typing your password in the dialog that appears. Click the View Account button and scroll the account page until you see the Gift Certificate button; click it to go to the Gift Certificate page.

Authorizing computers to play purchased music

The computer that you use to set up your account is automatically authorized by Apple to play the songs that you buy. Fortunately, the songs aren't locked to that computer — you can copy them to other computers and play them with iTunes. When you first play the songs on the other computers, iTunes asks for your Music Store account ID and password to authorize that computer. You can have up to five computers authorized at any one time.

If you want to delete one computer and add another computer, you can remove the authorization from a computer by choosing Advanced⇨Deauthorize Account on that computer.

After you set up an account, you can sign in to the Music Store at any time to buy music, view or change the information in your account, and see your purchase history. Each time you buy music, you get an e-mail from the iTunes Music Store with the purchase information. It's nice to know right away what you bought.

Chapter 5

Importing Music into iTunes

In This Chapter

▶ Setting importing preferences

▶ Ripping music from CDs

▶ Importing music files from other sources

*T*o immortalize your music, you need to import it into iTunes from your audio CDs and other sources. After the music is in your iTunes library, you can preserve it forever. A song in digital format can be kept in that format in a file on any number of digital media storage devices — so even if your CDs, DVDs, and hard drive fail, your backup copy (assuming that you made a backup copy on a safety CD or disk) is still as perfect as the original digital file. You can make any number of digital copies, and there are no technical limitations on *playing* the copies except those imposed by the iTunes Music Store for songs that you purchased.

Importing tracks from a CD is called *ripping* a CD. We're not sure why it's called that, but Apple certainly took the term to a new level with an ad campaign for Macs a while back that featured the slogan *Rip, Mix, Burn.* Burning a mix CD was the hip thing to do a few years ago. With iTunes, you can still rip and mix, but if you have an iPod, you no longer need to burn CDs to play your music wherever you go.

Ripping, in technical terms, is the process of extracting the song's digital information from an audio CD, but in common terms it also includes the process of compressing the song's digital information and encoding it in a particular sound file format. The ripping process is straightforward, but the import settings that you choose affect sound quality, hard drive space (and iPod space), and compatibility with other types of players and computers. In this chapter, we show you how to rip CDs, import music from the Internet, and provide suggestions for settings.

Setting the Importing Preferences

Although importing music from an audio CD takes a lot less time than playing the CD, it still takes time, so you want your import settings to be correct before starting. Pay a visit to the Importing Preferences window (iTunes⇨Preferences on a Mac, or Edit⇨Preferences in Windows), and then click the Importing button. The Importing preferences appear, as shown in Figure 5-1.

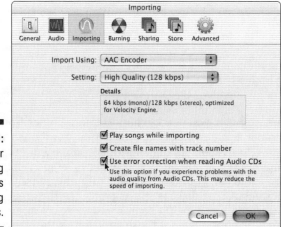

Figure 5-1:
Set your
importing
preferences
for ripping
CDs.

The Import Using pop-up menu gives you the opportunity to set the type of encoding — this is perhaps the most important choice — and the Setting pop-up menu offers different settings depending on your choice of encoder.

Encoding is a complicated subject and requires a whole chapter of its own. (In fact, Chapter 19 provides a more in-depth look if you want to know more.) For a quick and pain-free ripping session, select from among the following encoders in the Import Using pop-up menu based on how you plan to use your iTunes library:

- ✔ **AAC Encoder:** We recommend the AAC for all uses. (However, AIFF is better if you plan to burn another CD with the songs and not use them in your iPod.) Select the High Quality option from the Setting pop-up menu.

    You can convert a song that's been ripped in AIFF or WAV to AAC or MP3, as we describe in Chapter 20. However, ripping a CD with one encoder might be more convenient — and after that, you can rip it *again* with a different encoder. For example, you might import *Sgt. Pepper* with the

AAC encoder for use in your Mac and iPod, and then import it again with the AIFF encoder, calling the album "Sgt. Pepper-2" or something, in order to burn some songs on a CD. After burning the CD, you can delete "Sgt. Pepper-2" to reclaim the hard drive space.

✔ **AIFF Encoder:** Use AIFF if you plan on burning the song to an audio CD. AIFF offers the highest possible quality, but AIFF also takes up lots of space. If you use AIFF, select the Automatic option from the Setting pop-up menu. Don't use AIFF format for songs to be transferred to your iPod — convert them first to AAC or MP3, as we describe in Chapter 20.

✔ **Apple Lossless Encoder:** Use the Apple Lossless encoder for songs that you intend to burn onto audio CDs *and* for playing on iPods — the files are just small enough (about 60-70 percent of the size of the AIFF versions) that they don't hiccup on playback.

✔ **MP3 Encoder:** Use the MP3 format for songs that you intend to burn on MP3 CDs or use with MP3 players or your iPod — it's universally supported. If you use MP3, select the Higher Quality option from the Setting pop-up menu.

✔ **WAV Encoder:** WAV is the high-quality sound format that's used on PCs (like AIFF), and it also takes up a lot of space. Use WAV if you plan on burning the song to an audio CD or using it with PCs. If you use WAV, select the Automatic option from the Setting pop-up menu. Don't use WAV for songs to be transferred to your iPod — convert them first to AAC or MP3, as we describe in Chapter 20.

The Importing Preferences window offers the following options, which you set *before* ripping a CD:

✔ **Import Using:** Set this pop-up menu to the encoder. For more information about encoders, see Chapter 19.

✔ **Setting:** Set this pop-up menu to High Quality for most music. You can change this setting to get better quality or use hard drive space more efficiently, as we describe in Chapter 20.

✔ **Play Songs While Importing:** Select this check box to play the songs at the same time that you start ripping them. This option slows down the speed of importing, but hey — you get to listen to the music right away.

✔ **Create File Names with Track Number:** Select this check box to include the track number in the file names created by iTunes for the songs that you rip.

✔ **Use error correction when reading Audio CDs:** While it reduces the speed of importing, select this check box to use error correction if you have problems with audio quality or if the CD skips (not every skipping CD can be imported even with error correction, but it may help).

Ripping Music from CDs

After checking your Importing Preferences to be sure that your settings are correct, you are ready to rip. To rip a CD, follow these steps:

1. **Insert an audio CD.**

   The songs appear in your song list as generic unnamed tracks at first. If your computer is connected to the Internet, iTunes retrieves the track information. If you connect first by modem, go ahead and establish your connection, and then choose Advanced⇨Get CD Track Names.

2. **(Optional) Deselect the check boxes next to any songs on the CD that you don't want to import.**

   iTunes imports the songs that have check marks next to them; when you remove the check mark next to a song, iTunes skips that song.

3. **(Optional) To remove the gap of silence between songs that segue together, select those songs and choose Advanced⇨Join CD Tracks.**

   This happens often with music CDs — the tracks are separate, but the end of one song merges into the beginning of the next song. You don't want an annoying half-second gap between the songs. For example, in Figure 5-2, we joined the first two songs of the *Sgt. Pepper's Lonely Hearts Club Band* album because they run together. We also joined the last three songs of the CD for the same reason.

Figure 5-2:
Join songs to avoid the audible gap between them.

To select multiple songs, click the first one, hold down ⌘/Ctrl, and click each subsequent one. To select several consecutive songs in a row, click the first one, hold down Shift, and then click the last one.

Be sure to check the importing preferences before actually ripping the CD.

4. **Click the Import button.**

   The Import button is at the top-right corner of the iTunes window. The status display shows the progress of the operation. To cancel, click the small *x* next to the progress bar in the status display.

iTunes plays the songs as it imports them. You can click the Pause button to stop playback (but the importing continues). If you don't want to listen to the songs as they import, choose Preferences from the iTunes menu on a Mac or from the Edit menu in Windows. In the Preference window, click the Importing button. In the Importing Preferences window, deselect the Play Songs While Importing check box.

iTunes displays an orange, animated waveform icon next to the song that it's importing. As iTunes finishes importing each song, it displays a check mark next to the song, as shown in Figure 5-3. (On a color monitor, you see that the check mark is green.) iTunes chimes when it finishes the import list. When all the songs are imported, eject the CD by clicking the Eject button at lower-right corner of the iTunes window. You can also choose Controls⇨Eject Disc to eject the disc, or click the Eject icon next to the disc's name in the Source pane.

Figure 5-3:
iTunes
shows a
check mark
to indicate
it is done
ripping
the song.

Importing Music Files

The quality of the music that you hear depends on the quality of the source. Web sites and services offering music files vary widely. Some sites provide high-quality, legally derived songs that you can download, and some provide only streaming audio, which you can play but not save on your hard drive or on a CD (such as a Web radio station). The allegedly illegal file-sharing services offering MP3 files can vary in quality. Anyone can create MP3 files, so beware of less-than-high-quality knockoffs.

You can download the music file or copy it from another computer to your hard drive. After you save or copy an MP3 file — or for that matter an AIFF or WAV file — on your hard drive, you can simply drag it into the iTunes window to import it to your library. If you drag a folder or disk icon, all the audio files that it contains are added to your iTunes library. You can also choose File⇨ Add to Library as an alternative to dragging.

If you have your preferences set for iTunes to organize your library (the default setting) and you add a song to your iTunes library, a copy is placed inside the iTunes Music folder, which you can view in the Finder on a Mac or with Windows Explorer on a Windows PC. On the Mac, the iTunes Music folder lives in the iTunes folder inside the Music folder in your Home folder. The path to this folder is _your home folder_/Music/iTunes/iTunes Music. On a Windows PC, the iTunes Music folder resides in the iTunes folder inside the My Music folder of the My Documents folder in your user folder. The path to this folder is _your user folder_/My Documents/ My Music/iTunes/iTunes Music. These are the default locations — unless you turn off the default organization in iTunes by choosing iTunes⇨ Preferences on a Mac, or Edit⇨Preferences on a Windows PC, clicking Advanced in the Preferences dialog and unchecking the Keep iTunes Music Folder Organized option.

When you import a song file into iTunes, the song is copied into a new file in the iTunes library without changing or deleting the original file. You can then convert the imported song to another format — for example, you can convert an AIFF file to an MP3 file — while leaving the original intact. Find out about converting your songs to a different format in Chapter 20.

MP3 CDs are easy to import — since they are essentially data CDs, simply insert them into your CD-ROM drive, open the CD in the Finder, and drag-and-drop the MP3 song files into the iTunes window. Downloaded song files are even easier — just drag-and-drop the files into iTunes. If you drag a folder or CD icon, all the audio files it contains are added to your iTunes library.

You can import any sound into iTunes, even music from scratchy old vinyl records or sound effects recorded through a microphone. The *Pet Sounds Sessions* box set by the Beach Boys included just about every spoken word and sneeze in the studio during the recording, and you might have equally unusual sounds or rare music that can't be found anywhere else.

How do you get stuff like that into iTunes? On a Mac, you can use GarageBand, which is free (as part of iLife), or use a sound-editing program such as CD Spin Doctor (part of the Toast package) or Sound Studio. These programs typically record from any analog source device, such as a tape player or even a turntable. Sound Studio lets you record and digitize directly to your hard drive on a Mac running OS X. Some Mac models include a free copy of Sound Studio (you can find it in the Applications folder). You can also download a copy from Felt Tip Software (www.felttip.com/products/soundstudio) and use it for two weeks before having to pay $49.99 for it. Toast 6 Titanium from Roxio (www.roxio.com) for Mac OS X includes the CD Spin Doctor application for recording sounds.

There are many commercial applications to choose from that work on Windows PCs, including Roxio's Easy CD Creator 5 Platinum package, which includes CD Spin Doctor. You can also use MusicMatch Jukebox to record sound through a PC's line-in connection.

AIFF- or WAV-encoded sound files occupy too much space in your music library and iPod. Voice recordings and sound effects tend to be low-fidelity and typically don't sound any better in AIFF or WAV format than they do in formats that save hard drive space. Also, sound effects and voice recordings are typically mono rather than stereo. You can save hard drive and iPod space and still have quality recordings by converting these files to MP3 or AAC formats, changing them from stereo to mono in the process and leaving the original versions intact. We describe converting songs in Chapter 20.

Importing Audio Books

Do you like to listen to audio books and spoken magazine and newspaper articles? Not only can you bring these sounds into iTunes, but you can also transfer them to an iPod and take them on the road, which is much more convenient than taking cassettes or CDs.

Audible is a leading provider of downloadable spoken audio files. Audible lets you authorize computers to play the audio files, just like the iTunes Music Store (see Chapter 4). Audible does require that you purchase the files, and its content is also licensed by Apple to be included in the iTunes Music Store in the Audio Books category. Audible content includes magazines and radio programs as well as books.

To import Audible files, follow these steps:

1. **Go to** www.audible.com **and set up an account if you don't already have one.**

2. **Select and download an Audible audio file.**

   Files that end with .aa are Audible files.

3. **Drag the Audible file to the iTunes window.**

   If this is the first time that you've added an Audible file, iTunes asks for your account information. You need to enter this information once for each computer that you use with your Audible account.

To disable an Audible account, open iTunes on the computer that you no longer want to use with the account, and choose Advanced⇨Deauthorize Computer. In the Deauthorize Computer dialog that appears, select the Deauthorize Computer for Audible Account option and click OK.

You need to be online to authorize a computer or to remove the authorization from that computer.

Chapter 6

Sharing Music (Legally)

. . . .

In This Chapter

▶ Sharing music purchased from the iTunes Music Store

▶ Sharing music on a network

▶ Copying music files and folders to other drives

▶ Copying music files from Macs to PCs and vice versa

. . . .

*H*ey, it's your music after you buy it — that is, to the extent that you can make copies for yourself. You want to play your music anywhere and even share the music with your friends. It's only natural.

You can easily share the music that you rip from your CDs: After the music becomes digital, you can copy it endlessly with no loss in quality. You can also share the songs that you download from a service. Of course, if the songs are in a protected format (such as music bought from the iTunes Music Store), the computers that access the shared library must be authorized to play the music. However, iTunes lets you share a library over a local area network (LAN) with other computers running iTunes. You can even share your music library over a wireless network by using AirTunes and AirPort Express.

In this chapter, we show you how to bend the rules and share music with others. (After all, your parents taught you to share, didn't they?)

Sharing Music from the iTunes Music Store

To a limited extent, you can share the music that you buy online from the iTunes Music Store. Apple uses a protected form of the AAC encoder for the songs. (Read all about encoders in Chapter 19.) Thus, the rights of artists are protected while also giving you more leeway in how to use the music more than most other services (although by the time you read this, other services might have adopted this format with similar privileges).

I fought the law and the law won: Sharing and piracy

Apple CEO Steve Jobs gave personal demonstrations of the iTunes Music Store and the iPod to Paul McCartney and Mick Jagger. According to Steven Levy at *Newsweek* (May 12, 2003), Jobs said, "They both totally get it." The former Beatle and the Stones' frontman are no slouches — both conduct music-business affairs personally and both have extensive back catalogs of music. They know all about the free music-swapping services on the Internet, but they agree with Jobs that most people are willing to pay for high-quality music rather than download free copies of questionable quality.

We agree with the idea, also promoted by Jobs, that treating technology as the culprit with regard to violations of copyright law is wrong. Conversely, the solution to piracy is not technology because determined pirates always circumvent it with newer technology, and only consumers are inconvenienced.

We're not lawyers, but we think that the law already covers the type of piracy that involves counterfeiting CDs. The fact that you are not allowed to copy a commercial CD and sell the copy to someone else makes sense. You also can't sell the individual songs off a commercial CD.

Giving music away is, of course, the subject of much controversy, with services such as the original Napster closed by court order while others flourish in countries that don't have copyright laws as strict as the United States. (Napster is back, but it no longer provides the same type of music sharing.) While earlier versions of iTunes allowed the sharing of music across IP addresses outside a local network, that feature was removed at the request of record labels. The current version of iTunes doesn't enable the sharing of music at this level — you have to hack it somehow —

so we don't need to go into it, except to provide one observation: The songs that we hear from free sharing services such as KaZaa are (for the most part) low quality, on a par with FM radio broadcasts. They're nice for listening to new songs to see whether we like them, but they're not useful for acquiring as part of our real music collection. The iTunes Music Store is clearly superior in quality and convenience, and we prefer the original, authorized version of the song — not some knock-off that might have been copied from a radio broadcast.

As for making copies for personal use, the law is murky at best. It depends on what you mean by *personal use*. The iLife package allows you to use these music files in creative projects. You can, for example, put together a music video to show your friends by using iMovie to combine some video footage that you shot with your camcorder along with the latest hit by Eminem. However, don't expect to see it on MTV or VH1. Your local public access cable TV station can't even play it unless you first obtain the broadcast rights (which typically includes contacting the music publisher, the record label, and the artist — good luck).

Can you legally use a pop song as a soundtrack for a high school yearbook slideshow? It sounds legal to us, given the ability to use music for educational purposes, but that is a question only a lawyer can answer. If you're interested in obtaining the rights to music to use in semi-public or public presentations, or even movies and documentaries for public distribution, you can contact the music publisher or a licensing agent. Music-publishing organizations, such as the Music Publishers' Association (www.mpa.org), offer information and lists of music publishers, as well as explanations of various rights and licenses.

The protected form of AAC used with iTunes Music Store songs lets you do the following:

- ✔ **Create backups.** You can copy the music files and make as many copies as you want.
- ✔ **Copy music.** Play songs on up to five separate computers. See Chapter 4 to find out how to authorize your computers.
- ✔ **Share music over a network.** Those running iTunes on a LAN can play the music in your shared library, even over a wireless network using *AirPort Extreme,* Apple's wireless networking technology.

Regardless of whether you manage files on your hard drive on a regular basis, you might want to know where these songs are stored so that you can copy the music to other computers and to make a backup of the entire library. You might also want to move the library to another computer — after all, these computers just keep getting better year after year.

You can play your purchased music on any authorized computer, you can authorize up to five at once, and you can remove authorization from any computer that you don't use.

Sharing Music in a Network

If you live like the Jetsons — with a computer in every room, connected by a wireless or wired network — iTunes is made for you. You can share the music in your library with other computers in the same network. These computers can be PCs running Windows or Macs, as long as they are all running iTunes. If they can communicate with each other over the network, iTunes can share a music library with them.

When you share songs on a network, the song is *streamed* from the computer that contains the songs in its library (the *library computer*) to your computer over the network. The song is not copied to your music library. From your computer, you can't burn the shared-library songs onto a CD or copy the songs to your iPod.

You can share radio links, MP3, AIFF, and WAV files, and even AAC files and music purchased from the iTunes Music store, but not Audible spoken word files or QuickTime sound files.

To share your music library — turning your computer into the library computer — follow these steps:

1. **Choose Preferences (from the iTunes menu on a Mac, or from the Edit menu on a Windows PC), and click the Sharing tab.**

   The Sharing window appears, as shown in Figure 6-1, offering options for sharing music.

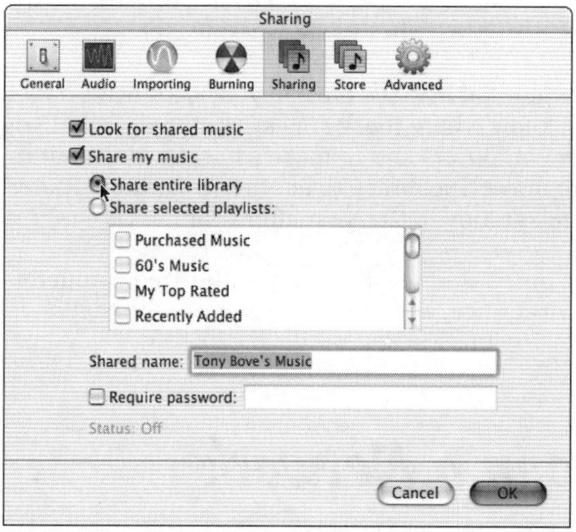

Figure 6-1:
Share your
music library
with other
computers
on the same
network.

2. **Select the Share My Music option.**

3. **Select either the Share Entire Library option or the Share Selected Playlists option (and then choose the playlists to share).**

4. **Type a name for the shared library and add a password if you want.**

   The name that you choose appears in the Source list for other computers that share it. The password restricts access to those who know it. Use a password that you don't mind letting others know — not the password for the online music store or any other secret password.

   Pick a password that you don't mind sharing with others; for example, your name is a good password, but your ATM PIN is not.

   iTunes displays a `Reminder: Sharing music is for personal use only` message.

5. **Click OK.**

You can access the music from the other computers on the network by following these steps:

1. **Choose Preferences (from the iTunes menu on a Mac, or from the Edit
   menu on a Windows PC), and click the Sharing tab.**

   The Sharing window appears, offering options for sharing music (refer to
   Figure 6-1).

2. **Select the Look for Shared Music option.**

   The shared libraries or playlists appear in the Source pane, as shown in
   Figure 6-2.

Figure 6-2:
Select
the music
library that
is shared
by iTunes
running on
another
computer on
the network.

3. **Click the shared library to select it.**

   Click the shared library in the Source pane (refer to Figure 6-2). iTunes
   fills the view on the right with the artists and songs from the shared
   library. Click the triangle next to a shared library entry in the Source
   pane, as shown in Figure 6-3, to see the shared playlists.

When you are finished sharing a music library, click the tiny Eject button that
appears to the right of the shared library name in the Source pane.

Before turning off sharing for your library, you must first notify anyone sharing
the library to eject the shared library before turning off the sharing feature.
Otherwise, iTunes displays a warning dialog allowing you to either continue
(and break off the connection to the shared library) or to leave sharing turned
on for the moment.

Figure 6-3:
Opening
the list of
playlists in
the shared
music
library.

Sharing a music library can be incredibly useful for playing music on laptops, such as PowerBooks, that support the wireless AirPort network.

Copying Songs to Other Computers

You can copy songs freely from your iTunes window to other hard drives and computers, or copy the song folders from the iTunes Music folder to other hard drives and computers. On the Mac, you can use the Finder to copy song files as well as dragging songs out of the iTunes window into folders or hard drives. Windows PCs offer several methods, including using Windows Explorer to copy files.

The files are organized in folders by artist name and by album within the iTunes Music folder. Copying an entire album, or every song by a specific artist, is easy — just drag the folder to a folder on another hard drive.

You can find out the location of any song by selecting the song in iTunes and choosing File⇨Get Info. Click the Summary tab in the Get Info dialog to see the Summary pane.

On the Mac, the iTunes Music folder can be found here:

```
Your Home folder/Music/iTunes/iTunes Music
```

On a Windows PC, the iTunes Music folder can be found here:

```
Your User folder/My Documents/My Music/iTunes/iTunes Music
```

Your playlists, including the library itself (which is in some ways a giant playlist), are stored as eXtensible Markup Language (XML) files in the iTunes folder along with your iTunes Music folder.

The easiest way to copy an album from a folder on a hard drive into your iTunes library is to drag the album's folder over the iTunes window and drop it there. To copy individual songs, you can drag the song files over the iTunes window and drop them. When you add a song to your iTunes library, a copy is placed inside the iTunes Music folder.

Copying Songs between PCs and Macs

Song files are not small, and album folders filled with songs are quite large. Copying a music library from a Mac to a PC, or vice versa, is not a simple task because of the enormity of the file sizes.

Don't even think about e-mail. *If the file is over four, it won't go through the door.* (Four megabytes, that is; and the door is the limitation of your Internet Service Provider's e-mail server.) And if you use a .Mac e-mail account, that limitation is more like 3MB.

Attaching a file to an e-mail message is the most popular method of transferring a file to someone, but there is a limit as to what you can attach. Most e-mail servers in the world won't accept an attachment larger than 5MB; some won't accept larger than 3MB.

Well, heck, just about every jazz tune and Grateful Dead jam we listen to in iTunes is larger than 3MB. A song compressed in the AAC or MP3 format is typically between 2 and 10MB, so you might get by with one pop song attached to an e-mail, but that's it.

How do you transfer larger amounts of music? One way would be with an external FireWire or a USB hard drive formatted for a PC — an iPod installed for Windows would do nicely, and you can learn all about using an iPod as a hard drive in Chapter 25. The Mac should recognize it when you plug it in, even though the drive is formatted for Windows, and you can copy files directly to the hard drive, and then take the hard drive over to your PC. You need FireWire or USB to connect an external drive. (USB is much slower.)

On a LAN you can share forever — if your computers communicate over a local-area network, they can share files . . . even large ones. To copy large song files or entire album folders between two Macs in a LAN, all you need to do is allow personal file sharing on your Mac. This sounds like a liberal thing to do, inviting all sorts of mischief and voyeurism, but you can control what others can do. (The converse is true: If someone wants to make a file or folder available to *you* over a LAN, all he has to do is enable personal file sharing.)

Mac OS X makes it very easy to share files and folders with Windows computers. You can enable Windows file sharing on the Mac, or access the Windows computer from a Mac. To access a Windows PC from a Mac, you need a valid user ID and password for an account on the Windows computer. You can go right to that account's Home directory on the Windows computer, and use your Mac to copy folders and files to and from the Windows computer. For more information about file sharing on a Mac and specifically between Mac and Windows computers on a network, see *Mac OS X Panther All-in-One Desk Reference For Dummies,* by Mark L. Chambers (Wiley).

Copying very large song files over the Internet is more complex, involving use of the File Transfer Protocol (FTP). Although it's easy to download an MP3 song file from a Web page or an FTP site with any browser (all you need is the Web or FTP address — and a user ID and password if the site is protected), you can't *send* the file to a protected site with most browsers unless the site is set up for this function. One easy way to share your files from a Mac is to use the .Mac service to create a Web page that accommodates anyone with the right password, even Windows-using folks, to visit and download files you put there. For information about setting up a .Mac account, see *iLife All-in-One Desk Reference For Dummies* by yours truly (Wiley).

To make it easy for others to copy files to and from a Mac at their convenience, enable FTP access for the Mac. To do this, open System Preferences, click the Sharing icon, and click the Services tab. Select the FTP Access option. A message appears at the bottom of the Sharing window providing the address of your FTP server on your Mac — something like `ftp://192.168.1.246/`. Give this address to those with an account on your computer, and they can access files and folders by using a Web browser, an FTP client such as Fetch, or Mac OS X.

How about transferring song files to other FTP sites, such as a password-protected site that requires use of an FTP client? Here are several options:

- **Use an FTP client,** such as Fetch. You can find Fetch at `http://fetchsoftworks.com` for $25 as of this writing. You can use it for several weeks before paying for it.

- **Use the FTP function inside another application,** such as Macromedia Dreamweaver.

> ✓ **Use the free Terminal application** supplied with Mac OS X, found in the Utilities folder inside your Applications folder, which offers FTP. For instructions, see *Mac OS X Panther All-in-One Desk Reference For Dummies,* by Mark L. Chambers (Wiley).

Fetch provides an easy drag-and-drop interface for transferring any type of file with FTP servers. After you establish a connection with the FTP server by typing the appropriate information (the FTP server name, your ID, your password, and the directory that you have access to), you can drag files to and from the FTP server window via the Finder, or you can browse folders to select files and then use the Get and Put Files buttons.

You can send an entire folder of files, such as an album of songs or an artist folder with multiple albums, by stuffing the folder (or even a set of folders) into a compressed file. StuffIt Deluxe from Aladdin Systems (www.stuffit.com) can compress the folder into one Zip or StuffIt file. (Zip is a standard compression format for Windows-based PCs.) You can then transfer the Zip file to the FTP server in one step. While the Zip or StuffIt file formats compress other types of files, if your music files are already compressed as MP3 or AAC the files won't get any smaller. However, the format offers a compact way of sending an entire folder of files.

Chapter 7

Using MusicMatch Jukebox

In This Chapter

▶ Installing the iPod software with MusicMatch Jukebox

▶ Setting the recording format in MusicMatch Jukebox

▶ Ripping CDs and importing music with MusicMatch Jukebox

▶ Playing songs in MusicMatch Jukebox

*I*f your PC is on the trailing edge rather than the leading edge, don't worry — you won't miss out on the iPod revolution. True, if you don't use Windows 2000 or Windows XP on your PC, you can't use iTunes for Windows. However, if you use Windows Me, you can use MusicMatch Jukebox, which is available on the iPod CD-ROM.

Because iTunes requires Windows 2000 or XP, a 500 MHz Pentium-class processor or faster, and 256MB of RAM, your only choice if you don't have that configuration (or a higher-performance configuration) is to use MusicMatch Jukebox, which requires only a 300 MHz or faster PC with at least 96MB of RAM running Windows Me, 2000, or XP (with at least 128MB of RAM).

You might want to use MusicMatch Jukebox for other reasons, such as its compatibility with other audio formats and its own MusicMatch MX radio. MusicMatch Jukebox offers high-quality MP3 encoders that produce excellent sound files that don't take up much hard drive or iPod space. Still, you must choose because your iPod can synchronize with only one program — iTunes *or* MusicMatch Jukebox. This chapter describes how to install and start using MusicMatch Jukebox. (See Chapter 2 for details on how to install iTunes.)

What You Can Do with MusicMatch Jukebox

With MusicMatch Jukebox, just like with iTunes, your computer is a vast jukebox limited only by your hard drive space. You can manage this library and keep a backup copy to preserve the music in high-quality format. iTunes and MusicMatch Jukebox are very similar in how they work. It's quick and easy to slip in a CD and *rip* (transfer and digitally encode) songs into your music library. The ripping process is very fast, and track information (including artist name and title) arrives automatically over the Internet.

Like iTunes, MusicMatch Jukebox gives you the power to organize songs into playlists and burn any songs in your library to CD, in any order. Both programs offer equalizers with preset settings for all kinds of music and listening environments as well as the ability to customize and save your own settings with each song. Songs that you rip from your CDs and import from Web sites and MP3 repositories can be burned onto another CD, copied to other computers, and transferred to your iPod freely.

You need the following to use MusicMatch Jukebox with the iPod:

- ✔ A PC with a 300 MHz or faster processor
- ✔ Windows Me, Windows 2000, Windows XP, or newer version of Windows
- ✔ 96MB of RAM (128MB for Windows XP)
- ✔ Built-in or Windows-certified FireWire (IEEE 1394) connection, or USB connection, as described in Chapter 1

MusicMatch Jukebox, as shown in Figure 7-1, looks a bit different than other Windows applications, and you can even customize the way it looks by assigning *skins* that represent designs of the graphical user interface, as we describe in Chapter 23.

MusicMatch Jukebox offers the following separate windows that you can drag to any position:

- ✔ **Library window:** Your music files appear in this window, sorted by artist. You can open artists just like folders in Windows Explorer to see songs organized by album.
- ✔ **Playlist window:** Drag songs or albums to this window to play them. You can also save playlists.
- ✔ **Recorder window:** Tracks on audio CDs appear here, ready to be ripped into your library when you click the Record button.

Playback Record
controls button   Playlist window

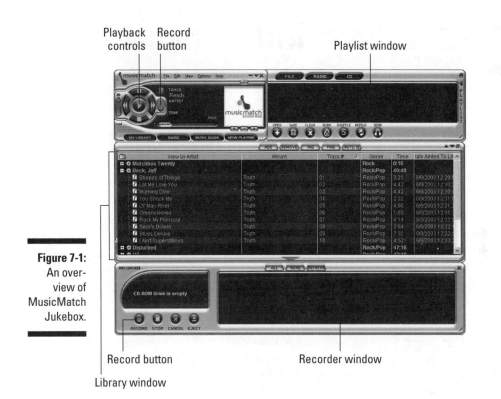

Figure 7-1:
An over-
view of
MusicMatch
Jukebox.

Record button   Recorder window

Library window

Installing MusicMatch Jukebox

Before installing the iPod software for Windows, make sure that you are
logged in as a Windows Administrator user if you're using Windows 2000
or Windows XP. Quit all other applications before installing, and disable
any virus protection software.

If you've installed an earlier version of MusicMatch Jukebox (especially if it's
a demo version provided free with your computer), you must use Add/Remove
Programs to remove the earlier version before installing the version that came
with your iPod. To remove the earlier version, click Start in your Windows
taskbar, choose Settings➪Control Panels➪Add/Remove Programs, and select
MusicMatch Jukebox to remove the program (called *uninstall* in some versions
of Windows).

When installing the iPod for Windows, be sure that you have the serial number
from the sleeve of your iPod's CD-ROM. When you install MusicMatch Jukebox,
you need to type in this serial number, which unlocks the Plus version of
MusicMatch Jukebox. The Plus version runs a bit faster and offers many more
features than the plain version, including the ability to save your playlists.

If you get a message recommending that you update MusicMatch Jukebox with a version that's newer than the one on your iPod's CD-ROM, *don't do it* unless you know what you are doing. Apple no longer provides support for any version but the one shipped with the iPod, which is version 7.50. Newer versions might not work with the iPod without performing some tricks with plug-ins. You can visit the MusicMatch Web site (www.musicmatch.com) for more information.

To install the proper software to make your iPod work with Windows and MusicMatch Jukebox, follow these steps:

1. **Insert the iPod for Windows CD-ROM into your Windows-based PC. Do not connect your iPod to your PC yet.**

   The appropriate version of MusicMatch Jukebox licensed by Apple (version 7.50 as of this writing) is available on the CD-ROM supplied with your iPod. The CD-ROM automatically starts running when you insert it into a PC.

2. **If the installer doesn't open automatically, double-click the CD-ROM icon in the My Computer window, and then double-click the Setup icon.**

3. **Click Install, following the instructions as they appear.**

   iPod for Windows software must be installed on the C: drive in order to work, but you can choose a destination folder.

4. **Connect your iPod.**

   The installation instructions tell you when it's time to connect your iPod to the PC. Go ahead and connect it to the PC, and follow the instructions to continue installation until installation is finished. If the PC doesn't recognize the iPod, see the troubleshooting instructions in Chapter 28.

After you first connect the iPod to a PC during the installation process, the iPod should be properly configured to work with Windows. The iPod for Windows software should automatically run MusicMatch Jukebox when it detects the iPod. If the program doesn't automatically run, you can launch it yourself by double-clicking the icon for MusicMatch Jukebox.

In MusicMatch Jukebox, your iPod should appear in the PortablesPlus window under the Attached Portable Devices folder, as shown in Figure 7-2. If the window is not yet open, choose File➪Send to Portable Device.

The iPod automatically synchronizes to the MusicMatch Jukebox library after you connect it, but you probably don't have anything in your music library yet. Your next step in building up your MusicMatch Jukebox library is to import music from CDs, buy music online, or import music from other sources. The next time that you connect your iPod, the music will transfer automatically.

Figure 7-2:
MusicMatch
Jukebox
adds your
iPod to the
portable
devices
list in the
Portables
Plus
window.

Importing Music into MusicMatch Jukebox

To get tunes into your iPod, you need to first import the music from your audio CDs or other sources. The importing process is straightforward, but the settings that you choose for importing affect sound quality, hard drive space (and iPod space), and compatibility with other types of players and computers.

Setting the recording format

Importing music from an audio CD takes less time than playing the CD. However, before you actually rip a CD, you should check your importing settings. To check your importing *(Recorder)* settings in MusicMatch Jukebox, follow these steps:

1. **Choose Options⇨Settings, and click the Recorder tab.**

   The Recorder pane of the Settings window appears, as shown in Figure7-3.

   From the Recording Format drop-down list, you can change the encoder used to create the digital sound files.

2. **Choose an encoding format and then make changes to its settings, which vary depending on the encoding format that you choose.**

   You have to do this only once; MusicMatch Jukebox keeps these settings for recording from audio CD until you change them.

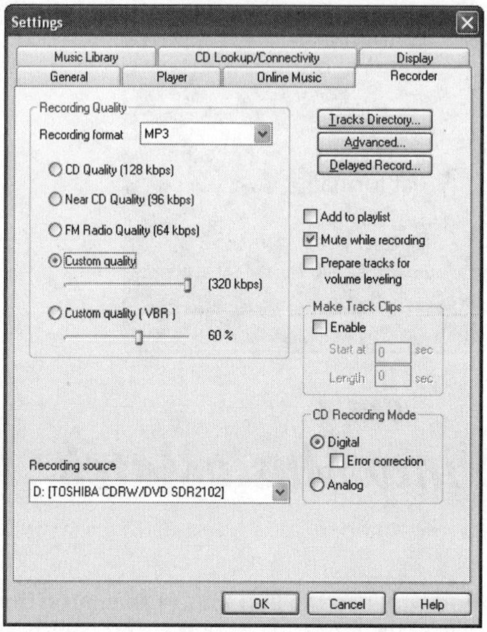

Figure 7-3:
Set your
importing
(Recorder)
settings
for ripping
CDs in
MusicMatch
Jukebox.

Use the MP3 recording format for songs that you intend to send to others over
the Internet, or burn an MP3 CD for use with MP3 CD players, or copy to an
iPod or other portable MP3 players. Select the quality option that you want:

- ✔ Choose CD Quality (128 kbps), or choose Custom Quality and move the
  slider up to 320 kbps (refer to Figure 7-3) for the highest bit rate provided for the MP3 format (higher bit rates mean higher quality audio).
  MusicMatch Jukebox also offers a version of CD Quality that offers
  Variable Bit Rate (VBR), which is described in detail in Chapter 19.

- ✔ Use Near CD Quality for songs that you want to compress more and
  don't mind the loss in audio quality.

- ✔ Use FM Radio Quality for voice recordings, narration, and very low quality audio but very high compression.

For more information about the MP3 format, see Chapter 19.

WAV, the high-quality recording format used on PCs, is more suitable for digital
song files that you burn onto an audio CD. However, songs encoded in WAV
occupy approximately 10MB per minute, which is many times more space than
MP3. As a result, WAV files also require more iPod battery power to play and

may skip when playing in an iPod because the skip protection cache fills up too quickly when playing uncompressed music. We recommend that you use WAV only to rip songs you intend to burn onto an audio CD or use with sound editing programs.

You can import songs from a CD using one encoding format, and then import them again by using a different format (or simply convert the songs, as we describe in Chapter 20). For example, you might use WAV to encode songs that you intend to burn onto a CD, and then use MP3 to encode the same songs for use on an iPod. After burning the CD, you could delete the WAV versions, which take up a lot of space.

Ripping songs from a CD

To rip a CD with MusicMatch Jukebox on a Windows PC, follow these steps:

1. **Choose View⇨Recorder to open the Recorder window, as shown in Figure 7-4.**

Figure 7-4:
Recording songs from an audio CD using MusicMatch Jukebox.

2. **Insert an audio CD.**

   The songs first appear in your song list as generic unnamed tracks. If your computer accesses the Internet at all times, MusicMatch Jukebox can connect to the Internet automatically and retrieve the track information every time you insert an audio CD. This takes only a few seconds. If for some reason this didn't happen and you are connected, or you have to connect first by modem, go ahead and establish your connection, making sure that CD Lookup is enabled. (To check, choose Options⇨Settings and click the CD Lookup/Connectivity tab.) Then click the Refresh button along the top of the Recorder window.

3. **(Optional) Remove the check mark next to any songs on the CD that you don't want to record (import).**

   MusicMatch Jukebox records the songs that have check marks next to them; when you remove the check mark next to a song, the program skips that song.

4. **Click the red Record button in the Recorder window or next to the playback controls to start importing the music.**

5. **MusicMatch Jukebox rips the CD.**

   When it's done, the program automatically ejects the CD.

During recording, the status area shows the progress of the operation. To cancel, click the Cancel button in the Recorder window.

Adding song files from other sources

After you save or copy an MP3 or WAV file to your hard drive from another sound-editing program or from the Internet, click the Add (+) button in the MusicMatch Jukebox Library window. You can then browse your hard drive to find folders of music files and either add music files separately or add entire folders of files at once.

You can also use MusicMatch Jukebox to automatically search your hard drive for music to add to your library. Choose Options⇨Music Library⇨ Search and Add Tracks From All Drives. You can use this function to import music from a network server as well as from your own hard drives.

Playing Songs in MusicMatch Jukebox

To play songs in MusicMatch Jukebox, click the song title, and click the Play button in the circle of playback controls in the upper-left corner of the MusicMatch Jukebox window, below the menu bar. This control panel offers the usual play, pause, forward, and reverse buttons, as well as a volume slider.

You can also click an artist name to select all the songs by the artist, and then click the Play button. As you select them and click the Play button, the songs appear in the order that you selected them in a list in the Playlist window, as shown in Figure 7-5. You can also drag songs or albums to the Playlist window in any order you choose; then click Play.

Figure 7-5:
After selecting songs in the MusicMatch Jukebox music library, you can drag them to the Playlist window.

To select a range of songs, click the first song and then hold down the Shift key while clicking the last song. To add single songs to your selection, hold down the Control/Ctrl key while clicking each.

Saving a playlist

If you installed the Plus version of MusicMatch Jukebox (by typing your iPod CD serial number during installation), you can use the Save Playlist feature. To save the songs in the Playlist window with a name for each playlist (essential for transferring playlists to the iPod, as we show in Chapter 11), click the Save button, and give the playlist a name.

After saving a playlist, click the Clear button to clear the Playlist window so that you can load a new set of songs to create another playlist.

To open a saved playlist, click the Open (+) button in the Playlist window and click the Playlists icon in the left column of the Open Music window. You can then select any named playlist, and MusicMatch Jukebox loads the playlist into the Playlist window for playback.

You can leave the option Clear Current Playlist When Adding New Tracks enabled so that you replace the current tracks in the Playlist window with the new playlist. If you want to add to the end of the current playlist, clear this option.

Playing albums

Although filling the Playlist window with all the songs by a particular artist is easy, you might instead want to play entire albums of songs without having to select each album or song.

To create a playlist of entire albums in a particular order, follow these steps:

1. **Select one or more albums in the Library window.**

2. **Drag the album or albums into the Playlist window, and then click Play.**

3. **(Optional) Save your playlist by clicking the Save button, and then type a name for your new playlist (such as the album name).**

4. **(Optional) After hearing the album, click the Clear button to clear the playlist for the next album you choose.**

To find out more about organizing your music library and adding song information in MusicMatch Jukebox, see Chapter 12.

Part II
Managing Your Music

The 5th Wave   By Rich Tennant

"I could tell you more about myself, but I think the playlist on my iPod says more about me than mere words can."

In this part . . .

*V*isit this part to find out how to organize your music.

- ✔ Chapter 8 describes how to browse your iTunes music library, change viewing options, and search for songs or artists.

- ✔ Chapter 9 describes how to add song information, artwork, and ratings, and then edit the info in iTunes.

- ✔ Chapter 10 shows you how to build playlists of songs and entire albums in iTunes, including smart playlists.

- ✔ Chapter 11 describes updating your iPod automatically or manually with iTunes and how to edit playlists and song information directly on your iPod.

- ✔ Chapter 12 describes how to organize your music in MusicMatch Jukebox and update your iPod.

- ✔ Chapter 13 shows you how to make backup copies of your iTunes or MusicMatch Jukebox libraries.

- ✔ Chapter 14 is a guide to burning audio and MP3 CDs.

Chapter 8

Searching, Browsing, and Sorting in iTunes

In This Chapter

▶ Browsing your music library

▶ Changing viewing options

▶ Sorting the song list

▶ Searching for songs or artists

You rip a few CDs, buy some songs from the iTunes Music Store, and then watch your music library fill up with songs. That song list keeps getting longer and longer — and as a result, your library is harder to navigate.

The iTunes library is awesome even by everyday jukebox standards — it can hold up to 32,000 songs (depending on how much space you have on your hard drive). And its companion, the 40GB iPod, can hold about 10,000 songs in the AAC format — enough music to last at least three weeks if played 24 hours a day! Even if you keep your iTunes library down to the size of what you can fit on your iPod, you still have a formidable collection at your fingertips. If you're a music lover and your music collection is getting large, you'll want to organize your collection to make finding songs easier. After all, finding U2's "I Still Haven't Found What I'm Looking For" is a challenge in a library of 32,000 songs.

This chapter shows you how to search, browse, and sort your music library in iTunes. You can find any song in seconds and display songs sorted by artist, album, genre of music, or other attributes. You can change the viewing options to make your library's display more useful.

Browsing by Artist and Album

You can switch from Song List view to Browse view to find songs more easily. Browse view is useful as long as you track information for the songs. You aren't overwhelmed by a long list of songs — for example, when you select an album, iTunes displays only the songs for that album.

To view albums in Browse view, click the Browse button in the upper-right corner. iTunes organizes your music library by genre, artist, and album, which makes finding just the right tunes easier, as shown in Figure 8-1. Click the Browse button again to return to the Song List view — the Browse button toggles between Browse view and the Song List view.

The Browse view sorts the songs by genre, artist, and album. This type of column arrangement is familiar to anyone who uses the Mac OS X Finder. Click a genre in the Genre column to see artists in that genre, or click All at the top of the Genre column to see all artists.

When you click an artist in the Artist column in the middle column (as shown in Figure 8-2), the album titles appear in the Album column on the right. At the top of the Album column, the All selection is highlighted, and the songs from every album by that artist appear in the song list below the Genre, Artist and Album columns.

To see more than one album from an artist at a time, hold down the ⌘ key on a Mac (Ctrl on a Windows PC), and click each album name.

As you click different albums in the Album column, the song list displays the songs from that album. The songs are listed in proper track order, just as the artist, producer, or record label intended them.

This is great for selecting songs from albums, but what if you want to look at *all* the songs by *all* the artists in the library at once? You can see all the songs in the library in Browse view by selecting All at the top of each of the columns — Genre, Artist, and Album.

Figure 8-1:
Click the
Browse
button to
browse the
iTunes
library.

Figure 8-2:
Select an
artist to see
the list of
albums for
that artist.

Note that iTunes considers "Clash" and "The Clash" to be different groups —
we edit the artist name and other information whenever necessary, as we
describe in Chapter 9.

Understanding the Song Indicators

As you make choices in iTunes, it displays an action indicator next to each
song to show you what it's doing. Here's a list of indicators and what they
mean:

- ✓ **Orange waveform:** iTunes is importing the song.

- ✓ **Green check mark:** iTunes has finished importing the song.

- ✓ **Exclamation point:** iTunes can't find the song. You might have moved or
  deleted the song accidentally. You can move the song back to iTunes by
  dragging it from the Finder to the iTunes window.

- ✓ **Broadcast icon:** The song is on the Internet and plays as a music stream.

- ✓ **Black check mark:** The songs are marked for the next operation, such as
  importing from an audio CD or playing in sequence. Click to remove the
  check mark.

- ✓ **Speaker:** The song is playing.

- ✓ **Chasing arrows:** iTunes is copying the song from another location or
  downloading the song from the Internet.

Changing Viewing Options

iTunes gives you the ability to customize the song list. The list starts out with the Song Name, Time, Artist, Album, Genre, My Rating, Play Count, and Last Played categories. You might have to drag the horizontal scroll bar along the bottom of the song list to see all these columns. You can display more or less information, or different information, in your song list. You can also display columns in a different order from left to right.

To make a column wider or narrower, drag the dividing line between the column and the next column to its right. As you move your cursor over the divider, it changes to a double-ended arrow; you can click and drag the divider to change the column's width.

You can also change the order of columns from left to right by clicking a column heading and dragging the entire column to the left or right — except that you can't change the position of the Song Name column and the narrow column to its left (which displays indicators). In addition, you can Control-click (Ctrl-click) any of the column headings to display a shortcut menu offering the same options as the View Options window, the Auto Size Column option, and the Auto Size All Columns option.

Maybe you don't like certain columns, like when they take up too much valuable screen space, or perhaps you want to display some other information about the song. You can add or remove columns such as Size (for file size), Date and Year (for the date the album was released, or any other date you choose for each song), Bit Rate, Sample Rate, Track Number, and Comment. To add or delete columns, choose Edit⇨View Options.

The View Options dialog appears, as shown in Figure 8-3, and you can select the columns that you want to appear in the song list. To pick a column, mark the check box next to the column's heading, indicating that column will be shown. Any unchecked column headings are columns that do *not* appear in the song list in iTunes. *Note:* The Song Name column always appears in the iTunes song list and can't be removed, which is why it doesn't appear in the View Options dialog. You can also change the view options by ⌘-clicking on a Mac (Ctrl-clicking on a PC) any of the column headings in the song list in either Browse or Song List view.

The viewing options that you choose depend on your music playing habits. You might want to display the Time column to know at a glance the duration of any song. Or maybe you want the Date or Year columns to differentiate songs from different eras, or the Genre column to differentiate songs from different musical genres.

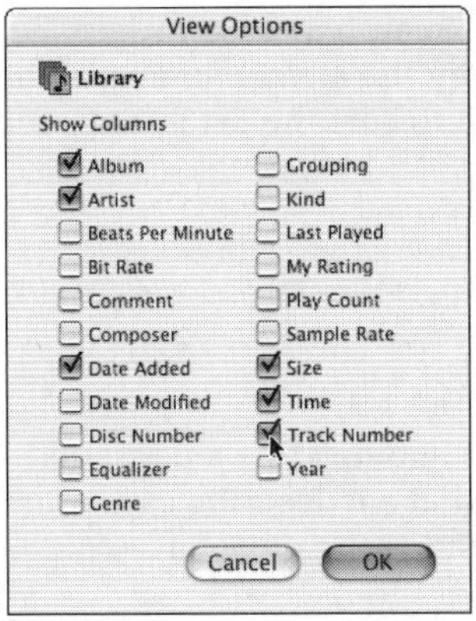

Figure 8-3:
The viewing
options for
the song list.

Browse view includes a Genre column on the left side. If you don't need a Genre column, you can remove it from the Browse view (or add it back) by choosing Preferences (from the iTunes menu on a Mac, or the Edit menu in Windows). Click the General button at the top of the Preferences window. In the General dialog, disable the Show Genre When Browsing option, which is on by default.

Sorting Songs by Viewing Options

Knowing how to set viewing options is a good idea because you can use the viewing options to sort the listing of songs. Whether you're in Browse view or viewing the song list in its entirety, the column headings double as sorting options.

For example, clicking the Time heading reorders the songs by their duration in ascending order from shortest to longest. If you click the Time header again, the sort is reversed, starting with the longest song. You can sort by any column heading, such as Artist, Album, Track, and Ratings. You might want to add the Date Added column to the Song List or Browse view, so that you can sort your library by the date you added the song.

You can tell which way the sort is sorting — ascending or descending order — by the little arrow indicator in the heading. When the arrow points up, the sort is in ascending order; when pointing down, it's in descending order.

Alternatively, you can sort the song list in alphabetical order. Click the Artist heading to sort all the songs in the list by the artist name, in alphabetical order (arrow pointing up). Click it again to sort the list in reverse alphabetical order (arrow pointing down).

Searching for Songs

As your music library grows, you might find locating a particular song by the usual browsing and scrolling methods that we describe earlier in this chapter too time-consuming. So . . . let iTunes find your songs for you!

If you want to search the entire library in Browse view, first click the All selections at the top of the Genre and Artist columns to browse the *entire* library before typing a term in the Search field. Or, if you prefer, click the Browse button again to return to the Song List view, which lists the entire library.

Locate the Search field — the oval field in the top-right corner, to the left of the Browse button — and follow these steps:

1. **Click in the Search field, and then type several characters of your search term, using these tips for best searching:**

    • You can search for a song title, an artist, or an album title.

    • Typing very few characters results in a long list of possible songs, but the search narrows down as you type more characters.

    • The Search features ignore case — for example, when we search for *miles,* iTunes finds "Eight Miles High," "She Smiles Like a River," and everything by Miles Davis.

2. **The results display as you type.**

    The search operation works immediately, as shown in Figure 8-4, displaying in the song list any matches in the Song Name, Artist, and Album columns.

    If you're in Browse view with an artist and a particular album selected, you can't search for another artist or song. Use browsing *with* searching to further narrow your search.

3. **Scroll through the search results and click a song to select it.**

    The search operation works immediately, searching for matches in the Song Name, Artist, and Album columns of the listing.

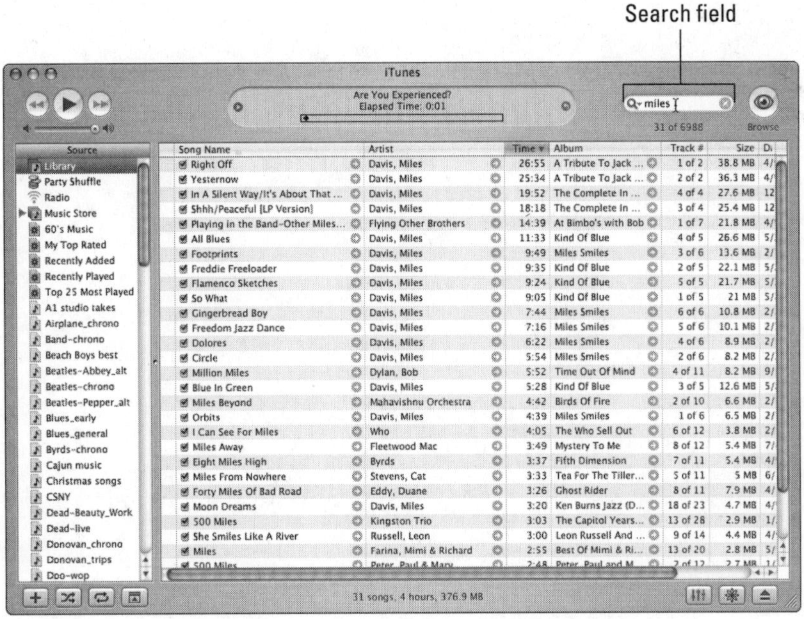

Search field

Figure 8-4:
Search for
any song
titles, album
titles, or
artists.

To back out of a search so that the full list appears again, you can either click the circled X in the Search field (which appears only after you start typing characters) or delete the characters in the Search field. You then see the entire list of songs in the library's song list, just as before you began your search. All the songs are still there and remain there unless you explicitly remove them. Searching only manipulates your view of the songs.

Chapter 9

Adding and Editing Song Information in iTunes

. . . .

In This Chapter

▶ Retrieving information from the Internet

▶ Entering song information

▶ Editing information for a selected song

▶ Editing information for multiple songs at once

▶ Adding more information, album artwork, comments, and ratings

. . . .

*O*rganization depends on information. You expect your computer to do a lot more than just store your music with *Untitled Disc* and *Track 1* as the only identifiers.

Adding all the song information for your tracks seems like a lot of trouble, but you can get most of the information automatically from the Internet — without all that pesky typing. Adding song information is important because you don't want your ripped CD music to have vague song titles like Track 1. You certainly don't want to mistakenly play "My Guitar Wants to Kill Your Mama" by Frank Zappa when trying to impress your classical music teacher with Tchaikovsky's 3rd Movement, Pathétique Symphony, do you?

This chapter shows you how to add song information to your music library in iTunes, and edit it for better viewing, so that you can organize your music by artist, album name, genre, composer, and ratings, and then sort the Song List or Browse view using this information by clicking on the column headings.

Retrieving Information from the Internet

Why bother entering song information if someone else has already done it for you? You can easily get information about most music CDs from the Internet. However, you do need to check your Internet connection first.

Retrieving information automatically

During the iTunes setup process that we describe in Chapter 2, you specify whether iTunes connects automatically to the Internet. If you have an always-on Internet connection, you probably set up iTunes to connect automatically; if you use a modem to manually connect, you probably set up iTunes to not connect automatically.

Even with a manual modem connection to the Internet, though, you can temporarily change the setup of your Internet connection to connect automatically at any time. Just follow these steps:

1. **Choose Preferences (from the iTunes menu on a Mac, or the Edit menu on a Windows PC).**

   The Preferences dialog appears.

2. **Click the General tab.**

   The General dialog appears.

3. **Select the Connect to Internet When Needed option.**

   With this option enabled for a modem connection, iTunes triggers your modem automatically (like a Web browser), calls your Internet service provider (ISP), and completes the connection process before retrieving the track information. With this option disabled (cleared), iTunes asks first before connecting to the Internet.

You can always stop an automatic modem connection at any time — a good idea if your ISP or phone service charges extra fees based on timed usage. When iTunes finishes grabbing the song information from the Internet, switch to your remote connection program without quitting iTunes, terminate the Internet connection, and then switch back to iTunes. That way, you can leave your Preferences setting to connect when needed and still terminate any connection right after using it.

Long distance information: Using the Gracenote database

The first time we popped an audio CD into the computer was like magic. iTunes, after thinking for a few moments, displayed the song names, album title, and artist names automatically. How did it know? This information isn't stored on a standard music CD — iTunes has to either recognize the disc somehow or read the liner notes.

The magic is that the software knows how to reach out and find the information on the Internet — in the Gracenote CDDB service. (CDDB stands for — you guessed it — *CD Database.*) The site (www.gracenote.com) hosts CDDB on the Web and offers the ability to search for music CDs by artist, song title, and other methods. The iTunes software already knows how to use this database, so you don't have to!

Gracenote recognizes an audio CD by taking into account the number of tracks and their durations (which is why the database can recognize CD-Rs that are burned with the identical songs in the same order). The database keeps track of information for most of the music CDs that you find on the market.

Although the database doesn't contain any information about personal or custom CDs, people can submit information to the database about CDs that the database doesn't know. You can even do this from within iTunes — type the information for each track while the audio CD is in your computer, and then choose Advanced⇨Submit CD Track Names. The information that you enter is sent to the Gracenote CDDB site, where the good people who work tirelessly on the database check out your information before including it. In fact, if you spot a typo or something erroneous in the information that you receive from the Gracenote CDDB, you can correct it, and then use the Submit CD Track Names command to send the corrected version back to the Gracenote site. The good folks at Gracenote appreciate the effort.

Retrieving information manually

You can connect to the Internet at any time manually (such as with a modem connection) and retrieve the song information when you are ready to use it. After you connect to the Internet, choose Advanced⇨Get CD Track Names.

Even if you automatically connect to the Internet, the song information database on the Internet (Gracenote CDDB) might be momentarily unavailable, or you might have a delayed response. If at first you don't succeed, choose Advanced⇨Get CD Track Names again.

ieving track information using a modem, your Internet
nected until the service hangs up on you. You might
r, without quitting iTunes, and surf the Web to make
d use iTunes to play music while you surf.

111

mation

manually enter the song information for CDs that are not known
the Gracenote CDDB or for custom CD-Rs. No big deal, though — just enter
a song's information in either Browse view or song list view. Click directly in
the information field, such as Artist, and then click again so that the mouse
pointer turns into an editing cursor. You can then type text into the field.

After you enter the information for a rare CD, consider submitting the song
information to the Gracenote CDDB for others to use. Enter the information
for each track while the audio CD is in your computer, and then choose
Advanced➪Submit CD Track Names. The information that you type is sent
to the Gracenote CDDB site, where it is checked first for accuracy and then
posted for others to use.

Editing the Information

Retrieving ready-made song information off the Internet is a great help, but
you might not always like the format it comes in. At some time or another, you
might want to edit artist and band names. For example, we like to list solo
artists by last name rather than by first name (as listings from the Gracenote
CDDB often are) — we routinely change *Miles Davis* to *Davis, Miles*.

Other annoyances sometimes occur in the CDDB, such as bands with *The* at
the beginning of their names, such as The Who, The Band, The Beatles, and
The Beach Boys. Even though these names sort correctly (in alphabetical
order under their proper name), we dislike having *The* before the band name,
so we routinely remove it.

In either Browse view or the Song List view, you can edit a song's information
by clicking directly in the specific track's field (such as the Artist field), and
clicking again so that the mouse pointer turns into an editing cursor. You can
then select the text and type over it, or use the Copy, Cut, and Paste commands
in the Edit menu, to move tiny bits of text around within the field. As you can
see in Figure 9-1, we changed the Artist field to be *Beck, Jeff*.

Figure 9-1:
Click inside
a field to
edit the
information.

You can edit the Song Name, Artist, Album, Genre, and My Ratings fields right in the song list. However, editing this information with File⇨Get Info is easier. Keep reading to find out.

Editing multiple songs at once

Editing in the song list is fine if you're editing the information for one song, but typically you need to change all the tracks of an audio CD. For example, if a CD of songs by Bob Dylan is listed with the artist as *Bob Dylan,* you might want to change all the songs at once to *Dylan, Bob.* Changing all the song information in one fell swoop is fast and clean, but like most powerful shortcuts, you need to be careful because it can be dangerous.

You can change a group of songs in either Browse view or the song list view. Follow these steps to change a group of songs at once:

1. **Select a group of songs by clicking the first song and then holding down the Shift key as you click the last song.**

   All the songs between the first and last are highlighted. You can extend a selection by Shift-clicking other songs or add to a selection by ⌘-clicking on a Mac, or Ctrl-clicking on a Windows PC. You can also remove songs already selected by ⌘-clicking on a Mac or Ctrl-clicking on a PC.

2. **Choose File⇨Get Info or press ⌘-I (Mac) or Ctrl-I (PC).**

   A warning message displays: `Are you sure you want to edit information for multiple items?`

   On a highway, speed can kill. Speed-editing the information in multiple songs at once can also be dangerous for your library organization. If, for example, you change the song title, the entire selection then has that song title. So be careful about what you edit when doing this. We recommend leaving the Do Not Ask Me Again check box cleared so that the warning appears whenever you try this.

3. **Click Yes to edit information for multiple items.**

   The Multiple Song Information dialog appears, as shown in Figure 9-2.

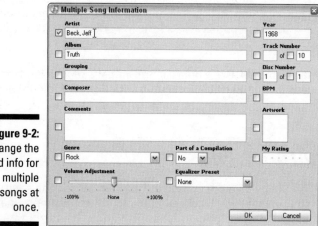

Figure 9-2:
Change the field info for multiple songs at once.

4. **Edit the field you want to change (typically the Artist field) for the multiple songs.**

   When you edit a field, a check mark appears automatically in the check box next to the field. iTunes assumes that you want that field changed in all the selected songs. Make sure that no other check box is selected except the field that you want, which is typically the Artist field (and perhaps the Genre field).

5. **Click OK to make the change.**

   iTunes changes the field for the entire selection of songs.

You can edit the song information *before* importing the audio tracks from a CD. The edited track information for the CD imports with the music. What's interesting is that when you access the library without the audio CD, the edited version of the track information is still there — iTunes remembers CD information from the CDs you previously inserted. Even if you don't import the CD tracks, iTunes remembers the edited song information until the next time you insert that audio CD.

Editing fields for a song

Although the track information grabbed from the Internet is enough for identifying songs in your iTunes library, some facts — such as composer credits — are not included. Composer information is important for iPod users because the iPod allows you to scroll music by composer as well as by artist, album, and song. Adding composer credits is usually worth your while because you can then search and sort by composer and create playlists.

After your songs import into the music library, locate a single song and choose File➪Get Info (or press ⌘-I). You see the song's information dialog, as shown in Figure 9-3.

While My Guitar Gently Weeps

| Summary | Info | Options | Artwork |

No Artwork Available

While My Guitar Gently Weeps (4:45)
Beatles
The Beatles [White Album] (Disc 1)

Kind: AAC audio file	**Profile:** Low Complexity
Size: 11 MB	**Channels:** Stereo
Bit Rate: 320 kbps	**Encoded with:** iTunes v4.0, QuickTime 6.2
Sample Rate: 44.100 kHz	
Date Modified: 5/25/03 3:53 PM	
Play Count: 7	
Last Played: 6/10/04 11:37 AM	

Where: Macintosh HD:Users:tony:Music:iTunes:iTunes Music:Beatles:The Beatles [White Album] (Disc 1):07 While My Guitar Gently Weeps.m4a

| Previous | Next | | Cancel | OK |

Figure 9-3:
The song's information dialog.

When you select one song, the Song Information dialog appears; when you select multiple songs, the Multiple Song Information dialog appears. Be careful when selecting multiple songs and using the Get Info command.

The Song Information dialog offers the following tabs:

- **Summary:** The Summary tab (as shown in Figure 9-3) offers useful information about the music file's format and location on your hard drive; the music file size; and information about the digital compression method (bit rate, sample rate, and so on).

- **Info:** The Info tab allows you to change the song name, artist, composer, album, genre, year, and other information, and you can also add comments, as shown in Figure 9-4.

- **Options:** The Options tab offers volume adjustment, choice of equalizer preset, ratings, and start and stop times for each song. You can assign up to five stars to a song (your own rating system, equivalent to the Top 40 charts).

- **Artwork:** The Artwork tab allows you to add or delete artwork for the song. The iTunes Music Store supplies artwork with most songs. Read how to add artwork in the upcoming section, "Adding Album Cover Art or Images."

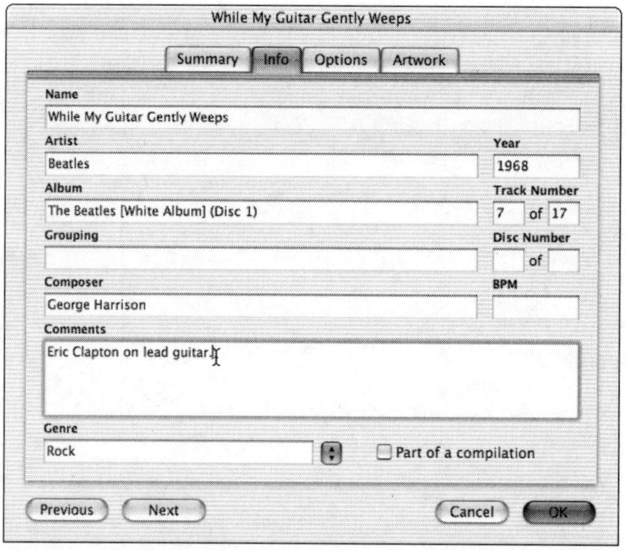

Figure 9-4:
View and edit song information from the Info tab.

While My Guitar Gently Weeps

Summary | Info | Options | Artwork

Name
While My Guitar Gently Weeps

Artist
Beatles

Year
1968

Album
The Beatles [White Album] (Disc 1)

Track Number
7 of 17

Grouping

Disc Number
of

Composer
George Harrison

BPM

Comments
Eric Clapton on lead guitar.

Genre
Rock

☐ Part of a compilation

Previous | Next | Cancel | OK

You can edit the song information one song at a time and still move quickly one song at a time through an album (without having to close the song information dialog and reopen it) by clicking the Previous or Next buttons in the bottom-left corner of the dialog to jump from song to song in an album.

Adding a rating

iTunes also allows you to rate songs, and the cool thing about ratings is that they're *yours*. You can use them to mean anything you want. For example, you can rate songs based on how much you like them, whether your mother would listen to them, or how they blend into a work environment. Then you can use the My Top Rated playlist to automatically play the top-rated songs in the library. You find out more about playlists in Chapter 10.

To add a rating to a song, click the Options tab, as shown in Figure 9-5. Drag inside the My Rating field to add stars — the upper limit is five stars (for best).

You might have noticed the My Top Rated playlist in the Source pane. This playlist is an example of a *smart playlist* — a playlist that updates itself when ratings are changed. The My Top Rated playlist plays all the top-rated songs in the library.

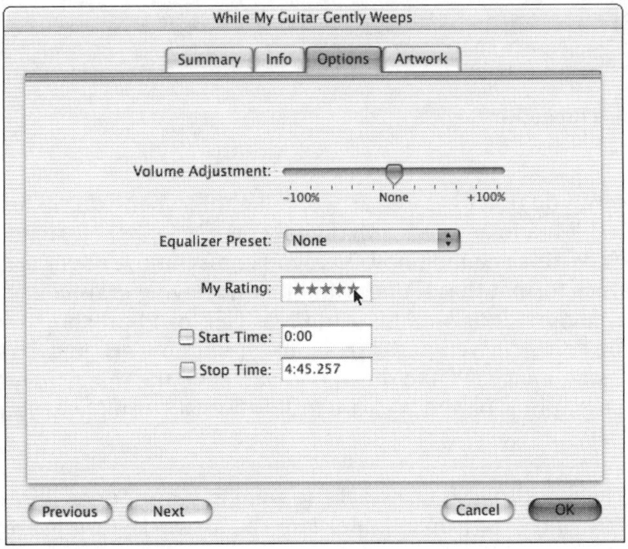

Figure 9-5:
Add a rating to a song from the Options tab.

While My Guitar Gently Weeps

Summary | Info | Options | Artwork

Volume Adjustment:
-100%   None   +100%

Equalizer Preset: None

My Rating: ★★★★★

☐ Start Time: 0:00
☐ Stop Time: 4:45.257

Previous   Next   Cancel   OK

Adding Album Cover Art or Images

Songs that you buy from the iTunes Music Store typically include an image of the album cover art or a photo of the artist. You can see the artwork in the lower-left corner of the iTunes window by clicking the Show/Hide Artwork button, as shown in Figure 9-6. The artwork changes for each song or album that you select.

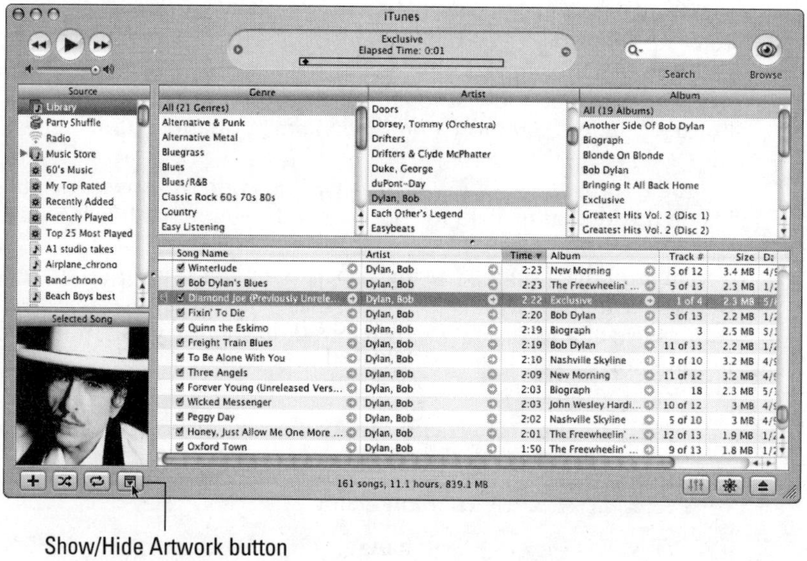

Figure 9-6: Show the artwork for a song bought from the iTunes Music Store.

Show/Hide Artwork button

Unfortunately, you don't get free artwork like this when you rip an audio CD — the discs aren't manufactured with digital cover art stashed somewhere on an empty track. With a scanner, however, you can scan the cover art and save it in a graphics format that iTunes (and its underlying graphics technology, QuickTime) understands — JPEG, GIF, PNG, TIFF, or Photoshop. Or with a Web browser, you can visit Web pages to scout for suitable art; just Ctrl-click (Mac) or right-click an image (PC) to download and save the image on your hard drive. (Most graphics on the Web are in JPEG or GIF format, so you don't have to convert anything.)

To add the artwork to a song, select the song in your iTunes library, and drag the artwork's image file from a folder into the artwork viewing area in the bottom-left corner of the iTunes window.

To add the same image as artwork for an entire album of songs (rather than just individual songs), select the album in Browse view first (or select all the songs in the album in song list view), and then drag the image file into the artwork viewing area.

You can also add the artwork to an album while editing multiple songs at once. Follow these steps:

1. **In Browse view, select the album in your iTunes library.**

   Click the Browse button to switch to Browse view so that an Album column appears on the right side of the iTunes window. Click an album to select it.

2. **Choose File⇨Get Info or press ⌘-I (Mac) or Ctrl-I (PC).**

   A warning message displays: `Are you sure you want to edit information for multiple items?`

3. **Click Yes to edit information for multiple items.**

   The Multiple Song Information dialog appears.

4. **Enable the Artwork field by selecting its check box.**

   When you add a check mark to a field, iTunes assumes you want that field changed in all the selected songs. Make sure that no other check box is selected except Artwork.

5. **Drag the graphics file to the Artwork panel.**

   Drag the graphics file directly over the blank Artwork well in the Multiple Song Information dialog.

6. **Click OK to make the change.**

   A warning message displays: `Are you sure you want to change the artwork for multiple items?`

7. **Click Yes to change the artwork.**

   iTunes adds the artwork for the entire album.

To remove the artwork from a song, view the artwork in a larger window, or resize the artwork, choose File⇨Get Info and click the Artwork tab. You can add a different image, add several images, delete the images with the Add or Delete buttons, or resize images with the size slider.

You can remove the artwork for an entire album by opening the Multiple Song Information dialog (choose File⇨Get Info after selecting the album), enabling the Artwork field, and then clicking OK. Because you haven't added anything to the Artwork field, iTunes replaces the artwork with nothing, effectively deleting the artwork.

Chapter 10

Organizing Music with Playlists

In This Chapter

▶ Creating a playlist of multiple songs

▶ Creating a playlist of albums

▶ Creating and editing smart playlists

▶ Deleting songs, albums, artists, and playlists

*T*o organize your music for different operations, such as copying to your iPod or burning a CD, you make a *playlist* — a list of the songs that you want.

You can use playlists to organize your music playback experience. For example, you can make a playlist of love songs from different albums to play the next time you need a romantic mood or compile a playlist of surf songs for a trip to the beach. We create playlists specifically for use with an iPod on road trips, and we generate other playlists that combine songs from different albums based on themes or similarities.

You can create as many playlists of songs, in any order, as you like. The song files themselves don't change, nor are they copied — the music files stay right where they are, with their names stored in the playlists.

You can even create a *smart playlist* that automatically includes songs in the playlist based on the criteria you set up and removes from the playlist songs that don't match the criteria. The song information you edited in Chapter 9 is very useful for setting up the criteria — for example, you can define the criteria for a smart playlist to automatically include songs from a particular artist, or songs that have the highest rating or fit within a particular musical genre.

Creating Playlists

You can create playlists of individual songs or entire albums. Not only do you save yourself a lot of browsing time by creating playlists, but you also need to create a playlist if you want to burn a CD.

Playlists of songs

You can drag individual songs into a playlist and rearrange the songs quickly and easily.

To create a playlist, follow these steps:

1. **Click the + button or choose File⇨New Playlist.**

   The + button, in the bottom-left corner of the iTunes window under the Source pane, creates a new playlist in the Source pane named *untitled playlist.*

2. **Type a descriptive name for the playlist.**

   The playlist appears in the Source pane. After you type a new name, iTunes automatically sorts it into alphabetical order in the Source pane, underneath the preset smart playlists and other sources.

3. **Select the library in the Source pane, and then drag songs from the library to the playlist.**

   Drag one song at a time (as shown in Figure 10-1) or drag a selection of songs, dropping them onto the playlist name in the Source pane. The initial order of songs in the playlist is based on the order in which you drag them to the list. Of course, you can rearrange the songs in any order after dragging them, as we show in the next step.

4. **Select the playlist in the Source pane, and then drag songs to rearrange the list.**

   To move a song up the list and scroll at the same time, drag it over the up arrow in the first column (the song number); to move a song down the list and scroll, drag it to the bottom of the list. You can move a group of songs at once by selecting them first (holding down Shift to select a range of songs, or press ⌘ on a Mac or Ctrl on a PC to select specific songs), and then dragging them into a new position.

You can drag songs from one playlist to another playlist. *Remember:* Only links are copied, not the actual files. Besides dragging songs, you can also rearrange a playlist by sorting the list — click the Song Name, Time, Artist column headings, and so on. And when you double-click a playlist, it opens in its own window, displaying the song list.

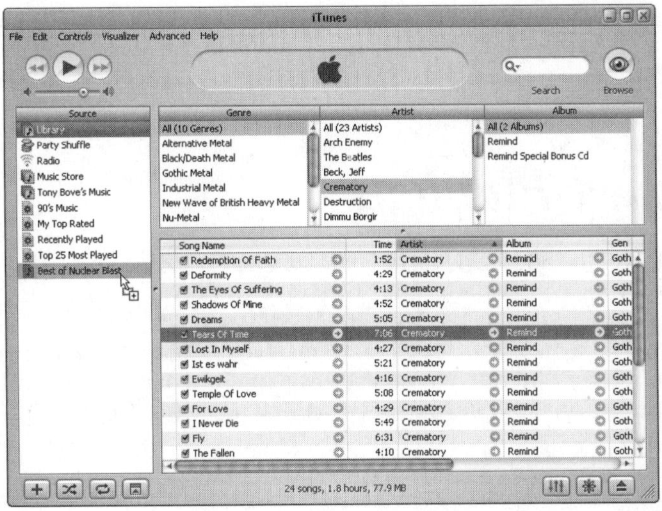

Figure 10-1:
Dragging
a song to
add it to a
playlist.

To create a playlist quickly, select the group of songs that you want to make into a playlist, and then choose File⇨New Playlist from Selection. A new playlist appears in the Source pane, and you can then type a name for the playlist.

Playlists of albums

You might want to play entire albums of songs without having to select each album as you play them. For example, you might want to use an iPod on that long drive from London to Liverpool to play Beatles albums in the order they were released (or perhaps the reverse order, reversing the Beatles' career from London back to Liverpool).

To create a playlist of entire albums in a particular order, follow these steps:

1. **Create a new playlist.**

   Create a playlist by clicking the + sign under the Source pane or by choosing File⇨New Playlist. Type a descriptive name for the new playlist.

2. **Select the library in the Source pane, and click the Browse button to find the artist.**

   The Album list appears in the right panel.

3. **Drag the album name over the playlist name.**

4. **Select and drag each subsequent album over the playlist name.**

   Each time you drag an album, iTunes automatically lists the songs in the proper track sequence.

You can rename a playlist at any time by clicking its name and typing a new one, just like you would rename any filename in the Mac Finder or Windows Explorer.

Using Smart Playlists

At the top of the Source pane, indicated by a gear icon, you can find what Apple (and everyone else) calls a *smart playlist.* iTunes comes with a few sample smart playlists, such as the My Top Rated playlist, and you can create your own. Smart playlists add songs to themselves based on prearranged criteria. For example, as you rate your songs, My Top Rated changes to reflect your new ratings. You don't have to set anything up — My Top Rated is already defined for you.

Of course, smart playlists are ignorant of your taste in music — you have to program them with criteria using the song information you edited in Chapter 9. For example, you can create a smart playlist that uses the Year field to grab all the songs from 1966, only to find that the list includes the Beatles ("Eleanor Rigby"), Frank Sinatra ("Strangers in the Night"), the Yardbirds ("Over Under Sideways Down"), and Ike and Tina Turner ("River Deep, Mountain High") in no particular order. Use other fields of the song information you entered, such as ratings, artist name, or comment to fine-tune your criteria. You can also use built-in functions such as the Play Count (the number of times the song was played) or the Date Added (the date the song was added to the library).

Creating a smart playlist

To create a new smart playlist, choose File⇔New Smart Playlist. The Smart Playlist dialog appears (as shown in Figure 10-2), offering the following choices for setting criteria:

- **Match the Following Conditions:** From the first pop-up menu (refer to Figure 10-2), you can select any of the categories used for song information. From the second pop-up menu, you can choose an operator, such as the greater than or less than operators. The selections that you make in these two pop-up menus combine to express a condition such as Year is greater than 1966. You can also add multiple conditions by clicking the + button, and then decide whether to match all or any of these conditions.

✓ **Limit To:** You can limit the smart playlist to a specific duration, measured by the number of songs, time, or size in megabytes or gigabytes, as shown in Figure 10-3. The songs can be selected by various methods such as random, most recently played, and so on.

✓ **Match Only Checked Songs:** This option selects only those songs that have a check mark beside them, along with the rest of the criteria. Checking and unchecking songs is an easy way to fine-tune your selection for a smart playlist.

✓ **Live Updating:** This allows iTunes to automatically update the playlist continually as you play songs, add or remove them from the library, change their ratings, and so on.

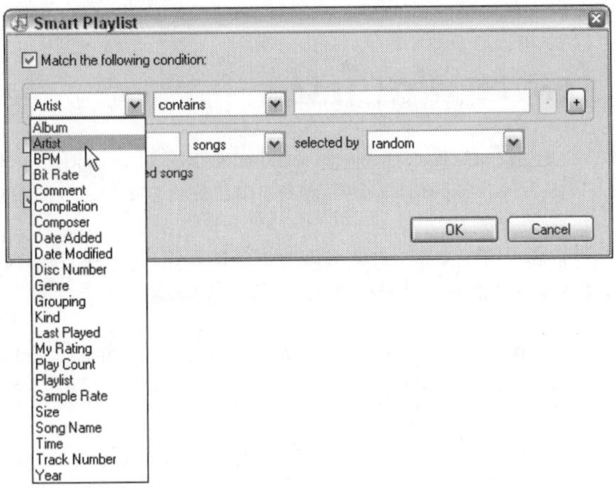

Figure 10-2:
Set the first match condition for a smart playlist.

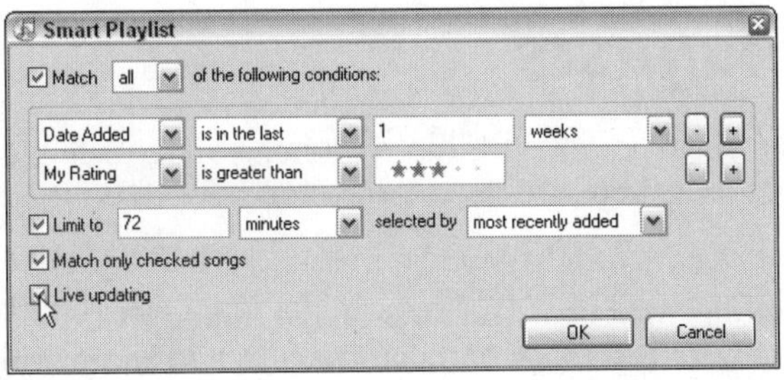

Figure 10-3:
Use multiple conditions and a time limit for a smart playlist.

After setting up the criteria, click OK. iTunes creates the playlist with a gear icon and the name *untitled playlist.* You can click in the playlist field and type a new name for it.

A smart playlist for recent additions

Setting up multiple criteria gives you the opportunity to create playlists that are way smarter than the ones supplied with iTunes. For example, we created a smart playlist with criteria shown in Figure 10-3 that does the following:

✔ Adds any song added to the library in the past week that *also* has a rating greater than three stars.

✔ Limits the playlist to 72 minutes of music (to fit on one audio CD), and refines the selection to the most recently added if the entire selection becomes greater than 72 minutes.

✔ Matches only checked songs.

✔ Performs live updating.

Editing a smart playlist

To edit a smart playlist, select the playlist and choose File⇨Edit Smart Playlist. The Smart Playlist window appears, with the criteria for the smart playlist.

To modify the smart playlist so that songs with a higher rating are picked, simply add another star or two to the My Rating criteria.

You can also choose to limit the playlist to a certain number of songs, selected by various methods such as random, most recently played, and so on.

Deleting Songs, Albums, Artists, and Playlists

Deleting songs can seem counterproductive when you're trying to build up your iTunes library, but there are times when you have to do it, such as the following:

✔ **Deleting versions of songs:** You might have ripped a CD twice — once in AIFF format to burn the songs onto another CD, and another in AAC format for your library and iPod. You can delete the AIFF versions in your library after burning your CD (as we describe in Chapter 14).

✔ **Deleting songs from playlists:** You can delete songs from playlists while keeping the songs in your library. When you delete a song from a playlist, the song is simply deleted from the list — not from the library. You have to switch to the Library in the Source pane in order to delete songs from the library. You can delete playlists as well, without harming the songs in those playlists.

✔ **Deleting a song, album, or artist you don't like:** You can select any song, group of songs, album, group of albums, artist, or group of artists, and then press Delete/Backspace or choose Edit⇨Clear. After clicking Yes to the warning message, the songs are gone from iTunes. (Why did you rip them in the first place? See Chapter 3 about how to play tracks first, before importing them.)

To delete a song from a playlist, select the playlist in the Source pane, and then select the song. Press Delete/Backspace (that's Delete on a Mac or Backspace on a Windows PC), or choose Edit⇨Clear. In the warning dialog that appears, click Yes to remove the selected item from the list.

To delete a playlist, select the playlist in the Source pane and press Delete/Backspace, or choose Edit⇨Clear.

To delete a song from the library, select Library in the Source pane, and then select the song. Press Delete/Backspace, or choose Edit⇨Clear. In the warning dialog that appears, click Yes to remove the selected item from the list.

Deleting a song removes the song from your iTunes library, but it doesn't remove it from your hard drive until you agree. iTunes displays another warning — Some of the selected files are located in your iTunes Music folder. Would you like to move these files to the Trash? — and you can click Yes to trash them, No to keep them in your music folder, or Cancel to cancel the operation.

You can delete multiple songs by first selecting them. Just hold down Shift as you click to select a range of songs, or hold down ⌘ (Mac) or Ctrl (PC) as you click each song to add it to the selection. Then press Delete/Backspace, or choose Edit⇨Clear.

To delete an entire album, first select the album in Browse view, press Delete/Backspace, or choose Edit⇨Clear. To delete everything by an artist, first select the artist in Browse view, and then press Delete/Backspace or choose Edit⇨Clear. If you choose to move the album or artist folder to the Trash, the album or artist folder is deleted from your hard drive; otherwise, it remains in your iTunes Music folder.

If you leave music files and folders in your iTunes Music folder, you can add them back to your iTunes library by dragging and dropping them into the iTunes window.

Chapter 11

Updating Your iPod with iTunes

In This Chapter

▶ Synchronizing your iPod with your iTunes music library

▶ Updating your iPod with selected playlists or selected songs

▶ Setting up your iPod to update manually

▶ Copying music directly to your iPod

▶ Deleting music from your iPod

▶ Managing playlists and editing song information on your iPod

*i*Tunes puts music on your iPod (actually more than just music — you can include audio books or anything stored as a song in iTunes), and iTunes can fill your iPod very quickly with the tunes in your library.

If you're too busy to copy specific songs to your iPod and your entire iTunes music library fits on your iPod anyway, why not just copy everything? Copying your library is just as fast as copying individual songs, if not faster, and you don't have to do anything except connect the iPod to your computer. This chapter shows you how to set up iTunes to automatically update your iPod.

This chapter also shows how you can update your iPod manually, choosing which songs to copy. iTunes is flexible in that you can use either option or *both* options to update your iPod. For example, you can update automatically with all the songs in playlists, go into iTunes, copy other music not in playlists directly to your iPod, and delete songs from your iPod if you need to make room. This chapter explains how to set your preferences for updating and change them when you need to.

If you use MusicMatch Jukebox on a Windows PC rather than iTunes, see Chapter 12 about updating your iPod.

Changing Your Update Preferences

If you've changed your iPod preferences to update manually, you can change them back to update automatically any time and vice versa. Change your iPod preferences by following these steps:

1. **Connect the iPod to your computer.**

   Your iPod must be connected for you to change the update preferences.

   iTunes starts automatically. If this is the first time connecting your iPod, it synchronizes automatically with the iTunes library. If you want to prevent this from happening, hold down the ⌘ and Option keys on the Mac (Ctrl and Alt keys on a PC) as you connect the iPod, keeping them pressed until the iPod name appears in the iTunes Source pane.

2. **Select the iPod in the iTunes Source pane.**

   Your iPod appears in the Source pane using the name you gave it when you installed the iPod software (see Chapter 2).

3. **Click the iPod Options button on the bottom-right side of the iTunes window.**

   The iPod Preferences dialog appears, as shown in Figure 11-1.

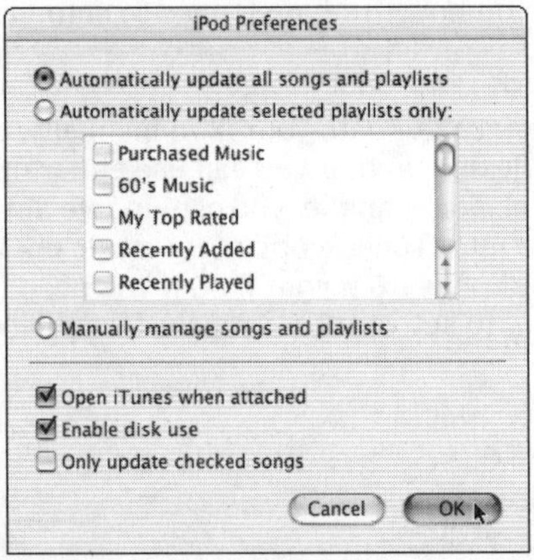

Figure 11-1:
Switch iPod
updating
methods
in the iPod
Preferences
dialog.

iPod Preferences

- ⦿ Automatically update all songs and playlists
- ◯ Automatically update selected playlists only:
  - ☐ Purchased Music
  - ☐ 60's Music
  - ☐ My Top Rated
  - ☐ Recently Added
  - ☐ Recently Played
- ◯ Manually manage songs and playlists

- ☑ Open iTunes when attached
- ☑ Enable disk use
- ☐ Only update checked songs

Cancel   OK

4. **Select the update preferences you want.**

   Set the update preferences, and click OK to the warning message that appears. For example, if you select the Automatically Update All Songs and Playlists option, iTunes displays a warning message asking you to confirm the update preference you chose (see Figure 11-2).

Figure 11-2:
Confirm that
you want
to update
your music
library auto-
matically.

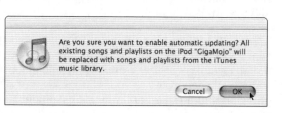

Are you sure you want to enable automatic updating? All existing songs and playlists on the iPod "GigaMojo" will be replaced with songs and playlists from the iTunes music library.

Cancel   OK

5. **Click OK to go ahead (confirming that you want to change to automatic update).**

6. **Change other iPod preferences as you wish.**

   Other preferences that you might want to change include Open iTunes When Attached, which launches iTunes automatically when turned on. If this is off, you have to start iTunes by clicking its icon in the Dock, or by double-clicking the application in the Applications folder.

7. **Click OK to close iPod Preferences.**

8. **Click the iPod Eject button, which appears in the bottom-right side of the iTunes window.**

   Another way to eject the iPod on a Mac is to drag the iPod icon on the Desktop to the Trash — or in Mac OS X 10.3, click the eject icon next to the iPod icon in the Finder Sidebar. In Windows, you can use various methods, including right-clicking the iPod icon and choosing Eject.

   After you eject the iPod, the iPod displays an OK to disconnect message in first- and second-generation models, or the iPod main menu in third-generation models. You can then disconnect the iPod from its dock, or disconnect the dock from the computer.

While the updating is in progress, don't disconnect your iPod from the computer until it tells you it is safe to do so. The iPod is a hard drive, after all, and hard drives need to be closed down properly in order for you not to lose any critical data. When it's safe, the iPod displays an OK to disconnect message in first- and second-generation models, or the iPod main menu in third-generation models.

Updating Your iPod Automatically

The default setting for a new iPod is to update itself automatically, *synchronizing* to your iTunes library: The iPod matches your library exactly, song for song, playlist for playlist. If you made changes in iTunes after the last time you synchronized, those changes are automatically made in the iPod when you synchronize again. If you added or deleted songs in your library, those songs are added or deleted in the iPod library.

If your iTunes music library is too large to fit on your iPod, you can still update automatically and keep your iPod synchronized to a subset of your library, adding new material under your control. For example, you can let iTunes select the music automatically according to your ratings, as described in the upcoming section, "Updating from a library larger than your iPod." You can even create a *smart playlist* that does it for you, as described in the later section, "Updating by playlist."

Before you actually connect your iPod to a computer to automatically update the iPod, keep these things in mind:

- ✔ iTunes remembers your updating preferences from the last time you updated your iPod. If you already set your preferences to update automatically, iTunes remembers and starts to automatically update your iPod. If you already set your preferences to update manually, iTunes remembers and makes your iPod active in the iTunes Source pane.

- ✔ To prevent your iPod from automatically updating, hold down the ⌘ and Option keys on a Mac (Ctrl and Alt keys on a PC) as you connect the iPod, and keep pressing until the iPod name appears in the iTunes Source pane. This works even if you choose to automatically update the iPod in the Setup Assistant.

- ✔ If you connect your iPod to another computer running iTunes, you might be in for a surprise. When you connect an iPod previously linked to another computer, iTunes displays the message: `This iPod is linked to another iTunes music library. Do you want to change the link to this iTunes music library and replace all existing songs and playlists on this iPod with those from this library?` If you don't want to change your iPod to have this other music library, click No. Otherwise, iTunes erases your iPod and updates your iPod with the other computer's iTunes library. By clicking No, you change that computer's iTunes preferences to manually update, thereby avoiding automatic updating.

- ✔ Songs stored remotely (such as songs shared from other iTunes libraries on a network) are not synchronized because they are not physically on your computer. See Chapter 6 for more info on how to share music over a network with iTunes.

When your iPod is set to update automatically (the entire library, or by playlist or selected song), the iPod song list and the iPod entry in the Source pane are grayed out in the iTunes window. Because you manage the contents automatically, you don't have direct access to the songs in the iPod using iTunes. For direct access, see "Updating Your iPod Manually," later in this chapter.

Synchronizing with your library

Your iPod is set up by default to automatically update itself from your iTunes library so that it can synchronize with it. Just follow these simple steps:

1. **Connect the iPod to your computer.**

   When you first connect the iPod to the computer, your iPod automatically synchronizes with your iTunes music library — unless you turned off the Automatic Update option in the Setup Assistant, or unless you hold down the ⌘ and Option keys on a Mac (Ctrl and Alt keys on a PC) while connecting the iPod.

2. **Wait for the updating to finish and then eject the iPod.**

   Wait until the iTunes status pane (up at the top) reads iPod update is complete. You can then click the iPod Eject button, which appears in the bottom-right side of the iTunes window.

You can also eject the iPod by dragging the iPod icon on the Desktop to the Trash on the Mac; in OS X 10.3, you can click the eject icon next to the iPod icon in the Finder Sidebar. In Windows, you can use various methods, including right-clicking the iPod icon and choosing Eject from the contextual menu.

While the updating is in progress and right after ejecting the iPod, don't disconnect your iPod from your computer until it tells you that it's safe to do so. As a reminder, the iPod displays the message Do not disconnect.

Updating from a library larger than your iPod

If your iTunes music library is too large to fit on your iPod, you can still update automatically and keep your iPod synchronized to a subset of your library. When you first use your iPod (which is set by default to automatic update), iTunes displays a message if your library is too large to fit, telling you that it has created a special playlist for your iPod.

s you only once choice, which is to click OK. iTunes creates
ᴄially designed for updating your iPod automatically. For
od is named GigaMojo, you will find a new playlist named
filled with all the songs that iTunes could fit in your iPod.

l, you have already been using your iPod and it's set to
e, iTunes displays a message that gives you a choice of
ıg a new playlist, or letting iTunes choose for you:

✔ If you click Yes, iTunes creates a new playlist (titled GigaMojo Selection, if your iPod is named GigaMojo like ours) and displays a message telling you so. Click OK, and iTunes updates your iPod using the new playlist.

✔ If you click No, iTunes updates automatically until it fills up your iPod. iTunes decides which songs and albums to include in this playlist using the ratings that you can set for each song in the iTunes song information, as we describe in Chapter 9. iTunes groups album tracks together and computes an average rating and play count for the album. It then fills the iPod, giving higher priority to albums with play counts and ratings greater than zero. You can therefore influence the decisions that iTunes makes by adding ratings to songs or entire albums.

Updating by playlist

Updating by playlist is useful when you want to copy selected sets of songs to your iPod every time you connect it to your computer. For example, you can define a set of playlists in your iTunes library to use just for updating an iPod that doesn't have enough capacity to hold your entire library. To do this, set up the iPod to update only selected playlists automatically.

Updating automatically by playlist is also an easy way to automatically update an iPod from an iTunes library that is larger than the iPod's capacity.

Before using this update option, create the playlists in iTunes (see Chapter 10) that you want to copy to the iPod. Then follow these steps:

1. **Connect the iPod to your computer.**

   If your iPod is set to automatically update, hold down the ⌘ and Option keys on a Mac (Ctrl and Alt keys on a PC) while connecting the iPod.

2. **Select the iPod name in the iTunes Source pane.**

3. **Click the iPod Options button.**

   The iPod Preferences dialog appears.

4. **Select the Automatically Update Selected Playlists Only option.**

5. **In the list box, select each playlist that you want to copy in the update.**

   Select the check box next to each playlist to select it for the update, as shown in Figure 11-3.

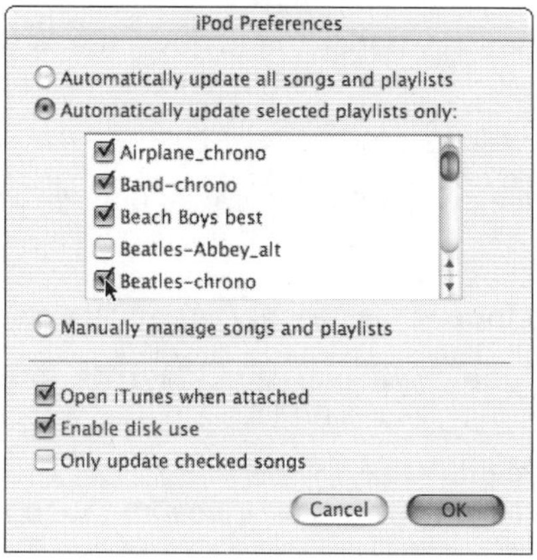

Figure 11-3:
Set the iPod to automatically update with only selected playlists.

iPod Preferences
○ Automatically update all songs and playlists
⦿ Automatically update selected playlists only:
☑ Airplane_chrono
☑ Band-chrono
☑ Beach Boys best
☐ Beatles-Abbey_alt
☑ Beatles-chrono
○ Manually manage songs and playlists
☑ Open iTunes when attached
☑ Enable disk use
☐ Only update checked songs
(Cancel) (OK)

6. **Click OK.**

   iTunes automatically updates the iPod by erasing its contents and copying only the playlists that you selected in Step 5.

7. **Wait for the updating to finish, and then eject the iPod.**

   Wait until the iTunes status pane reads `iPod update is complete`. Then you can click the iPod Eject button (the one with the eject triangle), which appears in the bottom-right side of the iTunes window.

Updating selected songs

You might want to update the iPod automatically but only with selected songs — especially if your iTunes library is larger than the capacity of your iPod. To use this method, you must first select the songs that you want to transfer to the iPod in the iTunes library and then deselect the songs that you don't want to transfer.

To select a song, mark the check box next to the song. To deselect a song, click the check box again so that the check mark disappears.

You can quickly select or deselect an entire album by selecting an album in Browse view and holding down the ⌘ key (Mac) or the Ctrl key (PC).

After you deselect the songs that you don't want to transfer and make sure that the songs you *do* want to transfer are selected, follow these steps:

1. **Connect the iPod to your computer.**

   If your iPod is set to automatically update, hold down the ⌘ and Option keys on a Mac (Ctrl and Alt keys on a PC) while connecting the iPod.

2. **Select the iPod name in the iTunes Source pane.**

   You can select the iPod name even when it's grayed out.

3. **Click the iPod Options button.**

   The iPod Preferences dialog appears (refer to Figure 11-1).

4. **Select the Automatically Update All Songs and Playlists option and click OK for the** `Are you sure you want to enable automatic updating` **message that appears.**

5. **Select the Only Update Checked Songs check box and then click OK.**

   iTunes automatically updates the iPod by erasing its contents and copying only the songs in the iTunes library that are selected.

6. **Wait for the updating to finish, and then eject the iPod.**

   Wait until the iTunes status pane reads `iPod update is complete`, and you can then click the iPod Eject button, which appears in the bottom-right side of the iTunes window.

Updating Your iPod Manually

With manual updating, you can add music to your iPod directly via iTunes, and you can delete music from your iPod as well. The iPod name appears in the iTunes Source pane, and you can double-click to open it, displaying the iPod playlists.

You might have one or more reasons for updating manually, but some obvious ones are the following:

✔ Your entire music library is too big for your iPod, and you want to copy individual albums, songs, or playlists to the iPod directly.

✔ You want to share a single music library with several iPods, and you have different playlists that you want to copy to each iPod directly.

✔ You share an iPod with others, and you want to copy your music to the iPod without wiping out their music.

✔ You want to copy some music from another computer's music library without deleting any music from your iPod.

✔ You want to edit the playlists and song information directly on your iPod without changing anything in your computer's library.

✔ You want to play the songs on your iPod using iTunes on the computer, where you can play your iPod through the computer's speakers and take advantage of iTunes playback features (such as cross-fading between two tracks — see Chapter 18).

When you set your iPod to update manually, the entire contents of the iPod is active and available in iTunes. You can copy music directly to your iPod, delete songs on the iPod, and edit the iPod playlists directly.

To set your iPod to update manually, follow these steps:

1. **Connect the iPod to your computer, holding down the ⌘ and Option keys on a Mac (Ctrl and Alt keys on a PC) to prevent automatic updating.**

   Continue holding the keys down until the iPod name appears in the iTunes Source pane.

2. **Select the iPod name in the iTunes Source pane.**

3. **Click the iPod Options button.**

   The iPod Preferences dialog appears (refer to Figure 11-1).

4. **Select the Manually Manage Songs and Playlists option.**

   iTunes displays the `Disabling automatic update requires manually unmounting the iPod before each disconnect` message.

5. **Click OK to accept the new iPod preferences.**

   The iPod contents now appear active in iTunes and not grayed out.

Don't disconnect your iPod while it is active in iTunes with the manual updating method. You have to eject the iPod and wait until the iPod displays the message `OK to disconnect` (in first- and second-generation models) or the iPod main menu.

Copying music directly

As soon as you set your iPod to manual updating, you can copy music directly. To copy music to your iPod directly, follow these steps (with your iPod connected to your Mac):

1. **Select the iTunes music library in the Source pane.**

   The library's songs appear in a list view or in Browse view.

2. **Drag items directly from your iTunes music library over the iPod name in the Source pane, as shown in Figure 11-4.**

   When you copy a playlist, all the songs associated with the playlist copy along with the playlist itself. When you copy an album, all the songs in the album are copied.

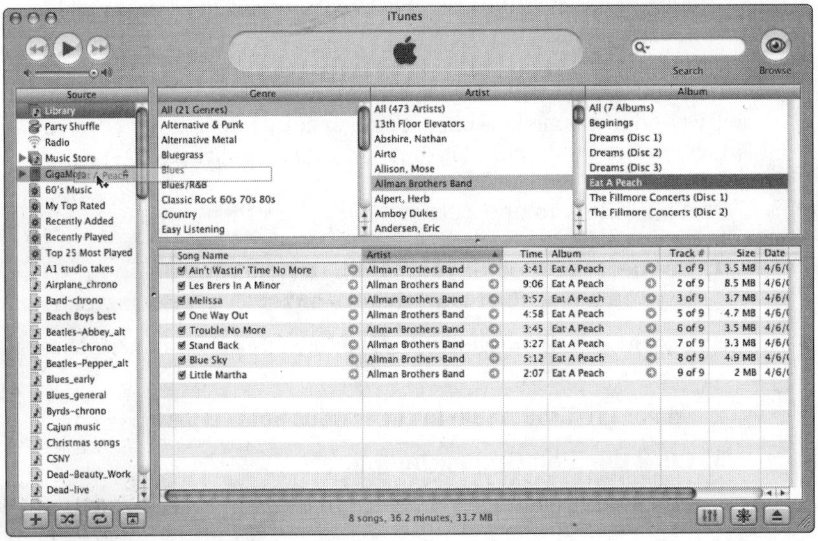

Figure 11-4:
Copy an album of songs directly from the iTunes library to the iPod.

3. **Wait for the copy operation to finish and then eject the iPod.**

   Wait until the iTunes status pane reads `iPod update is complete`; you can then click the iPod Eject button, which appears in the bottom-right side of the iTunes window.

Deleting music on your iPod

With manual updating, you can delete songs from the iPod directly. Manual deletion is a nice feature if you just want to go in and delete a song or an album to make room for more music.

Automatic synchronization with your iTunes library means that anything you delete in your iTunes library is also deleted when you update your iPod. However, if you update manually, you can delete songs from your iPod without changing your iTunes library.

To delete any song in the song list with your iPod set to manual updating, follow these steps:

1. **Select the iPod in the iTunes Source pane.**

2. **Open the iPod's contents in iTunes.**

3. **Select a song or album on the iPod in iTunes, and press Delete/Backspace or choose Edit➪Clear.**

   iTunes displays a warning to make sure you want to do this; click OK to go ahead or Cancel to stop. If you want to delete a playlist, select the playlist and press Delete or choose Edit➪Clear.

Like in the iTunes library, if you delete a playlist, the songs are not deleted — they are still on your iPod unless you delete them from the iPod song list or update the iPod automatically with other songs or playlists.

Managing Playlists on Your iPod

The song information and playlists for your iPod are automatically copied to your iPod when you update the iPod. However, you might want to edit your iPod's music library separately, perhaps creating new playlists or changing the song information manually, just on your iPod.

First you must connect your iPod to your computer, open iTunes, and set your iPod to update manually, as we describe earlier in "Updating Your iPod Manually."

Creating playlists directly on the iPod

You can create a playlist just on the iPod itself, using songs that are on the iPod. The songs must already be on the iPod.

To create a new playlist, follow these steps:

1. **Select the iPod in the iTunes Source pane.**

2. **Click the triangle next to the iPod name to open the iPod list of playlists, as shown in Figure 11-5.**

3. **Create a new playlist by clicking the + button in the bottom-left corner of iTunes under the Source list or choose File➪New Playlist.**

   Untitled playlist appears in the Source pane under the iPod entry.

Figure 11-5:
Create a
playlist here.

4. Type a name for the untitled playlist.

After you type a new name, iTunes automatically sorts it into alphabetical order in the list under the iPod.

5. Click the name of the iPod in the Source pane and drag songs from the iPod song list to the playlist.

You can also click the Browse button to find songs on the iPod more easily.

The order of songs in the playlist is based on the order in which you drag them to the list. You can rearrange the list by dragging songs within the playlist.

You can create smart playlists on the iPod in exactly the same way as in the iTunes music library. A *smart playlist* updates itself when you create it using iTunes, and then updates itself every time you connect and select your iPod with iTunes. Read all about smart playlists in Chapter 10.

Editing playlists

To edit an existing playlist on your iPod, do the following:

1. Select the iPod in the iTunes Source pane.

2. Click the triangle next to the iPod name to open the iPod list of playlists.

3. Scroll the Source pane to locate the playlist.

4. **Select the playlist to rearrange songs.**

5. **Click the name of the iPod in the Source pane and drag more songs from the iPod song list to the playlist.**

You can also click the Browse button to find songs more easily.

The songs and albums that you drag to an iPod playlist must already be on the iPod. If you want to copy songs from your iTunes library, see "Updating Your iPod Manually," earlier in this chapter.

Editing Song Information on Your iPod

With the iPod selected in iTunes and set for updating manually, you can edit song information just like you do in the iTunes library by scrolling down the song list and selecting songs.

After selecting the iPod in the Source pane, click the Browse button. In Browse view, you can browse the iPod library, and find the songs by artist and album.

You can edit information such as the Song Name, Artist, Album, Genre, and My Ratings information for the iPod songs directly in the columns in the song list. To edit song information, locate the song and click inside the text field of a column to type new text.

You might find it easier to edit this information by choosing File➪Get Info and typing the text into the Song Information dialog, as shown in Figure 11-6.

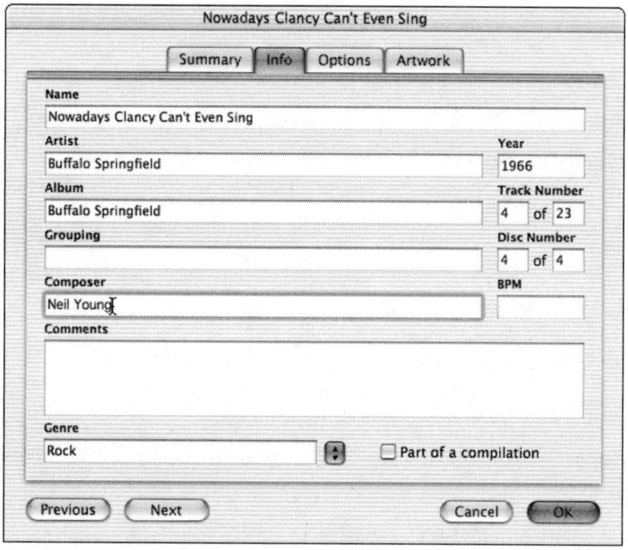

Figure 11-6:
Type the composer credits here.

Nowadays Clancy Can't Even Sing

Summary | Info | Options | Artwork

Name
Nowadays Clancy Can't Even Sing

Artist
Buffalo Springfield

Year
1966

Album
Buffalo Springfield

Track Number
4 of 23

Grouping

Disc Number
4 of 4

Composer
Neil Young

BPM

Comments

Genre
Rock

☐ Part of a compilation

Previous | Next | Cancel | OK

iTunes grabs song information from the Internet (as we describe in Chapter 9), but this information typically doesn't include composer credits. If you have the time and inclination to add composer credits, doing so is worth your while because you can then search, sort, and create playlists based on this information. This is particularly important for classical music lovers because iTunes and the iPod make it easy to find songs by the performer/artist but not by the composer — and sorting by composer is what many classical music fans prefer.

Chapter 12

Managing the MusicMatch Jukebox Library

....

In This Chapter

▶ Adding and editing song information with MusicMatch Jukebox

▶ Changing viewing options in MusicMatch Jukebox

▶ Updating your iPod with MusicMatch Jukebox

▶ Deleting songs and repairing broken links in MusicMatch Jukebox

....

*W*ith MusicMatch Jukebox, just like with iTunes, your computer is a vast jukebox limited only by your hard drive space. Like iTunes, MusicMatch Jukebox gives you the power to organize songs into playlists and update your iPod.

This chapter shows how to manage your MusicMatch Jukebox library and take advantage of its special organization features, such as super-tagging songs with song information, updating your iPod manually, and updating by saved playlist. This chapter also shows you how to set up MusicMatch Jukebox to automatically update your iPod and synchronize the iPod's library to the MusicMatch Jukebox library.

Managing Song Information

Organization depends on information. Your computer can do a lot more than store your songs with *Untitled Disc* and *Track 1* as the only identifiers. Song names, album titles, genre definitions, and composer credits might seem trivial, but you can use this information to browse songs on your iPod.

Using CD Lookup

You can get information about most music CDs from the Internet. However, you need to check your Internet connection first, keeping the following in mind:

- ✔ If you use an always-on broadband Internet service (for example, DSL or cable modem), you probably want MusicMatch Jukebox to connect and retrieve song information automatically.

- ✔ If you're using a dial-up modem, if your Internet service is intermittently off, or if your Internet service provider (ISP) charges prohibit using it all the time, you probably don't want this connection to be automatic.

In MusicMatch Jukebox, you can enable CD Lookup to grab song information from the Internet. Just choose Options➪Settings and click the CD Lookup/ Connectivity tab. Then select the Enable CD Lookup Service option.

You can set an optional timeout limit, in seconds, for how long MusicMatch Jukebox should spend trying to access the database before giving up. (Internet databases can be offline for a number of reasons, or your Internet connection might not be working.)

MusicMatch Jukebox lets you defer CD Lookup for another time, when your Internet connection is active. By default, MusicMatch Jukebox is set to enable deferred service, assuming that most users are intermittently connected to the Internet. This is set by default so that you can record CDs to your music library and have MusicMatch Jukebox look up the information later, when your computer is connected to the Internet. You can change this by disabling the Enable Deferred CD Lookup Service option.

When you record audio CDs, MusicMatch Jukebox connects to the Internet and retrieves the song information automatically, or defers this action until your computer is connected (unless you turned off these options). MusicMatch Jukebox refers to song information as *tags,* and you can always edit your tag information manually.

Editing information tags

The song information on the Internet might not be exactly the format you want it. For example, solo artists are listed by first and last names, as in *John Lennon,* but you might want to list them surname first, as in *Lennon, John.* You might also want to remove *The* from band names such as The Who, instead listing the band under *Who.*

The song information retrieved using the CD Lookup service can be changed after you record a CD into your MusicMatch Jukebox music library. You can edit the tag information for a single song or for an entire album of songs at once.

To edit the information for a single song, select the song and click the Tag button (or right-click the song and choose Edit Track Tags) to open the Edit Track Tag(s) window, as shown in Figure 12-1.

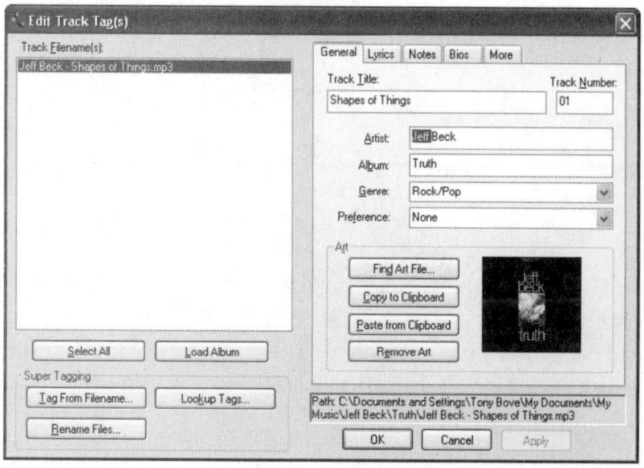

Figure 12-1:
Edit the
song (tag)
info here.

The Edit Track Tag(s) window opens with the General information (as shown in Figure 12-1). You can change the information for each tab in the Edit Track Tag(s) window — Lyrics, Notes, Bios, and More. The General tab shows information that appears in the Player window when you play a song, and some of this information is transferred to your iPod for sorting songs under the artist's name, the album name, and so on.

You can also edit the song information for multiple songs at once. To edit all the songs from a particular album, follow these steps:

1. **Select one of the songs, and click the Tag button (or right-click the song and choose Edit Track Tag) to open the Edit Track Tag(s) window.**

2. **Click the Load Album button in the lower-left side of the Edit Track Tag(s) window.**

   The Load Album button loads all the songs from the album into the list on the left side of the window.

At this point, you can click each song in the album and change its information. A quicker way is to click the Select All button to select all the songs in the album and thus change information for all the songs at once (such as the artist's name), as shown in Figure 12-2.

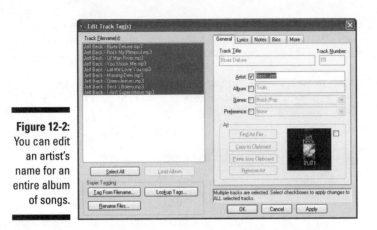

Figure 12-2:
You can edit
an artist's
name for an
entire album
of songs.

When you edit a tag for multiple songs, a check mark appears automatically in the box next to the tag. The check mark indicates that the tag will be changed when you click OK or Apply. Before clicking OK or Apply, make sure that no other box is checked except the tags you want to change. Then click OK, and MusicMatch Jukebox changes the tags for the entire album of songs.

In the music library, MusicMatch Jukebox lists your songs under the artist name. If you change the artist name for an album of songs, the location of the music in your library changes because the names are sorted in alphabetical order. However, the filenames do not change.

When you change the artist's name for an album of songs, you might also want to change the filenames stored on disk to reflect this change. See "Super-tagging songs with information" in this chapter.

Adding information about songs

Adding more information about songs enables you to use the criteria of your choice — such as genre of music or your personal ratings — to locate songs in the MusicMatch Jukebox library and on your iPod.

After your songs are recorded into the music library, locate a single song and click the Tag button (or right-click the song and choose Edit Track Tags). You should see the Edit Track Tag(s) window, which provides a list of songs for an album (if you click Load Album) and also shows the hard drive path to the file for the selected songs. You can change the information by clicking each of these tabs:

✔ **General:** This tab shows the track title, artist name, album title, genre, and preference. It also offers album artwork retrieved from the song information database on the Internet — or you can add your own artwork.

✔ **Lyrics:** This tab lets you add the lyrics to songs. You can copy the lyrics from a text editor (such as Notepad or Microsoft Word) or a Web page and paste them into the empty text box.

✔ **Notes:** This tab lets you add notes and comments. You can copy information from a text editor and paste it into the empty text box.

✔ **Bios:** This tab lets you add musician credits or other information (such as liner notes) to songs. You can copy this information from a text editor and paste it into the empty text box.

✔ **More:** This tab lets you categorize your songs by tempo, mood, and situation, specify the year of release, and add URLs (Internet addresses) for more information. You can also specify whether the song should be prepared for volume leveling.

Although most of this added information is not transferred to the iPod (only the information in the General tab is transferred), the information makes it easier to find music in the library and prepare playlists for different occasions. You can, for example, select all your up-tempo songs for a playlist and transfer that playlist to your iPod for listening on an upbeat day.

Super-tagging songs with information

You can tag your music with information automatically by using the super-tagging feature. After you transfer your songs into the music library, select a group of songs or an entire album, and right-click the selection to display the contextual menu — or choose Edit⇨Super Tag Playlist Track(s) with the album or songs already selected. Then choose one of the following:

✔ **Choose Super Tagging⇨Lookup Tags** to find and add information from the Internet. Even if you have partial song information, super-tagging can fill in the remaining tags. The Lookup Tags results window displays the tags found for each track. Choose the tag set that best represents your tracks.

✔ **Choose Super Tagging⇨Tag from Filename** to find and add information based on the music track's filename. For example, if the music file is `U2 - Beautiful Day.mp3`, the tags created are *U2* for the Artist field and *Beautiful Day* for the Track Title field.

✔ **Choose Super Tagging⇨Rename Files** to change the filenames stored on the hard drive to reflect a change in the artist's name. (Music files are stored by artist name.) MusicMatch Jukebox displays the current name and new name for each song, and you can click OK if you want to make the change.

Viewing Your Song Library

When you update your iPod automatically, all the songs in your library are transferred to your iPod. However, if you want to update your iPod manually with specific songs or albums, you need to be able to find these songs and albums in the library quickly. With MusicMatch Jukebox, you can sort the list of songs and locate songs or albums.

Browsing the library

When you first open MusicMatch Jukebox, the music library window displays songs in a similar fashion as Windows Explorer, with songs appearing as files within a folder that uses the artist's name, as shown in Figure 12-3 (showing the songs from the album *All That You Can't Leave Behind*, by the band U2).

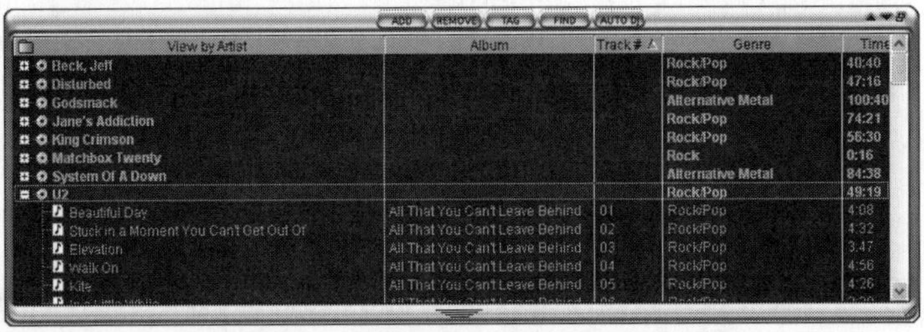

Figure 12-3:
Browse albums and songs by artist.

Clicking the plus sign next to an artist's name opens that listing like a folder; clicking the minus sign closes the folder.

To make a column wider or narrower in MusicMatch Jukebox, drag the dividing line between the column and the next column.

Changing views of your library

MusicMatch Jukebox let you customize the music library's display to show more or less information, or different information, in the columns. You can change your music library's display of songs to view by album, artist, genre, or even album art.

To change the viewing of songs for browsing, click the folder icon in the View By column, which displays a drop-down menu for choosing different ways to view the songs.

When you select to view by album cover art, the album covers appear in the music library, with pop-up text balloons appearing over each album as you move your mouse over them.

Double-click a song in the list or double-click an album, and the song or songs appear in the playlist window and start playing. You can clear the playlist by clicking the Clear button under the playlist.

To change the columns in the song list, choose Options⇨Settings⇨Music Library to display the Settings window. In the View By pop-up menu, you can change the first column of the song listing, which typically is the column used for sorting the list.

You can choose up to six more columns (for a total of seven) to display in the song list. To pick the type of information for a column, select the check box for the column and choose the type of information (tag) for that column. An unchecked column header indicates a column that will not appear.

You can also right-click any column heading in the MusicMatch Jukebox song list to change the type of information that it shows.

The column headers also act as sorting options; click once to sort in ascending order, and click again to sort in descending order. The arrow indicator in the header indicates whether the sort is in ascending or descending order — when the arrow points up, the sort is in ascending order; a down arrow indicates a descending order.

Searching for songs

To search for a song in MusicMatch Jukebox, click the Find button in the music library window to display the Find in Music Library dialog. Type part or all of a song name's characters and then click Find First (or OK).

MusicMatch Jukebox lists the first match for the characters in the Find window. You can continue to find more matches by clicking Find Next. Clicking the Add button adds the song to your current playlist.

You can use the Match Complete Name Only and Match Case options to refine your search. To match the complete name, you must type the entire song name. To match case, you must type the name exactly as it appears in the list, with uppercase and lowercase characters.

Updating Your iPod with MusicMatch Jukebox

You can set up your iPod to be updated with music in different ways depending on how much music you have in your library:

- ✔ **Automatically (entire library):** Update the iPod automatically to match your music library on your computer, adding or deleting songs as necessary.

- ✔ **Automatically by playlist:** Update the iPod with only the playlists you've selected, deleting everything else on your iPod.

- ✔ **Automatically by preselected songs:** Update your iPod with only the songs marked by a check mark, deleting everything else on your iPod.

- ✔ **Manually:** Update your iPod by dragging songs, albums, and/or playlists to the iPod, without deleting anything. You can also manually delete songs, albums, and playlists from your iPod and edit playlists and song information directly on the iPod with this method.

Updating automatically

Adding music to and deleting music from your iPod can be totally automatic. By default, the iPod is set up to update itself automatically, synchronizing itself with your music library.

With automatic update, your iPod matches your library exactly, song for song, playlist for playlist. MusicMatch Jukebox automatically copies everything in your music library to your iPod. If you made changes in your music library after the last time you updated your iPod, those changes are automatically made in your iPod when you connect it to the computer again. If you added or deleted songs in your library, those songs are added or deleted in your iPod's library (unless you use the Ignore All Content Deletions option).

By default, MusicMatch Jukebox is set up to automatically update your iPod unless you disabled the Complete Library Synchronization option in the Options window. Connect your iPod to the PC; if MusicMatch Jukebox does not launch by itself, start the program.

Wait a few minutes for MusicMatch Jukebox to recognize your iPod, which should appear in the PortablesPlus window under the Attached Portable Devices folder. If the window is not yet open, choose File➪Send to Portable Device to open it. When your iPod appears, select it and click the Sync button to update your iPod with the MusicMatch Jukebox music library. The PortablesPlus window displays a warning message — click Yes to continue.

When the synchronization is complete, click the Eject button at the bottom-left side of the PortablesPlus window to eject the iPod.

During updating, the iPod displays the warning Do not disconnect. Wait for the update to finish and also for the iPod to display the iPod main menu (or the message OK to disconnect in older iPods) before disconnecting it from your computer.

If you changed your iPod options to update manually or automatically by playlist, you can change it back to automatic update by following these steps:

1. **Connect your iPod to your PC, and wait for MusicMatch Jukebox to recognize your iPod.**

    Your iPod should appear in the PortablesPlus window under the Attached Portable Devices folder. If the window is not yet open, choose File➪Send to Portable Device.

2. **Select the iPod, click the Options button, click the Synchronization tab, and then select the Complete Library Synchronization option, as shown in Figure 12-4.**

    You can also enable the options to Automatically Synchronize on Device Connection and Ignore All Content Deletions.

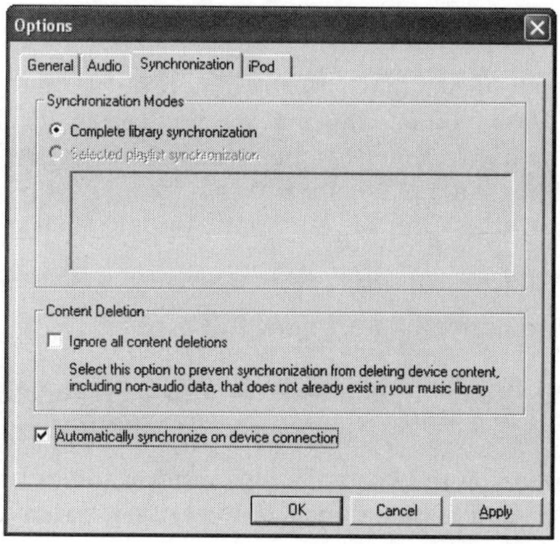

Figure 12-4:
Set your
iPod to
synchronize
with the
complete
library.

3. **Click OK to close the Options window.**

4. **Click the Sync button in the PortablesPlus window to update your iPod with the MusicMatch Jukebox music library.**

   The PortablesPlus window displays a warning message — click Yes to continue.

5. **When the synchronization is complete, click the Eject button at the bottom-left side of the PortablesPlus window to eject the iPod.**

The Options window offers two options for automatic updating: You can set your iPod to automatically synchronize on device connection so that each time you connect the iPod, the synchronization starts immediately. Or, you can set it to ignore all content deletions so that the update does not delete anything in your iPod — it simply adds more music, leaving the music on your iPod intact.

If you select the option to Automatically Synchronize on Device Connection, your iPod will update automatically when you connect it. However, if you don't want this to happen every time, go to the Options window to turn it off. (If you just connected, you have to wait for an update to happen before you can do this.) The alternative is to leave this option off and use the Sync button when you want to update your iPod.

Updating by MusicMatch playlist

If you have several iPods or music devices, or several people sharing one music library or one iPod, you might want to set up automatic updating by playlist so that you can determine which playlists (and associated music files) are copied to the iPod automatically. Before using this update option, create the playlists that you want to copy to the iPod. (See Chapter 7 for details on how to create and save playlists in MusicMatch Jukebox.)

MusicMatch Jukebox lets you save playlists and synchronize them with an iPod automatic update. When you use this feature, you can make changes to the defined playlists in the library, and the changes are automatically updated to the iPod's versions of the same playlists. You can create new playlists and define them for synchronization, and the automatic update then copies the new playlists and music to the iPod.

To define playlists for automatic update, follow these steps:

1. **Connect your iPod to your PC, and wait for it to be recognized by MusicMatch Jukebox.**

   Your iPod should appear in the PortablesPlus window under the Attached Portable Devices folder. If the window is not yet open, choose File⇨Send to Portable Device.

2. **Select the iPod, click the Options button, click the Synchronization tab, and then select the Selected Playlist Synchronization option.**

   You can also enable the options to Automatically Synchronize on Device Connection and Ignore All Content Deletions.

3. **Add a check mark in the box next to each playlist to define playlists for synchronization, and click OK to close the Options window.**

4. **Click the Sync button in the PortablesPlus window to update your iPod with the defined playlists.**

   The PortablesPlus window displays a warning message — click Yes to continue.

5. **When the synchronization is complete, click the Eject button at the bottom-left side of the PortablesPlus window to eject the iPod.**

In the iPod, playlists appear directly under the iPod's name on the left side of the PortablesPlus window. The contents of the iPod (or the contents of the selected playlist in the iPod) appear in the right side of the window.

Updating manually

You can copy music directly to your iPod without automatic updating and synchronization. The iPod's playlists appear directly under the iPod's name on the left side of the PortablesPlus window. The contents of the iPod (or the contents of the selected playlist in the iPod) appear in the right side of the window.

To copy music directly to your iPod, follow these steps:

1. **Connect your iPod to your PC, and wait for MusicMatch Jukebox to recognize your iPod.**

   Your iPod should appear in the PortablesPlus window under the Attached Portable Devices folder. If the window is not yet open, choose File➪Send to Portable Device.

2. **Select the iPod so that its contents appear in the right side of the window.**

3. **Drag entire albums or songs from the music library window to the PortablesPlus window.**

4. **When the copying is complete, drag more albums or songs, or click the Eject button at the bottom-left side of the PortablesPlus window to eject the iPod.**

Deleting Songs

Deleting songs or albums from the MusicMatch Jukebox library is easy. First select the song or album in the library window. Right-click to show the contextual menu and then choose Remove. The song files are not deleted — only the links to the library are deleted. You must still use Windows Explorer to locate and delete the song and album files. See "Searching for songs" earlier in this chapter for details on how to find the song files in MusicMatch Jukebox.

If you update your iPod automatically, song deletion is also automatic on the iPod. If you delete a song or album from your music library, the next time you update the iPod, the song or album is deleted automatically (unless you disable the Ignore All Content Selections option.

However, if you are manually updating your iPod, you also have to manually delete songs that you no longer want on your iPod.

In MusicMatch Jukebox, you can delete songs directly on the iPod. The iPod's playlists appear directly under the iPod's name on the left side of the PortablesPlus window. The contents of the iPod (or the contents of the selected playlist in the iPod) appear in the right side of the window.

To delete songs on the iPod, follow these steps:

1. **Connect your iPod to your PC, and wait for MusicMatch Jukebox to recognize your iPod.**

   Your iPod should appear in the PortablesPlus window under the Attached Portable Devices folder. If the window is not yet open, choose File⇨Send to Portable Device.

2. **Select the iPod so that its contents appear in the right side of the window.**

3. **Select one or more songs, right-click to show the pop-up menu, and then choose Remove.**

4. **When you're finished deleting songs, click the Eject button at the bottom-left side of the PortablesPlus window to eject the iPod.**

Repairing Broken Links to Songs

MusicMatch Jukebox can play songs located anywhere on your hard drive, but if changes occur to your hard drive's folder structure or to folder names, some of your songs might not be linked properly to MusicMatch Jukebox. Fortunately, you can repair these links automatically.

If you get the message <path\track . . . could not be found . . .
while trying to play a track from your library, you can repair the link by right-
clicking the track and choosing Repair Broken Links (or choosing Options⇨
Music Library⇨Repair Broken Links). MusicMatch Jukebox scans your library
for broken links and offers the following functions in a dialog:

- ✔ **Fix It:** This button browses your hard disk for the file to re-link it to the
  library.

- ✔ **Remove:** This button removes the link from your library but does not
  remove the music file from your computer.

- ✔ **Remove All:** This button removes all broken links. MusicMatch Jukebox
  searches your entire library and removes any links to tracks that are no
  longer active. However, it does not remove the music files from your
  computer.

- ✔ **Skip:** This button skips the current missing link and moves on to the
  next one.

- ✔ **Abort:** This button ends the repair process prematurely.

You should repair all broken links before synchronizing your iPod to your
MusicMatch Jukebox library so that you don't miss any songs.

Chapter 13

Gimme Shelter for My Music

In This Chapter

▶ Locating the iTunes music library

▶ Exporting playlists from iTunes

▶ Consolidating and backing up your iTunes music library

▶ Backing up MusicMatch Jukebox music libraries

*Y*ou might think that your music is safe, stored as it is on both your iPod and your hard drive. However, demons in the night are working overtime to render your hard drive useless, while at the same time someone left your iPod out in the rain. (No, not really, but it could happen.)

Copyright law and common sense prohibit you from copying copyrighted music and selling it to someone else. However, you *are* allowed to make copies of music for your personal use, including copies for your iPod and copies for backup.

In this chapter, you find out how to make a backup of your music library — a very important operation, especially if you purchase songs that don't exist anywhere else. That way, even if your hard drive fails, you still have your music.

You can't copy music files from your iPod to your computer using iTunes. While we describe third-party utility programs (not supported by Apple) in Chapter 27 that can do the job, the reason you can't copy music from your iPod using iTunes is that record companies won't allow indiscriminate copying. Most music is copyrighted and shouldn't be copied in this manner anyway (according to record labels). Instead, keep a backup of your iTunes library on your computer and on another hard drive or backup medium — don't rely on your iPod as a music storage device.

Some music that you can use in iTunes and with your iPod is protected. The iTunes Music Store uses Apple's FairPlay technology that protects the rights of copyright holders while also giving you some leeway in how you can use the music. You can copy the music files freely, so backup is easy and straightforward on either a PC or a Mac. The question of whether you can *play* the music after copying it is answered by reading the section on authorizing computers to play purchased music in Chapter 4. (**Hint:** You can play iTunes Music Store songs on up to five computers at the same time.)

Finding the iTunes Library

If you hate to be disorganized, you'll love iTunes and its nice, neat file storage methods. Songs are saved with descriptive filenames within album folders, which are in turn saved within artist folders, and these folders are stored in the iTunes Music folder.

For example, the song "Here, There and Everywhere" has the track name and song title in the filename (`05 Here, There And Everywhere.mp3`). The filename extension even tells you the type of encoding format — in this case, MP3. *Note:* Songs encoded in AAC have the extension `.m4a`. This song is saved in the Revolver folder (for the album), which is in the Beatles folder (for the artist).

What about songs performed by multiple artists, such as duets, or soundtrack albums with multiple artists? Albums and songs designated as part of a compilation are stored in album folders within the Compilations folder rather than within individual artist folders. You can designate a song as part of a compilation by selecting the song and opening the Song Information dialog (File↦Get Info), clicking the Info tab, and then selecting the Part of a Compilation option. You can designate an entire album as a compilation album (so that the album folder is stored in the Compilations folder) by selecting the album, opening the Multiple Song Information dialog (File↦Get Info), clicking Yes to edit multiple songs at once, and then selecting the Part of a Compilation option by choosing Yes (in the pop-up menu on a Mac or the drop-down menu in Windows). Even if the choice is already made, choose Yes again to set the check mark for updating.

You can find the location of any song by selecting the song and choosing File↦ Get Info, and then clicking the Summary tab in the Song Information dialog. Look in the Kind section of the Summary. If you see `(remote)` next to the file format description, the song is not on your hard drive. The Where section tells you where the song is, as shown in Figure 13-1.

```
                              Here, There And Everywhere
         ┌──────────┬──────┬──────────┬──────────┐
         │ Summary  │ Info │ Options  │ Artwork  │
         └──────────┴──────┴──────────┴──────────┘

                        Here, There And Everywhere (2:25)
                        Beatles
                        Revolver


               Kind:  MPEG audio file         Format:  MPEG-1, Layer 3
               Size:  5.6 MB               Channels:  Stereo
           Bit Rate:  320 kbps              ID3 Tag:  v2.2
        Sample Rate:  44.100 kHz       Encoded with:  iTunes v3.0
      Date Modified:  6/14/04 2:46 PM
         Play Count:  3
        Last Played:  3/8/04 1:47 PM


      Where:  Macintosh HD:Users:tony:Music:iTunes:iTunes Music:Beatles:Revolver:05 Here, There
              And Everywhere.mp3

      ( Previous )  ( Next )                      ( Cancel )  ( OK )
```

Figure 13-1:
Locate
a song's
file from
the Song
Information
dialog.

If you access shared libraries on a network, you probably have music in your library that's not actually _in_ your library at all, but rather part of a shared library or playlist on a network, as we describe in Chapter 6. When you look at the Summary tab of the Song Information dialog for a song in a shared library, the Where section does not appear.

All songs that you import are stored in the iTunes Music folder. Even music files that you drag to the iTunes window are stored here — iTunes makes a copy and stores the copy in the iTunes Music folder. You need to know where this folder is so that you can copy music folders or make a backup of your library.

iTunes maintains a separate iTunes folder (with a separate iTunes Music folder) in each Home folder (Mac) or user folder (PC). If you share your computer with other users who have Home folders, each user can have a separate music library on the same computer (and, of course, a separate iPod that synchronizes with it).

On a Mac, iTunes stores your music library inside your Home folder. The path to this folder is _your home folder_/Music/iTunes/iTunes Music.

On a Windows PC, iTunes stores your music library inside your User folder. The path to this folder is _your user folder_/My Documents/My Music/ iTunes/iTunes Music.

To change where iTunes stores your music library, choose Preferences (from the iTunes menu on a Mac/the Edit menu on PCs), click Advanced, and then click the Change button, which lets you select another location.

The iTunes Music Library file (`iTunes Music Library.xml`) must be located within the iTunes folder where iTunes can find it.

Consolidating the iTunes Library

If you have songs stored on different hard drives connected to the same computer, you can have iTunes consolidate your music library by copying everything into the iTunes Music folder. By consolidating your library first, you make sure that your backup is complete.

To consolidate your music library, choose Advanced⇨Consolidate Library. The original songs remain where they are, but copies are made in your Music folder.

The Consolidate Library command copies any file ending in `.aac`, `.m4a`, or `.mp3` into the Music directory and adds it to the iTunes library — including any `.mp3` sound files used in games, such as Quake. You might want to move files associated with games to another hard drive or backup disc before consolidating.

Exporting iTunes Playlists

With iTunes, you can export a playlist and import it into a different computer in order to have the same playlist in both places.

You must also copy the songs (or better yet, copy the entire artist folder containing the songs, to keep the songs organized) in order for the playlists on the other computer to work. Exporting a playlist does *not* copy the songs in the playlist. You get a list of songs in the XML (eXtensible Markup Language) format but not the songs themselves — you still need to copy the actual song files to the other computer.

To export a single playlist, select the playlist and choose File⇨Export Song List. On a Mac, choose the XML option from the Format pop-up menu in the Save: iTunes dialog, and click the Save button. On a Windows PC, choose the XML option from the Files drop-down menu in the Save window.

After exporting a playlist and copying it to another computer, you can import the playlist into iTunes on the other computer by choosing File⇨Import on that computer, selecting the XML file, and clicking the Choose button. You can also export all the playlists in your library at the same time by choosing File⇨Export Library; then import them into iTunes on the other computer by choosing File⇨Import and selecting the exported XML file.

Backing Up the iTunes Library

If you're like us, your iTunes library is huge. We've nearly filled the internal hard drives of two modern computers, each sporting 80GB of space. And you thought 80GB would be enough? What about the backup?

Yes, don't think twice: Backing up can be inconvenient, and it can eat up the capacity of all your external hard drives — but it must be done. Fortunately, it's easy to do. With iTunes, you can copy your library to another hard drive on your computer or to another computer. You can even copy a library from a Mac to a PC and vice versa.

Backing up on the same type of computer

To copy your entire music library to another hard drive, locate the iTunes folder on your computer. Drag this entire folder to another hard drive or backup device, and you're all set. This action copies everything, including the playlists in your library.

The copy operation can take some time if the library is huge. Although you can stop the operation anytime, the newly copied library might not be complete. Allowing the copy operation to finish is always best.

If you restore the backup copy to the same computer with the same names for its hard drive, the backup copy's playlists should work fine. Playlists are essentially XML lists of songs with pathnames to the song files — if the hard drive name is different, the pathnames won't work. However, you can import the playlists into iTunes by choosing File⇨Import, which realigns the playlist pathnames to the new hard drive. Alternatively, you can use the method described in "Backing up from Mac to PC or PC to Mac."

If you just copy just the iTunes Music folder, you are copying the music itself but not your playlists. You still have to export your playlists — see "Exporting iTunes Playlists," earlier in this chapter.

If you use a Mac and subscribe to the Apple .Mac service, you can download and use the free Backup 2 software, which allows you to save the latest versions of your files regularly and automatically so you never have to worry about losing important files. With Backup, you can quickly and easily store files on your iDisk (a portion of an Internet hard disk hosted by .Mac), or on CD or DVD as data files (not as CD songs — see Chapter 14 to read how to burn an audio or MP3 CD). The iDisk is perhaps the least convenient, even though you do get free space with a .Mac membership. It offers up to 100MB (barely enough for a few albums), and copying to the iDisk is slow with a modem connection. We use iDisk to transfer individual songs and other large files to other people and to back up very important documents, but you're better off using a CD-ROM or DVD-ROM (or a DVD-RW) as a backup medium for data, as well as an audio CD for your songs and albums.

Backing up from Mac to PC or PC to Mac

Maybe you use a Mac but you want to transfer your iTunes library to a PC running iTunes, or the other way 'round. Or perhaps you want a foolproof method of copying your entire music library to another computer, whether it's a Mac or a PC running Windows, or just a computer that uses a different name for its hard drive (or a different path to the Home folder or user folder).

To back up your iTunes music library no matter what the situation, follow these steps:

1. **Locate your iTunes Music folder on your old computer.**

   Locate your iTunes Music folder as we describe in "Finding the iTunes Library," earlier in this chapter. Call the first computer the *old* computer and the one to receive the copied library the *new* computer.

2. **Download and install iTunes on the new computer.**

   See Chapter 2 for instructions on installing iTunes. If the new computer already has an iTunes Music folder with music that you want to preserve, move the iTunes Music folder to another folder on the hard drive, or copy it to another hard drive or storage medium.

3. **Copy the iTunes Music folder from the old computer to the newly installed iTunes folder of the new computer.**

   If you have multiple users on the new computer, make sure that you choose the appropriate user folder for a Windows PC or Home folder for a Mac.

4. **Choose File⇨Export Library on the old computer, browse to a location on your hard drive or network, and click the Save button.**

When you export your entire library, iTunes creates an XML file called `iTunes Music Library.xml` that links to music files and stores all your playlists.

5. **Start iTunes on the new computer.**

6. **Choose File⇨Import on the new computer, and import the** `iTunes Music Library.xml` **file.**

The music library is now available on the new computer.

Backing Up the MusicMatch Jukebox Library

MusicMatch Jukebox libraries are actually collections of links to music files. Those files can be anywhere on your hard drive, not just in a special folder designated for such files. (We do recommend designating such a folder because otherwise you have to hunt for the music files when you want to copy them.)

You can maintain multiple libraries with MusicMatch Jukebox, without using much hard drive space, because each library is essentially a playlist with pathnames to the actual music files. You could also have music in your library that is not actually on your hard drive at all — it could be "streamed" to your computer over the Internet and never actually stored in a music file on your drive. (Of course, it also can't be copied to your iPod.)

Streaming is the process of sending audio to your computer in a protected set of bits over the network — your computer starts playing the audio as soon as the first set of bits arrive, and more sections are transferred while you listen, so that you hear it as a continual stream.

MusicMatch Jukebox stores music files created from recording CDs in folders inside the My Music folder in your My Documents folder unless you specify otherwise. The path to this folder on Windows XP or Windows 2000 is typically *your user folder*`/My Documents/My Music`, and inside this folder are folders organized by artist name.

Yes, consolidating all your song files in one place for easy backup might be time-consuming. Consider using disk backup software that copies all your files, or perhaps selectively copy the music files as you see fit. You can find out the location of any song's music file by selecting the song and right-clicking (using the alternate mouse button) to show the contextual menu, and choosing Open File Location.

Saving Multiple MusicMatch Jukebox Libraries

Because music libraries are essentially links to music files, they can be saved as separate library files as well as exported in a text database format. To save a music library, choose Options⇨Music Library⇨Save Music Library As. MusicMatch Jukebox saves the file with the filename extension `.ddf`, as in `yourlibrary.ddf`, which is the MusicMatch Jukebox-specific format for music library files.

You can save as many different music libraries as you want, such as libraries dedicated to specific types of music or libraries associated with different people. Each one can be used to synchronize with a separate iPod, or you can update one iPod manually from different libraries.

To load a saved music library, choose Options⇨Music Library⇨Open Music Library, and browse for the saved music library, which should have the `.ddf` extension. You can also import an entire music library into another music library — thus combining the two libraries — by choosing Options⇨Music Library⇨Import Music Library.

If you've moved your music files or renamed any folders in the path to your music files and MusicMatch Jukebox can't find the music file associated with a song, choose Options⇨Music Library⇨Repair Broken Links, and browse to the folder where the music file now resides.

Chapter 14

Burning CDs from iTunes

· ·

In This Chapter

▶ Creating a burn playlist

▶ Choosing the right format for burning a CD

▶ Setting the burn preferences

▶ Burning a CD

▶ Exporting song information

▶ Troubleshooting tips

· ·

*O*nce upon a time, when vinyl records were popular, rock radio disk jockeys who didn't like disco held *disco meltdown* parties. People were encouraged to throw their disco records into a pile to be burned or steamrolled into a vinyl glob. This chapter isn't about that; neither is it about anything involving fire nor heat.

Rather, *burning* a CD refers to the process in which the CD drive recorder's laser heats up points on an interior layer of the disc, simulating the pits pressed into commercial CDs that represent digital information.

People burn CDs for a lot of reasons — reason numero uno is to make a backup of songs on your computer. Perhaps having your 12 favorite love songs on one CD for your next romantic encounter is convenient, or perhaps you want to burn a few CDs of obscure songs to impress your friends on your next big road trip.

This chapter burns, er, boils everything down for you by telling you what kind of discs to use, which devices you can use to play the discs, how to get your playlist ready for burning, and what settings to use for burning. You find out what you need to know to make sure that your burns are not meltdowns — that the only melting is the music in your ears.

Selecting Recordable CDs

After importing music into your iTunes library, you can arrange any songs in your library into a playlist and burn a CD using that playlist (see Chapter 10 for more on creating playlists). If you have a CD-R, CD-RW, or DVD-R drive (such as the Apple SuperDrive for Macs), and a blank CD-R (R stands for *recordable*), you can create your own music CDs that play in most CD players.

Blank CD-Rs are available in most electronics and computer stores, and even supermarkets. You can also get them online from the Apple Store (not the music store — the store that sells computers and accessories). Choose iTunes⇨Shop for iTunes Products on a Mac or the Help⇨Shop for iTunes Products on a Windows PC to reach the Apple Store online.

The discs are called *CD-R* because they use a recordable format related to commercial audio CDs (which are not recordable, of course). You can also create a disc in the new MP3 format by creating a CD-R with data rather than music, which is useful for backing up a music library.

CD-Rs play just like regular audio CDs in most CD players, including car players and portable CD players. The CD-R format is the most universal and compatible with older players.

Many CD burners, such as the Apple SuperDrive, also burn CD-RWs (recordable, read-write discs) that you can erase and reuse, but CD players don't always recognize them as music CDs. Some burners can create data DVD-Rs and DVD-RWs also, which are useful for holding data files, but you can only use these discs with computers that have DVD drives. Most commercial DVD players won't read a data DVD-R or DVD-RW.

You can play MP3 files burned on a CD-R in the MP3 format on the new consumer MP3 disc players and combination CD/MP3 players as well as on many DVD players, and of course on computers that recognize MP3 CDs (including computers with iTunes).

What You Can Fit on a CD-R

You can fit up to 74 minutes of music on a high-quality CD-R; some can go as high as 80 minutes. The sound files on your hard drive might take up more space than 650 MB if they are uncompressed, but you can still fit 74 minutes (or 80 minutes, depending on the disc) because the CD format stores information more efficiently.

If you burn music to a CD-R in the MP3 format, the disc can hold more than 12 hours worth of music. You read that right — 12 hours on one disc. Now you know why MP3 discs are popular. MP3 discs are essentially CD-Rs with MP3 files stored on them.

If you have a DVD burner, such as the Apple SuperDrive, you can burn data DVD-Rs or DVD-RWs to use with other computers. This approach is suitable for making backup copies of music files (or any data files). A DVD-R can hold about 4,700,000,000 bytes (about 4.38GB), which is enough to hold part of a music library.

To burn a CD-RW or DVD-RW that already has data on it, you must first erase it by reformatting it using the application supplied with the drive. CD-RWs and DVD-RWs work with computers but won't work with consumer players.

TECHNICAL STUFF

The little Red Book that launched an industry

The typical audio CD and CD-R uses the CD-DA (Compact Disc-Digital Audio) format, which is known as *Red Book* — not something from Chairman Mao, but a document, published in 1980, that provides the specifications for the standard compact disc (CD) developed by Sony and Philips. According to legend, this document was in a binder with red covers.

Also according to legend, in 1979, Norio Ohga, honorary chairman and former CEO of Sony (who's also a maestro conductor), overruled his engineers and insisted that the CD format be able to hold Beethoven's *Ninth Symphony* (which is 74 minutes and 42 seconds — now the standard length of a Red Book audio CD).

CD-DA defines audio data digitized at 44,100 samples per second (44.1 kHz) and in a range of 65,536 possible values (16 bits).

To import music into the computer from an audio CD, you have to convert the music to digital sound files by a program such as iTunes. When you burn an audio CD, iTunes converts the sound files back into the CD-DA format as it burns the disc.

Creating a Burn Playlist

To burn a CD, you must first define a playlist for the CD. See Chapter 10 to find out how to create a playlist. You can use songs encoded in any format that iTunes supports; however, you get higher quality music with the uncompressed formats AIFF and WAV.

To copy an album you already have in your iTunes library onto an audio CD, you can quickly create a playlist for the album by switching to Browse view in your iTunes library and dragging an album from the Album list (in the top-right section of the window in Browse view) to the white area below the items in your Source pane. iTunes automatically creates a playlist with the album name. You can then use that playlist to burn a CD.

If your playlist includes music purchased from the iTunes Music Store or other online stores in the protected AAC encoding format, some rules might apply. For example, the iTunes Music Store allows you to burn ten copies of the same playlist containing protected songs to an audio CD, but no more. You can, however, create a new playlist and copy the protected songs to the new playlist, and then burn more CDs with the songs.

Calculating how much music to use

When you create a playlist, you find out how many songs can fit on the CD by totaling the durations of the songs, using time as your measure. You can see the size of a playlist by selecting it; the bottom of the iTunes window shows the number of songs, the amount in time, and the amount in megabytes for the currently selected playlist, as shown in Figure 14-1.

Figure 14-1:
Check the
duration of
the playlist
below the
song list.

In Figure 14-1, the selected playlist has 23 songs that total 1.1 hours and 724.1MB. (*Note:* The songs were encoded in the AIFF format.) You might notice the discrepancy between the megabytes (724.1) and what you can fit on an audio CD (650). Although a CD holds between 650MB and 700MB (depending on the disc), the music is stored in a special format known as CD-DA (or Red Book) that fills byte sectors more efficiently. Thus, you can fit a bit more than 650MB of AIFF-encoded music on a 650MB disc. We can fit 1.1 hours (66 minutes) of music on a 74-minute or 80-minute CD-R with many minutes to spare.

Always use the actual duration in hours, minutes, and seconds to calculate how much music you can fit on an audio CD — either 74 or 80 minutes for blank CD-Rs. Leave at least one extra minute to account for the gaps between songs.

You do the *opposite* for an MP3 CD — you use the actual megabytes to calculate how many songs can fit on a disc — up to 700MB for a blank CD-R. You can fit lots more music on an MP3 CD-R because you use MP3-encoded songs rather than uncompressed AIFF songs.

If you have too many songs in the playlist to fit on a CD-R, iTunes will burn as many songs in the playlist as will fit on the CD-R (either audio or MP3), and then it will ask you to insert another CD-R to continue burning the remaining songs in the playlist.

Importing music for an audio CD-R

Before you rip an audio CD of songs you want to burn to an audio CD-R, you might want to change the import settings. Check out Chapter 19 if you need to do so. Use AIFF or WAV for songs from audio CDs if you want to burn your own audio CDs with music.

AIFF is the standard digital format for uncompressed sound on a Mac, and you can't go wrong with it. WAV is basically the same thing for Windows. Both the AIFF Encoder and the WAV Encoder offer the same Custom settings dialog, with settings for sample rate, sample size, and channels. You can choose the automatic settings, and iTunes automatically detects the proper sample rate, size, and channels from the source.

Songs that you purchase from the iTunes Music Store come in the protected AAC format, which you can't convert to anything else.

The AAC music file format is a higher quality format than MP3, comparable to CD quality. We think that it offers a decent trade-off of space and quality and is suitable (although not as good as AIFF or Apple lossless) for burning to an audio CD.

Switching import encoders for MP3 CD-R

MP3 discs are essentially CD-Rs with MP3 files stored on them using the ISO 9660 file structure that is standard across computers and players. Consumer MP3 CD players are now on the market, including hybrid models that play both audio CDs and MP3 CDs.

You can fit an average of 12 hours of music on a CD using the MP3 format, although this amount can vary widely (along with audio quality) depending on the encoding options and settings you choose. For example, you might be able to fit up to 20 hours of mono (monaural) recordings because they use only one channel and carry less information. On the other hand, if you encode stereo recordings at high bit rates (above 192 bits per second), you will fit less than 12 hours. If you rip an audio CD, you can set the importing options to precisely the type of MP3 file you want (see Chapter 19).

You can use only MP3-encoded songs to burn an MP3 CD-R. Any songs not encoded in MP3 are skipped and not burned to the CD-R. Audible books and spoken-word titles are provided in an audio format that uses security technologies, including encryption, to protect purchased content. You can't burn an MP3 CD-R with Audible files; any Audible files in a burn playlist are skipped when you burn an MP3 CD-R.

Setting the Burning Preferences

Burning a CD is a simple process, and getting it right the first time is a good idea because when you burn a CD-R, it's done one time — right or wrong. You can't erase content on a CD-R like you can with a CD-RW. Because you can't play a CD-RW in as many CD players, if you want to burn an audio CD, we recommend using a CD-R. Fortunately, CD-Rs are inexpensive, so you won't be out more than a few cents if you burn a *coaster* (a bad CD-R).

Setting the sound check and gaps

Musicians do a sound check before every performance to check the volume of microphones and instruments and their effect on the listening environment. The aptly named Sound Check option in iTunes allows you to do a sound check on your tunes to bring them all in line, volume-wise.

To have all the songs in your library play at the same volume level all the time, choose iTunes⇨Preferences on a Mac or Edit⇨Preferences on a Windows PC. In the Preferences dialog, click the Audio tab. Select the Sound Check check box, as shown in Figure 14-2, which sets all the songs to the current volume controlled by the iTunes volume slider.

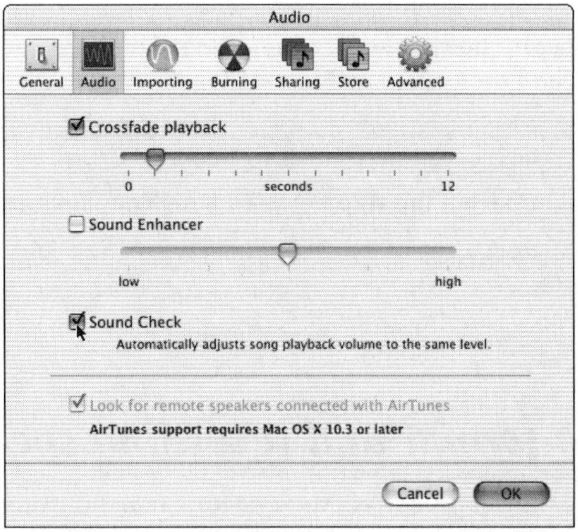

Figure 14-2:
Adjust the song playback volume of all songs to the same level.

After enabling Sound Check, you can burn your audio CD-R so that all the songs play back at the same volume, just like they do in iTunes. Choose iTunes➪Preferences on a Mac/Edit➪Preferences on a Windows PC, and then click the Burning button. Select the Use Sound Check option, as shown in Figure 14-3. *Note:* This option is active only if you are already using the Sound Check option in the Audio preferences.

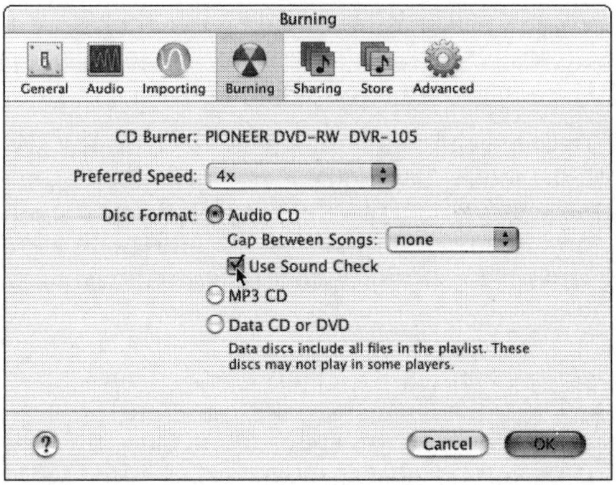

Figure 14-3:
Select the Use Sound Check option for the CD-R burn.

Consistent volume for all tracks makes the CD-R sound professional. Another professional touch is to add an appropriate gap between songs, just like commercial CDs. Follow these steps to control the length of the gap between the songs on your audio CD-R (not MP3 CD-R):

1. **Choose iTunes⇨Preferences on a Mac/Edit⇨Preferences on a Windows PC, and then click the Burning tab in the Preferences dialog.**

   The Burning Preferences appear (refer to Figure 14-3).

2. **Choose an amount from the Gap between Songs pop-up menu.**

   You can choose from a gap of 0 to 5 seconds. We recommend selecting a gap of 2 seconds.

3. **Click OK.**

Setting the format and recording speed

Before burning a CD-R, you have to set the disc format and the recording speed. Choose Preferences (from the iTunes menu on a Mac/Edit menu on a Windows PC), and then click the Burning tab in the Preferences dialog.

The Disc Format setting in the Burning dialog (refer to Figure 14-3) offers three choices:

- ✔ **Audio CD:** Choose this to burn a normal audio CD of up to 74 or 80 minutes (depending on the type of blank CD-R) using any iTunes-supported music files, including songs bought from the iTunes Music Store. Although connoisseurs of music might use AIFF-encoded or WAV-encoded music to burn an audio CD, you can also use songs in the AAC and MP3 formats.

- ✔ **MP3 CD:** Choose this to burn an MP3 CD with songs encoded in the MP3 format. No other formats are supported for MP3 CD.

- ✔ **Data CD or DVD:** Choose this to burn a data CD-R, CD-RW, DVD-R, or DVD-RW with the music files. You can use any encoding formats for the songs. *Important:* Data discs won't play on most consumer CD players — they are meant for use with computers. However, data discs are good choices for storing copies of music bought from the iTunes Music Store.

Blank CD-Rs are rated for recording at certain speeds. iTunes typically detects the rating of a blank CD-R and adjusts the recording speed to fit. However, if your blank CD-Rs are rated for a slower speed than your burner, or you have problems creating CD-Rs, you can change the recording speed setting to match the CD's rating. Choose iTunes➪Preferences on a Mac/Edit➪Preferences on a Windows PC, and then click the Burning tab in the Preferences dialog. From the Preferred Speed pop-up menu or drop-down list in the Burning Preferences, choose a specific recording speed or choose the Maximum Possible option to set the recording speed to your burner's maximum speed.

Burning a Disc

After you set the burning preferences, you're ready to start burning. Follow these steps to burn a CD:

1. **Select the playlist designated for burning a disc and click the Burn Disc button.**

   A message appears telling you to insert a blank disc.

2. **Insert a blank disc (label side up).**

   iTunes immediately checks the media and displays a message in the status window that the disc is ready to burn.

3. **Click the Burn Disc button again.**

   This time, the button has a radiation symbol. The burn process begins. The "radioactive" button rotates while the burning takes place, and a progress bar appears with the names of the songs displayed as they burn to the disc.

   When iTunes has finished burning the CD, iTunes chimes, and the CD is mounted on the Desktop.

4. **Eject the newly burned disc from your CD drive and test it.**

Burning takes several minutes. You can cancel the operation at any time by clicking the X next to the progress bar, but canceling the operation isn't like undoing the burn. If the burn has already started, you can't use the CD-R or DVD-R again.

If the playlist has more music than fits on the disc using the chosen format, iTunes burns as much as possible from the beginning of the playlist, and then asks you to insert another disc to burn the rest. To calculate the amount of music in a playlist, turn to the section, "Calculating how much music to use," earlier in this chapter.

If you choose the MP3 CD format, iTunes skips over any songs in the playlist that are not in the MP3 format.

Printing Liner Notes and CD Covers

Don't delete the playlist yet! You can print the CD liner notes and covers using any artwork you have assigned to the songs in the playlist (as described in Chapter 9).

Select the playlist, and choose File➪Print to see a print dialog box with choices for CD inserts and liner notes. You can print a CD jewel case insert, a song listing, or an album listing. If you choose a CD jewel case, you have a choice of themes such as Text Only (without song artwork), Mosaic (with artwork from songs arranged in a mosaic), Single Cover (with one song's artwork), and so on. If you choose a song listing, the Theme pop-up menu changes to provide options for columns in the song list

If you want to print liner notes in a layout that iTunes doesn't offer in its printing themes, you can export the song information for all the songs in a playlist to a text file, and then edit that information in a word processor or page layout program to make liner notes for the CD. iTunes exports all the song information for a single song, a playlist, an album, songs by an artist, or songs in the library into a text file. Select the songs or playlist and choose File➪Export Song List. In the Export Song List dialog, make sure that the Plain Text option is selected from the Format pop-up menu (unless you use a double-byte language, such as Japanese or Chinese, for which the Unicode option is the right choice).

Troubleshooting Burns

Murphy's Law applies to everything, even something as simple as burning a CD-R. Don't think for a moment that you are immune to the whims and treacheries of Murphy (no one really knows who Murphy is), who in all his infinite wisdom, pronounced that anything that *can* go wrong *will* go wrong. In this section, we cover some of the most common problems that you might encounter when burning CDs.

The best way to test your newly burned disc is to pop it right back into your computer's CD-ROM drive, or try it on a consumer CD player. On most CD players, an audio CD-R plays just like any commercial audio CD. MP3 CDs play fine on consumer MP3 CD players and also work in computers with CD-ROM and DVD drives.

If the CD works on the computer but not on a commercial CD player, you might have a compatibility problem with the commercial player and CD-R. We have a five-year-old CD player that doesn't play CD-Rs very well, and car players sometimes have trouble with them.

The following list gives some typical problems that you might run into when burning a CD, along with the solutions to those problems:

✔ *Problem:* The disc won't burn.

Solution: Perhaps you have a bum disc. Hey, it happens. Try using another disc or burning at a slower speed.

✔ *Problem:* In a consumer CD player, the disc doesn't play, or it stutters when playing.

Solution: This happens often with older consumer players that don't play CD-Rs well. Try the disc in your computer's CD-ROM drive. If it works there and you set the format to Audio CD, you probably have a compatibility problem with your consumer player.

✔ *Problem:* The disc doesn't show tracks on a consumer CD player, or it ejects immediately.

Solution: Be sure to use the proper disc format — choose iTunes➪ Preferences on a Mac/Edit➪Preferences on a Windows PC, and click the Burning tab to see the Disc Format setting in the Burning dialog. The Audio CD format works in just about all consumer CD players that can play CD-Rs. MP3 CDs work in consumer MP3 CD players and computer CD-ROM and DVD drives. Data CDs or DVDs work only in computer drives.

✔ *Problem:* Some songs in my playlist were skipped and not burned onto the disc.

Solution: Audio CD-Rs burn with songs encoded in any format, but you can use only MP3-encoded songs to burn an MP3 CD-R. Any songs not encoded in MP3 are skipped. (Any Audible files are also skipped, which can't be put onto an MP3 CD.) If your playlist for an audio CD-R includes music purchased from the iTunes Music Store, some rules might apply — see the section, "Creating a Burn Playlist," earlier in this chapter.

Don't violate copyright law.

Part III
Playing Tunes

The 5th Wave — By Rich Tennant

"I SAID, I THINK I FOUND YOUR iPOD!"

In this part . . .

*P*art III focuses on the many ways that you can use iTunes and an iPod to play music, and it covers the many different types of listening environments and accessories that accommodate them.

- ✔ Chapter 15 shows you how to locate and play your songs on your iPod, create playlists on the fly, and adjust the iPod's volume.

- ✔ Chapter 16 is about playing music over home stereos, headphones, and portable speakers with your iPod, and it includes cool accessories for using your iPod at home.

- ✔ Chapter 17 shows you how you can use your iPod in planes, on trains, and in automobiles with cool travel accessories.

- ✔ Chapter 18 shows you how to queue up and cross-fade songs like a professional DJ. In this chapter, we also share how to play songs that reside on an iPod using iTunes on your computer or another computer.

Chapter 15

Playing Your iPod

In This Chapter

▶ Locating songs by artist, album, or playlist

▶ Repeating and shuffling a song list

▶ Creating, clearing, and saving on-the-go playlists

▶ Changing the volume level

▶ Bookmarking Audible books

Your iPod is lightweight enough to carry everywhere but also heavy with thousands of songs, representing a cross-section of the history of rock music — a veritable museum in your hands. Or perhaps you have every popular song that made the charts in the last few years or every jazz note played between 1960 and 1966. You spent a few minutes creating playlists in iTunes that barely scratch the surface of the huge library you have in your hands. Now how do you switch songs or playlists while maintaining your jogging pace or avoiding wrecks on the freeway?

After you add music to your iPod, you can locate and play that music easily, browsing by artist and album, and even by composer. Selecting a playlist is simplicity itself, and if you don't have playlists from iTunes (or you don't want to hear those playlists), you can create a temporary On-The-Go playlist. This chapter shows you how to do all these things.

Locating Songs

With so many songs on your iPod, finding a particular one can be hard (like finding a needle in a haystack, or trying to find "Needle in a Haystack" by the Velvelettes in the Motown catalog) — even though you can narrow your search by genre, and also search by artist, composer, album, or playlist.

By artist

Your iPod organizes music by artist, and within each artist by album. Follow these steps to locate a song by artist and then album:

1. **Select the Browse item from the iPod main menu.**

   Scroll the main menu until Browse is highlighted, and then press the Select button. The Browse menu appears.

2. **Select the Artists item.**

   The Artists item is at the top of the Browse menu and should already be highlighted; if not, scroll the menu until Artists is highlighted, and then press the Select button. The Artists menu appears.

   To browse by genre, select the Genres item, and then select a genre from the Genres menu to get a reduced list of artists that have songs in that genre (in alphabetical order by artist name).

3. **Select an artist from the Artists menu.**

   The artists' names are listed in alphabetical order by first word. ***Note:*** Any leading *The* is ignored so that *The Beatles* appears where *Beatles* would be in the list. Scroll the Artists menu until the artist name (such as *Radiohead* or *Bowie, David*) is highlighted, and then press the Select button. The artist's menu of albums appears. For example, the Radiohead menu in our iPod includes the selections All, *OK Computer,* and *The Bends;* the Bowie, David menu includes All, *Heroes, Ziggy Stardust,* and many more).

4. **Select the All item or the name of an album from the artist's menu.**

   The All item is at the top of the artist's menu and should already be highlighted; you can press the Select button to select it or scroll until an album name is highlighted and then press the Select button. ***Note:*** Albums are listed in alphabetical order based on the first word. A leading *A* or *The* is *not* ignored, so the album *The Basement Tapes* is listed *after* the album *Stage Fright* in The Band's menu. A song list appears after you select a choice.

5. **Select the song from the list.**

   The songs in the album list are in album order (the order they appear on the album); in the All list, songs are listed in album order for each album. Scroll up or down the list to highlight the song.

By album

Follow these steps to locate a song by album directly:

1. **Select the Browse item from the iPod main menu.**

Scroll the main menu until Browse is highlighted, and then press the Select button. The Browse menu appears.

2. **Select the Albums item.**

   Scroll the Browse menu until Albums is highlighted, and then press the Select button. The Albums menu appears.

   Select the Composers item to choose a composer, and then select a composer from the Composers menu to get a list of songs for that composer.

3. **Select an album from the Albums menu.**

   The albums are listed in alphabetical order (without any reference to artist, which might make identification difficult). The order is by first word (a leading *A, An,* or *The* is not ignored, so the album *The Natch'l Blues* is listed after *Taj's Blues* in the T section rather than the N section). Scroll the Albums menu until the album name is highlighted and then press the Select button. A song list appears.

4. **Select the song from the list.**

   The songs in the album list are in the order in which they appear on the album. Scroll the list to highlight the song name and press the Select button. The artist name and song name appear.

By playlist

When you update your iPod automatically from your entire iTunes library, all of your playlists in iTunes are copied to the iPod. You can choose to update your iPod with only specified playlists, as we describe in Chapter 11.

Playlists make playing a selection of songs or albums in a specific order easy. The playlist plays from the first song selected to the end of the playlist.

Follow these steps to locate a song by playlist on your iPod:

1. **Select the Playlists item from the iPod main menu.**

   The Playlists item is at the top of the main menu and might already be highlighted. If not, scroll the main menu until Playlists is highlighted, and then press the Select button. The Playlists menu appears.

2. **Select a playlist.**

   The playlists are listed in alphabetical order. Scroll the Playlists menu to highlight the playlist name, and then press the Select button. A list of songs in the playlist appears.

3. **Select the song from the list.**

   The songs in the playlist are in *playlist order* (the order defined for the playlist in iTunes). Scroll up or down the list to highlight the song you want.

Playing a Song

After scrolling the song list until the song name is highlighted, press the Select button to play the selected song, or press the Play/Pause button — either button starts the song playing. When the song finishes, the iPod continues playing the next song in the song list.

While a song is playing, the artist name and song name appear, and you can use the scroll wheel to adjust the volume. See the section, "Adjusting the Volume," later in this chapter.

Press the Play/Pause button when a song is playing to pause the playback. Because the iPod is a hard drive, pause is the same as stop, and you won't find any delay in resuming playback.

Repeating Songs

If you want to drive yourself crazy repeating the same song over and over, the iPod is happy to oblige. More than likely, you'll want to repeat a sequence of songs, which you can easily do.

You can set the iPod to repeat a single song automatically by following these steps:

1. **Locate and play a song.**

2. **As the song plays, press the Menu button repeatedly to return to the main menu, and then select the Settings item.**

   The Settings menu appears.

3. **Scroll the Settings menu until Repeat is highlighted.**

   The Repeat setting displays Off next to it.

4. **Press the Select button once (Off changes to One) to repeat one song.**

   If you press the button more than once, keep pressing until One appears.

You can also press the Previous/Rewind button to repeat a song.

To repeat all the songs in the selected album or playlist, follow these steps:

1. **Locate and play a song in the album or playlist.**

2. **As the song plays, press the Menu button repeatedly to return to the main menu, and then select the Settings item.**

   The Settings menu appears.

3. **Scroll the Settings menu until the Repeat item is highlighted.**

   The Repeat setting displays Off next to it.

4. **Press the Select button twice (Off changes to All) to repeat all the songs in the album or playlist.**

Shuffling the Song Order

You can also shuffle songs within an album, playlist, or the entire library. By *shuffle,* we mean play in random order — like an automated radio station without a disk jockey talking between songs.

Follow these steps to shuffle songs in an album or playlist:

1. **Locate and play a song in the album or playlist.**

2. **As the song plays, press the Menu button repeatedly to return to the main menu, and then select the Settings item.**

   The Settings menu appears.

3. **Scroll the Settings menu until the Shuffle item is highlighted.**

   The Shuffle setting displays Off next to it.

4. **Press the Select button once (Off changes to Songs) to shuffle the songs in the selected album or playlist.**

You can set your iPod to repeat an album or playlist but still shuffle the playing order.

To shuffle all the albums in your iPod while still playing the songs in each album in normal album order, follow these steps:

1. **Press the Menu button repeatedly to return to the main menu, and then select the Settings item.**

   The Settings menu appears.

2. **Scroll the Settings menu until the Shuffle item is highlighted.**

   The Shuffle setting displays Off next to it.

3. **Press the Select button twice (Off changes to Albums) to shuffle the albums without shuffling the songs within each album.**

When the iPod is set to shuffle, it won't repeat a song until it has played through the entire album, playlist, or library.

Creating On-The-Go Playlists

If you don't have playlists from iTunes (or you don't want to hear those playlists), you can create a temporary On-The-Go playlist (which works in iPods using iPod software version 2.0 and newer, including iPod mini, but not in first-generation and second-generation iPods). You can select a list of songs or entire albums to play in a certain order, queuing up the songs or albums on the iPod. This is particularly useful for picking songs to play right before starting to drive a car. (Hel-*lo!* — you shouldn't be messing with your iPod while driving.)

Queued songs appear automatically in a playlist called *On-The-Go* in the Playlists menu. (To use the Playlists menu, see the sections, "Locating Songs" and "Playing a Song," earlier in this chapter.) This playlist stays in your iPod until you clear it (deleting the songs from the playlist) or update your iPod with new music and playlists. You can also save in your iTunes library the On-The-Go playlist that you created on an iPod.

Selecting songs for the playlist

To select songs or entire albums for an On-The-Go playlist, follow these steps:

1. **Locate and highlight a song or album title.**

2. **Press and hold the Select button until the title flashes.**

3. **Repeat Steps 1 and 2 in the order you want the songs or albums played.**

To play the On-The-Go playlist, scroll the main menu until Playlists is high-lighted, and then press the Select button. The Playlists menu appears. Scroll to the On-The-Go item, which you can always find at the very end of the list in the Playlists menu.

You can continue to add songs to the list of queued songs in the On-The-Go playlist at any time. Your iPod saves the On-The-Go playlist until you clear it.

Clearing songs from the playlist

To clear the list of queued songs, follow these steps:

1. **Press the Menu button repeatedly to return to the main menu, and then select the Playlists item.**

   The Playlists menu appears.

2. **Select the On-The-Go item.**

   The song list in the On-The-Go playlist appears.

3. **Scroll to the very end of the song list, and select the Clear Playlist item.**

   The Clear menu appears.

4. **Select the Clear Playlist item.**

   The songs disappear from the playlist. The songs are still in your iPod, of course — only the playlist is cleared.

Saving the playlist in iTunes

You can save the On-The-Go playlist — perhaps the songs you selected (or the order you selected them in) inspired you somehow, and you want to repeat the experience. You can save the On-The-Go playlist so that it shows up in iTunes as another one of your personal playlists, and you can give it a new name if you want. The playlist can then be transferred to the iPod during an update, just like your other playlists.

If you don't clear the list of queued songs in the On-The-Go playlist, the next time you automatically synchronize your iPod to iTunes (as we describe in Chapter 11), the playlist is automatically copied to your iTunes library as *On-The-Go 1* (the next list is *On-The-Go 2,* and so on). You can keep track of your On-The-Go playlists this way. Or if you want to save your On-The-Go playlists with a new name, you can rename them in iTunes, as shown in Figure 15-1.

When updating your iPod manually, as we describe in Chapter 11, you can drag the On-The-Go playlist from your iPod library to the iTunes library.

Figure 15-1: You can rename a saved On-The-Go playlist in iTunes.

Adjusting the Volume

The iPod is quite loud when set to its highest volume — you should turn it down before using headphones. To adjust the volume, follow these steps:

1. **Select and play a song on the iPod.**

2. **Change the volume with the scroll wheel.**

   A volume bar appears in the iPod display to guide you. Scroll with your thumb or finger clockwise to increase the volume, and counterclockwise to decrease the volume.

If you have the Apple iPod Remote — a handy controller that attaches by cable to the iPod headphone connection — you can use the volume button on the remote to adjust the volume. You can also use the remote controller to play or pause a song, fast-forward or rewind, and skip to the next or previous song. You can disable the buttons on the remote by setting the controller's Hold switch (similar to the iPod Hold switch).

Bookmarking Audible Audio Books

Audible books, articles, and spoken-word titles are stored and played just like songs in iTunes and your iPod. (You can download titles from www.audible. com.) When you play an Audible title, you can automatically bookmark your place in the text with the iPod. Bookmarks work only with Audible titles. If you have an audio book or spoken-word file in any other format, such as MP3, bookmarks are not available.

When you use the Pause/Play button to pause an Audible file, the iPod automatically bookmarks that spot. When you press the Play button again, the Audible file starts playing from that spot.

Bookmarks synchronize when you copy an Audible title to your iPod — whichever bookmark is farther along in iPod or iTunes becomes the effective bookmark.

Chapter 16

Getting Wired for Sound

. . . .

In This Chapter

▶ Finding your iPod's connections

▶ Connecting your iPod to home stereos

▶ Connecting portable speakers and headphones

▶ Using the Apple Remote or a wireless remote control

. . . .

Sound studio engineers try to make recordings for typical listening environments, so they have to simulate the sound experience in those environments. Studios typically have home stereo speakers as monitors so that the engineers can hear what the music sounds like on a home stereo. In the 1950s and early 1960s, when AM radio was king, engineers working on potential AM radio hits purposely mixed the sound with low-fidelity monaural speakers so that they could hear what the mix would sound like on radio. Thank goodness those days are over, and cars offer higher-quality FM radio as well as very high quality audio systems.

The point is that the quality of the sound is no better than the weakest link in the audio system. Songs from older times that were mixed to a mono (single) channel for car radios don't sound as good even when played on a home stereo.

The audio CD bridges the gap between home stereos, car stereos, and portable CD players by enabling you to listen to high-quality music anywhere as long as you have a decent pair of headphones. Music production changed considerably over the last few decades as more people listened to higher-quality FM radio; bought massive home stereos; and eventually bought CD players for their cars, and boats and purchased portable players to use while flying and jogging. At each step, popular music was reissued in the new medium, such as audio CD, and remixed in the process for the new sound systems.

The iPod represents a major leap forward in bridging the gap between home stereos, car stereos, and portable players. Picking up where CDs left off, the iPod offers nearly as high quality sound as an audio CD in a convenient device that can hold several weeks' worth of music. What's more, you can tweak the sound not just for home stereos, but for all listening environments.

Making Connections

The sleek iPod models enable you to connect headphones to your iPod, or connect your iPod to your home stereo, or connect your iPod to your Mac. The connections, as shown in Figure 16-1 (third-generation models) and Figure 16-2 (first- and second-generation models), are as follows:

- **FireWire:** Current (third-generation) models and iPod mini have a dock connection on the bottom for inserting into the dock or using with the dock connector cable, which has a dock connector on one end and a FireWire connector (or optional USB connector, or both FireWire and USB connectors with a split cable) on the other. First-generation and second-generation iPods have a six-pin FireWire connection on the top that works with any standard six-pin FireWire cable.

- **Headphone/line out (with remote control socket):** The combination headphone and control socket connection on the top of the iPod allows you to plug in the Apple iPod Remote, which in turn offers a headphone/line-out connection. (The Apple iPod Remote comes standard with the iPod). The remote offers playback and volume control buttons. You can also connect headphones, or a 3.5mm stereo mini-plug cable, to the headphone/line-out connection.

- **Dock connections:** For third-generation iPod models, the dock offers two connections: one for the special cable to connect to a FireWire (or USB) connection, and a headphone/line-out connection for a stereo mini-plug cable (or headphones).

You can connect the FireWire end to the computer (for synchronizing with iTunes and playing the iPod through iTunes, as we describe in Chapter 18) or to the power adapter to charge the iPod battery. The FireWire connection to the computer provides power to the iPod as long as the computer's FireWire hardware offers power to the device and the computer isn't in sleep mode.

Headphone/line out FireWire/USB Dock connector

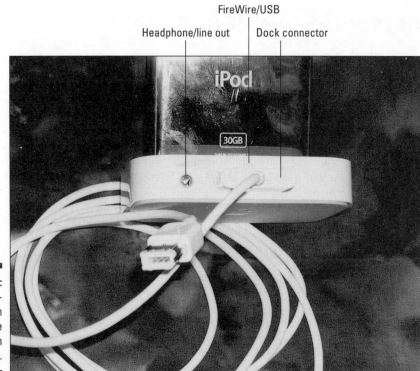

Figure 16-1:
A third-
generation
model of the
iPod with
its dock.

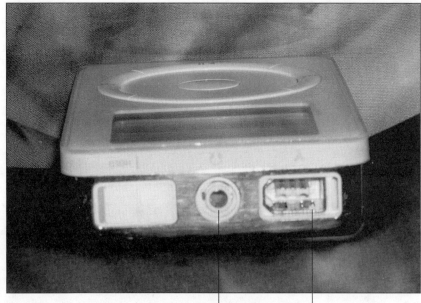

Figure 16-2:
A second-
generation
model of the
iPod with
connections
on top.

Headphone/line out FireWire

Connecting to a Home Stereo

Home stereo systems come in many shapes and sizes, from an audiophile's monster component racks to a kid's itty-bitty boom box. We're not talking about alarm-clock radios, but stereos with speakers that allow you to add another input device, such as a portable CD player.

Component-style stereo systems typically include a receiver (which offers a preamp/amplifier with a volume control, and a tuner to receive FM radio). Some separate these functions into separate components — such as a preamp, an amplifier, and a tuner. To find a place to connect your iPod or computer to a home stereo, look for RCA-type connections that are marked AUX IN (for auxiliary input), CD IN (for connecting a CD player), or TAPE IN (for tape deck input). All-in-one stereos and boom boxes that are all one piece typically don't have connections for audio input, although there are exceptions — look at the back and sides of the unit for any RCA-type connections.

You can connect a CD or tape player to most stereos with RCA-type cables — one (typically red or black) for the right channel, and one (typically white if the other is black, or white or black if the other is red) for the left channel. All you need is a cable with a stereo mini-plug on one end and RCA-type connectors on the other, as shown in Figure 16-3. Stereo mini-plugs have two black bands on the plug, but a mono mini-plug has only one black band.

The Monster high-performance iCable for iPod (formerly called the Monster Cable) available in the Apple Store, looks cool and offers high-quality sound for the discerning listener with excellent stereo equipment.

Connect the stereo mini-plug to the iPod dock headphone/line-out connection (refer to Figure 16-1), or to the headphone/line-out connection on the top of the iPod. Connect the left and right connectors to the stereo system's audio input — whatever connections are available, such as AUX IN (for auxiliary input); TAPE IN (for tape deck input); or CD IN (for CD player input).

Don't use the PHONO IN connection (for phonograph input) on most stereos. These connections are for phonographs (turntables) and aren't properly matched for other kinds of input devices. If you do this, you might get a loud buzzing sound that could damage your speakers.

Figure 16-3:
RCA-type connectors (left) and a stereo mini-plug (right).

You can control the volume from the iPod by using the scroll wheel, which we describe in Chapter 15. This controls the volume of the signal from the iPod. Stereo systems typically have their own volume control to raise or lower the volume of the amplified speakers. For optimal sound quality when using a home stereo, set the iPod volume at less than half the maximum output and adjust your listening volume by using your stereo controls. By doing this, you prevent over-amplification, which can cause distortion and reduce audio quality.

Connecting Headphones and Portable Speakers

Apple designed the iPod to provide excellent sound through headphones, and with the headphone/line-out connection, the iPod can also play music through portable speaker systems. The speaker systems must be self-powered or able to work with very little power (like headphones) and allow audio to be input through a 3.5mm mini-plug stereo connection.

The iPod includes a small amplifier powerful enough to deliver audio through the headphone/line-out connection. It has a frequency response of 20 Hz (hertz) to 20,000 Hz, which provides distortion-free music at the lowest or highest pitches. Hertz has nothing to do with rental cars — a hertz is a unit of frequency equal to one cycle per second. At pitches that produce frequencies of 20 cycles per second, or 20,000 cycles per second, the iPod responds with distortion-free sound.

Portable speaker systems typically include built-in amplifiers and a volume control, and offer a stereo mini-plug that you can attach directly to the iPod headphone/line-out connection or to the dock headphone/line-out connection. To place the external speakers farther away from the iPod, use a stereo mini-plug extension cable — available at most consumer electronics stores — which has a stereo mini-plug on one end and a stereo mini-socket on the other.

Portable speaker systems typically have volume controls to raise or lower the volume. Set your iPod volume to half and then raise or lower the volume of your speaker system.

When you travel, take an extra pair of headphones (or earbuds) and a splitter cable, such as the one in Figure 16-4, available in any consumer electronics store. The Monster iSplitter is available in the Apple Store. You can plug both headphones into the iPod and share the music with someone on the road.

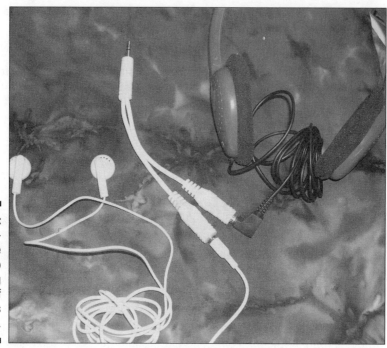

Figure 16-4:
This head-phone cable splits into two, allowing two sets of headphones to connect.

Accessories for the iHome

No home should be without an iPod on a pedestal, raising it above the desk clutter so that you can see its display and use its controls. Although you can play the music in your iTunes library from your computer, you might want to use the iPod in another room that has a stereo system, or you might want to play the iPod, freeing the computer to do other things.

Most of the accessories for the iPod (and hundreds of products are available) are designed for travel, and we describe the best in Chapter 17. However, companies also provide docks and stands for older iPods that don't have docks, as well as alternatives to the limited Apple Remote that connects by cable to the iPod.

The $30 iPodDock from Bookendz (www.bookendzdocks.com) supports the older iPod models in an upside down position on a desk or table and offers connection ports (audio and FireWire) for instant docking. The iPodCradle, also from Bookendz, supports the iPod in an upright position and is compatible with most cases on the market, so you can use your iPod in the cradle with or without the case. Bookendz also offers an iPodDock for third-generation iPods as an alternative to the standard Apple dock.

The Apple Remote, which is supplied with some models and optional with others, provides the usual CD player controls: Play/Pause, Next Track, Previous Track, and a volume button. It also has a Hold switch, just like the iPod, to render the controls useless and prevent accidental use. You connect the Apple Remote (shown in Figure 16-5) to the headphone/line out connection at the top of the iPod (not the dock). This connection has an outer ring for connecting remote control devices. The Apple Remote is tethered to the iPod by cable, so it isn't as useful in the home as it would be in a car — it has a clip for clipping the remote control to your shirt.

When your iPod is tethered to a dock and connected to your home stereo, you don't have to be within reach to control it remotely — you can control your iPod with a wireless remote control. For example, Ten Technology (www.tentechnology.com) offers the stylish $49.95 naviPod that provides wireless remote control of your iPod with standard Play/Pause, Next Track, Previous Track, and volume controls. The naviPod uses infrared wireless technology with a receiver unit that plugs directly into the top of the iPod, just like the Apple Remote (which we is describe in Chapter 17). The receiver has FireWire and headphone connections on the bottom, which allow you to connect your headphones or hook up your iPod to your computer without removing the naviPod receiver.

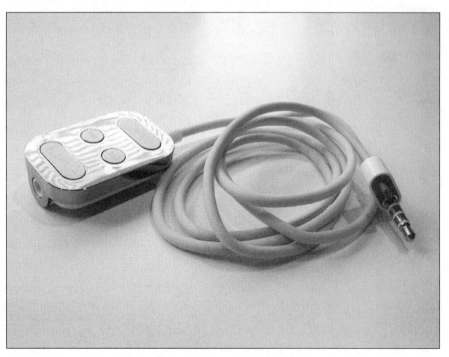

Figure 16-5:
The Apple Remote for controlling your iPod.

Engineered Audio (www.engineeredaudio.com) offers the RemoteRemote for $34.95. Unlike infrared wireless controls, RemoteRemote is an RF (radio frequency) wireless remote control that works around corners and through walls. RemoteRemote offers standard Play/Pause, Next Track, Previous Track, and volume controls, and it operates in a range of up to 100 feet.

Chapter 17

Listening While on the Move

In This Chapter

▶ Using adapters and mounts to play your iPod in cars

▶ Using wireless adapters to play your iPod on FM radios

▶ Protecting your iPod with carrying cases

▶ Using power accessories on the road

You can truly go anywhere with an iPod. If you can't plug it into a power source while it's playing, you can use the battery for up to eight hours of playing time before having to recharge. You can find all the accessories that you need to travel with an iPod in the Apple Store at www.apple.com.

Put on "Eight Miles High" by the Byrds while cruising in a plane at 40,000 feet. Ride the rails listening to "All Aboard" by Muddy Waters, followed by "Peavine" by John Lee Hooker. Or cruise on the Autobahn in Germany with Kraftwerk. Whatever. You have an entire music library with you wherever you go.

The iPod provides high-quality music no matter what the environment — even in an earthquake. With skip protection, you don't have to worry about turbulence, potholes, or strenuous exercise causing the music to skip. In addition to the hard drive, the 40GB iPod has a 32MB memory cache. The cache is made up of solid-state memory, with no mechanical or moving parts, so movement doesn't affect playback. Skip protection works by preloading up to 20 minutes of music to the cache at a time. The iPod plays music from the memory cache rather than the hard drive.

Playing Car Tunes

We always wanted a car that we could fill up with music just as easily as filling it up with gasoline, without having to carry dozens of cassettes or CDs. With an iPod, an auto-charger to save on battery power, and a way to connect the iPod to your car's stereo system, you're ready to pump music. (Start your engine and queue up "Getting in Tune" and then "Going Mobile" by The Who.) Go one step further and get a ncw BMW that offers an iPod installed and integrated into the car's stereo system so that you can control it from your steering wheel.

Getting in tune . . . with car adapters

While some new vehicles (particularly SUVs) offer 110-volt power outlets you can use with your Apple-supplied battery charger, most cars offer only a lighter/power socket that requires a power adapter to use with your iPod. Be careful to pick the right type of power adapter (shown in Figure 17-1) for your car's lighter/power socket. The automobile power adapters for older iPods provide a FireWire connector, but the adapters for the new dockable iPods use a dock connector cable.

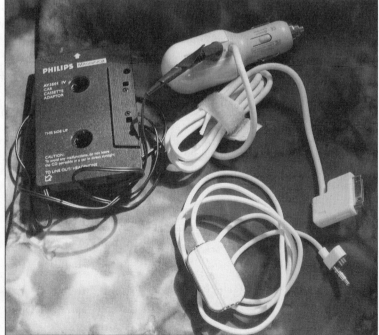

Figure 17-1:
Our car accessories: cassette-player adapter (left); power adapter (upper right); and Apple Remote (lower right).

Belkin (www.belkin.com) offers the Auto Kit for $49.95, and it includes a car power adapter with a convenient socket for a stereo mini-plug cable (which can connect directly to a car stereo if the stereo has a mini-socket for audio input). The adapter includes a volume-adjustable amplifier to boost the sound coming from the iPod before it goes into the cassette adapter or car stereo.

Unfortunately, not many car stereos offer a mini-socket for audio input, and as of this writing, the few accessories that integrate directly with car stereos require custom car installations. So far, there are no standard dock connectors for car stereos, which would be totally cool because the iPod is clearly designed for plugging into a "car dock" that offers both power and a connection to the car's stereo system.

You can, however, order a professional installation with the Dension ICE-Link ($149 to $239, depending on your car), which adds line-level audio output and recharging capability to almost any vehicle. It uses the CD-changer connections in car CD players to directly connect your iPod into the car's audio system. Dension (www.dension.com) assumes that the buyer is a professional installer, and although it's possible to install it yourself (especially if you use a CD changer in your trunk), most installations require taking apart the dashboard and installing the ICE-Link behind your CD stereo. ICE-Link can be combined with almost any mounting solution for the iPod itself (see the following section, "Going mobile . . . with car mounts").

Until you can get a car with a mini-socket for stereo audio input (also called a *stereo-in connection*) or a FireWire connection — or get one installed — you can use a cassette-player adapter to connect with your car stereo or a wireless device that we describe later in this chapter, in the section "Connecting by Wireless Radio." These solutions provide lower sound quality than custom installations or stereo-in connections but are inexpensive and work with most cars.

Many car stereos have a cassette player, and you can buy a cassette-player adapter from most consumer electronics stores or from the Apple Store (such as the Sony CPA-9C Car Cassette Adapter). The cassette-player adapter, shown previously in Figure 17-1, looks like a tape cassette with a mini-plug cable (which sticks out through the slot when you're using the adapter).

You can connect the mini-plug cable directly to the iPod, to the auto-charger if a mini-socket is offered, or to the Apple Remote that in turn is connected to the iPod. Then insert the adapter into the cassette player, being careful not to get the cable tangled up inside the player.

One inherent problem with this approach is that the cable that dangles from your cassette player looks unsightly. You also might have some trouble ejecting the adapter if the cable gets wedged in the door, but overall, this method is the best for most cars because it provides the best sound quality.

The Apple Remote, which is supplied with some models and optional with others, is more useful in a car than almost anywhere else — it provides the usual CD player controls: Play/Pause, Next Track, Previous Track, and a volume button (see Chapter 16), so you can pause a song, skip to the next or previous song, or adjust the volume without having to reach over to your iPod while driving. You can attach the Apple Remote to your shirt or the edge of something thin, such as an air-conditioner vent in your dashboard.

Going mobile . . . with car mounts

Unless you have one of the new BMW models that are iPod-ready, or opt for a custom installation of some kind involving your car stereo and car power (such as using a custom cable interface for a CD changer, which can be installed into your dashboard by a skilled car audio specialist), you have at best a clumsy solution that uses one cable (power) from a power adapter to the iPod, and another cable (audio) to your car stereo cassette adapter, audio input, or wireless adapter. Attached to these wires, your iPod needs a secure place to sit while your car moves — you don't want it bouncing around on the passenger seat.

You can fit your iPod securely in position in a car without getting a custom installation. The TuneDok ($29.95) from Belkin (www.belkin.com) holds your iPod securely and fits into your car's cup-holder (see Figure 17-2). The TuneDok's ratcheting neck and height-adjustment feature lets you reposition the iPod to your liking. The cable-management clip eliminates loose and tangled cables, and the large and small rubber base and cup fits most cup holders.

MARWARE (www.marware.com) offers an inexpensive solution for both car use and personal use. The $5.95 Car Holder, available when you select a MARWARE SportSuit case, attaches to the dashboard of your car, as shown in Figure 17-3, and lets you attach an iPod that's wearing one of the MARWARE SportSuit covering cases (see "Dressing Up Your iPod for Travel" in this chapter). The clip on the back attaches to the Car Holder.

ProClip (www.proclipusa.com) offers mounting brackets for clip-on devices. The brackets attach to the dashboard and can be installed in seconds. After you install the bracket, you can use different custom holders for the iPod models or for cell phones and other portable devices.

Figure 17-2:
The TuneDok
mount for a
car cup
holder.

Figure 17-3:
Mounting
the MAR-
WARE iPod
holder that
works with
the SportSuit
carrying
case.

Connecting by Wireless Radio

A wireless music adapter lets you play music from your iPod on an FM radio, with no connection or cable, although the sound quality might suffer a bit due to interference. We always take a wireless adapter with us whenever we rent a car — even if a rental car has no cassette deck (ruling out the use of our cassette adapter), the car probably has an FM radio.

You can use a wireless adapter in a car, on a boat, on the beach with a portable radio, or even in your home with a stereo system and tuner. We even use it in hotel rooms with a clock radio.

To use a wireless adapter, follow these steps:

1. **Set the wireless adapter to an FM radio frequency.**

   The adapter offers you a choice of several frequencies — typically 88.1, 88.3, 88.5, and 88.7 MHz. You choose the frequency and set the adapter according to its instructions.

2. **Connect the wireless adapter to the iPod headphone/line-out connector or to the line-out connector on the iPod dock.**

   The wireless adapter (see Figure 17-4) acts like a miniature radio station, broadcasting to a nearby FM radio. (Sorry, you can't go much farther than a few feet, so no one else can hear your Wolfman Jack impersonation.)

3. **Tune to the appropriate frequency on the FM dial.**

   Tune any nearby radio to the same FM frequency that you chose in Step 1.

Figure 17-4:
Two wireless adapters for playing your iPod with any FM radio.

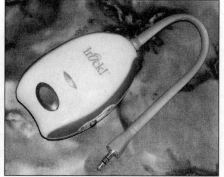
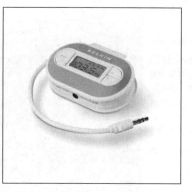

You need to set the adapter close enough to the radio's antenna to work, making it impractical for home stereos — you can get better quality sound by connecting to a home stereo with a cable.

Don't be surprised if the wireless adapter doesn't work as well in cities — other radio stations might cause too much interference.

Here are just a few wireless adapters that we recommend:

✔ For $29.99, the **irock 400FM Wireless Music Adapter** (www.myirock.com) from First International Digital requires standard replaceable batteries and offers a car power adapter.

✔ The **TuneCast II Mobile FM Transmitter** ($49.99) from Belkin (www. belkin.com) is particularly convenient in a car because it includes a 14-inch cable that delivers power when used with the Belkin Mobile Power Cord for iPod, so that you can preserve your batteries for times when you're away from an alternate source. It offers four programmable memory slots for saving the clearest radio frequency wherever you go.

✔ The **TransPod FM** ($99) from Digital Lifestyle Outfitters, available from Everything iPod (www.everythingipod.com), is an excellent all-in-one wireless FM transmitter, mounting system, and power adapter for using your iPod in a car, and it costs less than purchasing all three items separately.

Dressing Up Your iPod for Travel

The simple protective carrying case supplied with some iPod models is just not as stylin' as the myriad accessories that you can get for dressing up your iPod for travel. You can find different types of protective gear, from leather jackets to aluminum cases, in many different styles and colors. Some are designed primarily for protecting your iPod from harm; others are designed to provide some measure of protection while also providing access to controls.

On the extreme end of the spectrum are hardened cases that are ready for battlefields in deserts or jungles — the Humvees of iPod protective gear. The iPod Armor ($49.95) by Matias Corporation (www.ipodarmor.com) is a sturdy case that fits all models of iPod and offers possibly the best protection against physical trauma on the market. Your iPod rests within a hard, resilient metal exoskeleton that can withstand the abuse of bouncing down a flight of metal stairs without letting your iPod pop out. Of course, the very same feature that prevents your iPod from popping out also makes the iPod Armor difficult to open to get access to it — this is not a case to use while listening to music.

Business travelers can combine personal items into one carrying case. The iPod Leather Organizer from Belkin is made from fine-grain leather that even Ricardo Montalban would rave about. The case holds personal essentials, like business and credit cards, in four convenient slots. A handy mesh pocket keeps earphones easily accessible, and a billfold holds money and receipts.

On the sporty side, MARWARE (www.marware.com) offers the SportSuit Convertible case ($39.95) with a patented belt clip system offering interchangeable clip options for use with the MARWARE Car Holder or with an armband or belt for jogging or working out. The neoprene case has vulcanized rubber grips on each side and bottom for a no-slip grip and plastic inserts for impact protection, offering full access to all iPod controls and connections while the iPod is in the case. There's even space inside the lid to store earbud headphones.

If you like to carry a backpack with everything in it, consider the very first backpack ever designed to control an iPod within it: The Amp Pack ($199.95) from Burton (www.burton.com/Burton/gear/products.asp?productID=731) lets you switch songs on your iPod by pressing a button on the shoulder strap. Constructed from ballistic nylon, the Amp Pack offers a secure iPod storage pocket, a headphone port located on a shoulder strap, an easy-access side entry laptop compartment, and padded ergonomic shoulder straps with a soft, flexible control pad built into a strap. Perfect for listening to Lou Reed while hanging onto a pole in a subway car, or the Hollies while navigating your way to the back of the bus.

Using Power Accessories

If you want to charge your iPod battery when you travel abroad, you can't count on finding the same voltage as in your home country. However, you still need to plug your Apple power adapter into something to recharge your iPod. Fortunately, power adapters are available in most airports, but the worldly traveler might want to consider saving time and money by getting a travel kit of power accessories.

We found several varieties of power kits for world travel in our local international airport. Most kits include a set of AC plugs with prongs that fit different electrical outlets around the world. You can connect your iPod power adapter to these adapters. The AC plugs typically support outlets in North America, Japan, China, the United Kingdom, Continental Europe, Korea, Australia, and Hong Kong.

One way to mitigate the battery blues is to get an accessory that lets you use replaceable alkaline batteries — the kind that you can find in any convenience store. The Backup Battery Pack ($59.95) from Belkin (www.belkin.com) lets you power your iPod with four standard AA alkaline replaceable batteries — even when your internal iPod battery is drained. Discreet suction cups secure the unit to the back of your iPod without marring your iPod finish. A charge-level indicator tells you when your batteries are running low.

Another way to supply power to your iPod is to use your FireWire-equipped laptop to supply the power (make sure that you use FireWire hardware that provides power — see Chapter 1), and then use a power adapter with your laptop. You can use, for example, the Kensington Universal Car/Air Adapter from Apple to plug a Mac PowerBook or iBook into any car cigarette lighter or EmPower-equipped airline seat (the EmPower in-seat power system can provide either 110-volt AC or 15-volt DC power in an aircraft seat for passenger use). Then connect the iPod to the laptop with a FireWire cable.

If you fly often, the APC Travel Power ($79), available from the Apple Store, might be just the ticket. It includes an adapter that plugs into an airline seat power connection, as well as a car power adapter. The unit offers 75 watts of continuous power with built-in circuit protection. The flight attendant will still tell you to turn off your iPod before takeoff and landing, but you won't waste precious battery power during the flight.

Chapter 18

Spinning Tunes Like a DJ

. . . .

In This Chapter

▶ Changing the system sound volume for your computer

▶ Using Party Shuffle in iTunes to shuffle song playback

▶ Connecting your iPod to another computer

▶ Playing songs on your iPod through iTunes

▶ Playing songs on your stereo through a wireless AirTunes connection

▶ Playing songs on your iPod through MusicMatch Jukebox

. . . .

*I*f you like to entertain folks by spinning tunes at home or at parties, iTunes could easily become your DJ console. You could set up a laptop that connects to a home stereo and connect the iPods that your friends bring over to augment your iTunes library. Imagine how much music you could choose from by connecting several 40GB iPods to an iTunes library that already holds thousands of songs!

Your computer is a mean multimedia machine with the ability to mix sounds from different sources and play them through built-in speakers, external speakers, or headphones. Macs and PCs can play audio CDs, DVDs, and digital video files as well as iTunes music.

This chapter describes how you can play your iPod music on your computer, through your computer's speakers. It also shows how you can use a wireless connection with AirPort Express and AirTunes to transmit music to your home stereo or speakers without any wires. You could stroll through the party with your laptop, choosing songs, taking requests, and beaming the music directly to your stereo system.

Changing the Computer's Output Volume

You can control the volume and other characteristics of the sound coming out of your computer's speakers, headphones, or external speakers. Even if you connect your computer to a stereo amplifier with its own volume and equalizer controls, it's best to get the volume right at the source — your computer and iTunes — and then adjust the output volume as you please on your stereo or external speaker unit.

Volume is controlled by the computer system's audio controls. iTunes also controls the volume, but that control is within the range of the computer's volume setting. For example, if you set your computer's volume to half and set iTunes volume to full, you get half volume because the computer is limiting the volume to half. If you set your computer volume at half and also reduce the iTunes volume to half, you actually get *one-quarter* volume — half the computer' setting. The sound can be further adjusted after it leaves your computer by using the stereo system or external speakers with controls.

The appropriate volume depends entirely on your preferences for hearing music, but in general, the maximum level of output from your computer is preferable when connecting to a stereo system or speakers with volume controls. After setting your computer to the maximum volume, adjust the iTunes volume or your stereo or speaker volume (or both) to get the best sound. When using the computer's speakers or headphones, the computer's volume and the iTunes volume are the only volume controls that you have, so after adjusting the volume on your computer to the maximum level (or lower if you prefer), adjust the iTunes volume.

Adjusting the sound on a Mac

The Mac was built for sound from the very start. Making and playing music has been part of the Mac culture since day one, when Steve Jobs introduced the original Mac to an audience with music coming from its small speaker. (It played simple tones, but it was the first personal computer with built-in sound.)

Today's Mac comes with built-in or external speakers and at least one headphone/line-out connection that you can use to connect external speakers or a stereo system. Mac OS X lets you configure output speakers and control levels for stereo speakers and multichannel audio devices.

If you use external speakers, headphones, or a stereo system, make sure that you connect these devices properly before adjusting the volume. To adjust the volume on your Mac, follow these steps:

1. **Choose System Preferences from the Apple menu or the Dock, and then click the Sound icon.**

   You can have iTunes open and playing music while you do this.

2. **In the Sound preferences window, click Output.**

   If you have headphones attached, a Headphones option appears in the list of sound output devices; if not, an External Speakers option appears, as shown in Figure 18-1. If you have external speakers *and* a pair of headphones attached to your Mac, the external speakers disappear from the Sound preferences, but they're still enabled.

3. **Adjust the volume by dragging the Output Volume slider.**

   You can drag the slider to adjust the volume as you listen to music. You also have a Mute button in this window — click the Mute check box to silence your Mac. You can also adjust the stereo balance by dragging the Balance slider to put more music in the left or right channels.

4. **Close the Preferences window by choosing System Preferences⇨Quit System Preferences or by clicking the red button in the upper-left corner of the window.**

   The Sound preferences window isn't like a dialog — when you change settings, you can hear the effect immediately without having to click an OK button. (There isn't an OK button, anyway.)

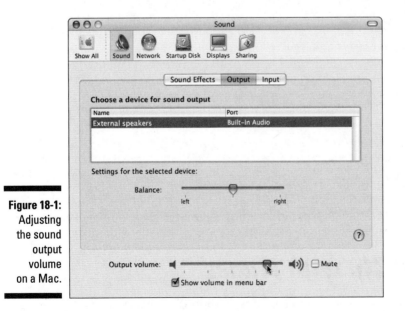

Figure 18-1:
Adjusting
the sound
output
volume
on a Mac.

Adjusting the sound in Windows

Windows XP and Windows 2000 let you configure output speakers and control levels for stereo speakers and multichannel audio devices.

Use the Sounds and Audio Devices Properties dialog to change the volume. To open this window, choose Start➪Control Panel, and click the Sounds and Audio Devices icon. Then click the Volume tab.

As shown in Figure 18-2, the Sounds and Audio Devices Properties dialog offers the Device volume slider — drag this slider to set the volume. You can also silence your PC by selecting the Mute check box.

If you select the Place Volume Icon in the Taskbar option, and your sound card supports changing the volume with software, a speaker icon appears in the notification area of Windows. You can then change the volume quickly without having to open the Sounds and Audio Devices Properties dialog — simply click the speaker icon and drag the slider that pops up. For more information about adjusting sound on a PC, see *PCs For Dummies,* 9th Edition by Dan Gookin (Wiley).

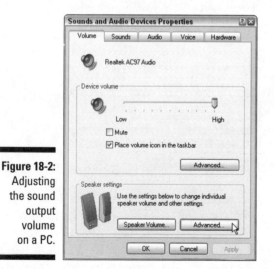

Figure 18-2:
Adjusting
the sound
output
volume
on a PC.

Mixing It Up with iTunes

You can choose songs to play manually, but iTunes also provides several automated features so that you can spend less time prepping your music selection and more time enjoying it.

Queuing up tunes with Party Shuffle

Playlists are great for organizing music in the order that you want to play it, but you can have iTunes serve up songs at random by using Party Shuffle. It's not a dance step or pub game — *Party Shuffle* is a dynamic playlist that automatically generates a semi-random selection in a list that you can modify on the fly. With Party Shuffle at work, you might even find songs in your library you forgot about or rarely play — Party Shuffle always throws a few rarely played songs into the mix.

To use Party Shuffle, follow these steps:

1. **Click Party Shuffle in the Source pane.**

   The Song List pane and Browse pane are replaced with the Party Shuffle track list and settings at the bottom, as shown in Figure 18-3.

Figure 18-3:
Adjusting
the settings
for Party
Shuffle.

2. **Select a source from the Source pop-up menu below the Party Shuffle track list.**

   You can select the entire library or any playlist (including smart playlists) as the source for music in the Party Shuffle. If you select a playlist, Party Shuffle limits its choices to songs from that playlist.

3. **Set the following options:**

   • *Recently played songs:* Choose how many songs should remain in the list after they are played. You can drag already-played songs (even though they are grayed out after playing) to a spot later in the list to play them again.

- *Upcoming songs:* Choose how many songs should be listed as upcoming (not yet played). By displaying upcoming songs first, you can decide whether to rearrange the list or delete songs before they are played.

- *Play higher rated songs more often:* Turn on this option to have iTunes add more high-rated songs to the random list. Using this option, you weight the randomness in favor of higher-rated songs. See Chapter 9 to learn how to add ratings to songs.

4. **(Optional) If you don't like the order of songs, you can rearrange it; any songs you don't like you can eliminate.**

   You can rearrange the order of songs in the Party Shuffle by dragging songs to different positions in the Party Shuffle list. Eliminate songs by selecting them in the Party Shuffle list and pressing Delete (or choosing Edit➪Clear).

5. **Play the Party Shuffle by selecting the first song and clicking the Play button or pressing the Space bar.**

   You can start playing from the first song or from any song on the list. (When you pick a song in the middle to start playing, the songs before it are grayed out to show that they won't play.)

6. **Add, delete, or rearrange songs even while the Party Shuffle plays.**

   While the Party Shuffle list plays, you can add songs in one of two ways:

   - Open the Party Shuffle in a separate window by double-clicking the Party Shuffle item in the Source pane. You can then drag songs from the main iTunes window — either from the Library or from a playlist — directly into position in the Party Shuffle track list.

   - Without opening Party Shuffle in a separate window, you can switch to the library or a playlist, and drag the song to the Party Shuffle item in the Source pane, just like dragging a song to a playlist. When you add a song to the Party Shuffle, it shows up at the end of the track list. You can then drag it to a new position.

You can add one or more albums to the Party Shuffle track list by dragging the albums; the songs play in album order. You can also add all the songs by an artist by dragging the artist name. Party Shuffle acts just like a playlist, except dynamically — you add, delete, and change the order of songs on the fly.

Cool DJs mix the Party Shuffle window with other open playlist windows — just double-click the playlist item in the Source pane to open it in a separate window. You can then drag songs from different playlist windows to the Party Shuffle window while the Party Shuffle plays, adding songs in whatever order you want in real time.

Cross-fading song playback

You can often hear a song on the radio fade out as another song immediately fades in right over the first song's ending. This is a *cross-fade*, and with iTunes, you can smoothly transition from the ending of a song to the beginning of the next one. Ordinarily, iTunes is set to have a short cross-fade of one second — the amount of time between the end of the fade in the first song and the start of the fade in the second song.

What's totally cool about this is that you can cross-fade between two songs in iTunes even if they're from different sources — the songs could be in your library, in a shared library, on CD or DVD, or even on one (or more!) iPods connected to your computer and playing through iTunes (as we describe in "Playing an iPod through iTunes," later in this chapter). You could play DJ at a party with a massive music library on a laptop and still augment that library with one or more iPods and any number of CDs, and the songs cross-fade to the next just like on the radio or at a dance party with a professional DJ.

You can change the amount of the cross-fade by choosing iTunes➪Preferences and then clicking the Audio button. The Audio dialog appears, as shown in Figure 18-4.

In the Audio dialog, you select the Crossfade Playback option, and then increase or decrease the amount of the cross-fade by dragging the slider. Each notch in the slider is one second. The maximum amount of cross-fade is 12 seconds. With a longer cross-fade you get a longer overlap from one song to the next — the second song starts before the first one ends. To turn off the cross-fade, deselect the check box.

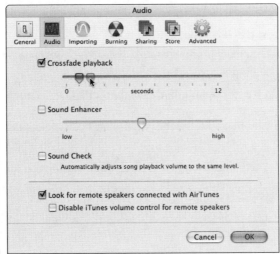

Figure 18-4:
Setting the cross-fade between songs to two seconds.

Playing an iPod through iTunes

You can't copy the songs from your iPod into your iTunes library using iTunes, but you can use iTunes on your computer to play the songs directly from the iPod. You can even bring your friend's iPod with you to a party, along with your laptop running iTunes, and include your friend's iPod songs in your Party Shuffle — include *anyone's* iPod songs in your Party Shuffle. Not only can you do that, but as you play songs from different iPods or from your library, you can cross-fade them, as we describe previously in "Cross-fading song playback," in this chapter.

When you set your iPod to manually update and connect the iPod to your computer, the iPod name appears in the iTunes Source pane, and when you select it, the iPod's songs appear in the iTunes window. You can connect someone else's iPod this way, as we describe in the following section, "Connecting your iPod to another computer."

To play music on your iPod in iTunes, follow these steps:

1. **Connect the iPod to your computer, holding down ⌘-Option on a Mac, or Ctrl-Alt on a PC, to prevent automatic updating.**

2. **Set the iPod to update manually.**

   To set the iPod to update manually, see Chapter 11. (The iPod updates automatically by default, but you can change that.)

3. **Select the iPod name in the iTunes Source pane.**

   After selecting the iPod in the iTunes Source pane, the list of songs on the iPod appears, as shown in Figure 18-5. You can scroll or browse the iPod's library just like the main iTunes library (as we describe in Chapter 8). Click the Browse button to browse the iPod's contents.

4. **(Optional) View the iPod playlists.**

   After selecting the iPod in the iTunes Source pane, you can click the triangle next to its name to view the iPod's playlists.

5. **Click a song in the iPod song list, and then click the iTunes Play button.**

When an iPod song is playing in iTunes, it's just like playing a song from the iTunes library or a track on a CD. The Status pane above the list of songs tells you the name of the artist and song (if known) and the elapsed time.

View playlists

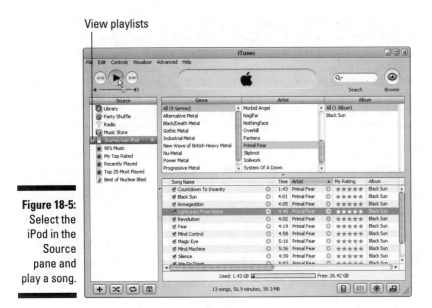

Figure 18-5:
Select the
iPod in the
Source
pane and
play a song.

Connecting your iPod to another computer

The previous section shows you how to connect your iPod to your computer. What if you want to connect your iPod to a computer other than your own? Or what if a friend arrives with an iPod filled with songs that you'd like to hear, and you want to hear them on your stereo system that's already connected to your computer?

You can connect your iPod to another computer, or connect someone else's iPod to your computer. Either way, iTunes starts up and recognizes that the iPod is not matched to the iTunes library (because it is matched to some other computer's iTunes library). iTunes displays a message asking whether you want to change the link to this iTunes music library and replace all existing songs and playlists. This is important: *click No.*

Unless you want to change the contents of your iPod to reflect this computer's music library, don't click Yes. *If you click the Yes button, iTunes erases the music library of your iPod* and then updates your iPod with the library on this computer. If you're using a public computer with no music in its iTunes library, you end up with an empty iPod. If you're using a friend's computer, your friend's library copies to your iPod, erasing whatever was on your iPod. So don't click Yes unless you really want to completely change the music on your iPod. You've been warned.

After clicking No, the iPod appears in the iTunes Source pane. Set the iPod to update manually (see Chapter 11) to play songs from your iPod.

You can use a Windows-formatted iPod with a Mac, but you can't use a Mac-formatted iPod with Windows. When you install an iPod with Windows, the iPod is formatted for Windows; but you are still in luck with a Mac because Macs can read Windows drives. If you want to be a laptop DJ and use other people's iPods in the mix, use a Mac laptop because it can access both types of iPods.

If you connected a Mac-formatted iPod to a Windows computer, you get a warning message about reformatting it. *Don't do it!* Click Cancel — otherwise, you reformat the iPod and clear all music from it. Then click the Safely Remove Hardware icon on the Windows taskbar to open the Safely Remove Hardware window. Select the iPod and click Stop. Wait for the list of devices in the Safely Remove Hardware window to be cleared. Then wait for your iPod to display a message that it's okay to disconnect (or until the iPod main menu appears). You can then disconnect the iPod.

Using AirTunes for wireless stereo playback

You want to play the music in your iTunes library (or on your iPod connected to your computer), but your stereo system is in another room, and you don't want wires going from one room to the other. What you need is an AirPort in your home — specifically, AirPort Express with AirTunes, which lets you play your iTunes music through your stereo or powered speakers in virtually any room of your house, without wires as it's within range of the AirPort Express Base Station.

AirPort is Apple's technology that provides Wi-Fi wireless networking for any AirPort-equipped Mac or PC that uses a Wi-Fi-certified IEEE 802.11b or 802.11g wireless card or offers built-in Wi-Fi. For more about AirPort, see *Mac OS X Panther All-in-One Desk Reference For Dummies* by Mark L. Chambers (Wiley).

AirPort Express uses the fast 802.11g wireless standard to deliver data rates up to 54 Mbps. It also works with the 802.11b wireless protocol, so that Macs and PCs with older Wi-Fi configurations can connect wirelessly.

To use a stereo system or powered speakers with AirTunes, connect the system or speakers to the audio port on the AirPort Express Base Station. iTunes automatically detects the connection. When you open iTunes on your

AirPort-equipped Mac or Wi-Fi-compliant PC, a pop-up menu appears in the lower-right corner of the iTunes window, showing your remote speakers. You can select the remote speakers or stereo system to play music.

If you already have a wireless network in place, you can add AirPort Express and AirTunes without changing anything. Connect the AirPort Express Base Station to the stereo system or powered speakers, and plug the Base Station into an electrical outlet. The AirPort Express Base Station wirelessly links to your existing wireless network without requiring any change to the network.

You can use several AirPort Express Base Stations — one for each stereo system or set of powered speakers, in different rooms — and then choose which stereo/speaker system to use in the pop-up menu.

To use AirTunes and the AirPort Express Base Station, follow these steps:

1. **Install the software supplied on CD-ROM, which includes support for AirTunes.**

2. **Connect your stereo or a set of powered speakers to the audio port of the AirPort Express Base Station.**

   You can use an optical digital or analog audio cable. (Both are included in the AirPort Express Stereo Connection Kit.) Which cable you use depends on whether your stereo or set of powered speakers has an optical digital or analog connection.

3. **Plug the AirPort Express Base Station into an electrical outlet.**

   Use the AC plug that came with the Base Station or the AirPort Express power extension cord included in the AirPort Express Stereo Connection Kit. The Base Station turns on automatically when connected to an electrical outlet. (The Base Station doesn't require a switch). The status light glows yellow while AirPort Express is starting up. When it starts up completely, the light turns green.

4. **On your computer, use the AirPort Express Assistant to set up iTunes.**

   The assistant detects the Base Station and walks you through the process of setting it up with iTunes.

The AirPort Express Base Station is small enough to fit in the palm of your hand — and it travels well because all it needs is a power outlet. You can take your laptop and AirPort Express to a friend's house or a party, connect the Base Station to the stereo system, and then use your laptop anywhere in its vicinity to play DJ. You can even use portable powered speakers wirelessly in a hotel room.

Playing iPod Songs through MusicMatch Jukebox

If you don't have the proper configuration to run the Windows version of iTunes, or you want to use MusicMatch Jukebox for other reasons (such as the encoders supplied with it), you can play your iPod's music directly on your Windows PC by using MusicMatch Jukebox. Normally, when you connect your iPod to a Windows-based PC by using MusicMatch Jukebox, the program starts up and displays the iPod in its PortablesPlus window. When you play an iPod song in MusicMatch Jukebox, it's similar to playing a song in the library or a track on a CD — you have the same flexibility with playback.

To play songs in MusicMatch Jukebox, first drag the selected songs from the iPod library in the PortablesPlus window to the MusicMatch Jukebox playlist window, which we cover in Chapter 7. The order of songs in the playlist is based on the order in which you selected them and dragged them to the list.

To play songs in the playlist, click the name of the song in the playlist window, and then click the Play button. When the song finishes, MusicMatch Jukebox continues playing the songs in the playlist in sequence until you click the Pause or Stop button. You can control song playback with MusicMatch Jukebox's Play, Stop, Pause, Next, and Previous buttons. The status area near the control buttons tells you the name of the artist and song (if known) and the elapsed time.

To rearrange songs in the playlist window, you can click and drag a song from one slot in the list to another. You can use the Repeat button to repeat the songs in a playlist, and use the Shuffle button to shuffle song playback in random order.

Part IV
Using Advanced Techniques

The 5th Wave   By Rich Tennant

"Margaret! Kyle's playing air bassoon the wrong way again! Doesn't iTunes have a help menu for this?"

In this part . . .

This part focuses on what you can do to improve the sound of your music.

- ✔ Chapter 19 gives you the info you need to make the right decisions for encoding and compressing sound files.

- ✔ Chapter 20 describes how to change your encoder and importing preferences to get the most out of the technology.

- ✔ Chapter 21 tells you about the iTunes and iPod equalizers and fine-tuning music playback in iTunes and on your iPod.

- ✔ Chapter 22 explains what you need to do to record sound from various analog sources (including vinyl LPs and tapes) for importing into iTunes or MusicMatch Jukebox.

- ✔ Chapter 23 covers other online music sources, how to play Web radio streams in iTunes, and how to enhance MusicMatch Jukebox.

Chapter 19

Choosing Your Encoding Format

· ·

In This Chapter

▶ Finding out the quality and space tradeoffs with sound encoders

▶ Understanding how encoders use compression

▶ Choosing the appropriate encoder and import settings

· ·

A s you discover more about digital audio technology, you find that you have more decisions to make about your music library than you previously thought, and this chapter helps you make them. For example, you might be tempted to trade quality for space — import music at average-quality settings that allow you to put more songs on your hard drive and iPod than if you chose higher-quality settings. This might make you happy today, but what about tomorrow, when iPods and hard drives double or triple in capacity?

On the other hand, you might be very picky about the sound quality, and with an eye toward future generations of iPods and cheap hard drives, you might decide to trade space for quality, importing music at the highest possible quality settings and then converting copies to lower-quality, space-saving versions for iPods and other uses. Of course, you need more hard drive space to accommodate the higher-quality versions.

This chapter explains which music encoding and compression formats to use for higher quality and which to use for cramming more songs into your hard drive space.

Trading Quality for Space

The encoding format and settings that you choose for importing music when ripping a CD affect sound quality, iPod space, and hard drive space on your computer. The format and settings might also affect the music files' ability to play on other types of players and computers.

The audio compression methods that are good at reducing space have to throw away information. In technospeak, these methods are known as *lossy* (as opposed to lossless) compression algorithms. For example, the AAC and MP3 encoding formats compress the sound using lossy methods — the compression algorithms reduce the sound quality by throwing away information to make the file smaller, so you lose information and some quality in the process. On the other hand, the Apple Lossless encoder compresses the sound without any loss in quality or information, but the resulting file is only a bit smaller than the uncompressed version — the main reason to use Apple Lossless is to maintain quality for burning CDs while also playing the songs on iPods. The AIFF and WAV encoders do not compress the sound and are the best choices for burning CDs.

With lossy compression using MP3 or AAC, the amount of compression depends on the *bit rate* that you choose, as well as the encoding format and other options. The bit rate determines how many bits (of digital music information) can travel during playback in a given second. Measured in kilobits per second (Kbps), a higher bit rate, such as 320KB, offers higher quality than a bit rate of 192KB because the sound is not compressed as much — which means the resulting sound file is larger and takes up more iPod and hard drive space.

Using more compression (a lower bit rate) means that the files are smaller, and the sound quality is poorer. Using less compression (a higher bit rate) means that the sound is higher in quality, but the files are larger. You can trade quality for space and have more music of lower quality, or trade space for quality and have less music of higher quality.

Also, power is an issue with the iPod. Playing larger files takes more power because the hard drive inside the iPod has to refresh its memory buffers more frequently to process information as the song plays — you might even hear hiccups in the sound.

We prefer a higher-quality sound overall, and we typically don't use the lower-quality settings for encoders except for voice recordings and music recorded before 1960 (which is already low in quality, so you don't hear that much of a difference when compressed). We can hear differences in music quality at the higher compression levels, and we prefer going out and buying another hard drive to store more music if necessary.

Choosing an Encoder

Your iPod's music software gives you a choice of encoders. This is perhaps the most important choice to make before starting to rip music CDs and build up your library. iTunes and MusicMatch Jukebox offer the same encoders — with some differences. Here we leapfrog years of technospeak about digital music file formats and get right to the ones that you need to know about.

iTunes encoders

Choose Preferences (from the iTunes menu on a Mac, or the Edit menu on a Windows PC) and click the Importing tab to see the Importing Preferences dialog. You can choose one of five encoders from the Import Using pop-up menu:

- **AAC Encoder:** All your purchased music from the iTunes Music store comes in this format. We recommend it for all uses except when ripping your own CDs to burn new audio CDs. Technically known as MPEG-4 Advanced Audio Coding, AAC is a higher quality format than MP3 at the same bit rate — meaning that AAC at 128 Kbps is higher quality than MP3 at 128 Kbps. (*MPEG* stands for Moving Picture Experts Group, a committee that recognizes compression standards for video and audio.) We think it offers the best tradeoff of space and quality for iPod users. It's suitable (though not as good as AIFF or Apple Lossless) for burning to an audio CD, and it's also excellent for playing on an iPod or from a hard drive. However, as of this writing, only Apple supports AAC.

- **Apple Lossless Encoder:** The Apple Lossless encoder is a compromise between the lower-quality encoding of AAC or MP3 (which results in lower file sizes) and the large file sizes of uncompressed, high-quality AIFF or WAV audio. The Apple Lossless encoder provides CD quality sound in a file size that's about 60 to 70 percent of the size of an AIFF or WAV encoded file. The virtue of this encoder is that you can use it for songs that you intend to burn onto audio CDs *and* for playing on iPods — the files are just small enough that they don't hiccup on playback, but are still much larger than their MP3 or AAC counterparts.

Using the Apple Lossless encoder is the most efficient method of storing the highest-quality versions of your songs. You can burn the songs to CDs without any quality loss and still play them on your iPod. You can't store as many songs on your iPod as with AAC or MP3, but the songs that you do store have the highest-possible quality.

✔ **AIFF Encoder:** The Audio Interchange File Format (AIFF) is the standard digital format for uncompressed sound on a Mac, and it provides the highest quality digital representation of the sound. Like the WAV encoder for Windows, the AIFF encoder uses a Mac-specific version of the original Pulse Code Modulation (PCM) algorithm required for compliance with audio CDs. Use AIFF if you plan to burn songs onto an audio CD or to edit the songs with a digital sound-editing program. Mac-based sound-editing programs import and export AIFF files, and you can edit and save in AIFF format repeatedly with absolutely no loss in quality. The downside is that AIFF files take up enormous amounts of hard drive and iPod space because they're uncompressed. Don't use AIFF for songs that you want to play on an iPod — use the Apple Lossless encoder instead.

✔ **MP3 Encoder:** The MPEG-1, Layer 3 format, also known as MP3, is supported by most computers and some CD players. Use the MP3 format for songs that you intend to use with other MP3 players besides your iPod (which also plays MP3 songs, obviously), or use with applications that support MP3, or to burn on an MP3 CD. (AIFF, WAV, or Apple Lossless formats are better for regular audio CDs.) The MP3 format offers quite a lot of different compression and quality settings, so you can fine-tune the format to get better quality, sacrificing hard drive (and iPod) space as you dial up the quality. Use the MP3 format for a song that you intend to use with MP3 players, MP3 CDs, and applications that support MP3.

✔ **WAV Encoder:** Waveform Audio File Format (WAV) is a digital audio standard that Windows PCs can understand and manipulate. Like AIFF, WAV is uncompressed and provides the highest quality digital representation of the sound. Like the AIFF encoder for the Mac, the WAV encoder uses a Windows-specific version of the original Pulse Code Modulation (PCM) algorithm required for compliance with audio CDs. Use WAV if you plan on burning the song to an audio CD or using the song with Windows-based digital sound-editing programs, which import and export WAV files (there is no difference between AIFF and WAV except that AIFF works with Mac applications and WAV works with Windows applications). WAV files take up enormous amounts of hard drive and iPod space because they're uncompressed. Don't use WAV for songs that you want to play on an iPod — use the Apple Lossless encoder instead.

If you want to share your music with someone who uses an MP3 player other than an iPod, you can import or convert songs with the MP3 encoder. As an iPod user, you can use the higher-quality AAC encoder to produce files that are either the same size as their MP3 counterparts but higher in quality, or at the same quality but smaller in size.

To have the best possible quality that you can get for future growth, and for music editing, consider not using compression at all (as with AIFF or WAV), or using Apple Lossless. You can import music at the highest possible quality — by using the AIFF or WAV encoders or the Apple Lossless encoder — and burn them to audio CDs; then convert the music files to a lesser-quality format for use in the iPod or other devices. If you use Apple Lossless for songs, you can use those songs on an iPod, but they take up much more space than AAC- or MP3-encoded songs. We describe how to convert music in Chapter 20.

MusicMatch Jukebox encoders

MusicMatch Jukebox offers several options for fine-tuning the CD-ripping process. When you first use the program, the MP3 recording format is selected by default, offering various quality options, which we describe in Chapter 20. You can change the recording format (properly known as the *encoder*) to mp3PRO, WAV, Windows Media, and other encoder formats that are associated with third-party plug-in software for MusicMatch Jukebox.

You have two basic choices for encoding formats in MusicMatch Jukebox that work with your iPod: MP3 (and its variations), and WAV. MP3 (or a variation such as mp3PRO) is the encoder to choose for songs to use on your iPod.

The WAV encoder, although it provides the highest quality sound, doesn't compress the audio, and is therefore not as useful for iPods. WAV is a digital audio standard for Windows-based PCs. Use WAV if you plan on burning the song to an audio CD or on using the song with PC-based digital sound-editing programs, which import and export WAV files. WAV files take up enormous amounts of hard drive and iPod space because they're uncompressed.

The mp3PRO encoder that's provided with MusicMatch Jukebox creates an MP3 file, only smaller. Use the mp3PRO encoder for even greater file compression than with the standard MP3 encoder. People typically use the mp3PRO encoder for songs that don't require extreme high-fidelity playback, because mp3PRO compresses files even further and allows more songs to fit on your iPod.

If you want to get the benefits of different formats, you can import a CD with one encoder, such as WAV, and then either import the CD again with a different encoder, such as MP3, or *convert* the music files to a lesser-quality format for use on the iPod or other devices. We describe how to convert music files in Chapter 20.

Although MusicMatch Jukebox lets you convert MP3 to WAV, or an MP3 at a lower bit rate to an MP3 with a higher bit rate, neither conversion improves song quality. You might have a reason for converting MP3 to WAV, but the song's quality remains exactly the same while taking up lots more space. The same is true about converting MP3s from a lower bit rate to a higher bit rate — the song remains at the same quality level but takes up more hard drive space. The most useful conversion is from WAV (the format used for burning CDs) to MP3 (the format used on the Web and iPod); this conversion slightly reduces the quality of the song, but shrinks the file size exponentially so that more songs can fit on your iPod.

The past, present, and future of music

Our suggestions for encoders and importing preferences for ripping CDs are based on our own listening experiences and our preference of the highest quality and the best use of compression technology. You might be quite happy with the results of using these suggestions, but listening pleasure depends entirely on you and the way the song itself was recorded. Some people can hear qualitative differences that others don't hear or don't care about. Some people can also tolerate a lower-quality sound in exchange for the convenience of carrying more music on their iPods. And sometimes the recording is so primitive-sounding that you can get away with using lower-quality settings to gain more hard drive space.

Just a century ago, people gathered at *phonography parties* to rent a headset and listen to a new invention called a phonograph, the predecessor to the record player. Before records, radio, and jukeboxes, these parties and live performances were the only sources of music, and the quality of the sound must have been crude by today's standards, but still quite enjoyable.

The choices of formats for sound have changed considerably from the fragile 78 rpm records from the phonography parties of the early 1900s and the scratchy 45 rpm and 33 rpm records of the 1940s through the 1980s to today's CDs. Consumers had to be on the alert then, as you do now, for dead-end formats that could lock up music in a cul-de-sac of technology, never to be played again. You know what we're talking about — dead-end formats, such as the ill-fated 8-track cartridge or the legendary quadraphonic LP. You want your digital music to last forever and play at high quality — not get stuck with technology that doesn't evolve with the times.

Digital music has evolved beyond the commercial audio CD, and computers haven't yet caught up to some of the latest audio formats. For example, iTunes can't yet import sound from these formats:

✔ **DVD-audio:** DVD-audio is a relatively new digital audio format developed from the format for DVD video. DVD-audio is based on PCM recording technology but offers improved sound quality by using a higher sampling frequency and longer word lengths. Neither iTunes nor MusicMatch Jukebox support the DVD-audio format, but you can import a digital video file containing DVD-audio sound into iMovie, extract the sound, and export the sound in AIFF or WAV format, which you can use with iTunes. You can also use Toast with Jam 6 from Roxio (www.roxio.com) to import and burn DVD-audio.

✔ **Super Audio CD (SACD):** Super Audio CD is a new format developed from the past audio format for CDs. The SACD format is based on Direct Stream Digital (DSD) recording technology that closely reproduces the shape of the original analog waveforms to produce a more natural, higher quality sound. Originally developed for the digital archiving of priceless analog masters tapes, DSD is based on 1-bit sigma-delta modulation, and operates with a sampling frequency of 2.8224 MHz (64 times the 44.1 kHz used in audio CDs). Philips and Sony adopted DSD as the basis for SACD, and the format is growing in popularity among audiophiles. However, neither iTunes nor MusicMatch Jukebox support SACD. If you buy music in the SACD format, choose the hybrid format that offers a conventional CD layer and a high-density SACD layer. You can then import the music from the conventional CD layer.

You might also want to take advantage of the compression technology that squeezes more music onto your iPod. Although the Apple-supported AAC format offers far better compression and quality than the MP3 format does (at the same bit rates), the MP3 format is more universal, supported by other players and software programs, as well as the iPod and iTunes. Sticking with AAC or Apple Lossless as your encoder might make you feel like your songs are stuck inside iTunes with the MP3 blues again. However, with iTunes and your iPod, you can mix and match these formats as you please.

Manic Compression Has Captured Your Song

Every person hears the effects of compression differently. You might not hear any problem with a compressed song that someone else says is tinny or lacking in depth.

Too much compression can be a bad thing. Further compressing an already-compressed music file — say, by converting a song — reduces the quality significantly. Not only that, but after your song is compressed, you can't uncompress the song back to its original quality. Your song is essentially locked into that quality.

The lossy-style compression used by MP3 and AAC loses information each time you use it, which means that if you compress something that has already been compressed, you lose even more information. This is bad. Don't compress something that's already compressed with a lossy method.

The Apple Lossless encoder doesn't use a lossy method, which is why it's called lossless. This is also why it reduces sound files to only two-thirds of their AIFF or WAV counterparts — which isn't as useful for saving space as the one-tenth compression that's common with MP3 or AAC.

MP3 and AAC use two basic lossy methods to compress audio:

- ✔ **Removing non-audible frequencies:** For non-audible frequencies, the compression removes what you supposedly can't hear (although this is a subject for eternal debate). For example, if a background singer's warble is totally drowned out by a rhythm guitar playing a chord, and you can't hear the singer due to the intensity of the guitar's sound, the compression algorithm loses the singer's sound while maintaining the guitar's sound.

- ✔ **Removing less important signals:** Within the spectrum of sound frequencies, some frequencies are considered to be less important in terms of rendering fidelity, and some frequencies most people can't hear at all. Removing specific frequencies is likely to be less damaging to your music than other types of compression, depending on how you hear things. In fact, your dog might stop getting agitated at songs that contain ultra-high frequencies that only dogs can hear (such as the ending of "Day in the Life" by the Beatles).

Selecting Import Settings

The AAC and MP3 formats compress sound at different quality settings. iTunes and MusicMatch Jukebox let you set the bit rate for importing, which determines the audio quality. You need to use a higher bit rate (such as 192 or 320 Kbps) for higher quality, which — all together now — increases the file size.

Variable Bit Rate (VBR) encoding is a technique that varies the number of bits used to store the music depending on the complexity of the sound. Although the quality of VBR is endlessly debated, it's useful when set to the highest setting because VBR can encode at up to the maximum bit rate of 320 Kbps in those rare cases where the sound requires it, while keeping the majority of the sound at a lower bit rate.

iTunes and MusicMatch Jukebox also let you control the *sample rate* during importing, which is the number of times per second the sound waveform is captured digitally (or *sampled*). Higher sample rates yield higher quality sound and large file sizes. However, never use a higher sample rate than the rate used for the source. CDs use a 44.100 kHz rate, so choosing a higher rate is unnecessary unless you convert a song that was recorded from Digital Audio Tape (DAT) or directly into the computer at a high sample rate, and you want to keep that sample rate.

Another setting to consider during importing is the Channel choice. *Stereo,* which offers two channels of music for left and right speakers, is the norm for music. However, *mono* — monaural or single-channel — was the norm for pop records before the mid-1960s. (Phil Spector was known for his high-quality monaural recordings, and the early Rolling Stones records are in mono.) Monaural recordings take up half the space of stereo recordings when digitized. Most likely, you want to keep stereo recordings in stereo, and mono recordings in mono.

Chapter 20

Changing Encoders and Encoder Settings

In This Chapter

▶ Changing your importing preferences in iTunes

▶ Changing settings for the AAC, MP3, AIFF, and WAV encoders in iTunes

▶ Importing voice and sound effects in iTunes

▶ Converting songs to a different encoding format in iTunes

▶ Changing your recorder settings in MusicMatch Jukebox

▶ Converting songs to a different encoding format in MusicMatch Jukebox

*Y*ou might want to change your import settings before ripping CDs, depending on the type of music, the source of the recording, or other factors, such as whether you plan to copy the songs to your iPod or burn an audio or MP3 CD. The encoders offer general quality settings, but you can also customize the encoders and change those settings to your liking. Whether you use iTunes or MusicMatch Jukebox, the software remembers your custom settings until you change them again.

This chapter provides the nuts-and-bolts details on changing your import settings to customize each type of encoder, importing sounds other than music, and converting songs from one format to another. With the choice of settings for music encoders, you can impress your audiophile friends, even ones who doubted that your computer could reproduce magnificent music.

You can also convert songs to another format as described in "Converting Songs to a Different Encoder in iTunes" in this chapter. However, you can't convert songs that you buy from the iTunes Music Store to another file format because they're encoded as protected AAC files. If you could, they wouldn't be protected, would they? You also can't convert Audible books and spoken-word content to another format. (However, you can burn them to an audio CD and re-import them, which might cause a noticeable drop in quality.)

Customizing the Encoder Settings in iTunes

To change your encoder and quality settings and other importing preferences before ripping an audio CD or converting a file in iTunes, follow these steps:

1. **Choose iTunes⇨Preferences on a Mac, or Edit⇨Preferences on a Windows PC, and then click the Importing tab.**

   The Importing Preferences dialog appears, allowing you to make changes to the encoding format and its settings.

2. **Choose the encoding format that you want to convert the song into and select the settings for that format.**

   The pop-up menus help you make your changes. The Setting pop-up menu offers different settings depending on your choice of encoder in the Import Using pop-up menu. See the sections on each encoding format later in this chapter for details on settings.

3. **Click OK to accept changes.**

   After changing your importing preferences, and until you change them again, iTunes uses these preferences whenever it imports or converts songs.

The AAC, MP3, AIFF, and WAV encoders let you change the settings for the encoders. The Apple Lossless encoder is automatic and offers no settings to change.

Changing AAC encoder settings

We recommend using the AAC encoder for everything except music that you intend to burn on an audio CD; AAC offers the best trade-off of space and quality for hard drives and iPods.

The Setting pop-up menu for the AAC encoder offers only two choices: High Quality and Custom, as shown in Figure 20-1. You might want to use the High Quality setting for most music, but for very intense music (such as complex jazz or classical music, recordings with lots of instruments, or your most favorite songs), you might want to fine-tune the settings. To customize your AAC encoder settings, select the Custom option from the Setting pop-up menu to see the AAC Encoder dialog, as shown in Figure 20-2.

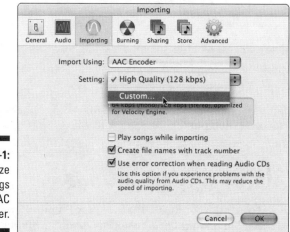

Figure 20-1:
Customize
the settings
for the AAC
encoder.

The custom settings for AAC (see Figure 20-2) allow you to change the following:

✔ **Stereo Bit Rate:** This pop-up menu allows you to select the bit rate, which is measured in kilobits per second (Kbps). Use a higher bit rate for higher quality, which also increases the file size. 320 Kbps is the highest-quality setting for this format; 128 is considered high quality.

✔ **Sample Rate:** This pop-up menu enables you to select the *sample rate,* which is the number of times per second the sound waveform is captured digitally (or *sampled*). Higher sample rates yield higher quality sound and larger file sizes. However, never use a higher sample rate than the rate used for the source. CDs use a 44.100 kHz rate.

✔ **Channels:** This pop-up menu enables you to choose how you want the music to play through speakers — in stereo or mono. Stereo offers two channels of music for left and right speakers, and mono offers only one channel but takes up half the space of stereo recordings when digitized. If the recording is in stereo, don't choose mono because you will lose part of the sound (you might lose vocals or guitar riffs, depending on the recording). Select the Auto setting to have iTunes use the appropriate setting for the music.

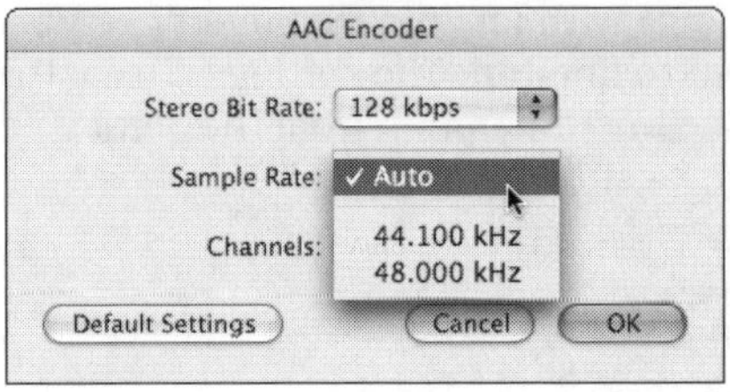

Figure 20-2:
Set the AAC
encoder to
import with
the highest
bit rate
and with
automatic
detection
of sample
rate and
channels.

AAC Encoder

Stereo Bit Rate: 128 kbps

Sample Rate: ✓ Auto
44.100 kHz
48.000 kHz

Channels:

Default Settings   Cancel   OK

We recommend selecting the highest bit rate in the Stereo Bit Rate pop-up menu and leaving the other two pop-up menus set to Auto.

Changing MP3 encoder settings

We prefer using the AAC encoder for music that we play on our iPods, but as of this writing, most other MP3 players don't support AAC. The iPod supports both AAC and MP3 encoders. You might want to use the MP3 encoder for other reasons, such as acquiring more control over the compression parameters and gaining compatibility with other applications and players that support MP3.

The MP3 encoder offers four choices for the Setting pop-up menu in the Importing Preferences dialog:

- **Good Quality (128 Kbps):** This is certainly fine for audio books, comedy records, and old scratchy records. You might even want use a lower bit rate for voice recordings.

- **High Quality (160 Kbps):** Most people consider this high enough for most popular music, but we go higher with our music.

- **Higher Quality (192 Kbps):** This one's high enough for just about all types of music.

- **Custom:** To fine-tune the MP3 encoder settings, select the Custom setting. Customizing your MP3 settings increases the quality of the sound and keeps file size low.

The MP3 encoder offers a bunch of choices in its custom settings dialog (see Figure 20-3):

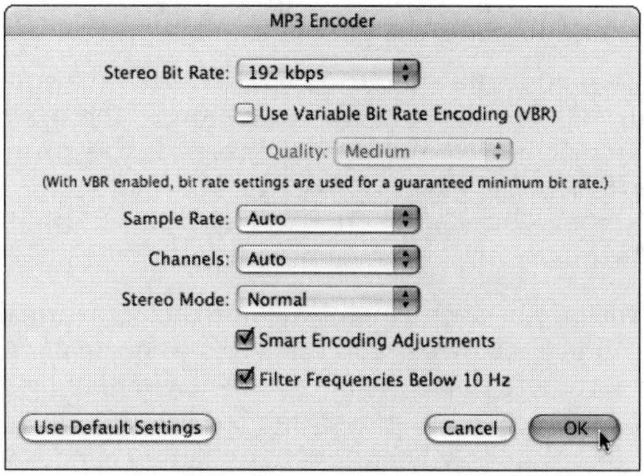

Figure 20-3: Customize the settings for the MP3 encoder.

MP3 Encoder
Stereo Bit Rate: 192 kbps
☐ Use Variable Bit Rate Encoding (VBR)
Quality: Medium
(With VBR enabled, bit rate settings are used for a guaranteed minimum bit rate.)
Sample Rate: Auto
Channels: Auto
Stereo Mode: Normal
☑ Smart Encoding Adjustments
☑ Filter Frequencies Below 10 Hz
Use Default Settings   Cancel   OK

✔ **Stereo Bit Rate:** This pop-up menu's choices are measured in kilobits per second; select a higher bit rate for higher quality, which increases the file size. The most common bit rate for MP3 files you find on the Web is 128 Kbps. Lower bit rates are more appropriate for voice recordings or sound effects.

We recommend at least 192 Kbps for most music, and we use 320 Kbps, the maximum setting, for songs that we play on our iPods.

✔ **Use Variable Bit Rate Encoding (VBR):** This option helps keep file size down, but quality might be affected. VBR varies the number of bits used to store the music depending on the complexity of the sound. If you select the Highest setting from the Quality pop-up menu for VBR, iTunes encodes at up to the maximum bit rate of 320 Kbps in sections of songs where the sound is complex enough to require a high bit rate. Meanwhile, iTunes keeps the rest of the song at a lower bit rate to save file space. The lower limit is set by the rate that you select in the Stereo Bit Rate pop-up menu.

Some audiophiles swear by VBR, but others don't ever use it. We use it only when importing at low bit rates, and we set VBR to its highest quality setting.

Although your iPod plays VBR-encoded MP3 music, other MP3 players might not support VBR.

- ✔ **Sample Rate:** This pop-up menu enables you to select the *sample rate* (the number of times per second that the sound waveform is captured digitally). Higher sample rates yield higher quality sound and larger file sizes. However, never use a higher sample rate than the rate used for the source — CDs use a 44.100 kHz rate.

- ✔ **Channels:** This pop-up menu enables you to choose how you want the music to play through speakers; in stereo or mono. Stereo, which offers two channels of music for left and right speakers, is the norm for music. Monaural (mono) recordings take up half the space of stereo recordings when digitized. Choose the Auto setting to have iTunes use the appropriate setting for the music.

- ✔ **Stereo mode:** This pop-up menu enables you to select Normal or Joint Stereo. Normal mode is just what you think it is — normal stereo. Select the Joint Stereo setting to make the file smaller by removing information that's identical in both channels of a stereo recording, using only one channel for that information while the other channel carries unique information. At bit rates of 128 Kbps and below, this mode can actually improve the sound quality. However, we typically don't use the Joint Stereo mode when using a high-quality bit rate.

- ✔ **Smart Encoding Adjustments:** This option, when selected, tells iTunes to analyze your MP3 encoding settings and music source and to change your settings as needed to maximize the quality of the encoded files.

- ✔ **Filter Frequencies Below 10 Hz:** This option, when selected, filters out low frequency sounds. Frequencies below 10 Hz are hard to hear, and most people don't notice if they're missing. Filtering inaudible frequencies helps reduce the file size with little or no perceived loss in quality. However, we think selecting this option and removing the low-frequency sounds detracts from the overall feeling of the music, and we prefer not to filter frequencies.

Changing AIFF and WAV encoder settings

We recommend that you use the AIFF, WAV, or Apple Lossless encoders for songs from audio CDs if you intend to burn your own audio CDs with the music. You get the best possible quality with these encoders because the music isn't compressed with a lossy algorithm. The Apple Lossless encoder (which is automatic and offers no settings to change) reduces file size to about 60–70 percent of the size of AIFF or WAV versions. However, AIFF or WAV files are preferable for use with digital sound-editing programs, and they offer settings that you can change, such as the number of channels (Stereo or Mono) and the sampling rate.

The difference between the AIFF and WAV encoders is only that AIFF is the standard for Mac applications and computers, and WAV is the standard for PC applications and computers.

You can import music with AIFF or WAV at the highest possible quality and then convert the music files to a lesser-quality format for use in your iPod.

AIFF and WAV files take up huge amounts of hard drive space (about 10MB per minute), and although you can play them on your iPod, they take up way too much space and battery power to be convenient for anyone but the most discerning audiophile who can afford multiple iPods. You can handle these large files by adding another hard drive or by backing up portions of your music library onto other media, such as a DVD-R (which can hold 4.7GB). However, if multiple hard drives and backup scenarios sound like unwanted hassles, use the AAC or MP3 encoders to compress files so that they take up less space on your hard drive.

The AIFF encoder and the WAV encoder offer similar custom settings dialogs; the AIFF Encoder dialog is shown in Figure 20-4. The pop-up menus offer settings for Sample Rate, Sample Size, and Channels. You can select the Auto setting for all three pop-up menus, and iTunes automatically detects the proper sample rate, size, and channels from the source. If you select a specific setting, such as the Stereo setting in the Channels pop-up menu, iTunes imports the music in stereo, regardless of the source. Audio CDs typically sample at a rate of 44.1000 kHz, with a sample size of 16 bits, and with stereo channels.

Figure 20-4:
The Chan-
nels pop-up
menu allows
you to import
regardless of
the source.

AIFF Encoder

Sample Rate: 44.100 kHz

Sample Size: 16 bit

Channels: ✓ Auto

Default Settings   Mono

Stereo   OK

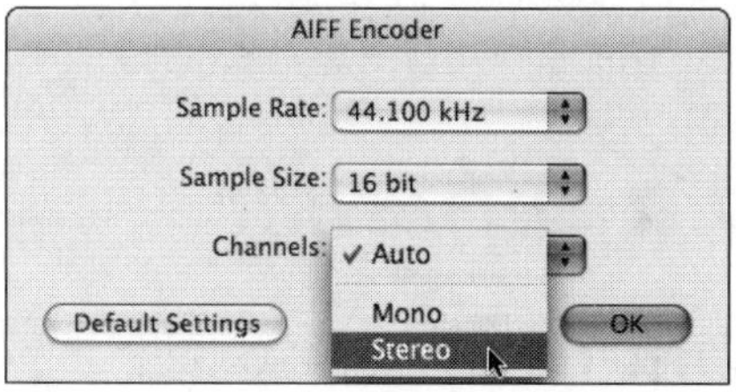

The Sample Rate pop-up menu for AIFF and WAV offers more choices than for AAC, down to a very low sample rate of 8.000 kHz, which is suitable only for voice recordings.

Importing Voice and Sound Effects in iTunes

Audio books are available from Audible (www.audible.com) in a special format that doesn't require any further compression, but you can also import audio books, spoken-word titles, comedy CDs, and other voice recordings in the MP3 format.

If the recording has any music at all or requires close listening to stereo channels (such as a Firesign Theatre or Monty Python CD), treat the entire recording as music and skip this section. ("Nudge-nudge, wink-wink. Sorry! Everything you know is wrong!")

By fine-tuning the import settings for voice recordings and sound effects, you can save a significant amount of space without reducing quality. We recommend the following settings depending on your choice of encoder:

- **AAC encoder:** AAC allows you to get away with an even lower bit rate than MP3 to achieve the same quality, thereby saving more space. We recommend a bit rate as low as 80 Kbps for sound effects and voice recordings.

- **MP3 encoder:** Use a low bit rate (such as 96 Kbps). You might also want to reduce the sample rate to 22.050 kHz for voice recordings. Filter frequencies below 10 Hz because voice recordings don't need such frequencies.

Converting Songs to a Different Encoder in iTunes

Converting a song from one encoder to another is useful if you want to use one encoder for one purpose, such as burning a CD, and a second encoder for another task, such as playing on your iPod.

Converting a song from one compressed format to another is possible (say from AAC to MP3), but you might not like the results. When you convert a compressed file to another compressed format, iTunes compresses the music *twice,* reducing the quality of the sound. You get the best results by starting with an uncompressed song that was imported using either the AIFF or WAV format, and then converting that song to the compressed AAC or MP3 format.

You can tell what format a song is in by selecting it and choosing File⇨Get Info. Then click the Summary tab to see the song's format. You might want to keep track of formats by creating CD-AIFF-version and iPod-MP3-version playlists for different formats.

To convert a song to another encoding format, follow these steps:

1. **Choose iTunes⇨Preferences on a Mac, or choose Edit⇨Preferences on a Windows PC, and then click the Importing tab.**

   The Importing Preferences dialog appears, allowing you to make changes to the encoding format and its settings.

2. **Select the encoding format that you want to convert the song into from the Import Using pop-up menu; in the custom settings dialog that appears, select the settings for that encoder.**

   For example, if you're converting songs in the AIFF format to the MP3 format, choose MP3 Encoder from the Import Using pop-up menu, and then select the settings that you want in the MP3 Encoder dialog that appears.

3. **Click OK to accept the settings for your chosen format.**

4. **In the iTunes window, select the song(s) that you want to convert, and then choose Advanced⇨Convert Selection.**

   The encoding format that you chose in Step 2 appears on the menu: Convert Selection to MP3, Convert Selection to AAC, Convert Selection to AIFF, or Convert Selection to WAV. Choose the appropriate menu operation to perform the conversion. When the conversion is complete, the newly converted version of the song appears in your iTunes library (with the same artist name and song name, so it's easy to find). iTunes doesn't delete the original version — both are stored in your music library.

If you convert songs obtained from the Internet, you may find MP3 songs with bit rates as low as 128 Kbps, and choosing a higher stereo bit rate doesn't improve the quality — it only wastes space.

The automatic copy-and-convert operation can be useful for converting an entire music library to another format — hold down the Option key on a Mac, or the Alt key in Windows, and choose Advanced⇨Convert Selection, and all the songs copy and convert automatically. If you have a library of AIFF tunes, you can quickly copy and convert them to AAC or MP3 in one step, and then assign the AIFF songs to the AIFF-associated playlists for burning CDs, and MP3 or AAC songs to MP3 or AAC playlists that you intend to copy to your iPod.

Changing Recorder Settings in MusicMatch Jukebox

In MusicMatch Jukebox, encoder settings are called *Recorder Settings,* and to change your Recorder Settings in MusicMatch Jukebox, choose Options➪ Settings➪Recorder, which displays the Settings dialog, as shown in Figure 20-5. From there you have several options, depending on what you want to do.

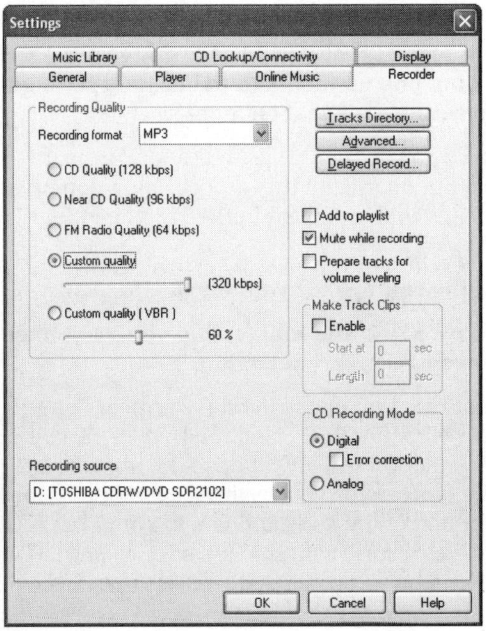

Figure 20-5: Customize the MP3-format recording settings for ripping CDs in MusicMatch Jukebox.

Selecting MP3 settings

You can select the following quality settings for MP3 recording in MusicMatch Jukebox:

✔ **CD Quality (128 Kbps):** Measured in kilobits per second, this option offers 128 Kbps, the most common bit rate for MP3 files on the Web. The notion that this is "CD quality" is subjective. With this setting, one minute of music takes up about 1MB of space.

✔ **Near CD Quality (96 Kbps):** This setting offers 96 Kbps, and one minute of music takes up about 700K. However, we find the quality to be poor. However, if you don't hear or mind the difference, you can certainly cram more music on your iPod with this setting.

✔ **FM Radio Quality (64 Kbps):** Bit rates lower than 96 Kbps are more appropriate for voice recordings or sound effects, not music. One minute takes up about 400K.

✔ **Custom Quality:** This option lets you set the stereo bit rate. A higher bit rate offers higher-quality sound and increases the file size. The most common bit rate for MP3 files you find on the Web is 128 Kbps. Lower bit rates are more appropriate for voice recordings or sound effects. We recommend at least 192 Kbps for most music, and we use 320 Kbps, the maximum setting, for songs we play on iPods.

✔ **Custom Quality (VBR):** This setting uses Variable Bit Rate (VBR) encoding to vary the number of bits used to store the music depending on the complexity of the sound. MusicMatch Jukebox offers a range from 1 (lowest quality with highest compression) to 100 (highest quality with least compression). At its highest setting, VBR might use the highest bit rate of 320 Kbps in sections of songs where the sound is complex enough to require a high bit rate, while keeping the rest of the song at a lower bit rate to save file space. We recommend using only the highest setting if you use VBR at all.

✔ **Digital:** MusicMatch Jukebox can record from a digital or analog source. When ripping CDs, select the Digital option. You can also use the Error correction option to filter out noise and produce better results with CDs that have minor scratches. If you hear clicks and pops or a jittery sound in the recorded digital music, try using this option, which minimizes the audio artifacts that occur from drive-seeking errors. Recording time takes longer, but the recording quality might be better with some CD-ROM drives.

✔ **Analog:** The Analog setting, which records in real time, is by far the slowest method and is provided for recording from slow CD-ROM drives to get higher-quality results.

Selecting WAV

Use WAV, which offers the highest possible quality, if you plan on burning the song to an audio CD. The files occupy lots more space than MP3 files because they aren't compressed. One minute of music in the WAV format occupies about 10MB of hard drive or iPod space. CD Quality is the only option for WAV.

Using the mp3PRO encoder

MusicMatch Jukebox also offers the mp3PRO encoder for creating smaller MP3 files that come close in quality to the larger files created by the default MP3 encoder. The mp3PRO encoder can create files that are nearly 50 percent smaller, but it offers low bit rate settings up to only 96 Kbps — suitable for mono records from before 1960 and voice recordings, but not much else. (Use the MP3 encoder for higher bit rate settings.)

The mp3PRO encoder offers the CD Transparency setting for 96 Kbps, which is the only setting we'd recommend. The lower settings are not useful as the sound quality is poor (in our opinion). You can also set a custom bit rate, but not higher than 96 Kbps. Variable Bit Rate (VBR) is also provided.

Using advanced recording options

MusicMatch Jukebox offers advanced settings, which are available by clicking the Advanced button in the Settings dialog (refer to Figure 20-5). The Advanced Recording Options dialog appears, and you can set a variety of recording options and special effects.

The following options improve the recording quality while ripping songs from CDs:

- **MP3 Encoding:** You can force recording into Stereo or Mono formats with this option. By default, MusicMatch Jukebox is set to use the appropriate setting that matches the source — Stereo for stereo sources and Mono for mono sources.

- **Maximum Bandwidth:** This option sets the range of frequencies allowed in the MP3 file. The human ear can theoretically hear frequencies up to 22 kHz, but many humans actually can't hear anything above 16 kHz. If you want frequencies higher than 16 kHz (often found in classical music), you can adjust this slider up.

- **Auto Config:** The Auto Config button automatically configures MusicMatch Jukebox for your CD-ROM drive and should be used whenever you change drives. You can select the sample size (short, medium, or long) in the drop-down list before configuring. Although most drives can be configured using the short or medium sample size, some need the long size.

✔ **Digital Audio Extraction (DAE):** If your audio files sound like they play too fast, it might be due to your CD drive not operating fast enough to keep up with the recording process — a drive speed/recording speed mismatch. Changing the DAE Speed setting to 4 (for a 4X recording speed) generally fixes this problem. If not, you can try 2X or real-time recording (1X). If you hear jitter in the sound even with error correction on, try turning the Multipass option on so that MusicMatch Jukebox reads the CD track multiple times, ensuring a successful recording (but also increasing recording time).

The following are special effects that you might want to use while recording songs:

✔ **Fade In:** You can record a song with a fade-in at the beginning and set the number of seconds for the fade-in. The fade-in is recorded along with the audio so that it is permanently part of the music file.

✔ **Fade Out:** You can record a song with a fade-out at the end and set the number of seconds for the fade-out. The fade-out is also permanently part of the music file.

✔ **Track Offset:** Use this option to start the recording process a number of seconds into the track instead of at the very beginning. For example, if a CD track has no sound or an introduction that you want to skip, you can specify the number of seconds to skip (or *offset*) before starting to record.

Chapter 21

Fine-Tuning the Sound

· ·

In This Chapter

▶ Setting the volume for songs in iTunes and your iPod

▶ Equalizing the sound in iTunes

▶ Adjusting the preamp volume and frequencies

▶ Creating and assigning equalizer presets to songs

▶ Using the iPod equalizer

▶ Using iTunes equalizer presets in your iPod

· ·

Sound is difficult to describe. Harder still to describe is how to adjust sound to your liking. Maybe you want more oomph in the lows, or you prefer highs that are as clear as a bell. If you've never mastered a stereo system beyond adjusting the bass and treble controls, the volume control, and the loudness button, you can use this limited knowledge of sound to quickly fine-tune the sound in iTunes, as we show in this chapter.

If you're a discerning listener, you might want to change the equalizer settings in iTunes and perhaps even use different settings for different songs. With iTunes, you have to change those settings only once. This chapter shows you how to make presets for each song in your library so that iTunes remembers them. What's more, you can use the iTunes settings on your iPod, which also offers an equalizer. This chapter shows you how.

Adjusting the Sound in iTunes

Some songs are just too loud. We don't mean too loud stylistically, as in thrash metal with screeching guitars; we mean too loud for your ears when you're wearing headphones or so loud that the music sounds distorted in your speakers. And some songs are just too soft, and you have to turn up the volume to hear them, then turn it down to hear other songs. Is there a way to set the volume in advance for a certain song or album?

Of course there is — you can set the overall volume in advance in the song information dialog by choosing File⇨Get Info. You can also make all the songs in your library play at the same volume by leveling the volume with the Sound Check option.

You can change the volume level at any time by sliding the volume slider in the upper-left section of the iTunes window. The maximum volume of the iTunes volume slider is the maximum set for the computer's sound in the Sound pane of System Preferences, as we describe in Chapter 18.

Setting the volume in advance for songs

With songs that you already know are too loud (or too soft), consider setting the volume for those songs (or certain albums) in advance, so that they always play with that volume adjustment.

To adjust the overall volume of a particular song in advance, so that it always plays at that setting, perform the following steps:

1. **Click a song to select it.**

2. **Choose File⇨Get Info.**

   The song information dialog appears.

3. **Click the Options tab.**

   Drag the Volume Adjustment slider left or right to adjust the volume lower or higher, as shown in Figure 21-1. You can do this while playing the song.

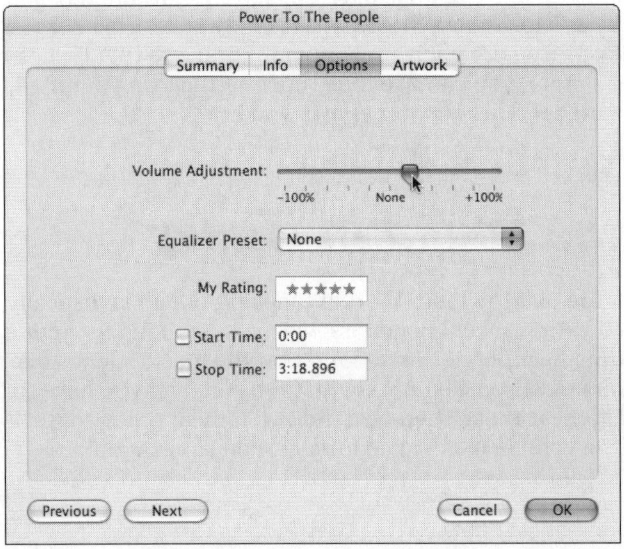

Figure 21-1:
Adjust the volume setting for a song here.

To set the volume for more than one song at once, you can select an entire album in iTunes Browse view or select multiple songs; then choose Get Info to open the Multiple Song Information dialog. The Volume Adjustment slider appears on the bottom-right corner of the dialog. Drag the slider as described earlier to set the volume adjustment for the entire album of songs or the selected songs.

Enhancing the sound

Audiophiles and sound purists frown on it, but many of you probably use the loudness button on home or car stereos to enhance the sound. iTunes offers a similar option — *Sound Enhancer* — that improves the depth of the sound by enhancing the high and low frequencies. Audiophiles and sound purists would most likely use the equalizer to boost frequencies, but you can use this brute force method to enhance the sound.

To turn on Sound Enhancer, choose Preferences (from the iTunes menu on a Mac/Edit menu on a Windows PC). Click the Audio button to show the Audio dialog, as shown in Figure 21-2.

To increase the sound enhancement (boosting the high and low frequencies), drag the Sound Enhancer slider to the right toward the High setting. This is similar to pressing the loudness button on a stereo or the equivalent of boosting the treble (high) and bass (low) frequencies in the equalizer (as we describe in "Equalize It in iTunes," later in this chapter). To decrease the high and low frequencies, drag the slider to the left toward the Low setting. The middle setting is neutral, adding no enhancement — the same as turning off the Sound Enhancer by clearing its check box.

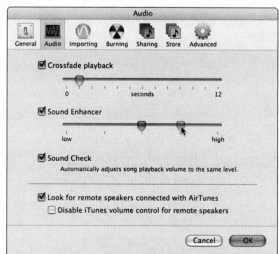

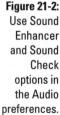

Figure 21-2:
Use Sound Enhancer and Sound Check options in the Audio preferences.

Sound-checking the iTunes volume

Because music CDs are mastered differently, there can be discrepancies in volume between them. Some CDs play more loudly than others; occasionally, individual tracks within a CD are louder than others.

You can standardize the volume level of all the songs in your iTunes music library with the Sound Check option. Hey, musicians do a sound check before every performance to check the volume of microphones and instruments and its effect on the listening environment. The aptly named Sound Check option in iTunes allows you to do a sound check on your tunes to bring them all in line, volume-wise. This option has the added benefit of applying the same volume adjustment when you play the songs back on your iPod, as described in the upcoming section, "Sound-checking the iPod volume."

To ensure that all the songs in your library ripped from CDs play at the same volume level, follow these steps:

1. **Drag the iTunes volume slider to set the overall volume for iTunes.**

   The volume slider is in the top-left corner of the iTunes window, under the Play button.

2. **Choose iTunes⇨Preferences on a Mac/Edit⇨Preferences on a Windows PC.**

   The Preferences dialog appears.

3. **Click the Audio button.**

   The Audio preferences dialog appears (refer to Figure 21-2).

4. **Select the Sound Check check box.**

   iTunes sets the volume level for all songs according to the level of the iTunes volume slider.

5. **Click OK.**

   The Sound Check option sets a volume adjustment based on the volume slider on all the songs so that they play at approximately the same volume.

Sound-checking the iPod volume

You can take advantage of volume leveling in your iTunes music library with the Sound Check option, and then turn Sound Check on or off on your iPod by choosing Sound Check in the iPod Settings menu.

This is useful especially when using your iPod in a car (or when jogging while listening to headphones) because you don't want to have to reach for the volume on the iPod or on the car stereo every time a song comes on that's too loud. However, the Sound Check option on your iPod works only if you've also set the Sound Check option in your iTunes library. (Audio purists frown on volume leveling as much as they frown on sound enhancement, preferring to adjust the volume only when they need to.)

In iTunes, select the Sound Check option as we describe in the preceding section, "Sound-checking the iTunes volume." Then, on the iPod, choose Settings⇨ Sound Check⇨On from the main menu to turn on the Sound Check feature. To turn it off, choose Settings⇨Sound Check⇨Off.

Equalize It in iTunes

The iTunes equalizer (EQ) allows you to fine-tune the specific sound spectrum frequencies in a more precise way than with the typical bass and treble controls you find on home stereos and powered speakers. (See the sidebar on equalizers, elsewhere in this chapter.) You can use the equalizer to improve or enhance the sound coming through a particular stereo system and speakers. With the equalizer settings, you can customize playback for different musical genres, listening environments, or speakers.

You might want to pick entirely different equalizer settings for car speakers, home speakers, and headphones. Fortunately, you can save your settings, as we describe in the upcoming "Saving your own presets" section.

To see the iTunes equalizer, click the Equalizer button, which is the icon with three mixer faders on the bottom-right side of the iTunes window. (On a Mac, you can also choose Window⇨Equalizer.)

Adjusting the preamp volume

The *preamp* in your stereo is the component that offers a volume control that applies to all frequencies equally.

Volume knobs generally go up to 10 — except, of course, for Spinal Tap's preamps, which go to 11.

The iTunes equalizer, as shown in Figure 21-3, offers a Preamp slider on the far-left side. You can increase or decrease the volume in 3-decibel (dB) increments up to 12 dB. *Decibels* are units that measure the intensity (or volume) of the frequencies. You can adjust the volume while playing the music to hear the result right away.

Figure 21-3:
Use the
Preamp
slider to
adjust the
volume
across all
frequencies.

You might want to increase the preamp volume for songs recorded too softly, or decrease it for songs that are so loud you can hear distortion. If you want to make any adjustments to frequencies, you might need to adjust the preamp volume first if volume adjustment is needed, and then move on to the specific frequencies.

Adjusting frequencies

You can adjust frequencies in the iTunes equalizer by clicking and dragging sliders that look like mixing-board faders.

The horizontal values across the equalizer represent the spectrum of human hearing. The deepest frequency ("Daddy sang bass") is 32 hertz (Hz); the midrange frequencies are 250 Hz and 500 Hz, and the higher frequencies go from 1 kilohertz (kHz) to 16 kHz (treble).

The vertical values on each bar represent decibels, which measure the intensity of each frequency. Increase or decrease the frequencies at 3 dB increments by clicking and dragging the sliders up and down. You can drag the sliders to adjust the frequencies while the music is playing, to hear the effect immediately.

Using iTunes' presets

iTunes offers *presets,* which are equalizer settings made in advance and saved by name. You can quickly switch settings without having to make changes to each frequency slider. iTunes comes with more than 20 presets of the most commonly used equalizer settings, for each musical genre from classical to rock. You can then assign the equalizer settings to a specific song or set of songs in your iTunes library.

These settings copy to your iPod along with the songs when you update your iPod.

To use an equalizer preset, click the pop-up menu in the Equalizer window at the top of the equalizer, as shown in Figure 21-4, to select a preset. If a song is playing, you hear the effect in the sound immediately after choosing the preset.

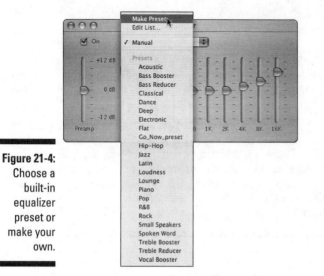

Figure 21-4: Choose a built-in equalizer preset or make your own.

Saving your own presets

You can create your own equalizer presets. When you make the changes that you want to the frequencies, and the pop-up menu automatically switches to Manual when you drag the sliders to change the frequencies. Then choose the Make Preset option from the pop-up menu (refer to Figure 21-4) to save your changes. The Make Preset dialog appears, as shown in Figure 21-5. Give your new preset a descriptive name. The name appears in the pop-up menu from that point on — your very own preset.

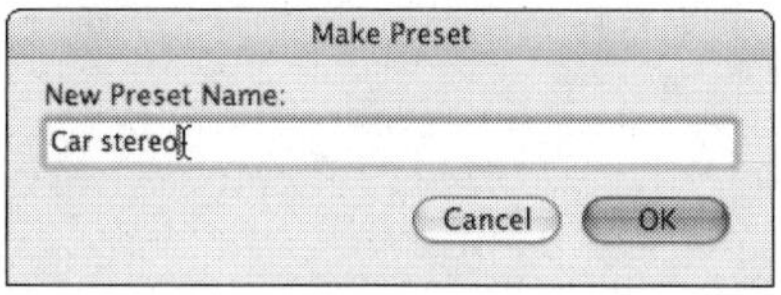

Figure 21-5: Save your adjustments as your own preset.

What's the frequency, Kenneth? The Equalizer opportunity

The Beach Boys were right when they sang "Good Vibrations" because that's what music is — the sensation of hearing audible vibrations conveyed to the ear by a medium such as air. The *frequency* of vibrations per second is how we measure pitch. The waves can fluctuate slowly and produce low-pitched sounds, or they can fluctuate rapidly and produce high-pitched sounds. The *amplitude* is a measurement of the amount of fluctuation in air pressure — therefore, amplitude is perceived as loudness.

When you turn up the bass or treble on a stereo system, you are actually increasing the volume, or intensity, of certain frequencies while the music is playing. The equalizer lets you fine-tune the sound

spectrum frequencies in a more precise way than with bass and treble controls. It increases or decreases specific frequencies of the sound to raise or lower highs, lows, and midrange tones. The equalizer does this with several band-pass filters all centered at different frequencies, and each filter offers controllable *gain* (the ability to boost the volume).

On more sophisticated stereo systems, an equalizer with a bar graph display replaces the bass and treble controls. An equalizer (*EQ* in audiospeak) enables you to fine-tune the specific sound spectrum frequencies, which gives you far greater control than merely adjusting the bass or treble controls.

You can rename or delete the presets by choosing the Edit List option from the pop-up menu, which displays the Edit Presets dialog for renaming or deleting presets, as shown in Figure 21-6. Click Rename to rename a preset, click Delete to delete a preset, and click Done when you're finished editing the list.

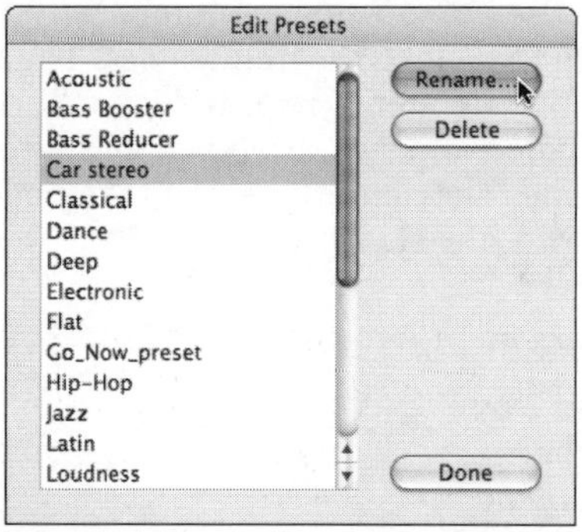

Figure 21-6:
Rename or delete presets.

Edit Presets

Acoustic
Bass Booster
Bass Reducer
Car stereo
Classical
Dance
Deep
Electronic
Flat
Go_Now_preset
Hip-Hop
Jazz
Latin
Loudness

Rename...
Delete
Done

You can rename or delete any preset, including the ones supplied with iTunes (which is useful if you want to recall a preset by another name).

Assigning equalizer presets to songs

One reason why you go to the trouble of setting equalizer presets is to assign the presets to individual songs. The next time you play the song, it will use the equalizer preset that you assigned.

When you transfer the songs to your iPod, the preset assignments stay assigned to them, and you can choose whether to use the preset assignments when playing the songs on your iPod.

Assign an equalizer preset to a song or set of songs by following these steps:

1. **Choose Edit⇨View Options.**

   The View Options dialog appears, as shown in Figure 21-7.

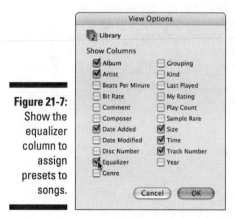

Figure 21-7: Show the equalizer column to assign presets to songs.

2. **Select the Equalizer check box and then click OK.**

   The Equalizer column appears in the song list in the iTunes window.

   You can combine Steps 1 and 2 by Control-clicking any song list column heading on a Mac (or right-clicking on a Windows PC), and then choosing Equalizer from the shortcut menu that appears.

3. **Locate a song in the song list and scroll the song list horizontally to see the Equalizer column, as shown in Figure 21-8.**

4. **Choose a preset from the pop-up menu in the Equalizer column.**

   The Equalizer column has a tiny pop-up menu that allows you to assign any preset to a song.

When you transfer songs with presets to the iPod, the presets can be used for song playback using the iPod equalizer.

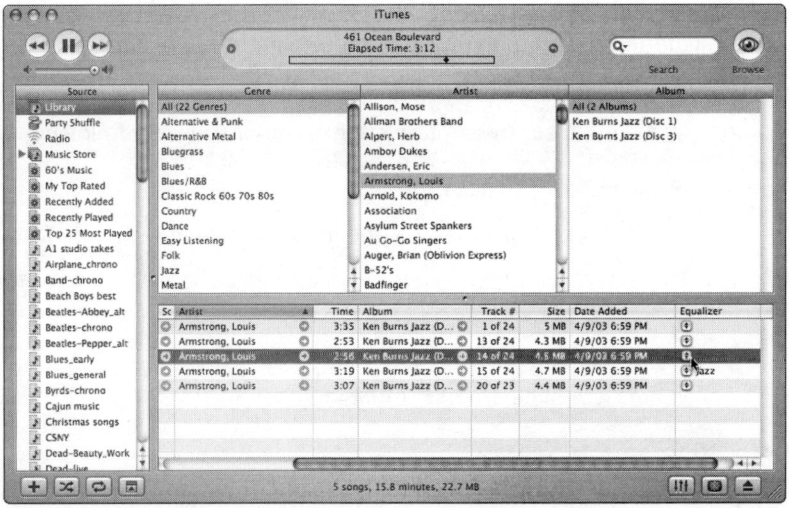

Figure 21-8:
Select a
song and
scroll the
iTunes song
list to see
the Equalizer
column.

Equalize It in Your iPod

You leave the back-road bliss of the country to get on the freeway, and now the music in your car doesn't have enough bass to give you that thumping rhythm you need to dodge other cars. What can you do? Without endangering anybody, you can pull over and select one of the iPod equalizer presets, such as Bass Booster.

Yes, your iPod also has a built-in equalizer. Like the iTunes equalizer, the iPod built-in equalizer modifies the volume of the frequencies of the sound. And although you don't have sliders for faders like the iTunes equalizer, you do get the same long list of presets to suit the type of music or the type of environment. You can use the iPod equalizer for on-the-fly adjustments.

The iPod equalizer uses a bit more battery power when it's turned on, so you might have less playing time on your iPod battery.

You can also use the iTunes equalizer to improve or enhance the sound, assigning presets to each song and then updating your iPod.

Choosing an EQ preset on your iPod

To select an iPod equalizer preset, choose Settings from the main menu and then choose EQ from the Settings menu. The EQ is set to Off until you select one of the presets.

Each EQ preset offers a different balance of frequencies designed to enhance the sound in certain ways. For example, Bass Booster increases the volume of the low (bass) frequencies; Treble Booster does the same to the high (treble) frequencies.

To see what a preset actually does to the frequencies, open the iTunes equalizer and select the same preset. The faders in the equalizer display show you exactly what the preset does.

The Off setting turns off the iPod equalizer — no presets are used, not even one you assigned in iTunes. You have to choose an EQ preset to turn on the iPod equalizer.

Applying the iTunes EQ presets

When you assign a preset to the song using iTunes, the iPod uses the assigned EQ preset from iTunes even when you choose an EQ preset on the iPod. That's right — the assigned EQ preset from iTunes takes precedence over the preset in the iPod.

Here's a workaround, though. If you know in advance that you need to use specific presets for certain songs, assign presets to the songs in iTunes before copying the songs to the iPod. If, on the other hand, you don't want the songs fixed to use a certain preset, *don't* assign presets to the songs in iTunes. You can then experiment with the presets in the iPod to get better playback in different listening environments.

To assign built-in or custom presets to songs with the iTunes equalizer, see "Assigning equalizer presets to songs," earlier in this chapter.

After assigning a preset to a song in iTunes, you turn on the iPod equalizer by choosing any EQ setting (other than Off), and the iPod uses the song's preset for playback.

Chapter 22

Recording and Editing Sound

. . . .

In This Chapter

▶ Recording cassettes, vinyl records, and other analog sources of sound

▶ Choosing a Macintosh or Windows application to record and edit sound

▶ Using MusicMatch Jukebox to record sound

▶ Defining start and stop times for a song

▶ Separating a long track into separate tracks in iTunes

. . . .

*Y*ou can find millions of songs on the Internet, and some digital recordings of songs might even be good enough to please audiophiles. With so many songs available in the iTunes Music Store for just 99 cents each, it doesn't make sense to spend a lot of time recording and digitizing the hits from your record collection, or even the B-sides and album cuts — most likely those songs are also available.

However, you might have sounds that were never released on CD or made available to the public. Rare record collectors and tape archivists — you know who you are — have sounds that you just can't find on the Internet or on CD, and if you create your own music, how do you get that stuff into your iTunes library so that you can burn a CD or include the songs on your iPod?

This chapter explains what you need to record and digitize sounds from other sources, such as tape players and turntables, and store the digital recordings in your iTunes library. It also shows you how to set the start and stop times of songs in your iTunes library, which is a trick you can use to edit the beginnings and endings of songs.

All the applications described in this chapter are commercially available for downloading from the Internet. Some are free to use, some are free for a limited time before you have to pay, and some require cash up front. Nevertheless, all are worth checking out if you have sounds you want to put into iTunes.

Recording Records, Tapes, and Analog Sources

Sound can be brought directly into your computer from a sound system or home stereo that offers a stereo audio output connection (such as Tape Out), or even directly from a cassette player or microphone. If you have old vinyl records with music that can't be found anymore, on CD or otherwise, you can convert the music to digital by using a phonograph connected to a stereo system with a Tape Out connection.

Songs already converted to digital can be copied into iTunes directly without any recording procedure. For example, MP3 CDs are easy to import. Because they're essentially data CDs, simply insert them into your CD-ROM drive, open the CD in the Finder, and drag and drop the MP3 song files into the iTunes window, as we describe in Chapter 5. Downloaded song files are even easier — just drag and drop the files into iTunes. If you drag a folder or CD icon, all the audio files that it contains are added to your iTunes library.

Before recording sound into your computer, be sure that you have enough disk space to record the audio in an uncompressed form (which is best for highest quality). If you're recording an hour of high-quality music, you need about 600MB of disk space to record it.

Connecting and setting up audio input

Most computers offer a Line In connection that accepts a cable with a stereo mini-plug. You can connect any kind of mono or stereo audio source, such as an amplifier or preamp, a CD or DVD player, or an all-in-one stereo system that offers recording through a Tape Out or similar connection.

Find the Line Out or Tape Out connection in your stereo system, and connect a cable that uses RCA-type left and right stereo plugs or a stereo mini-plug to this connection (see Chapter 16 for more information about audio cables). Connect the stereo mini-plug to your computer's Line In connection. You can then record anything that plays on your home stereo into your computer.

If your computer doesn't offer a Line In connection, you can purchase a Universal Serial Bus (USB) audio input device, such as the Griffin iMic or the Roland UA-30 for the Mac, or the Griffin PowerWave for Mac or Windows PC (www.griffintechnology.com). The PowerWave USB Audio Interface and Desktop Amplifier enables you to record any microphone or line input into your computer. The PowerWave is also an integrated desktop amplifier that you can use to connect any set of home speakers to your computer.

When recording from a phonograph (turntable for vinyl records), the phonograph must either include an amplifier or be connected to an amplifier in order to raise the signal to line levels and apply proper equalization curves.

After connecting the audio source to your computer, set the audio input for your computer and adjust the volume for recording.

On a Mac, follow these steps:

1. **Choose System Preferences from the Apple menu or the Dock, and then click the Sound icon.**

2. **Click the Input tab.**

   The Input tab displays the sound input preferences, as shown in Figure 22-1.

3. **Choose Line In from the list of input devices.**

   Use Line In to record into your computer. The alternative is to use the built-in microphone, which is useful for recording live performances — but not for records or tapes because it also picks up any noise in the room.

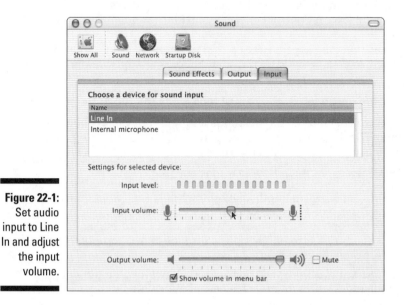

Figure 22-1:
Set audio
input to Line
In and adjust
the input
volume.

4. Adjust the volume for the Line In input.

To set the volume level for sound input, start playing the record, tape, or source of sound. As it plays, watch the input level meter. As the volume gets louder, the oblong purple dots seem to light up with highlights, from left to right. To adjust the volume, drag the slider underneath the input level meter. If all the dots are highlighted all the time, you're way too *hot* (studio tech talk for being too loud). If the dots are not highlighted at all, you're way too *low.* (For some reason, the studio techs don't say *cool* or *cold* — just *low.*) You want the dots to be highlighted about three-fourths of the way across from left to right for optimal input volume.

5. Quit System Preferences by choosing System Preferences⇨Quit System Preferences, or by clicking the red button in the top-left corner of the window.

On a Windows PC, you must have a Line In connection and an audio card driver that controls it. Some PCs are equipped only with microphone-controlling drivers, and some offer both Line In and microphone input. If you have the appropriate hardware, follow these steps:

1. Open the sound properties control panel.

In Windows XP, select Control Panel from the Start menu, and click the Sounds and Audio Devices icon. The Sounds and Audio Devices Properties window appears. Depending on your version of Windows, you might have a Control Panel specific for the audio driver and hardware, or Windows Mixer, or the Sound and Audio Devices control panel. You can open the appropriate control program by right-clicking the small speaker icon in your system tray, and choosing Adjust Audio Properties. In Windows Mixer, choose Options⇨Properties.

2. Click the Audio tab in the row of tabs along the top of the window.

As shown in Figure 22-2, the Sounds and Audio Devices Properties window offers sections for sound playback, sound recording, and MIDI (Musical Instrument Digital Interface) music playback.

3. Choose the input device for sound recording.

Use the drop-down list in the Sound recording section to choose the input device, which is the hardware for controlling the Line In connection or microphone. In Windows Mixer, select Recording under Adjust volume and then turn on the option for Line-In or Microphone to get to the Recording Control panel.

4. Click the Volume button in the Sound recording section to set the input volume.

Figure 22-2:
Set audio
input and
adjust the
volume of
input for a
Windows PC.

The Volume window offers a volume slider. Drag this slider to set the input volume (to the left is low, to the right is high).

5. Click OK to finish and save your settings.

After setting up the audio input and adjusting the volume, you need to launch an application that records sound.

Choosing a sound editing application

The Sound Studio application lets you record and digitize directly to your hard disk on a Mac running OS X. Some Mac models include a free copy of Sound Studio. (You can find it in the Applications folder.) You can also download a copy from Felt Tip Software (www.felttip.com/products/soundstudio). You can use it for two weeks before having to pay $49.99 for it.

Toast 6 Titanium from Roxio (www.roxio.com) for Mac OS X includes the CD Spin Doctor application for recording sounds. The Windows version of CD Spin Doctor is part of the Easy CD Creator 5 Platinum package from Roxio. CD Spin Doctor offers a Noise Reducer option to select filters for noise reduction: *de-click* removes loud distortions, which occur frequently with vinyl records; *de-crackle* removes surface crackling, which happens often with well-played vinyl records; and *de-hiss* removes the hissing noise that occurs with many different analog sources, including records and tapes.

Recording in Windows with MusicMatch Jukebox

You can also use MusicMatch Jukebox to record sound through a PC's Line In connection. Follow these steps:

1. **Choose Options⇨Settings and click the Recorder tab.**

2. **Select Line In from the Recording source pop-up menu.**

   Alternatively, you can choose Options⇨Recorder⇨Source ⇨Line In. MusicMatch Jukebox uses the Recorder Settings for recording the audio (which you can set by choosing Options⇨Settings⇨Recorder).

3. **Start the source sound player, and click the Record (record) button in the Recorder window to start recording from the analog source.**

   Each recorded segment is listed in the Recorder window as a separate song with a generic title.

MusicMatch Jukebox provides the Auto Song Detect option that can detect the end of a song from an analog source (such as a phonograph or tape player). To use it, choose Options⇨Settings⇨Recorder, and then click the Advanced button. Click the Active button to turn on Auto Song Detect. You can set the Gap Length, which is the amount of time between songs (typically about 1.5 seconds, or about 1,500 milliseconds [ms]) that MusicMatch Jukebox uses to determine when a song ends and another begins. You can also set the Gap Level, which tells MusicMatch Jukebox to listen for a certain volume level to determine when a song is over (typically about 10 percent of the total volume or less).

MusicMatch Jukebox saves the recording using the encoding format that you set in Recorder Settings (which you can set prior to recording by choosing Options⇨Settings⇨Recorder). The recording is automatically added to your MusicMatch Jukebox library, which you can use to update your iPod, as we describe in Chapter 12.

Modifying Songs in iTunes

Although iTunes was never meant to be a song editing application, it offers a simple control over the starting and stopping points for playing back a song. You can use this feature to cut out unwanted *intros* and *outros* of a song, such as announcers and audience applause. You can also use it in conjunction with the Convert feature to split a track into multiple tracks.

To do more significant modifications or editing, use the applications that we describe in "Recording Records, Tapes, and Analog Sources," earlier in this chapter, or use GarageBand on a Mac.

Setting the start and stop points in a song

iTunes will play only a portion of a song if you specify start and stop times within the song. To set the start and/or stop points in a song, select the song and choose File➪Get Info; then click Options to show the dialog that lets you specify the start and stop times, as shown in Figure 22-3.

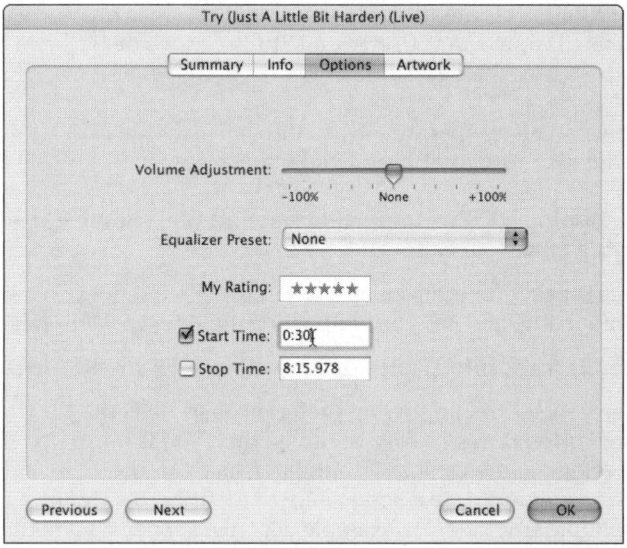

Figure 22-3:
Set the
start time
for a song.

Try (Just A Little Bit Harder) (Live)

Summary Info **Options** Artwork

Volume Adjustment: ─────────◯─────────
            –100%   None   +100%

Equalizer Preset: None

My Rating: ★★★★★

☑ Start Time: 0:30

☐ Stop Time: 8:15.978

Previous   Next   Cancel   OK

Click inside the Start Time field to set the start time; for example, in Figure 22-3, we set the Start Time to 0:30 (30 seconds). Click inside the Stop Time field to set the stop time. The time is in minutes, seconds, and hundredths of a second (decimal) — 8:15.978 is 8 minutes and 15.978 seconds.

To determine with accuracy the time for the start and stop points, play the song and look in the Status pane at the top-center part of the iTunes window for the Elapsed Time. You can drag the slider in the Status pane to move quickly through the song and find the exact times for the start and stop points you want to set. *Note:* If you click Elapsed Time in the Status pane, it toggles to Remaining Time; click it again for Total Time, and click it once more to see Elapsed Time again.

iTunes plays only the part of the song between the start and stop times. You can use this feature to your advantage because when you convert the song, iTunes converts only the part of the song between the start and stop times.

Splitting a track into multiple tracks

You might have a CD that was created with all the songs combined into one track, or you might have recorded an entire side of a vinyl record or cassette tape into one sound file. Either way, you probably want to separate the songs into separate tracks in iTunes.

The best way to split a long track into smaller tracks is to open the sound file in a sound editing program that lets you select sections and save them separately, such as CD Spin Doctor or Sound Studio, as we describe in "Recording Records, Tapes, and Analog Sources," earlier in this chapter.

However, you can also separate a track into smaller tracks in iTunes, as long as you use the AIFF format at first. Follow these steps:

1. **Before ripping a CD or importing a sound file, set the encoder in your importing preferences to AIFF.**

   Choose iTunes⇨Preferences on a Mac/Edit⇨Preferences on a Windows PC. Click Importing, and set your Importing encoder to AIFF (full quality).

2. **Rip the CD track into iTunes or import an AIFF sound file into iTunes.**

   Because you set the importing preferences to AIFF, the CD track is imported into iTunes as AIFF at full quality. You want to do this because you're going to convert it in iTunes later, and you need the uncompressed version to convert. Use a song name to identify this track as a long track with multiple tracks — for example, call it *side one* or something like that.

3. **Change your Importing preferences to AAC or MP3. (We use AAC mostly.)**

   Choose iTunes⇨Preferences on a Mac/Edit⇨Preferences on a Windows PC. Click Importing, and set your Importing encoder to AAC or MP3. Now you're ready to convert the song segments from the long track.

4. **Select the song in iTunes and choose File⇨Get Info.**

   The song information dialog appears.

5. **Click Options to show the Start Time and Stop Time fields.**

   You can set the start and stop times for the song (refer to Figure 22-3).

6. **Define the Start Time and Stop Time for the first song in the long track.**

   Play the song and look in the Status pane at the top-center part of the iTunes window for the Elapsed Time. You can drag the slider in the Status pane to move quickly through the song and find the exact times for the start and stop points you want to set. For example, if the first song were exactly 3 minutes and 12 seconds, you would define the first section to start at 0:00 and play to 3:12.

7. **Convert the defined segment of the long track from AIFF to AAC or MP3.**

   Select the long track *(side one)* and choose Advanced⇨Convert Selection to AAC (or Advanced⇨Convert Selection to MP3 if you chose the MP3 encoder in Step 6). iTunes converts only the section of the song defined by the Start Time and Stop Time fields that you set in Step 5, and creates a new song track in the AAC or MP3 format (depending on your choice in Step 3). iTunes converts the uncompressed AIFF segment into the compressed AAC or MP3 format.

8. **Change the song name of the newly converted track to the actual song name.**

   The converted section of the long track still has the same name *(side one)*. Change its name by clicking inside the song name in the iTunes song list, or by choosing File⇨Get Info, clicking the Info tab, and clicking inside the Name field. You can also enter a track number in the Track field. The converted song starts and stops as you specified in Step 5; because it's also converted to AAC or MP3, it's ready for use in your iTunes library and in your iPod.

9. **Repeat Steps 4 through 8 for each song segment.**

10. **When finished, delete the long track in AIFF format.**

    Delete the long track *(side one)* by selecting it and pressing Delete/Backspace. You don't need it anymore if you converted all the segments to separate songs.

Chapter 23

Enhancing Your Music Library

● ●

In This Chapter

▶ Downloading music from other sources

▶ Playing streaming broadcasts and Web radio in iTunes

▶ Changing the MusicMatch Jukebox look and feel

● ●

*Y*our music library is the center of your iPod and iTunes world — your control console for playing Master DJ at the party, your basement studio for burning CDs, and your archive of the most important music in the universe. Of course you would want to enhance it in any way possible.

In this chapter, we cover ways to enhance your iTunes or MusicMatch Jukebox library. We cover downloading music from online sources other than the iTunes Music Store as well as playing Web radio streams on your computer using iTunes.

Downloading Music from Other Sources

The iTunes Music Store isn't the only place to get music for your iPod online. With the launch of several digital music services over the past two years (including Napster 2.0, BuyMusic.com, MusicNow, and MusicMatch) and a growing list of new services queuing up to launch, the digital music landscape is rapidly evolving.

iTunes can store MP3, AIFF, Apple Lossless, and WAV files as well as protected AAC files. If you already have Windows Media Player version 9 or newer installed on your PC, the Windows version of iTunes can also convert unprotected Windows Media (WMA) files that don't include any digital rights management (DRM) wrappers of the sort found on files downloaded from services such as the relaunched Napster. (This is the same problem that Windows Media players have with iTunes AAC files.)

If you buy protected music in the Windows Media format or other protected format, you can always burn a CD of the music and then rip the CD into iTunes. It's a good practice to burn a CD of music that you buy online to have a backup copy in mint condition. If you download unprotected music (such as free promotions from bands), you can import the music files into iTunes if they are in the MP3 format, and with the Windows version of iTunes, you can also import unprotected Windows Media formats. See Chapter 5 for details on how to import music files into iTunes.

Music sources for iTunes and MusicMatch Jukebox

You can find music in the following types of places online:

- **From the source:** Artists and musicians are increasingly offering their music on their own Web sites for free. This is the best source of free music because it's legal and benefits the artists directly — they want you to listen and tell your friends. Examples include The Zen Tricksters (`www.zentricksters.com/home.html`), Little Feat (`www.littlefeat.net`), and the Flying Other Brothers (`www.flyingotherbros.com`).

- **Protected music:** Online music stores and services offer protected music for sale. Windows Media-protected songs and other protected formats can't be imported into iTunes because they're tied to the computer and player used for the format. However, you can burn a CD with the music (using a different player, such as Windows Media Player) and then rip the CD into iTunes. You lose no quality because burning a CD doesn't reduce the music's quality, and ripping the CD in iTunes doesn't reduce the music's quality if you use the AIFF format or the Apple Lossless encoder (or reduces quality only slightly if you use the AAC or MP3 encoders with the same or higher bit rate — see Chapter 20 for information about setting the AAC or MP3 encoder bit rate). You can also rip the CD into MusicMatch Jukebox using the WAV or MP3 encoders.

- **Unprotected music:** Some online services and Web sites offer unprotected music for sale or for free downloading as part of a promotion for artists. These sites and services typically offer MP3 or Windows Media (WMA) unprotected files that you can import directly into iTunes or MusicMatch Jukebox, and import WMA files into the Windows version of iTunes. For example, Warp Records (a prominent electronic music label) hosts Bleep.com (`www.warprecords.com/bleep`), which offers downloads of ordinary MP3s from several independent labels, without copy protection, for about $1.35 a song.

✔ **Swapped music:** Free and "pirate" networks using peer-to-peer technology allow users to "swap" music for free. That is, people can trade music, but the network essentially allows them to download music from others on the network for free. Some networks require registration for (cough) joining them so that they maintain the semblance of privacy. Others operate outside the legal jurisdiction of the U.S. copyright law and the laws of other countries. We don't like to recommend these networks for two reasons. One, the music might be pirated (and we believe copyright owners deserve to have some control over distribution, even free distribution). Two, the music might not be the highest quality because of compromises (such as lower bit rates for MP3 files, which make for poorer quality music).

If you have a choice of music formats to download, choose the highest quality format that you can download (depending on the bandwidth of your Internet connection) — typically MP3 at the highest bit rate offered. iTunes can import AIFF, WAV, AAC, Apple Lossless, and MP3 files, and the Windows version of iTunes can also import WMA (unprotected) files if you have Windows Media Player version 9 installed on your PC. MusicMatch Jukebox can import WAV, MP3, or WMA (unprotected) files. You can use AIFF, WAV, AAC, Apple Lossless, or MP3 files in your iPod, and convert files from other formats into these formats as we describe in Chapter 20.

Using the MusicMatch Jukebox Music Guide

The MusicMatch Music Guide helps you find free MP3 files on the Internet to listen to and commercial music to purchase. You can search for and download free music, music videos, and photos from popular artists. Music Guide can also make recommendations based on your personal preferences, matched to other users on the Internet with similar preferences.

Opening the Music Guide

To open Music Guide, launch MusicMatch Jukebox and choose View➪Music Guide. The Music Guide appears in place of your music library in MusicMatch Jukebox, as shown in Figure 23-1. You can find an artist or pick artists in a particular genre by clicking Browse Artist. Here you'll find an extensive list of genres (such as Rock, Classical, Bluegrass, Gospel, and so on), or you can enter an artist or album name. Click each artist to display a discography, the artist biography, and music that you can either download for free or purchase.

Figure 23-1:
Browse the
MusicMatch
Jukebox
Music Guide
on the
Internet.

Music-matching in the Guide

You can take advantage of the free music-matching service built into Music Guide, which finds music that suits your tastes based on your personal preferences. Music Guide compares your downloads and purchases with those of others who have downloaded or purchased music. Then it provides recommendations based on matches.

To use the music-matching service, click the Recommendations button in the Music Guide window, and then click the Sign Up Now button. Registration takes place automatically, and MusicMatch Jukebox compares your music with others that use the Music Guide. After a few minutes, the music-matching service has enough information, and recommendations start to appear that match the music others with similar tastes have bought or downloaded.

While installing MusicMatch Jukebox, the default setting is to opt into this service — meaning that it's automatically turned on. The service delivers recommendations based on personal preferences, but you might not want to share your information. If you choose to continue to participate in this feature, MusicMatch Jukebox periodically uploads your listening preferences so that the Music Guide can make better recommendations. However, if you don't want to participate, turn off the Personalize Music Recommendations option during installation.

Opting out of the Music Guide

To later opt out of this service, after installing the program, choose Options⇨ Settings and click the General tab for the program's general settings. Disable the Upload User Preference Information Based on Listening Profile option. To opt in at any time, you can turn this option back on. With this option enabled, MusicMatch Jukebox uploads to Music Guide the songs that you've played and compares them with other Music Guide users.

Playing Streaming Radio in iTunes

Radio stations from nearly every part of the world are broadcasting on the Internet. You can tune into Japan-A-Radio for the top 40 hits in Japan, or Cable Radio UK from the south coast of England, or Radio Darvish for Persian traditional music. You can also check out the local news and sports from your hometown, no matter where you are. You can listen to talk radio and music shows from all over the country and the world.

By *radio,* we really mean a *streaming broadcast;* of course, real radio stations make use of this technology to broadcast their programs over the Internet. A streaming broadcast sends audio to your computer in a protected stream of bits over the Internet. Your computer starts playing the stream as soon as the first set of bits arrive, and more sections are transferred while you listen, so that you hear it as a continual stream. Broadcasters can use this technology to continually transmit new content (like a radio station).

In addition, thousands of Web sites offer temporary streaming audio broadcasts all the time. A rock group on tour can offer a broadcast of a special concert, available for only one day. You might want to tune in weekly or monthly broadcasts such as high-tech talk shows, news programs, documentaries, or sporting events . . . the list is endless. You can even have access to private broadcasts such as corporate board meetings.

You can't record or save a song from a streamed broadcast without special software. Nor can you play a streaming broadcast on your iPod. But you *can* add your favorite stations to your iTunes music library to tune in quickly and easily. You can also tune in any MP3 streaming broadcast if you know the Web address.

iTunes offers a set links to radio stations on the Internet, so you might want to try these first. Follow these steps:

1. **Select the Radio option in the Source pane.**

   The iTunes window displays a list of categories of radio stations.

2. **Click the Refresh button to retrieve the latest radio stations.**

   More Web radio stations are added all the time. The Refresh button in the top-right corner of the iTunes window (taking the place of the Browse button) connects iTunes to the Internet to retrieve the latest list of radio stations for each category.

3. **Open a category to see a list of stations in that category.**

   Click the triangle next to a category name to open the list of radio streams in that category. Some large radio stations offer more than one stream.

4. **Select a stream and click the Play button.**

   To select a stream, click its name in the iTunes song list (actually, radio station list because you selected Radio in the Source pane). Then click the iTunes Play button. Within seconds, you hear live radio off the Web.

If you use a dial-up modem connection to the Internet, you might want to choose a stream with a bit rate of less than 56 Kbps for best results. The Bit Rate column shows the bit rate for each stream.

iTunes creates a buffer for the audio stream so that you hear continuous playback with fewer Internet-related hiccups than most Web radio software. The buffer temporarily stores as much of the stream as possible, adding more of the stream to the end of the buffer as you play the audio in the buffer. If you hear stutters, gaps, or hiccups when playing a stream, set your buffer to a larger size by choosing iTunes⇨Preferences on a Mac/Edit⇨Preferences on a Windows PC. In the Preferences dialog, click the Advanced button and then choose a size from the Streaming Buffer Size pop-up menu. Your choices are Small, Medium, or Large (sorry, no X-Large).

Car radios offer preset stations activated by you pressing a button. Of course, you first need to tune into the station of your choice to set that button. You can save your radio station choices in an iTunes playlist, and the process is just as easy:

1. **Select a radio station stream.**

2. **Create a playlist or scroll the Source pane to an existing playlist.**

   See Chapter 10 to discover how to create a playlist.

3. **Drag the stream name over the playlist name.**

   iTunes places the stream name in the playlist with a broadcast icon next to it. You can click the playlist name and rearrange the playlist as you want, dragging stream names as you would drag song names.

Drag as many steams as you like to as many playlists as you like. Radio streams in your playlists play only if you are connected to the Internet.

To quickly create a playlist from selected radio streams, first select the streams just as you would select multiple songs, and then choose File⇨New Playlist from Selection.

You can tune into any broadcast on the Internet. All you need to know is the Web address, also known as the *URL* (Uniform Resource Locator), which is the global address of documents and other resources on the Web. You can find most URLs from a Web site or e-mail about a broadcast.

Follow these steps to add a Web broadcast to a playlist:

1. **Choose Advanced⇨Open Stream.**

   The Open Stream dialog appears, with a URL text field for typing a Web address.

2. **Type the exact, full URL of the stream.**

   Include the `http://` prefix, as in `http://64.236.34.141:80/ stream/1014`.

   If you're connected to the Internet, iTunes automatically retrieves the broadcast and places it at the end of your song list.

3. **Click OK.**

As of this writing, iTunes supports only MP3 broadcasts. You can find lots of MP3 broadcasts from SHOUTcast (`www.shoutcast.com`) and Live365.com (`http://live365.com`).

Changing the MusicMatch Jukebox Look and Feel

Like many Windows applications, MusicMatch Jukebox can change its look and feel by adopting a different graphical user interface design. You can choose a *skin* that provides the same set of buttons to perform tasks such as increasing volume, opening the library, burning a music CD, and so on, but they are much cooler looking than the usual MusicMatch Jukebox look (which is itself a skin). Skins are changeable, and you can impress your friends by downloading new ones from the MusicMatch site.

To the tune, "Lose This Skin" by The Clash, follow these steps to change the MusicMatch Jukebox skin:

1. **Right-click inside the media panel.**

   A contextual menu appears, as shown in Figure 23-2.

2. **Choose a skin from the drop-down menu.**

   The pop-up menu offers skins that were downloaded or supplied with MusicMatch Jukebox.

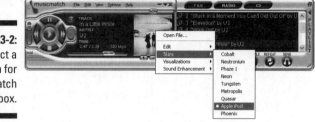

Figure 23-2:
Select a
new skin for
MusicMatch
Jukebox.

After selecting the skin, MusicMatch Jukebox changes its look and feel
automatically.

To download more skins from the Internet, first make sure that you're connected to the Internet, and then follow these steps:

1. Choose Download Skins from the View menu in MusicMatch Jukebox.

The Download Skins window appears with skins that you can download.

2. Click a skin in the Download Skins window.

The skin downloads and installs itself automatically, displaying a
progress window.

After installing the new skin, you can switch from the newly downloaded skin
to any other skin and back again, by right-clicking the media pane and choosing the skin from the Skins pop-up menu.

Part V
Have iPod, Will Travel

The 5th Wave By Rich Tennant

"Why can't you just bring your iPod like everyone else?"

In this part . . .

This part explains how you can use your iPod to take care of personal business the way people often use PDAs — especially on the road. It also covers how to troubleshoot problems with your iPod.

- ✔ Chapter 24 covers managing your life on the road waking up with the alarm clock, playing games, sorting your contacts, recording voice memos, and customizing the iPod menu and display settings.

- ✔ Chapter 25 is about using your iPod as a hard drive, and it includes saving files, storing notes and text, storing photos, and even saving a copy of the Mac system on your iPod.

- ✔ Chapter 26 shows you how to use both Apple and Microsoft applications to enter personal contact and calendar information in preparation for iPod synchronization.

- ✔ Chapter 27 describes synchronizing your iPod with personal information by using iSync. Here you can also find out about adding information manually to your iPod so that you don't miss any of your appointments or forget anybody's name.

- ✔ Chapter 28 gets into the nitty-gritty of troubleshooting iPod problems, including how to use the iPod Updater to update or restore your iPod.

Chapter 24

Sleeping with Your iPod

. . . .

In This Chapter

▶ Setting the time, date, and sleep functions

▶ Setting up your iPod as an alarm clock

▶ Changing the iPod display settings

▶ Playing games

▶ Checking your calendar and sorting your contacts

▶ Recording voice memos on your iPod

▶ Customizing your iPod menus and settings

. . . .

*Y*ou might have purchased an iPod simply to listen to music, but those thoughtful engineers at Apple who get to travel a lot with their iPods put a lot more into this device.

As we show in this chapter, your iPod keeps time, and you can use it as an alarm clock to awaken you to your favorite music (or just a beep). In particular, you can alleviate the boredom of travel with games, and check the time, date, and month (in case you're stranded for a long time). You can also check your calendar and To-Do list, and look up contact names, addresses, and phone numbers. You can even speak into your iPod and record dictation, conversations, or notes. You can also make your iPod more convenient to use while traveling by customizing the iPod menu.

Setting Date, Time, and Sleep Functions

All iPods running iPod software version 2.0 or newer have a digital clock that doubles as an alarm clock and a sleep timer. To access the clock, choose Extras⇨Clock from the main menu.

To set the date and time, follow these steps:

1. **Press the Menu button.**

2. **Choose Extras⇨Clock.**

   The clock appears with menu selections underneath (except in older models).

   You can also set the date and time by choosing Settings⇨Date & Time from the main menu.

3. **Select the Date & Time option.**

   The Date & Time menu appears.

4. **Select the Set Time Zone option.**

   A list of time zones appears in alphabetical order.

5. **Scroll the Time Zone list and select a time zone.**

   The Date & Time menu appears again.

6. **Select the Set Date & Time option.**

   The Date & Time display appears with up and down arrow indicators over the hour field, which is now highlighted.

7. **Change the field setting using the scroll wheel.**

   Scroll clockwise to go forward and counterclockwise to go backward.

8. **Press the Select button after scrolling to the appropriate setting.**

   The up and down arrow indicators move over to the minutes field, which is now highlighted.

9. **Repeat Steps 7 and 8 for each field of the date and time: minutes, AM/PM, the calendar date, calendar month, and year.**

When you finish setting the year by pressing the Select button, the Date & Time menu appears again. You can select the Time option and press the Select button to show the number of hours from 1 to 24 (military style).

You can also select the Time option, and press the Select button to show the time in the menu title of your iPod menus.

Just like a clock radio, you can set your iPod to play music for a while before going to sleep. To set the sleep timer, select the Sleep Timer option from the Clock menu. A list of intervals, from 0 (Off) to 120 minutes (2 hours) appears, in 15-minute increments. You can select a time amount or the Off setting (at the top of the list) to turn off the sleep timer. After the iPod shuts itself off (after you hold down the pause button, or it remains idle for a few minutes and shuts itself off), the preference for the Sleep Timer is reset to the default status, Off.

Setting the Alarm Clock

Time is on your side with the iPod Alarm Clock function, which is located in the iPod Clock menu (found only in newer models). To set the Alarm Clock, follow these steps:

1. **Choose Extras⇨Clock⇨Alarm Clock from the main menu.**

   The Alarm Clock menu appears, as shown in Figure 24-1.

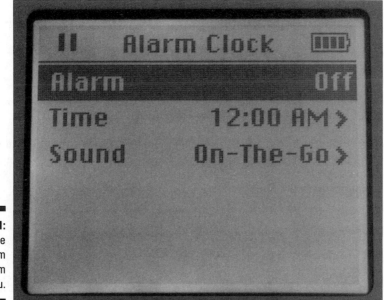

Figure 24-1:
Set the time
for the alarm
in the Alarm
Clock menu.

2. **Highlight the Alarm option and press the Select button (Off changes to On).**

3. **Select the Time option.**

   The Alarm Time menu appears with up and down arrow indicators.

4. **Change the time using the scroll wheel.**

   Scroll clockwise to go forward and counterclockwise to go backward.

5. **Press the Select button after scrolling to the appropriate alarm time.**

   The Alarm Clock menu appears again.

6. **Select the Sound option in the Alarm Clock menu.**

   A list appears, with the Beep option at the top of the list, followed by playlists on your iPod in alphabetical order.

7. **Choose an option as the alarm sound, and then press the Select button.**

   If you choose Beep, the alarm beeps without the need for any headphones or speakers. If you choose a playlist, when the alarm goes off, the playlist plays until you stop it by pressing the Play/Pause button. Of course, you need speakers or headphones to hear the music.

8. **You can return to the main menu by pressing Menu until you see the main menu.**

   When the alarm goes off, the playlist (or beep tone) plays until you stop the alarm by pressing the Play/Pause button.

Choosing Display Settings

Your future may be so bright that you got to wear shades, but your iPod display might need a bit of an adjustment to see it better in bright sunlight or the dark of night. With the iPod Settings menu, you can change the timer for the backlight and also set the contrast for better visibility. Choose the Settings menu from the iPod main menu.

Backlight timer

Ordinarily, your iPod display's backlight turns on when you press a button or use the scroll wheel, and then it turns off after a short amount of time. On third-generation iPods, the backlight also lights up the iPod buttons.

You can set the backlight to remain on for a certain interval of time. Choose Settings from the iPod main menu and then select Backlight Timer. A menu appears — 2 seconds, 5 seconds, 10 seconds, and so on. Select one by scrolling to highlight the selection, and then press the Select button.

The backlight drains the iPod battery; the longer you set the interval, the more frequently you need to recharge the battery.

You can turn off the backlight at any time by pressing and holding down the Menu button. You can also turn off the backlight and the iPod by pressing down and holding the Play/Pause button. The backlight turns on when you press any button or use the scroll wheel. You can also turn on the backlight by selecting Backlight from the iPod main menu.

You can also set the backlight to *always* be on or *always* be off. If you set it to always be off, the backlight doesn't turn on automatically when you press any button or use the scroll wheel. You can still turn it on, however, by pressing and holding the Menu button or by selecting Backlight from the main menu.

The backlight isn't that useful when the display is tilted toward direct sunlight. As we discuss in the next section, it's better to adjust the contrast to get better visibility in bright lighting conditions.

 Don't be alarmed if your backlight turns itself on at midnight for a brief flash. The iPod is just setting its internal clock. If you find this annoying, turn the Backlight Timer to off.

Contrast for better visibility

You can set the contrast of the iPod display to make the black characters appear sharper against the display background. You might need to adjust the contrast after a sharp temperature difference freezes or bakes your iPod. If you kept your iPod in your car overnight in the cold, or even in direct sunlight for a time, the contrast can change so much that you can't see your iPod display. Allow the iPod to warm up (slowly — don't use the oven or microwave) if it's cold, or cool down if the display is hot, and then adjust the contrast.

To adjust the contrast, choose Settings from the iPod main menu, and then choose Contrast from the Settings menu. The Contrast screen appears with a slider that shows the contrast setting, which ranges from low contrast (a black-and-white dot) to high contrast (a full black dot). Scroll clockwise to increase the contrast (toward the black dot) and counterclockwise to decrease the contrast (toward the black-and-white dot).

If you accidentally set the contrast too dark or too light, you can reset it to the halfway point between too dark and too light by pressing and holding down the Menu button for at least four seconds.

Playing Games

The games that come with the iPod — Brick, Parachute, and Solitaire — are a bit dorky for the information age, but hey, they're extras. Music Quiz, on the other hand, is a cool way to test your knowledge of your music library.

To find the games, choose Extras⇨Games (Extras⇨Game on older iPods). And of course you can listen to music while you play.

Brick and Parachute

Brick is like the original version of Breakout for the Atari. To access this game, choose Extras⇨Games⇨Brick (Extras⇨Game on older iPods), and press the Select button to start the game. Move the paddle from side to side along the bottom of the display by scrolling with the scroll wheel. You get a point for each brick you knock out. If you break out — knock out all the bricks — you move up a level in the game, and the game starts again.

Parachute is a crude shoot-'em-up game where you play the role of an antiaircraft gunner. Choose Extras⇨Games⇨Parachute, and press the Select button to start the game. You pivot the gun at the bottom with the scroll wheel. Press the Select button to fire on helicopters and paratroopers. Don't let the paratroopers reach the ground, or else they'll heave grenades at you. War is hell.

Solitaire

Rather than playing the card game *'til one, with a deck of 51,* try the iPod version of Solitaire (known as "Klondike"). Choose Extras⇨Games⇨Solitaire, and press the Select button to start the game. To move cards, place the hand pointer over a card by scrolling the scroll wheel, and press the Select button to select the card. Then scroll again to move the hand pointer to the new location for the card, and press Select to place the card at that position. To deal out another round of three cards, move the hand pointer over the card deck in the top-left corner of the display, and press the Select button. After going through an entire deck, the game places the remaining cards into a new deck so that you can continue dealing cards. The game improves considerably in a smoke-filled room with take-out pizza nearby; gangsters are optional.

Music Quiz

Music Quiz tests your knowledge of your music library and is probably the greatest time-waster of them all. The game plays the first few seconds of a song picked at random from your iPod. Choose Extras⇨Games⇨Music Quiz, put on your headphones or connect your iPod to speakers, and press the Select button to start the game. As the song plays, you have ten seconds to pick the song title from a list of five titles. If you choose the wrong title, the game displays Incorrect! and moves on to the next one. If you choose the right title, you gain points and move on to the next one. ("Life's a Long Song" by Jethro Tull would be appropriate.)

Checking Your Calendar

Imagine a musician going backstage after a performance and meeting a promoter who says he can get him ten more gigs if he can confirm the dates *right now.* This musician happens to carry around an iPod, and amid the backstage craziness, he scrolls through his calendar for the entire year, finding all the details he needs about gigs and recording sessions, right down to the minute, including travel directions to each gig. "No problem," the musician says.

Your iPod has a standard calendar that you can view by choosing Extras⇨ Calendars⇨All. Select a calendar and then use the scroll wheel to scroll through the days of the calendar. Select an event to see the event's details. Press the Next and Previous buttons to skip to the next or previous month. To see your To-Do list, choose Extras⇨Calendars⇨To Do.

If your calendar events use alarms, you can turn on the iPod's calendar alarms. Choose Extras⇨Calendars⇨Alarms. Select Alarms once to set the alarm to Beep, or once again to set it to Silent (so that only the message for the alarm appears), or one more time to set if to Off. (The Alarms choices cycle from Beep to Silent to Off and then back to Beep.)

Calendars are far more useful if you enter your personal information as we describe in Chapter 26.

Sorting Your Contacts

The most likely bits of information that you might need on the road are someone's phone number or address (or both). The iPod stores up to 1,000 contacts right alongside your music. To see how to put your personal contacts into your iPod, see Chapter 26.

The iPod contact list is sorted automatically, and the iPod displays contact names in alphabetical order when you select Extras⇨Contacts. You can choose whether to display contacts by last or first name. Choose Settings⇨Contacts⇨ Display; then press the Select button in the scrolling pad for each option:

- ✔ **First Last:** Displays the contact list by first name and the last name, as in *Ringo Starr.*

- ✔ **Last, First:** Displays the contact list by last name followed by a comma and the first name, as in *McCartney, Paul.*

You can also change how the contacts sort so that you don't have to look up people by their first names (which can be time-consuming with so many friends named Elvis). The sort operation uses the entire name, but you decide whether to use the first name or the surname first. Choose Settings⇨ Contacts⇨Sort. Press the Select button in the scrolling pad for each option:

✔ **First Last:** Sorts the contact list by first name, followed by the last name, so that *Mick Jagger* sorts under *Mick* (after Mick Abrahams but before Mick Taylor).

✔ **Last, First:** Sorts the contacts by last name, followed by the first name, so that *Brian Jones* sorts under *Jones.* (*Jones, Brian* appears after *Jones, Alice* but before *Jones, Norah.*)

Speaking into Your iPod

Do you record conversations and interviews on the road? Throw out that tape recorder. Your iPod can record hundreds of hours of voice-quality memos, meetings, notes, and interviews with a touch of a button. All you need is an accessory that includes a microphone, such as the tiny Belkin iPod Voice Recorder (www.belkin.com), $59.95, which fits right on top of your iPod. The voice memos are stored on your iPod where you can review them immediately using the built-in speaker of the accessory or your head-phones or speakers. Even better, the voice memos are automatically trans-ferred to your iTunes library for archiving or reviewing on your computer.

The Belkin iPod Voice Recorder attaches to the remote connector on the top of full-size third-generation and fourth-generation iPods (updated by version 2.1 of the iPod software or newer).

Recording voice memos

To record voice memos, connect the Belkin iPod Voice Recorder to the iPod and choose Extras⇨Voice Memos⇨Record Now. The iPod displays the Record screen. Press the Play/Pause button to begin recording, and hold the iPod as you would a microphone, with the Voice Recorder pointing at the sound source (or your mouth for your voice). The green LED on the Voice Recorder turns on when you are recording. You can pause the recording by pressing the Play/ Pause button again.

When you finish recording, press the Menu button. The audio files for voice memos are stored on your iPod in the Recordings folder, using the date and time of the recording as the filename.

Playing back voice memos

To play back a voice memo, choose Extras⇨Voice Memos and choose the voice memo from the list. (The Voice Memos menu doesn't appear unless you have already connected the Belkin Voice Recorder at least once.) Then select Play (or press the Play/Pause button).

The voice memo plays just like any other song on your iPod — you can press Play/Pause to pause playback, and press it again to resume. You hear the playback in the Belkin Voice Recorder's tiny speaker, attach headphones to your iPod, or connect your iPod to a home stereo, car stereo, or self-powered speakers.

You can play music through the Belkin Voice Recorder's speaker by connecting the accessory to your iPod and playing. This comes in handy if you set your iPod as an alarm clock to play a music playlist; you can hear music when you wake up without having to connect the iPod to speakers. See the earlier section, "Setting the Alarm Clock."

Managing voice memos in iTunes

Just like your music, your voice memos synchronize automatically with your iTunes library if you set your iPod to update automatically. (See Chapter 11 to discover how to set your iPod to update automatically.) iTunes stores the voice memos in the library and creates a playlist named Voice Memos, as shown in Figure 24-2, so that you can find them easily.

If you update your iPod manually, you can drag voice memo files directly from the Recordings folder to your hard drive, or drag and drop them over the iTunes window. *Note:* The iPod must already be enabled as a hard drive. (Flip to Chapter 25 to see how to enable your iPod as a hard drive.)

Voice memos are stored as WAV files. If you want to archive them in a format that takes up less hard drive space, convert them by using the AAC or MP3 encoder, as we describe in Chapter 20.

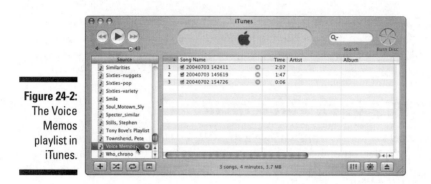

Figure 24-2:
The Voice
Memos
playlist in
iTunes.

Customizing the Menu and Settings

When traveling or using your iPod in situations or environments where porta-bility is important, you might want to customize your iPod menu and display to make doing things easier, such as selecting certain albums, displaying the time, displaying menus with backlighting turned on longer than usual, and so on.

The Settings menu in the iPod main menu offers ways to customize your iPod experience by changing the main menu to have more choices. Choose the Settings menu from the main menu, and then choose Main Menu. The iPod displays a list of menus; each menu is set to either On or Off. On means the menu appears in the iPod main menu; Off means the menu does not appear in the main menu. (Don't worry; the menus are still where they are supposed to be. Turning one to On simply adds it to the main menu as well.)

Other ways to customize your experience include setting the clicker sound and setting the language to use for the menus. The options in the Settings menu include

- **About:** This displays information about the iPod, including number of songs, how much space is used, how much space is available, the soft-ware version in use, and the serial number.

- **Main Menu:** This allows you to customize the main menu on iPods that use iPod software 2.0 or newer. For example, you can add items from other menus, such as Artists or Songs from the Music menu (Browse menu in older iPods), to the main menu.

- **Backlight Timer:** You can set the backlight to remain on for a certain amount of time by pressing a button or using the scroll wheel. Specify two seconds, five seconds, and so on. You can also set it to always be on.

The backlight drains the iPod battery; the longer you set the interval, the more you need to recharge the battery.

✔ **Contrast:** You can set the contrast of the iPod display by using the scroll wheel to increase or decrease the slider in the Contrast screen. If you accidentally set the contrast too dark, you can reset it by holding down the Menu button for at least four seconds.

✔ **Clicker:** When this setting is on, you hear a click when you press a button; when it's off, you don't hear a click.

✔ **Language:** This sets the language used in all the menus. See Chapter 1 for how to set the language.

✔ **Legal:** This displays the legal message that accompanies Apple products.

✔ **Reset All Settings:** This resets all the Settings menu settings in your iPod, returning them to the state they were in originally. However, your music and data files on the iPod are not disturbed. This is not the same as resetting (and restarting) the iPod software itself; Reset All Settings simply returns all settings to their defaults. See Chapter 1 for how to reset the iPod itself.

Chapter 25

Using the iPod as a Hard Drive

In This Chapter

▶ Mounting your iPod as a hard drive for a Mac or a Windows PC

▶ Copying notes and text files to your iPod

▶ Storing photos on your iPod

▶ Storing Mac OS X on your iPod for emergencies

*Y*ou have a device in your pocket that can play weeks of music, sort your contacts, remind you of events, wake you up in the morning, and tuck you in at night. Did you also know that you can use your iPod to keep a safe backup of your most important files?

You read that right. Mac users can even put a version of the Mac system on the iPod in case of emergencies. (Unfortunately, you can't do this with Windows.) Apple doesn't recommend putting the Mac system on the iPod because using the iPod as a startup hard drive might make your iPod too hot from overuse, but you can do it. You can also copy applications and utility programs that you might need on the road or even copy your entire User folder to the iPod if you have room after putting music on it.

But that's not all. With full-size third-generation and fourth-generation iPods (which can connect with the dock-type connector), you can use accessories to extend your iPod's capabilities. For example, you can use the Belkin Media Reader for iPod to store photos from digital camera memory cards. There's even software, such as Pod2Go, that offers synchronized feeds that supply your iPod with news, weather forecasts, and even sections of Web pages that you can read on the iPod screen.

The key to these capabilities is the fact that the iPod serves as an external hard drive. After you mount the iPod on your Mac or Windows desktop, you can use it as a hard drive, but do so sparingly.

We don't recommend using the iPod regularly as a hard drive to launch applications. The iPod is designed more for sustained playback of music, and you can eventually burn out the device by using it to launch applications all the time. Instead, use it as an external hard drive for backing up and copying files, and use it in emergency situations for starting up the system.

Mounting the iPod as a Hard Drive

Your iPod can double as an external hard drive. And like any hard drive, you can transfer files and applications from your computer to your iPod and take them with you wherever you go. The iPod is smart enough to keep your files separate from your music collection so that you don't accidentally erase them when you update your music. And because your iPod is *with you,* it's as safe as you are.

The iPod, as shipped, is formatted as a Macintosh hard drive and can be connected to any Mac. When you connect it to Windows, the iPod is reformatted as a Windows hard drive. You can then connect it to any Windows PC or any Mac. (Macs can read hard drives that are formatted for PCs.)

Setting up the hard drive iPod on a Mac

To use your iPod as an external hard drive on a Mac, follow these steps:

1. **Connect your iPod to your Mac.**

2. **Select the iPod name in the iTunes Source pane.**

3. **Click the iPod Options button.**

   The iPod Preferences dialog opens, as shown in Figure 25-1.

4. **Select the Enable Disk Use option and click OK.**

   The Enable Disk Use option is available if your iPod is set to automatically update. You must select this option to use your iPod as a hard drive. If you already set your iPod to manual updating (as we describe in Chapter 11), this option is grayed out because it isn't needed — setting the iPod to update manually automatically enables you to use it as a hard drive.

5. **Open the iPod icon in the Finder to see its contents.**

   The iPod hard drive opens up to show three folders — Calendars, Contacts, and Notes, as you can see in Figure 25-2. You can add new folders, rename your new folders, and generally use the iPod as a hard drive, but don't rename these three folders; they link directly to the Calendar, Contacts, and Notes functions on the iPod.

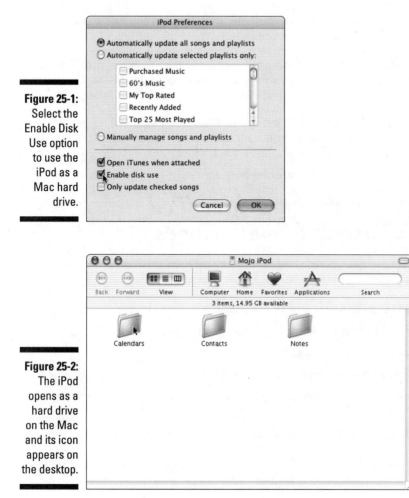

Figure 25-1:
Select the
Enable Disk
Use option
to use the
iPod as a
Mac hard
drive.

Figure 25-2:
The iPod
opens as a
hard drive
on the Mac
and its icon
appears on
the desktop.

6. *Optional:* **Drag files or folders to the iPod window.**

   To keep data organized, create new folders on the iPod, and then drag files and folders that you want to copy to the newly created folders.

7. **Before disconnecting the iPod, eject the iPod from the system.**

   Click the Eject button next to the iPod name in the Finder or drag the iPod icon to the Trash.

After ejecting the iPod, its display shows the `OK to disconnect` message on older models, or the main menu. You can then disconnect the iPod from its dock or disconnect the dock from the computer. Don't ever disconnect an iPod before ejecting it. You might have to reset your iPod. (If you do, head to Chapter 1.)

To delete files and folders from the iPod, drag them to the Trash just like an external hard drive.

Don't use a hard drive utility program, such as Disk Utility or Drive Setup, to erase or format the iPod's hard drive. If you erase your iPod's hard drive in this way, it might be unable to play music.

To see how much free space is left on the iPod, you can use the Finder. Select the iPod icon on the desktop, and then choose File⇨Show Info. You can also choose Settings⇨About from the iPod's main menu.

Setting up the hard drive iPod on a Windows PC with iTunes

You can set up your iPod to use as an external hard drive on a Windows PC by using iTunes. If you use iTunes, follow these steps:

1. **Connect your iPod to your computer.**

2. **Select the iPod name in the iTunes Source pane.**

3. **Click the iPod Options button.**

   The iPod Preferences dialog opens, as shown in Figure 25-3.

4. **Select the Enable Disk Use option and click OK.**

   The Enable Disk Use option is available if your iPod is set to automatically update. You must select this option to use your iPod as a hard drive. If you already set your iPod to manual updating (as we describe in Chapter 11), this option is grayed out because it isn't needed — setting the iPod to update manually automatically enables you to use it as a hard drive.

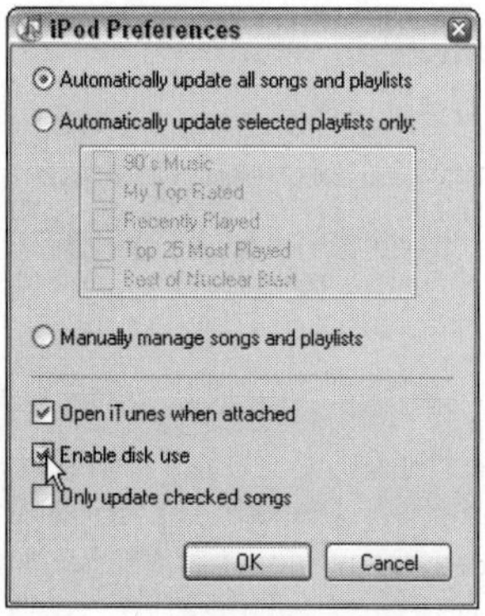

Figure 25-3:
Select the Enable Disk Use option to use the iPod as a Windows hard drive.

5. **Double-click the iPod icon in the My Computer or Windows Explorer window to see its contents.**

   If you open the My Computer window, the iPod appears as an external hard drive, as shown in Figure 25-4. The iPod in the figure is named *Journeyman* and assigned to drive G. Windows automatically assigns the iPod hard drive to a Windows drive letter.

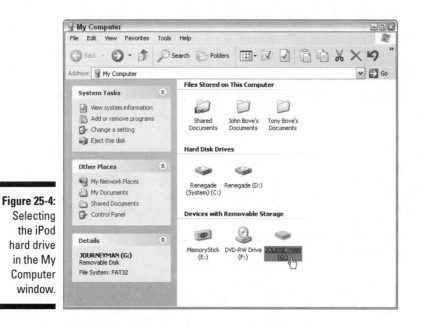

Figure 25-4: Selecting the iPod hard drive in the My Computer window.

The iPod hard drive opens up to show three folders — Calendars, Contacts, and Notes. You can add new folders, rename your new folders, and generally use the iPod as a hard drive, but don't rename these three folders; they link directly to the Calendar, Contacts, and Notes functions on the iPod.

6. *Optional:* **Copy files or folders to the iPod.**

   To keep data organized, create new folders on the iPod, and then copy files and folders to the newly created folders by using the drag-and-drop method in the My Computer window or Windows Explorer, or by copying and pasting.

7. **Before disconnecting the iPod, eject the iPod from Windows.**

   Right-click the iPod name or icon and choose Eject from the shortcut menu. You can do this from within iTunes by clicking the Eject button next to the iPod's name in the Source pane.

After ejecting the iPod, it displays the `OK to disconnect` message on older models, or the main menu. You can then disconnect the iPod from its dock or disconnect the dock from the computer. Don't ever disconnect an iPod before ejecting it. You might have to reset your iPod. (If you do, head to Chapter 1.)

To delete files and folders from the iPod, select the filename and press Delete, or choose File⇨Delete from the Windows Explorer menu, just like you do on your internal hard drive.

Don't use the Windows formatting utility or third-party hard drive utility program to erase or format the iPod's hard drive. If you erase the hard drive in your iPod in this way, it may be unable to play music.

To see how much free space is left on the iPod, select the iPod icon in My Computer and choose File⇨Properties. You can also choose Settings⇨ About from the iPod's main menu.

Setting up the hard drive iPod on a Windows PC with MusicMatch Jukebox

If you use MusicMatch Jukebox, you can enable the iPod to work as a hard drive in Windows by using MusicMatch Jukebox or the iPod Manager utility installed with MusicMatch Jukebox. Follow these steps:

1. **Connect your iPod to your PC and wait for MusicMatch Jukebox to recognize it.**

   Your iPod should appear in the PortablesPlus window under the Attached Portable Devices folder. If the PortablesPlus window isn't yet open, choose File⇨Send to Portable Device.

2. **Select the iPod, click the Options button, and then click the iPod tab.**

3. **Select the Enable Disk Mode option.**

4. **Click OK to close the Options window.**

You can use the iPod Manager utility, installed with iPod for Windows and MusicMatch Jukebox, to change iPod settings, launch the software updater, check the Apple site for updates, and change the home application for the iPod (set to MusicMatch Jukebox by default). To use iPod Manager, follow these steps:

1. **Connect your iPod to the Windows PC.**

2. **Launch iPod Manager.**

   To launch iPod Manager, you can right-click the iPod icon and choose iPod Manager from the shortcut menu, or open iPod Manager directly by choosing Start Menu⇨All Programs⇨iPod⇨iPod Manager. The iPod Manager dialog appears, as shown in Figure 25-5.

3. **Select the Enable Disk Mode option in the iPod Manager dialog.**

4. **Click OK to close the iPod Manager dialog.**

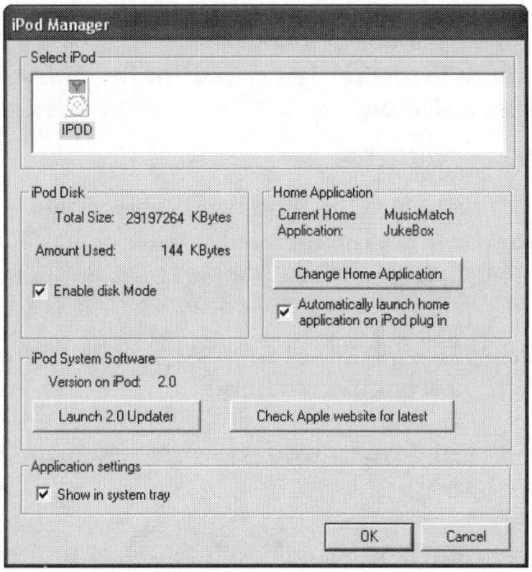

Figure 25-5:
Using iPod
Manager to
enable the
iPod as a
hard drive in
Windows.

To see how much free space is left on your iPod, check the iPod Disk area in the iPod Manager dialog, which shows you the total amount of storage space on your iPod and the amount already used.

You can now open your iPod in the My Computer window to see its contents and use it as an external hard drive, just like any storage device connected to your Windows PC. The iPod is assigned a drive letter, such as E. (The letter chosen depends on how many devices you already have connected to the PC.)

When you finish using your iPod as a hard drive, eject the iPod by using one of the following ways:

   ✔ Click the Eject button in MusicMatch Jukebox.

   ✔ Use the Safe Remove Hardware icon in the system tray.

Due to the way iPod for Windows works with MusicMatch Jukebox, use only one of the above methods to eject your iPod. Do *not* use the Eject option on the shortcut menu that pops up if you right-click the iPod icon in the My Computer window. This Eject option doesn't work with iPod for Windows and MusicMatch Jukebox.

To eject your iPod by using MusicMatch Jukebox, follow these steps:

1. **Close any application other than MusicMatch Jukebox (such as iPod Manager) that is using the iPod.**

2. **Select iPod in the MusicMatch Jukebox PortablesPlus window.**

3. **Click the Eject button in the lower-left corner of the MusicMatch Jukebox PortablesPlus window.**

4. **An alert dialog appears, click Yes.**

   It takes about 15 seconds before the iPod can be disconnected. The PortablesPlus window displays the message `Ejecting iPod. Please wait . . .` until it finishes, and then it displays `It is now safe to disconnect iPod`.

5. **Wait until the iPod displays** `OK to disconnect` **or its main menu, and then disconnect the iPod from the computer.**

Follow these steps to eject your iPod by using the Safely Remove Hardware icon in the Windows system tray:

1. **Close any applications (such as MusicMatch Jukebox and iPod Manager) that are still using the iPod.**

2. **In the bottom-right corner of the screen, click the Safely Remove Hardware icon.**

   The Safely Remove Hardware shortcut menu appears.

3. **Select the Apple IEEE 1394 (FireWire) device if you use FireWire, or the USB Mass Storage device if you use USB, from the short-cut menu.**

4. **An alert dialog appears. Click OK.**

5. **Wait until the iPod displays** `OK to disconnect` **or its main menu, and then disconnect the iPod from the computer.**

Never disconnect an iPod before ejecting it. If you do, you might have to reset your iPod, as we describe in Chapter 1.

Adding Notes and Text

You can add text notes to your iPod so that you can view them on the iPod display — all sorts of notes, such as driving directions, weather information, or even news items. If you just use your iPod for music, you might want notes about the music. This feature works with iPods that run iPod software 2.0 or newer (including iPod mini and third- and fourth-generation iPods that use the dock connector).

Using the Notes folder

In a perfect world you could rip audio CDs and also capture all the information in the liner notes — the descriptions of who played which instruments, where the CD was produced, and other minute detail. Then, while sharing your iPod music with others, you could view the liner notes on the iPod screen whenever a question arises about the music.

You can almost achieve the same result by typing some of the liner notes or any text you want (or copy or export song information from iTunes, as we describe in Chapter 14) into a word processing program, such as TextEdit on a Mac or NotePad on a Windows PC. You can then save the document as a text-only file (with the filename extension .txt) and drag it to the Notes folder of the iPod.

Documents must be saved as text-only files to be viewed on the iPod display. If you use a word processor, such as Microsoft Word, choose File⇨Save As, and select the Text Only option (or the Text Only with Line Breaks option) from the Save As Type drop-down list in Windows or the Format pop-up menu on a Mac. Each text file must be smaller than 4K.

Text files in the Notes folder are organized by filename. You can view these notes files by choosing Extras⇨Notes. Make sure that you name your notes with descriptive filenames so that you can easily scroll the list of notes files to find the liner notes for the album you're listening to.

Your iPod can also display a folder hierarchy in the Notes folder, allowing you to organize your notes by creating folders (using the Finder with your iPod mounted as a hard drive) and putting notes files within the folders in the Notes folder. The size of any single note is limited to 4K; any text beyond 4K is truncated. You can transfer up to 1,000 notes. Your notes can include basic HTML tags (used on Web pages) such as paragraph markers (<P> and </P>) and line break (<BR>).

Adding news feeds, books, and Web pages

Do you want the latest news, weather, sports scores, or driving directions available at the touch of a button of your iPod? Enterprising software entrepreneurs have moved in to fill the vacuum left by Apple with accessories that provide displayable text on your iPod screen, such as the following:

- ✔ **Pod2Go** (available at www.kainjow.com/pod2go/website) for the Mac offers synchronized feeds for news, weather forecasts, movie listings, stock quotes, horoscopes, sections of Web pages, and driving directions.

- ✔ **NewsMac 3** (available at www.thinkmac.co.uk/newsmac), also for the Mac, lets you keep tabs on world news Web sites and lets you transfer entire Web pages.

- ✔ **EphPod** for Windows (available at www.ephpod.com) also lets you update your iPod with news, weather, and other information updates.

- ✔ **Book2Pod** (available at www.tomsci.com/book2pod) is a shareware program for the Mac that allows you to read entire books on your iPod display. There's also a similar shareware program for Windows called **iPodLibrary** (available at www.ipodlibrary.com).

- ✔ You can also take advantage of the Notes folder and other iPod features by using some of the handy AppleScripts provided for iTunes and the iPod, which you can download from the Apple site (www.apple.com/applescript/ipod).

Storing Photos on Your iPod

If you're traveling with your digital camera and your iPod, you can shoot all the pictures you want without worrying about filling up your camera's memory card. Shoot all the pictures you want, and then connect the camera to your full-size iPod with the Belkin Media Reader for iPod, and transfer the photos to your iPod. Then delete the pictures from your camera's memory card and go snap some more. You could travel for weeks on end, shooting thousands of photos in locations around the world without running out of space in your iPod.

The Belkin Media Reader for iPod connects to the iPod's FireWire dock connector and transfers photos quickly to the iPod hard drive, which can hold hundreds or even thousands of photos (depending on how much music is already stored on the iPod). Available from the Apple Store, this accessory works only with full-size iPod models with dock connectors.

To transfer the photos to the iPhoto library on a Mac, mount the iPod as a hard drive, as we describe earlier in this chapter. Then import the photos by dragging the files directly from the iPod hard drive and dropping them over the iPhoto window.

Taking Your Mac System on the Road

Although the iPod is the road warrior's dream weapon for combating road fatigue and boredom, if you update and maintain its hard drive contents wisely, it can also be invaluable as a tool for providing quick information and for saving your computer from disaster. Don't let hard drive space go to waste: Fill up your iPod and let the iPod be your road manager. You can put your most important applications, utilities, and files on the iPod hard drive as a backup.

You can even use your iPod to save your Mac in a system crisis. Although this operation isn't officially supported by Apple, you can load the iPod with a minimally configured Mac system and then use the iPod to start up your Mac. Depending on the size of your iPod, you should be able to fit both a minimal system and a considerable amount of music on the iPod.

Life on the road can be hazardous to your laptop's hard drive, and if any portion of the hard drive containing system files is damaged, your system might not start up. When this happens, you ordinarily use the installation CDs to start the Mac, scan and fix the hard drive trouble spots, and reinstall the Mac operating system. With your iPod, you can at least start the Mac and scan and fix the hard drive trouble spots, and you can also use any other files or applications that you previously put on your iPod.

Mac models introduced after January 2003 can't start up with Mac OS 9, so you need to save Mac OS X to your iPod unless you use an older Mac.

To get the most functionality from your iPod, make sure that you have the latest version of iPod software. To find out which version of software your iPod uses, choose Settings➪About from the iPod main menu. To update your iPod software to the latest version, see Chapter 28.

To copy files and applications to your iPod, first mount the iPod as a hard drive, as we describe earlier in this chapter.

Installing Mac OS 9

To install a custom version of OS 9 on your iPod, connect your iPod as a hard drive, and then follow these steps:

1. **Insert your Mac OS 9 installation CD into your Mac and follow the directions to start up the installation process.**

   You have to restart the Mac with the installation CD while holding down C to start the computer from the CD.

2. **When the installer asks you to select a destination, select the iPod hard drive.**

3. **After the installation finishes, quit the installation program.**

   That's all you have to do — the installer does everything for you.

To start up a Mac from an iPod that holds Mac OS 9, connect the iPod, hold down Option, and choose Restart from the Apple menu (or if your system is already hosed, use the Power button to reboot while holding down Option). Eventually, as the Mac resets and scans itself for any startup drives, all the startup drives appear as icons in a row, with a right-pointing arrow underneath the icons. Click the icon representing the iPod hard drive, and then click the right-pointing arrow to start the system from that drive.

Installing Mac OS X

To install a custom version of OS X older than version 10.2 on your iPod (such as 10.0 or 10.1), connect your iPod as a hard drive, as we describe earlier in this chapter, and then follow these steps:

1. **Insert your Mac OS X installation CD into your Mac and follow the directions to start up the installation process.**

   You have to restart the Mac with the installation CD while holding down C to start the computer from the CD.

2. **When the installer asks you to select a destination, choose the iPod hard drive.**

Don't use the option to erase and format the hard drive, because the hard drive of your iPod is specially formatted for playing music, and formatting it in this manner prevents it from playing music again. So *don't* format it! If you format or erase the iPod's hard drive by mistake, you must restore it to its factory condition, as we describe in Chapter 28.

3. **Specify a custom installation rather than a standard installation.**

   To make sure that you don't use up too much hard drive space on your iPod, choose a custom installation of OS X. In the custom installation section, choose only the languages that you need. These language options take up a lot of space, and you probably don't need them.

4. **After installation finishes and the Mac restarts from the iPod, continue through the setup procedure, and then use Software Update in System Preferences to update the Mac system on your iPod.**

   Most likely a lot of system updates are waiting for you — updates released after the date of your installation CDs. Take the time to update your system because these updates might make a difference in how your computer performs with certain applications.

To install a custom version of OS X version 10.2 (Jaguar) on your iPod, you need to use Carbon Copy Cloner, a $5 shareware program (available from `www.bombich.com/software/ccc.html`). Although you could clone your system by using the Unix ditto command in the Terminal window of Mac OS X, this process is tedious and you could easily make a mistake. Carbon Copy Cloner lets you specify what parts of the system you don't need cloned, and you can use its Preferences dialog to make the target disk (your iPod) bootable.

To install a custom version of OS X version 10.3 (Panther) on your iPod, connect your iPod as a hard drive, and then use the Disk Utility program supplied with OS X. (It's in the Utilities folder inside your Applications folder.) Using Disk Utility, drag the icon for a source hard drive with a version of OS X 10.3 to the Source text box in the Disk Utility dialog, and then drag your iPod hard drive icon into the Destination text box. Then click Restore, and the program does everything for you.

To start up a Mac from an iPod that runs Mac OS X, connect the iPod, hold down Option, and choose Restart from the Apple menu (or if your system is already hosed, use the Power button to reboot while holding down Option). Eventually, as the Mac resets itself and scans itself for any startup drives, all the startup drives appear as icons in a row, with a right-pointing arrow underneath the icons. Click the icon representing the iPod hard drive, and then click the right-pointing arrow to start the system from that drive.

While you're at it, copy the Disk Utility program to your iPod so that you can repair any Mac's hard drive by using your iPod as the startup drive.

Removing the system

Removing Mac OS 9 from an iPod is easy: Simply drag the System Folder from the iPod hard drive to the Trash when your iPod is connected as a hard drive.

Removing Mac OS X isn't as easy because OS X installs hidden files and directories, and there is no easy way to drag them to the Trash. (Perhaps that's why Apple doesn't support this feature.) The quickest and easiest way to remove OS X from an iPod is to restore the iPod, as we describe in Chapter 28. Restore erases and reformats the iPod to its original factory condition. Be sure to copy any important files stored on your iPod before doing this. Although all your music and files are erased in this one step, it's much easier to then add your music from iTunes, your calendars and contacts, and your files, than it is to try to delete files associated with OS X. Restore, and then copy everything back to your iPod as needed.

Chapter 26

Entering Personal Information

· ·

In This Chapter

▶ Adding calendar appointments and To-Do lists with iCal

▶ Adding calendar appointments and To-Do tasks with Microsoft Outlook

▶ Storing contacts in Address Book (Mac)

▶ Storing contacts in Outlook and Microsoft Address Book (Windows or Mac)

· ·

*Y*our iPod is capable of helping you manage your activities on the road to the point where it competes in some respects with personal digital assistants (PDAs). You can manage your address book, calendar, and To-Do list for the road all on your computer, and then update or synchronize your iPod to have all the information that you need for viewing and playback. As a result, you might not ever need an additional PDA — especially if you prefer typing data into your computer before loading it into the device. Your iPod is a *player* — not just in the world of music, but also in the world of personal productivity.

The most likely bit of information that you might need on the road is a phone number, an address, or information related to an event or calendar appointment. Your iPod can store your personal information right alongside your music so that the information is available at your fingertips. After entering and managing your personal information on your computer, you can then copy the information to your iPod or synchronize with information already on your iPod.

The iPod accepts industry-standard iCalendar and vCalendar files for calendars and To-Do lists, which you can export from most applications that offer calendars and To-Do lists. It also accepts industry-standard *vCards,* or *virtual business cards,* which are records containing contact information for people, including physical addresses, e-mail addresses, phone numbers, and so on. Again, most applications that offer address books or contact lists can export vCards.

If you're a Mac user, you have it easy: You can use the free iCal and Address Book applications and automatically synchronize the information with your iPod calendar and contact list with iSync (see Chapter 27). Mac users can also choose other applications and export (or drag) the information to your iPod.

If you're a Windows user, you have a variety of choices for managing contacts and calendar information, and you also have choices of third-party utilities for putting the information on an iPod, as well as the tried-and-true technique of exporting (or dragging) information to the iPod.

This chapter shows you how to enter your personal information into the computer by using Address Book and iCal (on a Mac) or Microsoft Outlook and Microsoft Address Book (on a Windows PC).

Keeping Appointments with iCal on the Mac

iCal, the free desktop calendar application that you can download from Apple's software download page (www.info.apple.com/support/downloads.html), creates calendars that you can copy to your iPod. iCal requires Mac OS X version 10.2.3 or newer. You can create custom calendars for different activities, such as home, office, road tours, exercise and diet schedules, mileage logs, and so on. You can view them separately or all together. After editing your calendars on the Mac, you can synchronize your iPod to have the same calendars by using iSync, as we describe in Chapter 27.

 If you use another application to manage your personal calendar, you might still want to use iCal just to transfer your calendar information to the iPod painlessly. You can import calendars from other applications that support the iCal or vCal format, such as Microsoft Entourage, Microsoft Outlook, and Palm Desktop. When your information is in iCal, you can synchronize your entire calendar with your iPod by using iSync.

Launch iCal by double-clicking the iCal application or clicking its icon in the Mac OS X Dock. iCal displays a calendar, as shown in Figure 26-1, and you can switch the view from an entire month to just one week or one day by clicking the Day or Week buttons at the bottom of the window.

iCal starts you off with two calendars: Home and Work. Their names have check marks next to them in the upper-left corner of the iCal window, indicating that both are visible, and they're merged into the calendar view. To see only your Home calendar, deselect the Work option in the Calendars pane on the left, and vice-versa. It's easy to set up appointments and events for either calendar.

Figure 26-1:
View your
personal
calendar
with iCal.

Setting up an appointment or event

Some appointments and events are a drag, and some are fun, but either way you
can drag your mouse to create one. Click the Week button at the bottom of the
window to see just an entire week, and then click and drag over a period of time
to create an appointment. You can choose File➪New Event to do the same thing.

To see the details of an event or appointment, do one of these things:

- Double-click the event or appointment.
- Click the event or appointment to select it, and then click the i button in
  the lower-right corner.
- Click the event or appointment to select it, and then choose Window➪
  Show Info.

The detail for the event or appointment appears in the info drawer that sticks
out on the right side of the iCal window, as shown in Figure 26-2.

In the info drawer, you can type over the filler "New Event" and "location" text,
change the date and time, add attendees, specify the status and whether the
event or appointment should be repeated, and so on. You can add type a note
in the Notes section at the bottom and assign the event to a specific calendar
(in this case, the Home calendar). If you have created custom calendars within
iCal (as we describe in "Creating a custom calendar"), select the calendar that
you want to add the event to from the Calendar pop-up menu. You can set the
event to automatically repeat every day, week, month, or year by using the
Repeat pop-up menu.

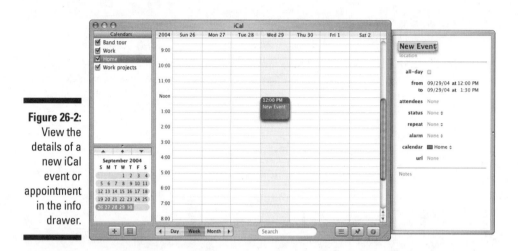

Figure 26-2:
View the details of a new iCal event or appointment in the info drawer.

Need to be reminded? Set an alarm for an event in iCal by selecting an option from the Alarm pop-up menu. If you select the Message with Sound option, the alarm works with your iPod when you synchronize your calendar with your iPod with iSync, as we describe in Chapter 27.

iPod as PDA: You can play, but you can't type

We could never get used to tiny portable computers and PDAs. We use computers for all our information needs, but we've never really gone smaller than a laptop because the keyboards on smaller devices are too small for touch-typists.

People who use the hunt-and-peck method of typing can quickly adapt to using forefingers and thumbs or a stylus to type reasonably well on a cell phone or PDA. However, PDAs can be hard to use for people who are trained to hold their hands a certain way and touch-type with all fingers.

There's true irony in this. The original reason for the QWERTY arrangement of keys on the keyboard, standard to this day, was to *slow down* the human typist and place commonly used letter combinations on opposite sides of the keyboard so that the mechanical arms of the typewriter wouldn't jam. Efforts to change this during the computer age were ignored even if they did allow for increased typing speed and higher productivity. People assimilated the original arrangement and learned to type quickly with it, and they simply refused to change.

Small keyboards and clumsy human interfaces hamper the use of PDAs for input, raising the question for the laptop users: "Why bother?" Laptops (and possibly the new tablet computers) are excellent for input and organizing information. Besides, if you use more than one device to enter input, you run the risk of being out of sync — most often you end up accidentally overwriting the new stuff put into the PDA with the stuff from your laptop.

A Mac laptop and iPod combo is our answer to this dilemma. We input and edit all information with a Mac laptop and update the iPod as necessary. We can then take the iPod into situations in which we need to view but not change the information. And we don't need PDAs — except to play with as gadget freaks.

Adding a To-Do item

If you're petrified like the White Rabbit in Carroll's *Alice in Wonderland* with so little time and so much to do, iCal can keep track of your To-Do list. Click the thumbtack icon to view the To Do items pane of the iCal window (or choose Window⇨Show To Dos). Choose File⇨New To Do to add an item to the list.

You can set the priority of the To-Do item so that it sorts to the top (highest priority) or bottom (no priority) of the To-Do list. You can also set its due date in the Due Date pop-up menu — if you set a due date, the alarm pop-up appears so that you can also set an alarm for the To-Do item. (The alarm also works in your iPod when you synchronize your calendar with your iPod.) iCal lets you assign the To-Do item to a specific calendar and even add a Web address to the URL field to link the To-Do item to a Web page. To mark a To-Do item as finished, select the Completed option for the item.

Creating a custom calendar

You can create custom calendars in iCal that show only the events that are assigned to the custom calendar. For example, you might create one custom calendar for work events, another for family events, another for an exercise plan, and so on. Your custom calendars are maintained by iCal so that you can see them all at once or individually in the calendar view. The list of custom calendars appears in the top-left corner of the iCal window, with a check box next to each calendar. When you select the check box, the custom calendar's events show up in the calendar view. If you select more than one custom calendar, the events from all selected custom calendars are merged in the calendar view.

To create a custom calendar, follow these steps:

1. **Choose File⇨New Calendar, or click the plus (+) button in the bottom-left corner of the iCal window.**

    An Untitled item appears in the list of calendars in the top-left corner.

2. **Type a new name for the Untitled item.**

    Click inside the Name text box and type a new name.

3. **Turn on or off the custom calendar.**

    Deselect the custom calendar if you don't want its events to be displayed. Select it to display the custom calendar along with other selected custom calendars (merged with the other custom calendar events).

Keeping Appointments with Microsoft Outlook

Microsoft Outlook is offered as part of Microsoft Office (Windows version), and Microsoft Outlook Express is offered free with Windows. In addition, a Mac version of Outlook is available from Microsoft. You can use any of these applications to create calendars and export the calendar information to your iPod.

Outlook provides extensive calendar and scheduling functions and task management. You need only a fraction of Outlook's features to keep a calendar and To-Do list that can be viewed on your iPod. Many of the more advanced functions, such as scheduling conferences and meetings to coincide with the schedules of other people on a network, have no meaning on an iPod. Nevertheless, the iPod is useful for viewing the results of Outlook activity. If you use those features, any event, appointment, or meeting that displays in your Outlook calendar is also copied to your iPod along with the calendar.

With your calendar and To-Do tasks set up in Outlook, you can export the information to your iPod, as we describe in Chapter 27.

Setting up an appointment or event

To set up an appointment or event in Microsoft Outlook, first launch Outlook, and then follow these steps:

1. **Click the Calendar icon and click any time slot to select it in the Outlook calendar.**

   The time slots in the Outlook calendar, as shown in Figure 26-3, appear when you click the Calendar icon.

2. **Choose File⇨New⇨Appointment to create an appointment or event, and then fill in the information.**

   Alternatively, you can right-click the selected time slot and choose New Appointment (or choose New Recurring Appointment for appointments that repeat often). Specify start and end times and a location, as shown in Figure 26-4.

3. **Click the Save and Close button to save the appointment or event.**

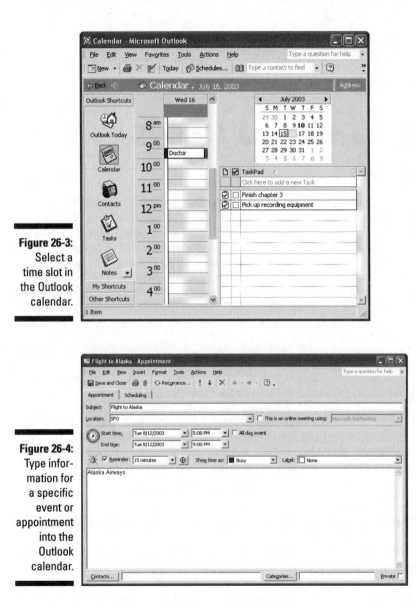

Figure 26-3:
Select a time slot in the Outlook calendar.

Figure 26-4:
Type information for a specific event or appointment into the Outlook calendar.

Adding a To-Do task

The outlook for your future plans might be bright, but you need more than a crystal ball to keep them that way. If you already use Outlook for your e-mail and calendar functions, you might also want to use it to keep track of your To-Do list.

To create a To-Do task in Outlook, choose New⇨Task, and type a subject name for the task. To make the task a recurring task, select the Recurrence option and choose a frequency (Daily, Weekly, Monthly, or Yearly) for the recurring task. Finally, click the Save and Close button to save the task.

Storing Contacts in the Mac OS X Address Book

Address Book, a free application that's provided with OS X for the Mac, has just about all the features you could ever want for storing names, addresses, phone numbers, e-mail addresses, and physical addresses. You can drag and drop addresses and phone numbers from incoming e-mails to avoid having to type the information, and you can wirelessly copy cards from your address book to cell phones, PDAs, and other Bluetooth-enabled devices. Keeping your iPod synchronized with your addresses and phone numbers is simple and automatic. You can then have your friends addresses and phone numbers with you at all times, right on your iPod.

If you use some other application for storing contact information, you might want to use Address Book in addition to your other application so you can import contact information from other applications that support vCards or the LDIF format (LDIF is the file format for LDAP, which stands for Lightweight Directory Access Protocol). To do so, launch Address Book and choose File⇨ Import, select the format that you used from the submenu, and select the file that contains the exported information. When your information is in Address Book, you can synchronize the information with your iPod by using iSync, eliminating the hassle of dragging vCards to the iPod individually.

Adding and editing contact information

Launch Address Book by double-clicking the Address Book application or by clicking its icon in the Mac OS X Dock. To add a new card, follow these steps:

1. **Choose File⇨New Card or click the plus (+) button at the bottom of the Name pane.**

   A new blank card appears, ready for you to add information.

2. **Type the person's first and last name over the placeholder first and last name text boxes, and add contact information to the other text boxes.**

You can type addresses, phone numbers, e-mail addresses, and so on, as shown in Figure 26-5. To add multiple addresses, phone numbers, or other text boxes, click the tiny plus (+) icon next to each type of information to add more. If some of the text boxes don't apply, skip them and they won't show up in the edited card. You can even enter a two-line address by pressing Return to continue to the second line.

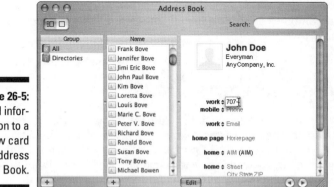

Figure 26-5: Add information to a new card in Address Book.

3. **To save your changes, click the Edit button, and Address Book saves the edits.**

To edit a card, select the person in the Name pane and click the Edit button. To save your changes, click the Edit button again, and Address Book saves the edits.

You can also add new people to your address book from the Mail program by selecting an e-mail message and choosing Message⇨Add Sender to Address Book. You can then open Address Book, click the name in the Name pane, and click the Edit button to edit the person's card.

If you receive a vCard as an e-mail attachment (with the .vcf extension), you can simply drag the attachment to your Address Book window to add the vCard to your address book. Wouldn't it be nice if all your friends sent you vCards to keep you up to date, and you never had to retype the information?

Be careful with vCards from unknown persons — vCards can be used to carry viruses.

Merging cards

One of the coolest features of Address Book is its ability to merge cards. You might occasionally end up with multiple cards for the same person in Address Book, typically by saving the sender's e-mail address from the Mail application while also dragging a vCard from the same person. To fix that, you can hold down Shift and click cards in the Name pane to select the ones that you want to combine. Then choose Card⇨Merge Cards. Address Book creates a new card that combines all the unique information. You can then delete the excess cards.

Searching in Address Book

Can't find the person you're looking for? Address Book lets you search for any text in any of the text boxes of any card. If you're searching for a person, and all you have is part of a phone number or even just part of the person's name, type the text in the Search text box at the top-right corner of the Address Book window. As you type, Address Book displays the names of the people who have the text fragment anywhere in their cards. Address Book searches all the information on the cards, including the Notes text box, and it searches *fast,* displaying names immediately. If more than one matching card is found, click the arrow buttons at the bottom of the window to switch between the cards. Or, choose View⇨Card And Columns to see a list of all the cards. To see all your cards again, delete the text from the Search text box.

Managing contacts in groups

You can combine address cards in Address Book into a *group* to make it easy to select all the addresses at once. For example, you might want to group together all your local friends or all your co-workers. You can then send an e-mail to all of them at once by choosing the group as the e-mail recipient.

You can also use a group to keep track of a subset of contacts. For example, you might want only a subset of your contact list on your iPod rather than the entire list. To do this, create a group for the subset of contacts and export the group as a single vCard file that you can then use on your iPod.

To create a group of contacts in Address Book

1. **Click the plus (+) sign at the bottom of the Group pane.**

   Address Book creates a new entry in the Group column with a highlighted text box so that you can type a new name for the group.

2. **Type a name for the group.**

3. **Select the All item in the Group pane to see your entire list of names.**

4. **Drag and drop names over the group name to add them to your new group.**

After creating a new group, you can see the names in the group by clicking the group name in the Group pane. Select the All item in the Group pane to see all the names in the address book.

To put your addresses on the iPod, you can export a vCard file to the iPod Contacts folder or use the iSync application, as we describe in Chapter 27.

Storing Contacts in Microsoft Address Book or Outlook

Microsoft Outlook, provided with the Windows version of Microsoft Office and also available on the Mac as Outlook Express, provides extensive features for managing contacts with e-mail and address information. You can also import address books and contact information into Outlook from programs such as Eudora, Lotus Organizer, Netscape Messenger, Microsoft Mail, or Microsoft Schedule+.

Outlook actually uses another application, Microsoft Address Book, to store the contact information. Microsoft Address Book lets you gather address books from other sources, including Microsoft Exchange Server and Internet directory services (depending on how you've set up Outlook). It also includes all the contacts in your Outlook Contacts folder. When you update the information in your Outlook Contacts folder, the Microsoft Address Book is updated as well, so you can make all your changes in the Outlook Contacts folder.

To create a contact in Outlook, which saves the contact information in Microsoft Address Book, launch Outlook and then follow these steps:

1. **Click the Contacts icon to open the Contacts folder.**

   The Contacts icon appears in the Outlook Shortcuts pane on the left of the Outlook display (refer to Figure 26-5).

2. **Choose New⇨Contact, and then type a name for the contact.**

   The Contact window appears (Windows version). To enter multiple entries for a text box, such as more than one physical address or e-mail address, click the down-arrow next to the text box to display more lines for that text box. Enter all the information you want (or as little as you want).

3. **Click Save and Close to save the contact.**

   Your contacts are displayed in the Contact window of Outlook.

You can also create a new contact automatically for the sender of an e-mail message that you receive. Open the e-mail message, and in the From text box, right-click the name that you want to add to your Contacts folder, and then choose Add to Contacts.

You can export the contact information from Microsoft Outlook (and Microsoft Address Book) to your iPod, and for more on that, flip to Chapter 27.

Chapter 27

Synchronizing Information with Your iPod

In This Chapter

▶ Putting calendars and contacts on your iPod automatically with iSync (Mac)

▶ Putting calendars and contacts on your iPod automatically from Microsoft Outlook (Windows)

▶ Copying calendar and contact files manually

▶ Exporting calendars and contact information

*W*e chose the iPod for music, but we also find it useful while traveling for viewing the personal information — contacts, appointments, events, and To-Do tasks — that we manage on our computers.

If you've already read Chapter 26, you know how to manage your calendar activities and your contacts on your computer. In fact, you're probably knee-deep in vCards (virtual business cards) for your Address Book, and the calendars in your vCalendar files look like they were drawn up in the West Wing. Information changes often, and new information accumulates quickly, but you're well armed with an iPod that can be kept up to date. This chapter shows you how to *synchronize* your iPod to have all the information that you need for viewing and playback. We also show you how to simply copy the information to your iPod to update it.

Not 'N Sync? Try iSync (Mac Only)

Chances are that you make a lot of changes to addresses, phone numbers, calendar events, and To-Do lists on your Mac. Even though you can update your iPod with this information manually, remembering to copy each file you need is difficult. iSync performs this function automatically and keeps all your information updated on multiple devices, including your iPod. iSync is available as a free download from Apple at www.apple.com.

After installing iSync, follow these steps:

1. **Connect your iPod to the Mac, and open iSync.**

2. **Choose Devices⇨Add Device.**

   iSync searches for devices (such as iPods, cell phones, and PDAs) that are compatible with the Mac.

3. **Select the iPod from the list of devices.**

   The iPod icon appears in the iSync window, as shown in Figure 27-1. (The figure shows two different iPods connected at the same time.)

Figure 27-1: The iSync window displays icons for each device.

Click the iPod icon, and the iSync window expands to show the synchronization settings for the selected iPod, as shown in Figure 27-2.

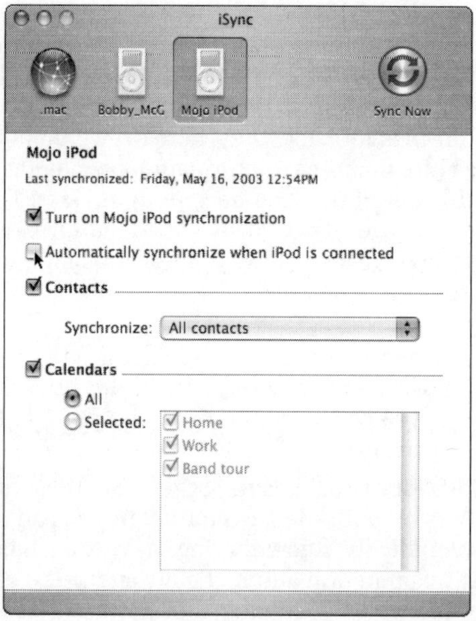

Figure 27-2: The iPod synchronization settings.

You can synchronize all contacts and calendars, or just the ones you select. Select the Automatically Synchronize When iPod Is Connected option, and every time you connect your iPod, iSync goes to work. If you don't want that level of automation, you can launch iSync anytime and click the Sync Now button.

iSync performs its magic automatically, but it pauses to inform you if you're changing your iPod information, as shown in Figure 27-3. This is a warning so that you don't overwrite information that you meant to keep.

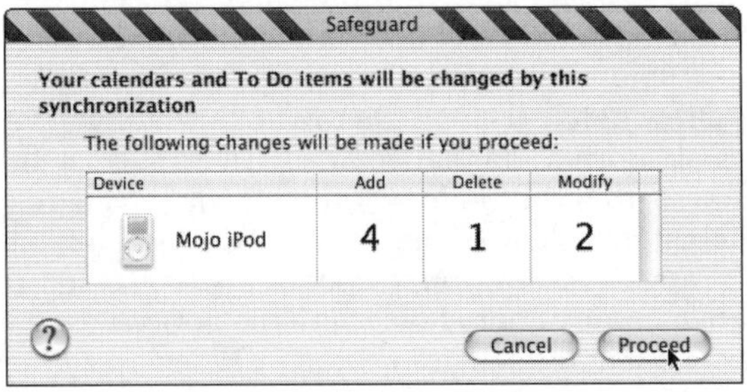

Figure 27-3:
iSync warns
you before
you update.

Device	Add	Delete	Modify
Mojo iPod	4	1	2

Safeguard

Your calendars and To Do items will be changed by this synchronization

The following changes will be made if you proceed:

Cancel   Proceed

After you finish synchronizing, be sure to eject the iPod (by dragging the iPod icon to the Trash, or in OS X 10.3 or newer, by clicking the Eject icon next to the iPod icon in the Finder Sidebar) before disconnecting it. If you forget this, your iPod's hard drive might freeze up, and you might need to reset your iPod, as you find out in Chapter 1.

After updating and ejecting the iPod, you can view your addresses and phone numbers by choosing Extras⇨Contacts, and then choosing a name.

You can look at your calendars by choosing Extras⇨Calendar⇨All. Just select a calendar, and then use the scroll wheel to scroll through the days of the calendar. You can also select an event to see the event's details. Use the Next and Previous buttons to skip to the next or previous month. To see your To-Do list, choose Extras⇨Calendar⇨To Do.

If your calendar events use alarms, you can turn on the iPod's calendar · alarms. Choose Extras⇨Calendar and select Alarms in the Calendar menu once to set the alarm to Beep, or once again to set it to Silent (so that only the message for the alarm appears), or one more time to set if to Off. The Alarms choices cycle from Beep to Silent to Off and then back to Beep.

Synchronizing Microsoft Outlook (Windows)

Third-party programs are available for Windows iPod users that will automatically synchronize your iPod with contacts and calendar info from Microsoft Outlook.

For example, iPodSync (available at `http://iccnet.50megs.com/iPodSync`) is a utility for Windows that lets you keep your Outlook calendar, contacts, and To-Do tasks synchronized between your PC and your iPod.

iPodSync displays a row of icons along the top of its window. The icons represent different types of information that you can synchronize with your iPod. These include contacts from the Outlook Contacts folder (Microsoft Address Book), calendar appointments and events from the Outlook Calendar, and To-Do tasks from Outlook Tasks. Click an icon to choose the type of information (such as Contacts), and then modify your choice with the options available (such as including birthdays in the notes field for contacts). When everything is set, click the Sync iPod button to automatically synchronize your iPod. iPodSync exports contacts into a single vCard file for your iPod Contacts folder and exports calendar information for the iPod Calendar folder.

Outlook can export contacts and calendar information, but it's a tedious process of exporting each contact and appointment individually. This failing of Outlook opens a window of opportunity for entrepreneurs, and several utilities and applications provide a way to export contacts and calendar data all at once. The following are samples of enterprising shareware utilities:

- **OutPod:** (`http://outpod.stoer.de`) This utility lets you export contact and calendar information in bulk from Microsoft Outlook to vCard and vCalendar files, which you can then drag to the iPod, as we describe in "Adding Calendars Manually" and "Adding Contacts Manually" in this chapter.

- **EphPod:** (`www.ephpod.com`) This utility lets you update your iPod with contacts from Outlook. EphPod is a full-featured Windows application that you can use in place of MusicMatch Jukebox. It supports standard WinAmp (`.m3u`) playlists and can synchronize the iPod with a library of music files. It imports Microsoft Outlook contacts and lets you create and edit your own contacts. EphPod can also download the latest news, weather, eBooks, and movie listings to an iPod.

Adding Calendars Manually

If you use your iPod as a hard drive, as we describe in Chapter 25, you can copy calendar files directly to the Calendar folder on your iPod. You can copy industry-standard iCalendar or vCalendar files, which can be exported by many applications including Microsoft Entourage, Microsoft Outlook, and Palm Desktop.

In most cases, you can drag an iCalendar file (with the filename extension .ics) or a vCalendar file (with the filename extension .vcs) to your iPod Calendars folder, as shown in Figure 27-4.

Figure 27-4: Add exported calendars in the iCalendar format to the Calendars folder on the iPod.

To save calendar information in the iCalendar format from Microsoft Outlook, you must save each appointment separately as an ICS (iCalendar) file. Select the appointment in the calendar view or open the appointment by double-clicking it. Use the Save As command and select iCalendar from the Save As Type pop-up menu, and then select a destination for the ICS file. The destination can be a folder on your hard drive, or it can be the iPod's Calendars folder. If you select a folder on your hard drive, be sure to copy the files to the iPod's Calendars folder.

Some applications, such as Microsoft Entourage, don't offer a convenient way to export calendar information (except perhaps by dragging each appointment or event onto the desktop). However, iCal for the Mac can import Entourage calendars, so you can import into iCal (choose File➪Import), and then use iSync to synchronize your iPod, as we describe earlier in this chapter.

You can look at your calendars on the iPod by choosing Extras⇨Calendar⇨All. Select a calendar and then use the scroll wheel to scroll through the days of the calendar, or select an event to see the event's details. Press the Next and Previous buttons to skip to the next or previous month. To see your To-Do list, choose Extras⇨Calendar⇨To Do.

To remove a calendar from your iPod, connect the iPod to your computer and enable the iPod as a hard drive (see Chapter 25). You can then open the Calendars folder on the iPod and delete the calendar file. You can also copy calendar files from the iPod to your hard drive.

Adding Contacts Manually

If you use your iPod as a hard drive, as we describe in Chapter 25, you can copy contacts in vCard files directly to the Contacts folder on your iPod.

A vCard, or *virtual card,* is a standard format for exchanging personal information. The iPod sorts and displays contacts in the vCard format — you can use separate vCard files for each person or use a group vCard file that contains records for many people.

After enabling the iPod as a hard drive, simply export your contacts as vCards directly into the Contacts folder of your iPod. In most cases, you can drag vCard-formatted contacts from the application's address book to the iPod Contacts folder.

You might want to copy contacts manually rather than using iSync because iSync takes longer to synchronize contact information than it takes to copy new contacts over to the iPod in the Finder.

You can copy one card, a group of cards, or even the entire list as a vCard file (with a .vcf extension) by dragging the vCard file into the Contacts folder. Contacts must be in the vCard format to use with the iPod.

You can use applications to export vCard files directly to your iPod. For example, in Microsoft Outlook, you can export a vCard file for a contact directly into your iPod's Contacts folder by following these steps:

1. **Choose File⇨Export to vCard.**

2. **Use the Save In drop-down menu in the dialog to select the iPod as the destination drive.**

3. **Then select the Contacts folder to save the contacts file.**

As of this writing, the iPod supports only a portion of what you can put into a vCard. For example, you can include photos and sounds in vCards used by other applications, but you can't open up those portions of the vCard by using the iPod.

Using Utilities to Copy Files and Music

The iPod has spawned a thriving industry of third-party accessories and products. Some of the most useful products are utility programs that expand the capabilities of the iPod or your ability to update the iPod, and even full-featured programs that are designed as replacements for iTunes and MusicMatch Jukebox. With so many programs to check out, you might be overwhelmed. We've selected three of the best programs for the Mac and Windows (as of this writing).

Keep in mind, with programs that allow music copying functions, that copying copyrighted material to other computers without permission is illegal. Don't steal music — or anything else, for that matter.

Mac utilities

On the Mac, third-party offerings have focused on extending the capabilities of the iPod and its software to do things like copying music from the iPod to the computer and updating the iPod with contacts and calendar information. Take a glance at the following examples:

- ✔ **iPod It 2.3.2:** (www.zapptek.com/ipod-it) With this software, you can transfer personal information to your iPod from Entourage, Stickies, Mail, Address Book, and iCal. You can even download weather forecasts and news headlines directly to your iPod.

- ✔ **iPod Access v3.1.5:** (www.findleydesigns.com/ipodaccess) This utility lets you transfer songs from an iPod to a Mac. iPod Access is available from Findley Designs, Inc.

- ✔ **iPodRip 3.3.1:** (www.thelittleappfactory.com/software/ipodrip. php) This third-party utility, available from The Little App Factory, lets you transfer music from your iPod back to your iTunes library and listen to music on your iPod through your computer (saving hard drive space). It supports all iPod song formats including MP3, AAC, Protected AAC, and Audible.com books.

Windows utilities

On Windows, third-party offerings fill a void left by the lack of an iSync-like program. Lots more third-party programs exist for Windows, and they do everything from extending the capabilities of the iPod and updating contacts and calendar information to replacing the need for MusicMatch Jukebox and iTunes.

✔ **iPodSync:** (http://iccnet.50megs.com/iPodSync) Keep Microsoft Outlook calendars, contacts, tasks, and notes synchronized between a Windows PC and an iPod. iPodSync exports industry standard vCards for contacts, and uses the iCalendar format for appointment information. iPodSync can even synchronize Outlook notes and tasks. For more information, see the iPodSync Web site.

✔ **EphPod 2.75:** (www.ephpod.com) This shareware utility lets you update your iPod with contacts from Outlook. It's a full-featured Windows application that can be used in place of MusicMatch Jukebox or iTunes. It supports standard WinAmp (.M3U) playlists and can synchronize the iPod with a library of music files. It imports Microsoft Outlook contacts and also lets you create and edit your own contacts. EphPod can also download the latest news, weather, e-books, and movie listings to an iPod.

✔ **XPlay 2:** (www.mediafour.com/products/xplay) This utility, from Mediafour Corp., provides read and write access to your iPod hard drive for documents and data files, plus the ability to organize your music from the Explorer-based XPlay interface or from Windows Media Player, as an alternative to MusicMatch Jukebox or iTunes. XPlay makes your iPod appear as a normal drive under Windows for the sharing of data files, and it makes your songs, playlists, artists and albums appear in custom folders in Explorer, so they're easy to access and manipulate and organized similarly to how the iPod organizes them. XPlay is available from Mediafour Corp.

Chapter 28

Updating and Troubleshooting

· ·

In This Chapter

▶ Your first steps for troubleshooting iPod problems

▶ Updating the iPod system software and firmware for Mac or Windows by using iTunes

▶ Restoring an iPod to its original factory condition and settings

▶ Troubleshooting the MusicMatch Jukebox configuration with iPod for Windows

· ·

*T*his chapter describes some of the problems that you might encounter with your iPod and computer and how to fix them. If your iPod fails to turn on, or if your computer fails to recognize it, you can most likely find a solution here.

This chapter also covers updating the firmware and software on your iPod, and restoring your iPod to its factory default condition. (*Firmware* is software encoded in hardware.) That last option is a drastic measure that erases any music or information on the iPod, but it usually solves the problem if nothing else does.

Before Apple introduced iTunes for Windows, PC users had no other choice except MusicMatch Jukebox, which included the iPod for Windows utility and the iPod Updater for updating and restoring an iPod. Apple revamped the iPod Updater along with developing iTunes for Windows, and now offers a new version of the iPod Updater, which is virtually the same for Mac and Windows. As a result, the troubleshooting instructions are different for iTunes and MusicMatch Jukebox configurations. Here's how to use this chapter:

✔ If you use iTunes, you can skip "Troubleshooting iPod for Windows and MusicMatch Jukebox."

✔ If you use MusicMatch Jukebox, you can skip "Using iPod Updater."

First Troubleshooting Steps

Problems can arise with electronics and software that can prevent the iPod from turning on at all or from turning on properly with all its music and playlists. You can also have problem in the connection between your iPod and your computer.

When you turn on your iPod, built-in startup diagnostic software checks the iPod hard drive for damage and attempts to repair it if necessary. If the iPod finds an issue when it is turned on, it automatically uses internal diagnostics to check for and repair any damage. You might see a disk scan icon on your iPod screen after turning it on, indicating that a problem was fixed. If this happens, update your iPod firmware and software, as we describe in "Updating the iPod with the iPod Updater," later in this chapter.

Checking the Hold switch

If your iPod refuses to turn on, check the position of the Hold switch on top of the iPod. The Hold switch locks the iPod buttons so that you don't accidentally activate them. Slide the Hold switch away from the headphone connection, hiding the orange layer, to unlock the buttons. (If you see the orange layer underneath one end of the Hold switch, the switch is still in the locked position.)

Checking the power

Got power? The battery might not be charged enough. If the battery is too low for normal operation, the iPod doesn't turn on. Instead, a low battery screen appears for about three seconds, and then disappears. At that point, your only choice is to connect the iPod to an AC power source, wait for a moment, and then turn the power on by pushing any button on the iPod. If your source of AC power is your computer (using the FireWire connection), make sure that the computer is on and not set to go to sleep. The battery icon in the upper-right corner of the display indicates whether it's full or recharging. For more information about maintaining a healthy battery, see Chapter 1.

Resetting the iPod

This operation resets the operating system of the iPod and restarts the system. Sometimes when your iPod gets confused or refuses to turn on, you can fix it by resetting it. Follow these steps:

1. **Toggle the Hold switch.**

   Push the Hold switch to hold (lock), and then set it back to unlock.

2. **Press the Menu and Play/Pause buttons simultaneously and hold for at least five seconds until the Apple logo appears; then release the buttons when you see the Apple logo.**

   The appearance of the Apple logo signals that your iPod is resetting itself, so you no longer have to hold down the buttons.

It's important to release the Menu and Play/Pause buttons as soon as you see the Apple logo. If you continue to hold down the buttons after the logo appears, the iPod displays the low battery icon, and you must connect it to a power source before using your iPod again.

After resetting, everything should be back to normal, including your music and data files.

Draining the iPod battery

Certain types of battery-powered devices sometimes run into problems if the battery hasn't drained in a while. In rare cases, the iPod might go dark and can't be reset until the battery is drained. If the above steps didn't resolve the issue, disconnect the iPod from any power source and leave it disconnected for approximately 24 hours. After this period, connect it to power and reset.

Try to keep the iPod at room temperature — generally near 68 degrees Fahrenheit (20 degrees Celsius), but you can use iPod anywhere between 50 to 95 degrees Fahrenheit (10 and 35 degrees Celsius). If you have left the iPod in the cold, let it warm up to room temperature before waking it from sleep. Otherwise, a low-battery icon might appear, and the iPod won't wake up properly. If the iPod doesn't wake from sleep after warming up, connect the power adapter and reset the iPod, as we describe in the previous section.

Hitting the panic button

Actually it's never a good idea to hit the panic button, even if there is one, but if you have tried the solutions above and your iPod still doesn't turn on, check the following:

- ✔ Make sure that the iPod is the only device in your FireWire or USB chain. Although you can connect a FireWire or USB device to another FireWire or USB device that has a connection, forming a chain, it isn't a good idea to do this with an iPod.

- ✔ Make sure that you use the FireWire or USB cable that came with your iPod and that the cable is in good condition.

- ✔ Try connecting the iPod to the built-in FireWire or USB connection of a different computer to see if the symptom persists.

If, after turning on the iPod, all you see on the display is the Apple logo and iPod name, and the device seems to be restarting over and over, try these steps if you use a FireWire connection to your Mac or PC:

1. **Connect the iPod to your computer's FireWire connection.**

   This procedure doesn't work with a USB connection because it requires power. Make sure that the computer is on and is not set to go to sleep.

2. **Reset the iPod, as we describe in "Resetting the iPod," earlier in this chapter.**

3. **When the Apple icon appears on the display, immediately press and hold the Previous and Next buttons until the Do Not Disconnect screen or FireWire icon appears.**

   You can now restore the iPod — see "Restoring an iPod with iPod Updater," later in this chapter.

If the Do Not Disconnect screen or FireWire icon doesn't appear, repeat Steps 2 and 3. (You might need to press and hold the Previous and Next buttons even more quickly.) If, after repeating these steps, the Do Not Disconnect screen or FireWire icon still doesn't appear, the iPod might need to be repaired. You can get more information, updated troubleshooting instructions, and links to the iPod repair site by visiting the Apple support site for the iPod (www.apple.com/support/ipod).

Using iPod Updater

The iPod Updater can update the system software that controls the iPod and can also update the firmware for the iPod's hard drive, if necessary. The update doesn't affect the music or data stored on iPod's drive. iPod Updater is provided on the CD-ROM that comes with your iPod. To find out whether a new version is available for downloading, go to the Apple Web page for the iPod (www.apple.com/ipod).

If you use MusicMatch Jukebox rather than iTunes on your Windows PC, skip this section and see "Troubleshooting iPod for Windows and MusicMatch Jukebox," later in this chapter.

If you use a Mac and you've turned on the Software Update option in your System Preferences, Apple automatically informs you of updates to your Apple software for the Mac, including iTunes, iCal, Address Book, iSync, and the iPod system software. All you need to do is select which updates to download and click the Install button to download them.

Before downloading the iPod Updater from the Apple Web site, make sure that you pick the appropriate version — Mac or Windows. The iPod Updater includes updates for all generations of iPods and can detect which iPod you have. As of this writing it offers version 3.0 for fourth-generation iPods, version 2.2 (for third-generation iPods), and version 1.4 (for first- and second-generation iPods).

Updating the iPod with iPod Updater

Be sure that your iPod has the most recent iPod firmware update installed. To determine which version of the iPod software is installed on your iPod, press the Menu button until you see the iPod main menu, and then choose Settings⇨About. (With first-generation and second-generation iPods, choose Settings⇨Info.) You see information next to the word Version that describes the software version installed on the iPod.

You can also determine the software version on your iPod by using iPod Updater. Connect the iPod to your computer and launch iPod Updater. The iPod Updater window appears. The software version appears next to the Software Version heading. If this version of the iPod Updater application has a newer software version that it can install on the iPod, you see (needs update) next to the version number. If not, you see (up to date).

To update the iPod's firmware and software, follow these steps for both the Mac and Windows versions:

1. **Connect the iPod to your computer.**

   iTunes opens, and if you set your iPod for automatic update, iTunes synchronizes the iPod with music and playlists from its library. The iTunes display notifies you when the iTunes music update is complete.

2. **Quit iTunes.**

   On a Mac, quit by choosing iTunes⇨Quit iTunes. On a Windows PC, choose File⇨Exit.

3. **Launch the iPod Updater application.**

   On a Mac, this application is located in the Utilities folder, which is in your Applications folder. On a Windows PC, you can find it under iPod in the Start menu. The Updater dialog appears, as shown in Figure 28-1 (Windows version).

Figure 28-1:
The iPod
Updater
utility lets
you update
or restore
your iPod.

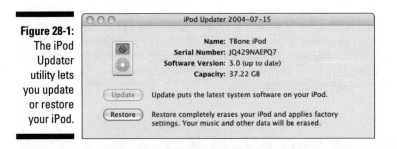

4. **Click the Update button.**

   (In Mac OS X, you might need to click the padlock and type an administrator account name and password first.) If the Update button is grayed out, the software on the iPod is the same version or a newer version than the iPod Updater application.

5. **Follow the instructions to disconnect and reconnect your iPod, if required.**

   Some iPod models need to be disconnected temporarily during the process of updating the software; others do not. If you see a message asking you to disconnect the iPod, follow the instructions displayed with the message.

The iPod Updater notifies you when the update is finished, and the Update button is grayed-out, indicating that your iPod no longer needs an update.

6. **When the update is finished, quit iPod Updater.**

   On a Mac, you can quit by choosing iPod Updater➪Quit iPod Updater. On a Windows PC, quit by clicking the dialog's Close button (refer to Figure 28-1).

7. **Eject the iPod.**

   When you quit iPod Updater, iTunes might launch again because your iPod is still connected. You can eject the iPod by clicking the iPod Eject button in iTunes.

   If iTunes doesn't launch, you can eject the iPod on a Mac clicking the Eject button next to the iPod name in the Finder or by dragging the iPod icon to the Trash. On a Windows PC, right-click the iPod name or icon and choose Eject from the shortcut menu.

After ejecting the iPod, wait for its display to show the main menu or the OK to disconnect message. You can then disconnect the iPod from its dock or disconnect the dock from the computer. Don't ever disconnect an iPod before ejecting it. You might have to reset your iPod, which we describe earlier in this chapter.

Restoring an iPod with iPod Updater

Restoring the iPod erases the iPod's hard drive and restores the device to its original factory settings, so make sure that you back up any important data that you keep stored on your iPod. To replace music that was erased by the restore operation, synchronize or update your iPod from your computer's music library, as we describe in Chapter 11.

To restore an iPod, follow these steps for both the Mac and Windows versions:

1. **Connect the iPod to your computer.**

   If your iPod is working, iTunes opens, and if you set your iPod for automatic update, iTunes synchronizes the iPod with music and playlists from its library. The iTunes display notifies you when the iTunes music update is complete. If your iPod isn't working, skip to Step 3.

2. **Quit iTunes.**

   On a Mac, quit by choosing iTunes⇨Quit iTunes. On a Windows PC, choose File⇨Exit.

3. **Launch the iPod Updater application.**

   On a Mac, this application is located in the Utilities folder, which is in your Applications folder. On a Windows PC, you can find it under iPod on the Start menu. The Updater dialog appears (refer to Figure 28-1).

4. **Click the Restore button.**

   (In Mac OS X, you might need to click the padlock and type an administrator account name and password first.) An alert dialog appears to confirm you want to restore iPod.

5. **Click the Restore button to confirm the restore operation.**

   A progress bar appears, indicating the progress of the restore operation.

6. **When the restore operation is finished, quit iPod Updater.**

   On a Mac, you can quit by choosing iPod Updater⇨Quit iPod Updater. On a Windows PC, quit by clicking the dialog's Close button (refer to Figure 28-1).

7. **Set up your iPod by using the iTunes Setup Assistant.**

   In the iTunes Setup Assistant dialog, type a name for iPod in the space provided, and then proceed with setting up iTunes with your iPod, as we describe in Chapter 2.

8. **Quit iTunes Setup Assistant, and update your iPod from your music library.**

   When you quit iTunes Setup Assistant, iTunes might launch again because your iPod is still connected. You can use this opportunity to update your iPod with the music in your library, as we describe in Chapter 11. You can also copy data to the iPod while it's mounted as a hard drive (see Chapter 25).

9. **When you're finished updating the iPod with music and data, eject the iPod.**

   You can eject the iPod by using the iPod Eject button in iTunes.

   If iTunes doesn't launch, you can eject the iPod on a Mac by clicking the Eject button next to the iPod name in a Finder window Sidebar or by dragging the iPod icon to the Trash icon (which turns into an Eject icon). On a Windows PC, right-click the iPod name or icon and choose Eject from the shortcut menu.

Troubleshooting iPod for Windows and MusicMatch Jukebox

It's no secret that Windows is somewhat different than the Mac, and troubleshooting a complex and varied Windows system can be a daunting task. Installing the latest updates and service packs from Microsoft ensures that your Windows system is up to date.

If you use MusicMatch Jukebox with your iPod on a Windows PC, you use an older version of the iPod Updater application to update or restore your iPod. This software was installed when you installed iPod for Windows by using the iPod for Windows CD-ROM, as we describe in Chapter 7. The iPod Updater can update the software that controls iPod and can also update the firmware for the iPod's hard drive, if necessary. The update doesn't affect the data stored on iPod's hard drive.

Updating the iPod with the MusicMatch Jukebox configuration

To update the iPod's firmware and software with the version of iPod Updater supplied on CD-ROM with MusicMatch Jukebox, follow these steps:

1. **Connect the iPod to your computer.**

   MusicMatch Jukebox opens, displaying the iPod in the PortablesPlus window. If you set your iPod for automatic update, MusicMatch Jukebox synchronizes the iPod with music and playlists from its library. MusicMatch Jukebox notifies you when the music update is complete.

2. **Quit MusicMatch Jukebox.**

   Quit by clicking the Close button in its window, or choose File➪Exit.

3. **Open the iPod Updater application by choosing Start➪iPod➪iPod Updater.**

4. **Click the Update button.**

   If the Update button is dimmed, the software on the iPod is the same version or a newer version than the iPod Updater.

   A progress bar appears. When the progress bar shows that the update is finished, the Update button is dimmed, indicating that your iPod no longer needs an update.

5. Click the Close button in the iPod Updater to quit.

6. Eject the iPod.

When you quit iPod Updater, MusicMatch Jukebox might launch again because your iPod is still connected. You can eject the iPod by clicking the Eject button at the bottom-left side of the MusicMatch Jukebox PortablesPlus window.

If MusicMatch Jukebox doesn't launch, you can eject the iPod in one of two ways:

- Right-click the iPod Watcher icon in the taskbar at the bottom of the Windows desktop to see a contextual menu. Choose Unmount from the contextual menu.

- Right-click the Safe Remove Hardware icon in the taskbar. From the contextual menu, select the Apple IEEE 1394 (FireWire) device if you're using FireWire, or select the USB Mass Storage device if you're using USB, and then click the Unmount button.

Because of the way iPod for Windows works with MusicMatch Jukebox, you should use only one of the two eject methods (or the Eject button in MusicMatch Jukebox) to eject your iPod. Do *not* right-click the iPod icon in the My Computer window and choose Eject from the shortcut menu that appears. This Eject option doesn't work with iPod for Windows and MusicMatch Jukebox.

After ejecting the iPod, wait for its display to show the main menu or the OK to disconnect message. You can then disconnect the iPod from its dock or disconnect the dock from the computer. Don't ever disconnect an iPod before ejecting it. You might have to reset your iPod, which we cover earlier in this chapter.

Restoring an iPod with the MusicMatch Jukebox configuration

To restore an iPod by using the version of iPod Updater that's supplied on CD-ROM with MusicMatch Jukebox, follow these steps:

1. Connect the iPod to your computer.

If your iPod is working, MusicMatch Jukebox opens, displaying the iPod in the PortablesPlus window. If you set your iPod for automatic update, MusicMatch Jukebox synchronizes the iPod with music and playlists from its library. MusicMatch Jukebox notifies you when the music update is complete. If your iPod is not working, see the following section, "If your iPod doesn't appear."

2. **Quit MusicMatch Jukebox.**

   Quit by clicking the Close button or by choosing File⇨Exit.

3. **Open the iPod Updater application by choosing Start⇨iPod⇨iPod Updater.**

4. **Click the Restore button.**

   An alert dialog appears to confirm that you want to restore iPod.

5. **Click the Restore button to confirm the restore operation.**

   A progress bar appears, indicating the progress of the restore operation.

6. **When the restore operation finishes, quit iPod Updater.**

   Quit by clicking the window's close box.

7. **Launch MusicMatch Jukebox, and in the MusicMatch Jukebox Device Setup dialog, type a name for iPod in the space provided.**

   The Complete Library Synchronization option and the Automatically Synchronize on Device Connection option are selected by default, but you can turn them off if you prefer, as we describe in Chapter 12.

8. **Click OK to finish device setup.**

9. **Select the iPod in the PortablesPlus window and click the Sync button to synchronize the iPod with the library of this computer.**

   Wait until the synchronization is complete before ejecting the iPod.

10. **Eject the iPod.**

    Click the Eject button at the bottom-left side of the MusicMatch Jukebox PortablesPlus window.

After ejecting the iPod, wait for its display to show the main menu or the OK to disconnect message. You can then disconnect the iPod from its dock or disconnect the dock from the computer. Don't ever disconnect an iPod before ejecting it. You might have to reset your iPod, as we describe earlier in this chapter.

If your iPod doesn't appear

Sometimes MusicMatch Jukebox fails to recognize an iPod through the FireWire connection. Don't panic — follow these steps first:

1. **Follow the instructions in the "First Troubleshooting Steps" section at the beginning of this chapter.**

   Make sure that your connection from the iPod to the computer is properly secure and that your iPod has power.

2. **Wait until activity stops on your iPod.**

   You can observe a lot by watching the iPod's display. The hard drive activity indicator (two arrows spinning in a circle) appears in the upper-left corner of the display. Before ejecting or disconnecting, wait for the arrows to stop spinning.

3. **Eject the iPod.**

   You can eject the iPod in one of two ways:

   - Right-click the iPod Watcher icon in the taskbar at the bottom of the Windows desktop to see a contextual menu. Choose Unmount from the contextual menu.

   - Right-click the Safe Remove Hardware icon in the taskbar. From the contextual menu, select the Apple IEEE 1394 (FireWire) device if you're using FireWire, or select the USB Mass Storage device if you're using USB, and then click the Unmount button.

4. **Restart your PC.**

5. **Disconnect the iPod and reconnect it.**

6. **Launch MusicMatch Jukebox if it doesn't launch automatically.**

If MusicMatch Jukebox still doesn't recognize the iPod, try restoring the iPod, which we cover in the section "Restoring an iPod with the MusicMatch Jukebox configuration."

As shipped from the factory, the iPod's hard drive is formatted as a Mac hard drive. When you install the iPod with MusicMatch Jukebox, iPod for Windows 2.0 software reformats the drive by using the Windows (FAT32) format. If the iPod doesn't appear in MusicMatch Jukebox the first time you connect it after installing the software, the iPod might be still formatted as a Mac hard drive. You can check the format on your iPod by choosing Settings➪About. If the About display doesn't say "Windows," then reinstall the iPod software as described in Chapter 7, and check again to make sure it formatted the drive using the Windows (FAT32) format.

If the iPod doesn't appear in MusicMatch Jukebox, but the Do Not Disconnect screen appears on the iPod display, open the iPod Manager utility and make sure that MusicMatch Jukebox is the home application. The iPod Manager utility is provided with iPod for Windows to change iPod settings, launch the software updater, check the Apple site for updates, and change the home application for the iPod (set to MusicMatch Jukebox by default). To change the home application with iPod Manager, follow these steps:

1. **Click the iPod Watcher icon in the taskbar.**

   Alternatively, you can right-click the icon and choose iPod Manager from the shortcut menu, or choose Start⇨iPod⇨iPod Manager.

2. **Click the Change Home Application button and select MusicMatch from the drop-down menu.**

3. **Click OK to close the iPod Manager window.**

4. **Eject the iPod.**

5. **Disconnect the iPod and reconnect it.**

6. **Launch MusicMatch Jukebox if it doesn't launch automatically.**

If the iPod doesn't appear in MusicMatch Jukebox, but you see menus on the iPod's display, make sure that "disk mode" is enabled in the iPod Manager utility.

If your iPod still doesn't appear in MusicMatch Jukebox, restart the Windows system while the iPod is connected. Occasionally the FireWire connection on a PC conflicts with another device or fails to work for some mysterious reason. You can tell when this happens: Use the System control panel to view the Hardware panel, and then click Device Manager. The Apple iPod IEEE 1394 device should be listed, and if it has a yellow exclamation point next to it, a conflict exists. You might be able to temporarily resolve the conflict by restarting Windows.

Part VI
The Part of Tens

The 5th Wave   By Rich Tennant

" He stepped outside, said he wanted to listen to his iPod on the way home, but then accidentally pulled out his iLightning Rod instead."

In this part . . .

*I*n this part, you find three chapters chock-full of information.

- ✔ Chapter 29 offers ten common iPod problems and their solutions.
- ✔ Chapter 30 provides *eleven* tips on using the equalizer.
- ✔ Chapter 31 offers *twelve* Web sources for finding more iPod information.

Chapter 29

Ten Problems and Solutions for Your iPod

- -

In This Chapter

▶ What to do if your iPod doesn't wake up

▶ How to keep your battery from running out so quickly

▶ How to keep the scroll wheel from exhibiting erratic behavior

▶ What to do if your iPod displays a problem icon

▶ How to restore your iPod to its original factory condition

▶ What to do if your iTunes music library is larger than your iPod's capacity

▶ What to do if your computer doesn't recognize the iPod

- -

*U*nfortunately, this isn't a perfect world. Even though we think the iPod comes as close to perfection as possible, at some point, your iPod isn't going to work as you expect it to. When that happens, turn to this chapter because here we show you how to fix the most common problems.

How Do I Get My iPod to Wake Up?

If your iPod doesn't turn on, don't panic — at least not yet. Try the following suggestions to get your iPod to respond:

✔ **Check the Hold switch's position on top of the iPod.** The Hold switch locks the iPod buttons so that you don't accidentally activate them. Slide the Hold switch away from the headphone connection, hiding the orange layer, to unlock the buttons.

✔ **Check to see whether the iPod has enough juice.** Is the battery charged up? Connect the iPod to a power source and see whether it works.

✔ **Reset your iPod if the iPod still doesn't turn on.** First toggle the Hold switch, and then press the Menu and Play/Pause buttons simultaneously. Hold them for at least five seconds until the Apple logo appears. Release the buttons as soon as you see the Apple logo. If that doesn't work, see Chapter 28.

How Do I Get My Battery to Last Longer?

You can do a lot to keep your battery going longer (much to the envy of your friends), including the following:

✔ **Press the Play/Pause button to pause (stop) playback.** Don't just turn off your car or home stereo or take out your headphones — if you don't also pause playback, your iPod continues playing until the playlist or album ends. When playback is paused, the power-save feature turns off the iPod after two minutes of inactivity.

✔ **Hold down the Play/Pause button to turn off the iPod when not using it.** Rather than wait for two minutes of inactivity for the power-save feature to turn off the iPod, you can turn it off yourself and save battery time.

✔ **Turn off the backlighting.** If you don't need to use backlighting, turn it off. It can drain the power.

✔ **Avoid changing tracks by pressing the Previous/Rewind or Next/Fast-Forward buttons.** The iPod uses a memory cache to load and play songs. If you frequently change tracks by pressing the Previous or Next buttons, the cache has to turn on the hard drive to load and play the songs, which drains the battery.

✔ **Use compressed AAC or MP3 files.** Playing larger uncompressed AIFF or WAV files takes more power because the hard drive inside the iPod has to refresh its memory buffers more frequently to process more information as the song plays.

How Do I Keep My Scroll Wheel from Going Crazy?

Second-generation and third-generation iPods use a nonmoving scroll wheel that works like the *trackpad* (also sometimes called a *touchpad*) of a laptop computer. Although the trackpad-style scroll wheel is far better than the first-generation moving wheel (which could be hampered by sand or dirt and had moving parts that could be damaged), it has problems of its own: it goes crazy sometimes, and it can be very sensitive — not sensitive to criticism, but to the touch of your finger.

The trackpad-style scroll wheel translates the electrical charge from your finger into movement on the iPod display. If you use more than one finger or have another finger nearby, the scroll wheel might detect the signal and skip over selections or go backwards while scrolling forwards, and so on. If the scroll wheel has excessive moisture on it, from humidity or a wet hand, wipe the wheel with a soft, dry cloth.

Don't use lotion or moisturizer on your hand right before touching the scroll wheel. Don't try to use pencil erasers, pen caps, or other types of pointers to scroll the scroll wheel (they won't work with trackpad-style scroll wheels and may damage other types of scroll wheels). Don't use your ring finger or the hand that sports a heavy bracelet or similar jewelry — these can throw off the sensors in the scroll wheel.

How Do I Get My Computer to Recognize My iPod?

Follow the first troubleshooting steps outlined in Chapter 28. If iTunes or MusicMatch Jukebox still does not recognize the iPod, you can use the iPod Updater to restore the iPod.

Also, make sure that your FireWire or USB cable is in good condition. Try connecting your iPod to another computer by using the same type of connection to see whether the same problem occurs. (Your computer might be to blame.) If the same type of connection (FireWire or USB) to the other computer works, the problem is your computer's connection or software. If it doesn't work, the problem is your iPod or cable. You can try a new cable to see whether that works.

What Do I Do if a Strange Icon Appears on My iPod?

When you turn on your iPod, built-in diagnostic software checks the iPod hard drive. If the iPod finds a problem when it's turned on, it automatically uses internal diagnostics to check for and repair any damage. You might see a disk scan icon on your iPod screen after turning it on, indicating that a problem was fixed. If this happens, restore your iPod to its original factory condition (see Chapter 28), and load it again with music.

If the iPod displays any other strange icon, such as a backwards Apple logo, a disk icon with a flashing question mark, or the dreaded disk-with-magnifying glass icon, it might need to be repaired. You can arrange for repair by visiting the Apple support site for the iPod (`www.apple.com/support/ipod`).

How Do I Restore My iPod to its Original Condition from the Factory?

Restoring the iPod erases your iPod's hard drive and returns the device to its original factory condition. Restore erases all of the data on the hard drive, so make sure that you back up any important data that you have stored on your iPod. You can use the iPod Updater utility to restore your iPod, as we describe in Chapter 28. When finished, add music back to your iPod from the iTunes library or from your MusicMatch Jukebox library, and then resynchronize your iPod with calendar and contact information.

How Do I Update My iPod to Have the Newest Software?

To determine which version of the iPod software is installed on your iPod, press the Menu button until you see the iPod main menu, and then choose Settings⇨About (in earlier versions, choose Settings⇨Info). Look at the version number that describes the software version installed on your iPod.

You can use the iPod Updater application to update or restore your iPod (see Chapter 28).

How Do I Update My iPod with Music When My Library Is Larger than My iPod's Capacity?

If you have less space on your iPod than music in your iTunes library, you can update manually (by album, artist, or songs), update automatically by selected songs only, or update automatically by playlist.

When you update by playlist automatically, you can create playlists exclusively for your iPod. A smart playlist can be limited to, for example, 18GB (for a 20GB iPod).

By combining the features of smart playlists (in Chapter 10) and updating automatically by playlist (in Chapter 11), you can control the updating process while also automatically limiting the amount of music you copy to your iPod.

You can also update automatically and keep your iPod synchronized to a subset of your library. iTunes creates a new playlist specially designed for updating your iPod automatically. iTunes decides which songs and albums to include in this playlist by using the ratings that you can set for each song in the iTunes song information, as we describe in Chapter 11.

How Do I Cross-Fade Music Playback with My iPod?

You can fade the ending of one song into the beginning of the next one to slightly overlap songs, just like a radio DJ, when you use iTunes. The *cross-fade setting* is the amount of time between the end of the fade-out from the first song and the start of the fade-in to the second song.

To cross-fade songs on your iPod, you have to play your iPod songs through iTunes on your computer. Connect your iPod to your computer and connect your computer to a stereo or connect speakers (or headphones) to your computer. Hold down ⌘-Option (on a Mac) or Ctrl-Alt (on a PC) as you launch iTunes and you can then select iPod in the iTunes Source pane.

By default, iTunes is set to have a short cross-fade of one second.

If you're playing songs on an iPod that's connected to your computer and also playing songs from your iTunes library (or even on a second iPod, both connected to your computer), your songs cross-fade automatically.

You can change this cross-fade setting by choosing iTunes⇨Preferences (on a Mac) or Edit⇨Preferences (on a PC), and then clicking the Audio button. You can then increase or decrease the amount of the cross-fade with the Crossfade Playback option.

How Do I Get Less Distortion with Car and Portable Speakers?

The 40GB iPod model designed for the Unites States has a powerful 60-milliwatt amplifier to deliver audio signals through the headphone connection. It has a frequency response of 20 Hz to 20 kHz, which provides distortion-free music at the lowest or highest pitches, but it might cause distortion at maximum volume depending on the recorded material.

For optimal sound quality, set the iPod volume at no more than three-quarters of the maximum volume and adjust your listening volume by using the volume control or equivalent on your car stereo or portable speaker system. (If no volume control exists, you have no choice but to control the volume from the iPod.) By lowering the iPod from maximum volume, you prevent over-amplification, which can cause distortion and reduce audio quality.

Chapter 30

Eleven Tips for the Equalizer

In This Chapter

▶ Adjusting the equalizer on your home stereo

▶ Taking advantage of the iPod's equalizer preset

▶ Getting rid of unwanted noise

*Y*ou play your iPod in many environments. The same song that sounds like music to your ears in your car might sound like screeching hyenas on a plane. In this chapter, we show you can fix most sound problems that occur with iPods. Soon you'll be cruising to the beat all the time — no matter where you are.

Setting the Volume to the Right Level

Before using the iPod equalizer (EQ) to refine the sound, make sure the volume of the iPod is set to about half or three-quarters (not more) so that you don't introduce distortion. Then set your speaker system or home stereo volume before trying to refine the sound with equalizers.

Adjusting Another Equalizer

When you have the iPod connected to another system with an equalizer, try adjusting that equalizer:

✔ **Home stereo system:** Refine the sound with your home stereo's equalizer because it might offer more flexibility and can be set precisely for the listening environment.

✔ **Car stereos:** The same rule applies as your home stereo — adjust the car stereo's equalizer first.

Setting Booster Presets

When playing music with your iPod through a home stereo or speakers (without a built-in equalizer) in a heavily draped and furnished room, try the iPod's Treble Booster EQ preset or create a your own EQ preset (see Chapter 21) that raises the frequencies above 1 kHz. Boosting these higher frequencies makes the music sound naturally alive.

Reducing High Frequencies

When using your iPod to play music through a home stereo (without a built-in equalizer) in a basement with smooth, hard walls and concrete floors, you might want to use the iPod's Treble Reducer EQ preset, which reduces the high frequencies to make the sound less brittle.

Increasing Low Frequencies

If you use high-quality acoustic-suspension compact speakers, you might need to add a boost to the low frequencies (bass) with the Bass Booster EQ preset so that you can boogie with the beat a little better. The Small Speakers EQ preset also boosts the low frequencies and lowers the high frequencies to give you a fuller sound.

Setting Presets for Trucks and SUVs

We use our iPods in different types of cars — one is a sedan; the other a 4-wheel drive truck. Trucks need more bass and treble, and the Rock EQ preset sounds good for most of the music that we listen to. We also recommend the Bass Booster EQ preset when using your iPod in a truck if the Rock preset doesn't boost the bass enough. In the sedan, the iPod sounds fine without any equalizer adjustment.

Setting Presets When You're Eight Miles High

When using your iPod on an airplane where jet noise is a factor, try using the Bass Booster EQ preset to hear the lower frequencies in your headphones and compensate for the deficiencies of headphones in loud environments. You might want to use the Classical EQ preset, which boosts both the high and low frequencies for extra treble and bass. Try the Bose QuietComfort 2 Acoustic Noise Canceling headphones (www.bose.com) for plane travel — they work great!

Reducing Tape Noise and Scratch Sounds

To reduce the hiss of an old tape recording (or the scratchy sound of songs recorded from an old vinyl record), reduce the highest frequencies with the Treble Reducer EQ preset.

Reducing Turntable Rumble and Hum

To reduce the low-frequency rumble in songs recorded from a turntable (for vinyl records) or recorded with a hum pickup, choose the Bass Reducer EQ preset.

Reducing Off-Frequency Harshness and Nasal Vocals

To reduce a particularly nasal vocal sound reminiscent of Donald Duck (caused by off-frequency recording of the song source, making the song more harsh-sounding), try the R&B EQ preset, which reduces the midrange frequencies while boosting all the other frequencies.

Cranking Up the Volume to Eleven

If you want that larger-than-life sound, use the Loudness preset, and then jack up the Preamp slider to the max, turn up your stereo all the way, and put your fingers in your ears to protect them. Then consult the DVD *This is Spinal Tap* or the Spinal Tap fan site, http://spinaltapfan.com/.

Chapter 31

Twelve Web Sources for More iPod Information

In This Chapter

▶ Finding iPod products and accessories

▶ Purchasing music and audio books online

▶ Getting support and troubleshooting information

The Internet contains a lot of information, and finding resources for the iPod is no exception. Try out these Web sites.

The Apple iPod Web Site

Your first stop for everything iPod, including iPod information and accessories, is the iPod Web page on the Apple Web site: `www.apple.com/ipod`. You can find tips, troubleshooting information, software to download, and information about the newest iPod accessories.

The Audible Web Site

Get audio books and documents for the iPod from the Audible site: `www.audible.com`. The iPod supports the Audible book format to allow automatic bookmarking, and iTunes supports the format for allowing book sharing. You can purchase and download digital audio books, audio magazines, radio programs, and audio newspapers.

The iTunes Music Store

We talk about the iTunes Music Store throughout this book, but this chapter wouldn't be complete if we didn't include it. Visit the Web site for the iTunes Music Store to find out all about online music purchasing: `www.apple.com/music/store`. You can create your account with the store from the Web site as well as from within iTunes. You can also download the newest version of iTunes.

The iPod Support Web Site

For those times when you need to send in your iPod for repair, go to the iPod Support Web site: `www.apple.com/support/ipod`. Follow the directions for troubleshooting your iPod and getting it repaired.

Apple Software Download

You can obtain the iPod Updater application and current information about iPod software updates at the Apple Software Downloads page: `www.info.apple.com/support/downloads.html`.

The iPod Troubleshooting Guide

To solve problems with your iPod, visit the Apple iPod troubleshooting guide: `www.info.apple.com/usen/ipod/tshoot.html`. You find a long list of diagnostic issues and solutions involving specific iPod models. You can also find troubleshooting information for using your iPod with Windows.

The MusicMatch Jukebox Site

For information about MusicMatch Jukebox and access to MusicMatch MX, including downloadable skins and plug-ins, visit the MusicMatch site: `www.musicmatch.com`.

Version Tracker

You can get loads of free software, including iPod utilities, synchronizing utilities, alternatives to Address Book and iCal, and iTunes visual effects plug-ins (also known as Visualizers) by visiting Version Tracker: `www.versiontracker.com/macosx` for Mac software. For Windows software, go to `www.versiontracker.com/windows`. Version Tracker is an accurate and up-to-date source of Mac software updates. The Version Tracker content team tracks over 30,000 applications with hundreds more added every week.

iPodHacks

For comprehensive iPod information, tips, and tricks, as well as a lively user forum, visit iPodHacks: `www.ipodhacks.com`. One of the first sites to support the iPod, the site focuses on hacks, modifications, and other alternate uses of the iPod. Don't forget — opening the iPod voids the warranty.

iPoding

For an excellent source of information about iPod accessories and third-party products, including downloads, visit iPoding: `www.ipoding.com`. The site offers late-breaking news about iPod software and accessories and hosts a lively forum for helping owners with support questions. You can also find more information about technical issues, such as the iPod's built-in diagnostics.

iPod Lounge

For the latest in iPod news and reviews of accessories and software, or just to hang out with other Pod People, visit the iPod Lounge at `www.ipodlounge.com`. The site offers excellent articles about iPod promotions and how owners are using their iPods, and you can find extensive reviews as well as an informative forum that includes lots of support questions.

Apple Developer Connection

This is for those who feel the need to push the envelope by developing products that work with iTunes.

You can download the iTunes Visual Plug-ins software developer kit (SDK) for free from `http://developer.apple.com/sdk`. (You must sign up for a free membership in the Apple Developer Connection.) The SDK contains the files that you need to develop code and includes documentation and sample code. The sample code is a fully functional Visual Plug-in developed for Mac OS 9 with Metrowerks CodeWarrior Pro 6 and for Mac OS X with ProjectBuilder.

Index

• *Numerics* •

1-Click purchasing, iTunes music store,
    62–64
1Disk, 162
78 rpm records, 224

• *A* •

AAC encoded file
  battery, conserving, 338
  copying onto CD, 168, 169
  described, 14, 72–73, 221
  iTunes setup, 37
  lossy method, 226
  protected form, 79, 81
  settings, changing, 230–232
  StuffIt files, 87
  voice and sound effects, 236
AC plugs, 202
accessories
  iHome connections, 192–194
  necessary, 16–17
  power, 202–203
  Web site, 349
account, Audible audio books, 77–78
account, iTunes music store
  benefits, 54
  setting up, 56–57
  viewing and changing information, 66
adapters
  battery power, 21
  car tunes, 196–198
  FireWire cable, 19–20
Address Book (Mac OS X)
  cards, merging, 310
  contact information, adding and editing,
    308–309
  groups, managing contacts in, 310–311
  searching, 310

AIFF encoded file
  Apple Lossless Encoder file versus, 221
  described, 73, 169, 222
  file size, 77
  settings, changing, 234–235
  tracks, splitting into multiple tracks,
    262–263
airplane presets, 344–345
AirPort, 214
AirTunes wireless stereo playback, 214–215
alarm, calendar, 281, 304, 315
Alarm Clock, 277–278
album
  browsing in iTunes, 101–103
  copying onto CD, 168
  cover art or images, 47, 118–119
  deleting, 126–127
  finding songs by, 59–60, 180–181
  iTunes music store, browsing for, 57–59
  playing in MusicMatch Jukebox, 98
  playlists, 123–124
alkaline batteries, 202
allowances, iTunes music store, 67–68
alphabetical order, sorting songs by, 106
America Online (AOL), 54, 55, 57
Amp Pack (Burton), 202
amplifier
  car stereo, 342
  turntable, need for, 257
analog devices
  connecting and setting up audio input,
    256–259
  editing application, choosing, 259
  in Windows with MusicMatch Jukebox, 260
analog sources
  connecting and setting up audio input,
    256–259
  editing application, choosing, 259
  recording, 77
  in Windows with MusicMatch Jukebox, 260

animation, light show with library music, 51–52
AOL (America Online), 54, 55, 57
APC Travel Power (Apple Store), 203
appearance, MusicMatch Jukebox, 271–272
Apple Developer Connection Web site, 350
Apple iPod Web site, 347
Apple iTunes Web page, 32
Apple .Mac service, 162
Apple online store, 16
Apple software download Web site, 348
Apple troubleshooting guide Web site, 348
applying presets, 253–254
appointment tracking
  iCal, 302–305
  Microsoft Outlook, 306–308
artist
  all songs by, playing, 96–97
  browsing iTunes, 101–103
  deleting, 126–127
  finding songs by, 58–60, 180
  iTunes music store browsing, 57–59
  multiple, 158
  playing song, 50
  renaming files by, 147
artwork, 47, 118–119
assigning presets to songs in iTunes
    equalizer (EQ), 251–252
Atari Breakout, game like, 280
Audible audio books
  bookmarking, 186
  buying, 54
  inability to share, 81
  music, 77–78
  voice and sound effects, 236
  Web information source, 347
audio CD
  format, choosing, 172
  import settings, changing, 169
audio input setup, 256–259
authorizing computers to play purchased
    music, 69
Auto Config button, 240
Auto Kit (Belkin), 197

• B •

backlight
  battery, conserving, 23, 338
  menu, 25
  on/off switch, 27
  timer, 278–279, 284–285
backpack, iPod-carrying, 202
Backup Battery Pack (Belkin), 202
backup, library
  consolidating, 160
  exporting playlists, 160–161
  finding, 158–160
  legality of, 81
  from Mac to PC or PC to Mac, 162–163
  multiple MusicMatch Jukeboxes, 164
  MusicMatch Jukebox, 163
  need for, 65
  protected music, 158
  reasons for, 157
  on same type of computer, 161–162
backwards Apple logo icon, 340
bandwidth, MP3 file, 240
bass, 250
battery
  backlight usage, 278
  charging, 20, 21–24
  draining, 323
  international adapters, 202
  life, maintaining, 22–23
  most current iPod, 16
  replaceable alkaline, 202
  replacing, 24
  tips for long life, 338
Billboard Charts, 59
billing address, changing, 66
bit rate
  choosing, 231–232
  compression, 220
  older Internet downloaded songs, 237
  stereo, 231, 232
  streaming broadcast, 269
  VBR encoding, 226
Bleep Web site, 266
bookmarking audible audio books, 186
Book2Pod Web site, 296

booster equalizer presets, 344
Brick and Parachute game, 280
broadband Internet connection, 34
broken links, repairing, 154–155
Browse menu, 26
browsing in iTunes
  by artist and album, 101–103
  searching for songs, 106–107
  song indicators, 103
  sorting songs by viewing options,
    105–106
  viewing options, changing, 104–105
browsing MusicMatch Jukebox library, 148
burning CDs
  described, 71, 165
  discs, selecting, 166
  format and recording speed, 172–173
  playlist, 168–170
  printing liner notes and covers, 174
  size, 167
  sound check and gaps, setting, 170–172
  steps, 173
  troubleshooting, 174–175
Burton Amp Pack, 202
business cards, virtual (vCards),
    301, 309, 318
buttons
  clicker, setting, 285
  iPod, 26–27
  iTunes playback, 47

• **C** •

cables, 14, 339
cache, 23, 195
calendar
  adding and synchronizing, 317–318
  alarm, setting, 281
  appointment or event, setting up, 303–304
  custom, creating, 305
  described, 302–303
  to-do item, adding, 305
calibrating battery, 22
car
  adapters, 196–198
  CD player, 175
  equalizer, adjusting, 343

  mounts, 198–199
  On-The-Go playlist, creating, 184–185
  radio station choices, 270
  speaker distortion, minimizing, 342
  volume, presetting, 247
Car Holder (MARWARE), 198, 199
Carbon Copy Cloner, 299
card game, 280
cards, Mac OS X Address Book, 310
carrying case, 22, 201–202
cassette-player adapter, 197
CD burning
  described, 71, 165
  discs, selecting, 166
  format and recording speed, 172–173
  playlist, 168–170
  printing liner notes and covers, 174
  size, 167
  sound check and gaps, setting, 170–172
  steps, 173
  troubleshooting, 174–175
CD Lookup, 144
CD player
  commercial, 175
  connecting to home stereo, 190
CD Spin Doctor (Roxio), 259
CD tracks
  importing music, 74–75
  MusicMatch Jukebox, 95–96
  playing with iTunes, 48–52
  rearranging and repeating, 50
  repeating song list, 50–51
  skipping, 50
  visual effects, 51–52
CD-RWs, 166
celebrity playlists, browsing iTunes music
    store, 61
central processing unit (CPU), 89
Chambers, Mark (*Mac OS X Panther All-in-
    One Desk Reference For Dummies*),
    86, 87
channel choice, 227, 231, 234
charts, browsing by, 59
check marks
  importing songs from CDs, 74
  removing from list, 50
classical music search tip, 142

clicker, button pressing, 285
clock, alarm, 277–278
closing down iPod, 131
coding format
  compression problems, 225–226
  converting to different, 236–237
  import settings, choosing, 226–227
  quality, trading for space, 220
  settings, changing, 230–235
  software tools, 221–225
cold storage, 21
columns
  song list, changing, 149
  viewing options, 104
component-style stereo systems, 190
composer credits, 142
compression
  encoding problems, 225–226
  folder, 87
  iPod mini, 14
computer
  connecting iPod to another, 213–214
  copying songs to another, 84–85
  dock connector, 13–14
  library backup among different types, 161–162
  multiple, using with Music Store account, 64
  older, way to use, 89
  recognizing iPod, 339
  volume output, changing for DJ console, 206–208
confused iPod, resetting, 28–29
connections
  accessories for iHome, 192–194
  audio input for recording records, tapes, and analog sources, 256–259
  dock, 13–14
  headphones and portable speakers, 191–192
  to home stereo, 190–191
  iPod to another computer, 213–214
  wires, discussed, 188–189
consolidating library backup, 160
contacts
  iPod, sorting, 281–282
  Mac OS X Address Book, 308–311

  Microsoft Address Book or Outlook, 311–312
  synchronizing, 316, 318–319
contrast display setting, 279, 285
converting encoded files, 72–73, 224, 236–237
copying music
  to iPod directly, 137–138
  to other computers, 81, 84–85
  between PCs and Macs, 85–87
copying vCards, 318
copyright law, 80, 157
correction, error, 73
cover art or images. *See* artwork
covers, printing, 174
CPU (central processing unit), 89
credit card
  allowances, setting up, 67
  changing, 66
cross-fading music playback, 211, 341
cup holder mount, 198
custom calendar, creating, 305

• D •

DAE (Digital Audio Extraction), 241
dashboard brackets, 198
data player, 11
date functions, 275–276
decibels, 247–248
de-click, 259
de-crackle, 259
de-hiss, 259
deleting
  calendar, 318
  computer from authorized list, 69
  file and folders, 290
  intros and outros, 260–261
  Mac OS 9, 300
  presets, 250–251
  Shopping Cart items, 63
deleting songs
  from iPod, 138–139
  MusicMatch Jukebox library, 154
  On-The-Go playlists, 184–185
  from Party Shuffle, 210
  playlists, 126–127

Digital Audio Extraction (DAE), 241
digital rights management (DRM), 265
disabling iPod buttons, 26
disco meltdown parties, 165
discs, CDs, 166
disk icon with flashing question mark, 340
disk-with-magnifying-glass icon, 340
display settings
  backlight timer, 278–279
  contrast, 279
  temperature and, 21
DJ console
  described, 205
  mixes, creating with iTunes, 208–211
  volume, changing computer output,
    206–208
dock connector
  described, 13–14, 188, 189
  for older iPods, 192
downloads
  iSync, 313
  iTunes music store, resuming
    interrupted, 65
  latest iTunes version, 32–33, 38
  music library, 265–268
  Web site, 349
DRM (digital rights management), 265
drop-down menu, 56
DV terminal. *See* FireWire
DVD, 172
DVD-audio, 225
DVD-Rs, 166

● *E* ●

Easy CD Creator (Roxio), 77
editing
  application, choosing, 259
  playlists, 140–141
  smart playlists, 126
editing song information
  fields, 115–117
  on iPod, 141–142
  multiple songs at once, 113–115
  MusicMatch Jukebox library tags,
    144–146
  ratings, adding, 117
  reasons for, 112–113

educational purposes, using music for, 80
Eject button, 47, 50, 75
ejecting iPod as hard drive, 47, 293–294
e-mail
  redeeming gift certificate sent by, 66
  sender, creating new contact for, 312
  vCards, handling, 309
e-mail addresses
  cards, merging, 310
  contact information, adding and editing,
    308–309
  groups, managing contacts in, 310–311
  iPod, sorting, 281–282
  Mac OS X Address Book, 308–311
  Microsoft Address Book or Outlook,
    311–312
  searching, 310
  synchronizing, 316, 318–319
encoding format
  compression problems, 225–226
  converting to different, 236–237
  import settings, choosing, 226–227
  quality, trading for space, 220
  settings, changing, 230–235
  software tools, 221–225
end of song, detecting, 260
English, switching iPod to, 27
enhancing sound, 245
Entourage (Microsoft), 317
EphPod Web site, 296, 316, 320
EQ (iTunes equalizer)
  assigning presets to songs, 251–252
  frequencies, 248
  preamp volume, 247–248
  presets, 248–249, 253
  saving your own presets, 249–251
equalizer
  adjusting another, 343
  airplane presets, 344–345
  assigning presets to songs, 251–252
  booster presets, 344
  buttons, 47
  frequencies, 248
  high frequencies, reducing, 344
  larger-than-life sound, 345
  low frequencies, increasing, 344
  off-frequency harshness and nasal vocals,
    reducing, 345

equalizer *(continued)*
  preamp volume, 247–248
  presets, 248–249
  saving your own presets, 249–251
  tape noise and scratch sounds,
      reducing, 345
  truck and SUV presets, 344
  turntable rumble and hum, reducing, 345
  volume, setting, 343
error correction, audio CD, 73
events, alarms for, 281
exporting playlists to library, 160–161
Extras menu, 25

• F •

factory condition, restoring original,
    28, 340
fading, 241
Fetch, 87
fields, editing song information, 115–117
file
  copying utilities, 319–320
  iTunes organization, 34, 37
  music, importing, 76–77
  naming setup, 73
filename, tagging from, 147
filtering low frequencies, 234
finding
  backup, library, 158–160
  game playing, 279
  iPod songs, 179–181
FireCard 400 CardBus card (Unibrain), 18
FireWire
  cable problems, 339
  computer minimum requirements, 17
  connection, 188
  models of iPod, 12–13
  recognition, failed, 331–333
  troubleshooting, 324
  USB versus, 18
firmware refresh, 43
first names
  contacts, 282
  library's use of artists', 58
first-generation models, 12
Flying Other Brothers Web site, 266
FM radio, wireless connection, 199–201

folder
  adding, 288–289
  compression, 87
  iTunes organization, 34, 37
foreign language, switching iPod from,
    27–28
format
  burning CDs, 172–173
  iPod recognition, 10–11
  Mac OS X, 298
  third-party software, 292
fourth-generation models, 15–16, 25
frequencies
  bass or treble, 250
  boosting high and low, 245
  filtering below 10 Hz, 234
  iTunes equalizer, 248
frozen iPod, resetting, 28–29
FTP access, enabling, 86–87

• G •

game playing
  Brick and Parachute, 280
  finding, 279
  music files, separating, 160
  Music Quiz, 280
  Solitaire, 280
gap of silence, removing, 74–75
GarageBand software, 77
genre
  browsing for music, 105
  searching for music by, 57, 58
gift certificates, iTunes music store
  redeeming, 65–66
  sending, 68
Gracenote database
  described, 49
  retrieving information manually, 111
groups, managing contacts in, 310–311

• H •

hand lotion, 339
hard drive
  crashed, losing music on, 65
  Mac setup, 288–290

news feeds, books, and Web pages, adding, 296
Notes folder, 295
photos, storing, 296–297
traveling with, 297–300
Windows PC setup with iTunes, 290–292
Windows PC setup with MusicMatch Jukebox, 292–294
headphones
    connections, 188, 191–192
    volume, setting, 186
high frequencies, reducing, 344
Hold switch
    checking, 21, 28, 322
    using to conserve battery power, 23
home stereo
    connections, 13, 190–191
    equalizer, 343–344
    recording from, 256
HPod (Hewlett-Packard), 11

● *I* ●

iCable for iPod (Monster), 190
iCal
    appointment or event, setting up, 303–304
    custom calendar, creating, 305
    described, 302–303
    to-do item, adding, 305
ICE-Link (Denison), 197
icon
    appearance of strange, 339–340
    battery power display, 22
    importing songs, 75
IEEE 1394. *See* FireWire
iHome accessories, 192–194
iLife software package, 80
images, cover, 118–119
iMic (Griffin) audio input device, 256
import settings, encoding format, 226–227
importing music
    audio books, 77–78
    CDs, ripping, 74–75
    described, 71
    files, 76–77
    preferences, setting, 72–73
    voice and sound effects, 236

inactive iPod, need to recharge, 23
information sources
    Apple Developer Connection, 350
    Apple iPod site, 347
    Apple software download, 348
    Apple troubleshooting guide, 348
    Audible site, 347
    iPod Lounge, 349
    iPod Support site, 348
    iPodHacks site, 349
    iPoding site, 349
    iTunes Music Store, 348
    MusicMatch Jukebox, 348
    Version Tracker, 349
information tags
    adding about songs, 146–147
    editing, MusicMatch Jukebox library, 144–146
    super-tagging songs, 147
installing
    Mac OS 9, 298
    Mac OS X, 298–299
    MusicMatch Jukebox, 31, 91–93
Internet
    automatic information retrieval, 110
    Gracenote database, 111
    manual information retrieval, 111–112
interrupted iTunes music store downloads, resuming, 65
intros, 260–261
iPod
    accessories, necessary, 16–17
    battery, charging, 21–24
    bookmarking audible audio books, 186
    buttons, 26–27
    connecting to another computer, 213–214
    described, 10–11
    language, setting, 27–28
    library, synchronizing, 133
    locating songs, 179–181
    Mac, FireWire or USB cables with, 17–19
    Mac OS 9, installing, 298
    Mac OS X, installing, 298–299
    Mac setup, 38–40
    menus, 24–26
    models, comparing, 11–16
    On-The-Go playlists, 184–185

iPod *(continued)*
PC, FireWire or USB cables with, 19–20
playing songs, 182, 212–213, 216
power, 20–21
repeating songs, 182–183
resetting, 28–29
shuffling song order, 183
volume, 186, 246–247
Windows PC setup, 40–43
wireless stereo playback, AirTunes,
214–215
iPod Access (Findley Designs), 319
iPod Armor (Matias Corporation), 201
iPod equalizer
applying iTunes EQ presets, 253–254
described, 252–253
iPod It (Zapptek), 319
iPod Leather Organizer (Belkin), 201
iPod Lounge Web site, 349
iPod service FAQ, 24
iPod Support Web site, 348
iPod Updater
restoration, 327–328
using, 325–327
iPod Voice Recorder (Belkin), 282
iPodDock (Bookendz), 192
iPodHacks Web site, 349
iPoding Web site, 349
iPodLibrary Web site, 296
iPodRip (The Little App Factory), 319
iPodSync, 320
irock 400FM Wireless Music Adapter
(First International Digital), 201
ISO 9660 file structure, 170
iSplitter (Monster), 191–192
iSync
suggested, 17
synchronizing Mac with, 313–315
iTunes. *See also* importing music
CD tracks, playing, 48–52
described, 10
library, updating, 340–341
on Mac, 33–35
music sources, 266–267
playing iPod through, 212–213
setup, 32–33
uses, 45–46

version required, 17
volume, 246
window, 46–48
on Windows PC, 35–38
iTunes equalizer (EQ)
assigning presets to songs, 251–252
frequencies, 248
preamp volume, 247–248
presets, 248–249, 253
saving your own presets, 249–251
iTunes Music Store
account, setting up, 56–57
allowances, setting up, 67–68
artists, songs, and albums, browsing for,
57–59
authorizing computers to play purchased
music, 69
celebrity and published playlists,
browsing, 61
charts, browsing by, 59
described, 53–54
interrupted downloads, resuming, 65
music videos and movie trailers, playing,
60–61
1-Click purchasing, 62–64
opening, 54–56
power-searching, 59–60
preferences, changing, 64
previewing songs, 62
purchase history, viewing, 67
redeeming gift certificates and prepaid
cards, 65–66
sending gift certificates, 68
sharing music, 79, 81
viewing and changing account
information, 66
visiting directly after iTunes setup,
34, 37–38
Web information sources, 348
iTunes Visual Plug-ins SDK (software
developer kit), 350

• J •

Jagger, Mick (artist), 80
Jobs, Steve (Apple founder), 53, 80

jumping over
  beginning of track, 241
  CD tracks, 50
  quality issue, 73
  to song points, 27

• *K* •

KaZaa, 80
keyboard, 304

• *L* •

LAN (Local Area Network) music sharing,
    81–84, 86
language, setting, 27–28, 285
laptop, running iPod from, 203
larger iTunes library, updating from,
    133–134
larger-than-life sound, 345
legal issues
  Apple products, 285
  copyright infringement suits, 53
  privacy and copyright, 80, 157
library
  changing entire iPod, 213
  deleting songs, 127
  downloading from other sources, 265–268
  importing music files, 76
  iPod, synchronizing, 133
  larger iTunes, updating from, 133–134
  quizzing, 280
library, MusicMatch Jukebox
  automatic update, 150–152
  backup, 163
  broken links, repairing, 154–155
  browsing, 148
  deleting songs, 154
  manual updates, 153
  playlist updates, 152–153
  searching for songs, 149–150
  song information, managing, 143–147
  views, changing, 148–149
  window, 90
light
  battery, conserving, 23, 338
  menu, 25

on/off switch, 27
  timer, 278–279, 284–285
light show, synchronizing with library
    music, 51–52
Line In/Line Out connection, 256, 257–259
liner notes
  folder, organizing, 295
  printing, 174
links, repairing broken, 154–155
lithium ion battery, 22
Little Feat Web site, 266
Local Area Network (LAN) music sharing,
    81–84, 86
logo, backwards Apple, 340
Lookup Tags, 147
Lossless encoder (Apple)
  described, 73, 221
  limitations, 226
lotion, 339
loudness, 243–244
low frequencies
  filtering, 234
  increasing, 344

• *M* •

Mac
  file and music copying utilities, 319
  FireWire or USB cables with, 17–19
  hard drive, 288–290
  iPod setup, 38–40
  iSync utility, 313–315
  iTunes set up, 33–35
  library backup to or from PC, 162–163
  minimum iTunes requirements, 16–17
  music library folder, 159
  recording and editing sound, 257–258
  reformatting, caution against, 214
  sharing songs with PCs, 85–87
  synchronizing calendar and address
    book, 302
  USB versus FireWire connections, 18
  volume, changing computer output,
    206–207
Mac OS 9
  deleting, 300
  installing on iPod, 298

Mac OS X
  deleting, 300
  installing on iPod, 298–299
  sharing with Windows computers, 86
Mac OS X Panther All-in-One Desk Reference
  For Dummies (Chambers), 86, 87
matching Music Guide service, 268
McCartney, Paul (artist), 80
Media Reader for iPod (Belkin), 296
memory
  cache, 23, 195
  less than optimum, alternative
    software, 89
  minimum required on computer, 16
  sufficient room for recording, 256
memos, voice
  managing, 283–284
  playing back, 283
  recording, 282–283
menu
  customizing, 284–285
  iPod, 24–26
  pop-up and drop-down, described, 56
Menu button, 26, 278
microphone, 257
Microsoft Entourage, 317
Microsoft Outlook. *See* Outlook (Microsoft)
Microsoft Windows. *See* Windows
    (Microsoft)
midnight, backlight flashing, 279
mini models, 14–15, 25
mini-plug, stereo, 190
mixes, 208–211
mobility
  in car, 196–199
  power accessories, 202–203
  protective cases, 201–202
  volume, presetting, 247
  wireless radio adapter, 199–201
models
  first-generation, 12
  fourth-generation, 15–16
  mini, 14–15
  second-generation, 12–13
  third-generation, 13–14
modifying songs in iTunes
  described, 260–261
  start and stop points, setting, 261–262
  tracks, splitting, 262–263

mono/monaural channel, 227, 231
mounts, car, 198–199
movie trailers, playing, 60–61
moving music library, 160, 164
MP3 file
  Apple Lossless Encoder file versus, 221
  battery, conserving, 338
  CD, burning, 169, 173, 175
  CD format, choosing, 172
  CD-R import encoders, switching, 170
  converting, 224
  copying, 256
  described, 73, 222
  downloading files, choosing, 267
  encoder settings, changing, 232–234, 240
  importing files, 76
  iTunes setup, 37
  lossy method, 226
  players, 166
  recorder settings, changing, 238–239
  saving or copying, 96
  streaming radio broadcast, 271
  StuffIt files, 87
  VBR-encoded, 233
  voice and sound effects, 236
mp3PRO encoder, 223, 240
music. *See* song
music copying utilities
  for Mac, 319
  for Windows, 320
Music Guide
  matching service, 268
  opening, 267
  opting out, 268
music library. *See* library
music link, iTunes Music Store, 54
Music menu, 25
Music Quiz game, 280
Music Store, iTunes
  account, setting up, 56–57
  allowances, setting up, 67–68
  artists, songs, and albums, browsing for,
    57–59
  authorizing computers to play purchased
    music, 69
  celebrity and published playlists,
    browsing, 61
  charts, browsing by, 59
  described, 53–54

interrupted downloads, resuming, 65
music videos and movie trailers, playing, 60–61
1-Click purchasing, 62–64
opening, 54–56
power-searching, 59–60
preferences, changing, 64
previewing songs, 62
purchase history, viewing, 67
redeeming gift certificates and prepaid cards, 65–66
sending gift certificates, 68
sharing music, 79, 81
viewing and changing account information, 66
visiting directly after iTunes setup, 34, 37–38
Web information sources, 348
music videos, playing, 60–61
musician. *See* artist
MusicMatch Jukebox
  appearance, changing, 271–272
  CD, ripping, 95–96
  described, 40, 89–91
  encoders, 223–224
  installing, 31, 91–93
  Music Guide, 267–268
  music sources, 266–267
  playing songs, 96–98, 216
  recorder settings, changing, 238–241
  recording format, setting, 93–95
  records, tapes, and analog sources, 260
  restoration with, 330–331
  song files, adding from other sources, 96
  updating with, 329–330
  Web information sources, 348
  Windows PC hard drive with, 292–294
MusicMatch Jukebox library
  automatic update, 150–152
  backup, 163
  broken links, repairing, 154–155
  browsing, 148
  deleting songs, 154
  manual updates, 153
  playlist updates, 152–153
  searching for songs, 149–150
  song information, managing, 143–147
  views, changing, 148–149
My Computer window, 293–294

• N •

name
  finding song by, 59–60
  playlist, changing, 124
  presets, changing, 250–251
  sorting contacts, 281–282
Napster, 80
nasal vocals, reducing, 345
naviPod (Ten Technology), 193
network
  finding music on, 159
  sharing music, 81–84
  swapping music, 267
news
  feeds, 296
  Web site, 349
NewsMac 3 Web site, 296
Next/Fast-Forward button, 26
noise, reducing from vinyl records, 259–260
Notes folder hard drive, 295
Now Playing menu, 25

• O •

off-frequency harshness, reducing, 345
Ohga, Norio (Sony honorary chairman and former CEO), 167
1-Click purchasing, iTunes music store, 62–64
1Disk, 162
online sources
  Apple Developer Connection, 350
  Apple iPod site, 347
  Apple software download, 348
  Apple troubleshooting guide, 348
  Audible site, 347
  iPod Lounge, 349
  iPod Support site, 348
  iPodHacks site, 349
  iPoding site, 349
  iTunes Music Store, 348
  MusicMatch Jukebox, 348
  Version Tracker, 349
On-The-Go playlists
  clearing songs, 184–185
  saving in iTunes, 185
  selecting songs, 184

opening
  iTunes music store, 54–56
  Music Guide, 267
opting out, Music Guide, 268
organizing. *See* playlist
OS 9 (Mac)
  deleting, 300
  installing on iPod, 298
OS X Address Book (Mac)
  cards, merging, 310
  contact information, adding and editing,
    308–309
  groups, managing contacts in, 310–311
  searching, 310
OS X (Mac)
  deleting, 300
  installing on iPod, 298–299
  sharing with Windows computers, 86
Outlook (Microsoft)
  appolntment or event, setting up, 306–307
  synchronizing with Windows, 316
  To-Do task, adding, 307–308
OutPod, 316
outros, 260–261

• *P* •

page, Web, 296
Party Shuffle, 209–210
password, network sharing, 82
Pause button, 49, 186
pause playback, 23, 75
PC, Microsoft Windows
  copying songs from Macs, 85–87
  file and music copying utilities, 320
  FireWire or USB cables with, 19–20
  hard drive setup, 290–294
  iPod compatibility, 10, 11, 12
  iPod setup, 40–43
  iTunes requirements, minimum, 17
  iTunes set up, 31, 35–38
  library backup to or from Mac, 162–163
  Mac OS X, sharing with, 86
  Microsoft Outlook, synchronizing, 316
  music library folder, 159
  MusicMatch Jukebox, recording records,
    tapes, and analog sources, 260
  MusicMatch Jukebox requirements,
    minimum, 90

recording and editing sound, 258–259
synchronizing calendar and address
  book, 302
USB versus FireWire, 18
volume, changing computer output, 208
PDA (personal digital assistant),
    using iPod as
  described, 11, 301–302
  iCal, 302–305
  Mac OS X Address Book, 308–311
  Microsoft Address Book or Outlook,
    311–312
  Microsoft Outlook, 306–308
  typing, absence of, 304
personal digital assistant. *See* PDA, using
    iPod as
personal use, 80
Philips Red Book, 167
phone numbers
  cards, merging, 310
  contact information, adding and editing,
    308–309
  groups, managing contacts in, 310–311
  searching, 310
phonograph
  amplifier, need for, 257
  connection, 190
  recording sound from, 255
  rumble and hum, reducing, 345
phonography parties, 224–225
photos, storing, 296–297
piracy, music sharing and, 80
playback button, 47
playing games
  Brick and Parachute, 280
  finding, 279
  music files, separating, 160
  Music Quiz, 280
  Solitaire, 280
playing music
  albums in MusicMatch Jukebox, 98
  battery-conserving method, 23
  CD tracks, 48–50
  described, 182
  music videos and movie trailers, 60–61
  on MusicMatch Jukebox, 96–98, 216
  through iTunes, 212–213
  voice memos, 283

playing video, 60–61
playlist
  album, 123–124
  burning CDs, 168–170
  buttons, 47
  CD, calculating, 168–169
  celebrity and published, browsing, 61
  creating directly on iPod, 139–140
  deleting songs, 126–127
  described, 121
  editing, 126, 140–141
  finding songs by, 181
  library, exporting, 160–161
  menu, 26
  MusicMatch Jukebox window, 90
  recent additions, smart, 126
  saving in MusicMatch Jukebox, 97
  smart, creating, 124–125
  of songs, 122–123
  streaming radio broadcast, 270
  updating by, 134–135, 152–153
  Voice Memos, 283, 284
Play/Pause button, 26, 338
Pod2Go Web site, 296
pointers, 339
pop-up menu, 56
portable speaker
  connecting, 191–192
  distortion, minimizing, 342
power
  accessories, 202–203
  basic iPod, 20–21
  dock connector, 13–14
  high-quality sound and, 220
  tips on saving, 23
  troubleshooting, 322
power-searching iTunes music store, 59–60
PowerWave (Roland) audio input device,
    256–257
pre-1960 music, quality of, 220
preamp volume, iTunes equalizer (EQ),
    247–248
preferences
  importing music, setting, 72–73
  iTunes music store, changing, 64
  updating iPod with iTunes, 130–131

prepaid cards, redeeming at iTunes music
    store, 65–66
presets
  airplane, 344–345
  assigning to songs, 251–252
  booster, 344
  deleting, 250–251
  iTunes EQ, 248–249
  saving your own, 249–251
  truck and SUV, 344
previewing songs, iTunes music store,
    54, 62
Previous/Rewind button, 26, 182–183
printing liner notes and covers, 174
priority, To-Do items, 305
protected music
  backup, library, 158
  sources, 266
protective case, 22, 201–202
published playlists, browsing iTunes music
    store, 61
purchase history, viewing iTunes music
    store, 67

● *Q* ●

quality
  audio, correcting, 73
  copied music, 10
  file formats, comparing, 169
  multiple CD copies, 266
  trading for space, encoding format, 220
QuickTime
  inability to share, 81
  music videos and movie trailers, 60–61
  need for, 16–17

● *R* ●

radio
  streaming, 269–271
  wireless adapter, 199–201
random order, playing
  iPod, 15, 183
  iTunes button, 51
  menu, 25
  Party Shuffle, 209–210

ratings, adding to song information, 117
RCA-type connectors, 190
rearranging CD tracks, 50
recognition, failed, 331–333
Record Industry Association of America
    (RIAA), 53
recording
  from analog sound devices, 77, 256–269
  format, setting, 93–95
  MusicMatch Jukebox window, 90
  streaming broadcast, 269
  voice memos, 282–283
recording speed, burning CDs, 172–173
records
  connecting and setting up audio input,
    256–259
  converting, 224
  editing application, choosing, 259
  need to transfer to digital, 255
  in Windows with MusicMatch
    Jukebox, 260
Red Book, 167
Remote (Apple)
  in cars, 198
  described, 193
remote, iPod, 186, 188
RemoteRemote (Engineered Audio), 194
repair Web site, 348
repeating
  CD tracks, 50
  song list, 50–51
  songs, 182–183
replacing battery, 24
resetting
  all settings, 285
  battery, 24
  iPod, 26, 28–29
  troubleshooting, 323
restoration
  iPod Updater, 43, 327–328
  with MusicMatch Jukebox configuration,
    330–331
retrieving information manually, 111–112
reviews, Web site, 349
RIAA (Record Industry Association of
    America), 53
ripping CDs, 46, 71

• S •

SACD (Super Audio CD), 225
sample rate, 227, 231, 234, 235
saving
  On-The-Go playlists in iTunes, 185
  playlist in MusicMatch Jukebox, 97
  your own presets in iTunes equalizer,
    249–251
scheduler
  adding and synchronizing, 317–318
  alarm, setting, 281
  appointment or event, setting up, 303–304
  custom, creating, 305
  described, 302–303
  to-do item, adding, 305
scroll wheel
  described, 11
  first-generation iPod, 12
  iPod mini, 15
  managing, 338–339
  menus, viewing, 24–26
  volume, controlling, 191
searching
  for classical music by composer, 142
  field for music library, 47
  hard drive, 96
  in iTunes, 106–107
  iTunes music store, advanced, 59–60
  Mac OS X Address Book, 310
  in MusicMatch Jukebox library, 149–150
second-generation models, 12–13
serial number, iPod, 91
settings
  customizing, 284–285
  encoding format, 230–235
  resetting, 29
Settings menu, 25
setup
  audio input, 256–259
  hard drive, 288–294
  iPod, 38–43
  iTunes, 32–33
78 rpm records, 224
sharing music
  from iTunes Music Store, 79, 81
  to other computers, 84–85

over network, 81–84
between PCs and Macs, 85–87
piracy and, 80
with two headphone sets, 191–192
shoot-'em-up game, 280
Shopping Cart option, 63
shuffling song order
iPod, 15, 183
iTunes button, 51
menu, 25
Party Shuffle, 209–210
silence, removing gap, 74–75
singer. *See* artist
size, burning CDs, 167
skin, MusicMatch Jukebox, 271
skip protection, 195
skipping
beginning of track, 241
CD tracks, 50
quality issue, 73
to song points, 27
sleep functions, 275–276
sleep mode, 21
smart encoding adjustments, 234
smart playlists, 117, 124–125
software. *See also* iTunes
conserving battery power, 23
encoding format, 221–225
free, 349
MusicMatch Jukebox, 92
recording analog sound, 77
updating with newest, 340
software developer kit, iTunes, 350
Solitaire game, 280
song
cross-fading playback, 211
deleting, 126–127
files, adding to MusicMatch Jukebox from
other sources, 96
indicators, browsing by, 103
iTunes music store, browsing for, 57–59
playlists, 122–123
skipping to any point, 27
volume, presetting, 244–245
song information
album cover art or images, 118–119
editing, 112–117, 141–142

entering, 112
Internet, retrieving from, 110–112
MusicMatch Jukebox library, managing,
143–147
reasons to add, 109
song list
repeating, 50–51
sources, displaying, 46–47
Sony 1.Link. *See* FireWire
Sony Red Book, 167
sorting songs by viewing options in iTunes,
105–106
sound
check and gaps, setting before burning
CDs, 170–172
enhancing, 245
equalizing, 247–252
iPod volume, 246–247
iTunes volume, 246
loudness, 243–244
song volume, presetting, 244–245
sound effects, 236
Sound Studio software (Felt Tip Software),
77, 259
source
connecting and setting up audio input,
256–259
editing application, choosing, 259
music, 266–267
MusicMatch Jukebox, adding from
other, 96
need to transfer to digital, 255
protected music, 266
viewing, 46
in Windows with MusicMatch
Jukebox, 260
space bar, 49
space, trading quality for, 220
speaker
connecting, 191–192
distortion, minimizing, 342
specifications page, Apple iPod Web site, 11
speed
recording CDs, 172–173
ripping versus playing CDs, 72
USB versus FireWire, 18
sport utility vehicle (SUV) preset, 344

SportSuit case (MARWARE), 198
SportSuit Convertible case (MARWARE), 22, 202
start point, setting in iTunes, 261–262
startup hard drive, warning against using as, 287, 288
status
  playing artist and song, 50
  ripping CDs, 47, 96
stereo bit rate, 231, 233
stereo channel, 227, 231, 234
stereo system
  connections, 13, 190–191
  equalizer, 343–344
  recording from, 256
stop points, setting in iTunes, 261–262
streaming audio, 76, 163
streaming broadcast, 269
StuffIt Deluxe (Aladdin Software), 87
sunlight, 279
Super Audio CD (SACD), 225
SuperDrive (Apple), 166
super-tagging songs, 147
SUV (sport utility vehicle) preset, 344
swapped music, 267
synchronizing
  calendars, 317–318
  contacts, 318–319
  deletes, 138
  disabled, 152
  display light show with library music, 51–52
  iPod updates, 132
  Mac with iSync, 313–315
  Microsoft Outlook with Windows, 316
  MusicMatch Jukebox, 92

• T •

tape
  collection of rare, 255
  connecting and setting up audio input, 256–259
  editing application, choosing, 259
  noise, reducing, 259, 345
  in Windows with MusicMatch Jukebox, 260

tasks to do
  iCal, 305
  Microsoft Outlook, 307–308
telephone numbers
  cards, merging, 310
  contact information, adding and editing, 308–309
  groups, managing contacts in, 310–311
  searching, 310
temperature
  battery and, 22
  display settings, 21
  startup hard drive, using as, 287
Terminal application, 87
testing newly burned CDs, 174
third-generation models, 13–14, 24
time
  elapsed by song, 50
  functions, 275–276
  sorting song by, 105
Time Zone, 276
timer, sleep, 276
title, finding song or album by, 59–60
Toast software (Roxio), 77, 259
To-Do task
  iCal, 305
  Microsoft Outlook, 307–308
touchpad/trackpad, 338–339
tracks
  changing, battery conservation, 338
  gaps, removing between, 74–75
  importing music, 74–75
  MusicMatch Jukebox, 95–96
  numbering imported song files, 73
  offset recording, 241
  playing with iTunes, 48–52
  rearranging and repeating, 50
  repeating song list, 50–51
  skipping, 50
  splitting songs in iTunes, 262–263
  visual effects, 51–52
  volume, importance of consistent, 172
TransPod FM (Digital Lifestyle Outfitters), 201
travel
  airplane presets, 344–345
  Alarm Clock, 277–278
  hard drive, 297–300

On-The-Go playlist, creating, 184–185
power accessories, 202–203
protective cases, 22, 201–202
troubleshooting
  battery, draining, 323
  burning CDs, 174–175
  FireWire connection, 324
  Hold switch, checking, 322
  power, 322
  resetting, 323
truck preset, 344
trunk-based CD changer, 197
TuneCast II Mobile FM Transmitter
    (Belkin), 201
TuneDok (Belkin), 198, 199
turning on/off iPod, 26
turntable
  amplifier, need for, 257
  connection, 190
  recording sound from, 255
  rumble and hum, reducing, 345
type, music
  browsing for, 105
  searching for, 57, 58
typing, absence of, 304

• *U* •

Uniform Resource Locator (URL) streaming
    radio broadcast, 271
unmounting hard drive, 47, 293–294
updating
  automatically from MusicMatch Jukebox
      library, 150–152
  manually from iTunes library, 283, 340–341
  with MusicMatch Jukebox configuration,
      329–330
  MusicMatch Jukebox library, 153
  by playlist, 134–135, 152–153
  selected songs, 135–136
  software, 340
updating iPod with iTunes
  automatic, 132–136
  described, 129–130
  manual, 136–139
  preferences, 130–131

URL (Uniform Resource Locator) streaming
    radio broadcast, 271
USB
  audio input device, 256
  cable problems, 339
  computer minimum requirements, 17
  FireWire versus, 18
user forum, 349
utilities, free, 349

• *V* •

VBR (Variable Bit Rate) encoding, 226, 233
vCards (virtual business cards),
    301, 309, 318
Version Tracker Web site, 349
video, playing, 60–61
viewing
  iTunes browsing, 104–105
  iTunes music store account
      information, 66
  MusicMatch Jukebox library, 148–149
  sorting songs in iTunes, 105–106
vinyl records. *See* records
virtual business cards (vCards),
    301, 309, 318
viruses, vCards and, 309
visual effects, CD tracks, 51–52
Visualizer menu, 52
voice
  compression, 220
  importing, 236
voice memos
  managing, 283–284
  playing back, 283
  recording, 282–283
volume
  button, 27
  car stereo, 342
  DJ console, changing computer output,
      206–208
  equalizer, 343
  headphones and portable speakers, 191
  iPod, 186, 191
  record input, 257–259
  sound check and gaps, setting, 170–172

• W •

waking iPod, 337–338
warming up iPod, 21
Warp Records (electronic music label), 266
WAV encoded files
  converting, 224
  described, 73, 222
  file size, 77
  recorder settings, changing, 239
  saving or copying, 96
  settings, changing, 234–235
  voice memos, 283
  when to use, 94–95, 223
Web address, streaming radio
      broadcast, 271
Web information sources
  Apple Developer Connection, 350
  Apple iPod site, 347
  Apple software download, 348
  Apple troubleshooting guide, 348
  Audible site, 347
  iPod Lounge, 349
  iPod Support site, 348
  iPodHacks site, 349
  iPoding site, 349
  iTunes Music Store, 348
  MusicMatch Jukebox, 348
  Version Tracker, 349
Web page, saving to hard drive, 296
Web sites, artists', 266
Wi-Fi wireless networking, 214
window
  iPod, 10–11, 24–26
  iTunes, 46–48
  Source pane, adjusting, 48
Windows (Microsoft)
  copying songs from Macs, 85–87
  file and music copying utilities, 320
  FireWire or USB cables with, 19–20
  hard drive setup, 290–294
  iPod compatibility, 10, 11, 12
  iPod setup, 40–43
  iTunes requirements, minimum, 17
  iTunes set up, 31, 35–38
  library backup to or from Mac, 162–163
  Mac OS X, sharing with, 86
  Microsoft Outlook, synchronizing, 316
  music library folder, 159
  MusicMatch Jukebox, recording records,
      tapes, and analog sources, 260
  MusicMatch Jukebox requirements,
      minimum, 90
  recording and editing sound, 258–259
  synchronizing calendar and address
      book, 302
  USB versus FireWire, 18
  volume, changing computer output, 208
wired connections, 188–189
wireless radio adapter, 197, 199–201
wireless remote control, 193
wireless stereo playback, AirTunes,
      214–215
WMA (Windows Media audio) files
  organizing, 37
  unwrapped, copying, 265

• X •

XPlay (Mediafour), 320

• Z •

The Zen Tricksters Web site, 266
Zip file, 87